Electronic and Computer Music

# Electronic and Computer Music

*Second Edition*

PETER MANNING

CLARENDON PRESS · OXFORD
1993

*Oxford University Press, Walton Street, Oxford* OX2 6DP

*Oxford New York*
*Athens Auckland Bangkok Bombay*
*Calcutta Cape Town Dar es Salaam Delhi*
*Florence Hong Kong Istanbul Karachi*
*Kuala Lumpur Madras Madrid Melbourne*
*Mexico City Nairobi Paris Singapore*
*Taipei Tokyo Toronto*
*and associated companies in*
*Berlin Ibadan*

*Oxford is a trade mark of Oxford University Press*

*Published in the United States*
*by Oxford University Press Inc., New York*

*© Peter Manning 1985, 1993*
*Second edition first published 1993*
*New as Paperback 1994*

*British Library Cataloguing in Publication Data*
*Data available*

*Library of Congress Cataloging in Publication Data*
*Manning, Peter, 1948–*
*Electronic and computer music / Peter Manning.—2nd ed.*
*Originally published in hardcover in 1993.*
*Includes bibliographical references (p.   ) and index.*
*Discography: p.*
*1. Electronic music—History and criticism.   2. Computer music—*
*History and criticism.   I. Title.*
*ML1380.M36   1994      786.7'09—dc20      94–3546*
*ISBN 0–19–816328–2*
*ISBN 0–19–816329–0 (pbk.)*

*Printed in Hong Kong*

To Liz

# Contents

# Illustrations

Photographs are reproduced by kind permission of the following:

(1) John Morton, Darlington; (3) photo Serge Lido, Paris; (4) Universal Edition (London) Ltd.; (5) RAI Radiotelevisione Italiana, Milan; (6) Philips Press Office, Eindhoven; (7) RCA, New York; (10) Daphne Oram, Wrotham, Kent; (11) Instituut voor sonologie, Utrecht; (12) Electronic Music Studio, University of Toronto (UTEMS); (13) Cunningham Dance Foundation (photo Hervé Gloaguen); (14) Massachusetts Institute of Technology (photo Jim Harrison); (15) IRCAM, Paris (photo Philippe Gontier); (16) Bell Laboratories, Murray Hill, NJ; (17) Peter Zinovieff, Swaffham Prior, Cambs.; (18) Yamaha-Kemble Music (UK) Ltd.; (19) Bandive Ltd., London; (20) Fairlight Instruments Pty, Sydney.

# 1 The Background, to 1945

Buried amongst the records of the United States patent office for the year 1897 is a rather unusual entry, no. 580.035, registered in the name of Thaddeus Cahill. The invention described has long since passed into obscurity, but in several respects it was to prove as significant a landmark for electronic music as the more celebrated phonograph patents of Edison and Berliner registered some twenty years previously.

Cahill's entry described an electrically based sound-generation system, subsequently known as his Dynamophone or Telharmonium, the first fully developed model being presented to the public early in 1906 at Holyoke, Massachusetts. As the former title suggests, the machine was essentially a modified electrical dynamo, employing a number of specially geared shafts and associated inductors to produce alternating currents of different audio frequencies. These signals passed via a polyphonic keyboard and associated bank of controls to a series of telephone receivers fitted with special acoustic horns.

The Dynamophone was a formidable construction, about 200 tons in weight and some 60 feet in length, assuming the proportions of a power-station generator. The quoted cost, some $200 000, provides another startling statistic. For all its excessive proportions and eccentricities the machine offered sound-production features which were both new and flexible to a degree not to be emulated by subsequent designs for some considerable time. Cahill saw his invention not merely as a substitute for a conventional keyboard instrument but as a powerful tool for exploring an enlarged world of pitched sounds, where it would become possible 'to produce the notes and chords of a musical composition with any timbre desired out of their electrical elements'. This claim highlighted the ability of the performer to vary the musical quality of the selected sounds in terms of the relative strengths of each of the primary harmonics associated with a particular note. Such a facility necessitated the use of separate inductors for each overtone, adding greatly to the complexity of the system.

News of Cahill's work travelled far, attracting the attention of no less a composer than Ferruccio Busoni. In an extended essay entitled *Sketch of a New Aesthetic of Music* (1907) he championed the Dynamophone as a powerful tool for exploring new concepts of harmony. Sadly, however, Busoni did not choose to pioneer investigations himself. Cahill, and the New England Electric Music Company which funded the venture, intended to sell production models of the machine to large cities and towns throughout America for the transmission of 'Telharmony' to hotels, restaurants, theatres, and private homes via the local telephone exchange. This visionary quest to provide a music broadcasting network for the nation was not to become a reality, however, for in addition to the excessive capital outlay required, it was discovered that the machine seriously interfered with other telephone calls. Faced with such impossible commercial odds the venture ran into financial difficulty, and eventually failed just before the outbreak of the First World War in Europe.

Advances in the newly established field of electronics were, nevertheless, preparing the way for less costly and more compact approaches to the generation of synthetic sound. The direct current arc oscillator appeared in 1900, and by 1906, the same year as the first demonstration of the Dynamophone, Lee De Forest had patented the vacuum-tube triode amplifier valve. Progress was slow but steady, and by the end of the war, with the industry well established, several engineers were able to investigate the possibility of using the new technology for the construction of electronic musical instruments. The primary motivation behind most of these designs was a desire to create additions to the conventional orchestral range, with an underlying hope that composers could be persuaded to provide a suitable repertoire. The devices which emerged were thus intended primarily to satisfy traditional ideas of musical writing. Some indeed, such as the Neo-Bechstein Piano (1931), were little more than modified acoustical instruments, using special pick-ups to capture naturally produced vibratory characteristics and subject them to processes of electronic amplification and modification. The best known modern example of this class of instrument is the electric guitar.

The majority relied on an electronic method of sound generation, for example the Thérémin (1924), the Sphärophon (1927), the Dynaphone (not to be confused with the Dyna*mo*phone) (1927–8), the Ondes Martenot (1928), and the Trautonium (1930). Most were keyboard orientated, providing a single melodic output and an ancillary means of controlling volume, usually taking the form of a hand-operated lever or a foot pedal. The Thérémin was a notable exception, having no keyboard at all. Instead two capacitive detectors were employed, one a vertical rod, the other a horizontal loop. These controlled pitch and amplitude, respectively, by generating electrical fields which altered according to the proximity of the hands of the performer.

Electronic instruments of this type flourished briefly during the inter-war period. Despite contributions from composers such as Hindemith, Honegger, Koechlin, Milhaud, and Messiaen, only a limited repertoire emerged. Rather more sustained interest was shown by writers of film music, but outside this sphere these instruments failed to establish any lasting position of significance. Today the Ondes Martenot is the only example of these original designs in concert use, its position being sustained by works such as Messiaen's *Turangalîla* symphony and *Trois Petites Liturgies*.

The Givelet (1929), soon to be overshadowed by the Hammond Organ (1935), heralded a rather different and commercially more successful line of development, for these instruments were polyphonic, designed in the first instance as comparatively cheap replacements for the pipe organ. The Givelet combined the principles of the Pianola or 'player piano' with those of electronic sound generation, for it could be controlled via a pre-punched tape. This ability to program the production of sound foreshadowed devices such as the RCA synthesizers and more generally the use of computers in sound production a quarter of a century or more later. The Hammond Organ, although a more conventional instrument from the performer's point of view, gained a reputation for its distinctive if not entirely authentic sound quality. This was largely due to the method of tone generation employed, involving the rotation of suitably contoured discs in a magnetic field in a manner reminiscent of the Dynamophone. The potential of the Givelet and the Hammond Organ as substitutes for the piano in the field of popular music was quickly recognized and exploited. Applications such as these, however, contributed very little to an appreciation of the artistic potential of this new medium of sound production. It was perhaps inevitable that the first excursions into such an unknown sphere should be so closely modelled on traditional instrumental practice. There were, nevertheless, a few pioneers who were anxious to explore the possibilities of an expanded sound world in a less restricted manner.

One of the earliest attempts to employ non-traditional sound-generation techniques as part of a communicative art form arose from the activities of the members of the Futurist movement, initiated by the Italian poet Filippo Marinetti in February 1909 with the publication of his *Manifesto of Futurist Poetry*. Their musical objectives were outlined by Balilla Pratella in the *Manifesto of Futurist Musicians*, published in October 1910. Echoing the revolutionary spirit of the movement, this document called for the rejection of traditional musical principles and methods of teaching and the substitution of free expression, to be inspired by nature in all its manifestations.

Five months later to the day, in another document, the *Technical Manifesto of Futurist Music*, Pratella suggested that composers should 'master all expressive technical and dynamic elements of instrumentation and regard the orchestra as a sonorous universe in a state of constant mobility, integrated by an effective fusion of all its constituent parts'. Further, he considered that their work should reflect 'all forces of nature tamed by man through his continued scientific discoveries', for example, 'the musical soul of crowds, of great industrial plants, of trains, of transatlantic liners, of armoured warships, of automobiles, of aeroplanes'.

Exactly two years later another Futurist, Luigi Russolo, published a related manifesto entitled *The Art of Noises* as an open letter to Pratella. This proposed the composition of works based entirely on the use of sound sources from the environment:

Musical sound is too limited in qualitative variety of timbre. The most complicated of orchestras reduce themselves to four or five classes of instruments differing in timbre: instruments played with the bow, plucked instruments, brass-winds, wood-winds and percussion instruments . . . we must break out of this narrow circle of pure musical sounds and conquer the infinite variety of noise sounds.

This document is notable for its appreciation of the relevance of acoustic laws to the generation of musical structures from noise sources:

We must fix the pitch and regulate the harmonics and rhythms of these extraordinarily varied sounds. To fix the pitch of noises does not mean to take away from them all the irregularity of tempo and intensity that characterizes their vibrations, but rather to give definite gradation of pitch to the stronger and more predominant of these vibrations. Indeed noise is differentiated from musical sound merely in that the vibrations that produce it are confused and irregular, both in tempo and intensity. Every noise has a note—sometimes even a chord—that predominates in the ensemble of its irregular vibrations. Because of this characteristic pitch it becomes possible to fix the pitch of a given noise, that is, to give it not a single pitch but a variety of pitches without losing its characteristic quality—its distinguishing timbre. Thus certain noises produced by rotary motion may offer a complete ascending or descending chromatic scale by merely increasing or decreasing the speed of motion.

The practical manifestations of his proposal involved the construction of specially designed noise instruments, Intonarumori, in collaboration with the percussionist Ugo Piatti. The first public performance of the 'Art of Noises' took place in June 1913 at the Teatro Storchi, Milan, barely three months after the publication of the manifesto, and with only some of the Intonarumori completed. A second, altogether more successful, performance using the full complement of instruments was given as part of a concert of Futuristic music, presented by Marinetti and Russolo at the Teatro dal Verne, Milan, in April 1914.

The historical interest in this venture lies not so much in the acoustical design features of the Intonarumori themselves, instruments which in any event have long since been destroyed, but more in the motivation which led to their construction. The Futurist movement did not succeed in its attempt to produce a major revolution in the path of new music, but its challenging of traditionally accepted relationships between the science of acoustics and the art of musical sound production was to prove singularly prophetic.

Busoni had already attacked traditional nineteenth-century musical practices in his *Sketch of a New Aesthetic of Music*, advocating a reappraisal of the whole language of music 'free . . . from architectonic, acoustic and aesthetic dogmas'. This book caught the attention of a young French composer, Edgard Varèse, who, having rebelled against the traditional outlook of the Paris Conservatoire, was eager to explore new concepts of musical expression. Varèse, more than any other composer of his time, pioneered in his instrumental music the aesthetics which were necessary for the acceptance of electronic sound-processing techniques in musical composition. It is thus particularly tragic that it was not until the 1950s, towards the end of his life, that he gained access to the facilities he so fervently desired.

As early as 1916 he was quoted in the New York Telegraph as saying: 'Our musical alphabet must be enriched . . . We also need new instruments very badly. . . . In my own works I have always felt the need for new mediums of expression.' He was quick, however, to deny suggestions that his efforts were directed towards the Futurist movement.

The Futurists (Marinetti and his noise artists) have made a serious mistake . . . Instruments, after all, must only be a temporary means of expression. Musicians should take up this question in deep earnest with the help of machinery specialists . . . What I am looking for are new technical means which can lend themselves to every expression of thought.

Varèse had become acquainted with the electronic designer René Bertrand[1] in May 1913, and this marked the start of a long and lasting friendship. In 1922, during the composer's first stay in America, he declared in an interview for the *Christian Science Monitor*:

What we want is an instrument that will give us continuous sound at any pitch. The composer and electrician will have to labor together to get it . . . Speed and synthesis are characteristics of our own epoch.

During the 1920s Varèse continued his search for new sound textures, but without the aid of any technical facilities. His work with natural instrumental resources in his first published compositions was nevertheless singularly prophetic, for he was concerned to use procedures which were to become primary characteristics of electronic sound processing; analysis and re-synthesis. He experimented, for example, with altered attack characteristics for brass instruments, where the initial transient would be suppressed by making the entry of a sound *piano*, and its central portion or body heavily accentuated by means of a rapid crescendo. Such an effect is remarkably similar to that achieved easily today by running recordings of normally articulated notes backwards, the decay thus becoming the attack. He was also particularly concerned to use instruments as component building-blocks for sound masses of varying quality, density, and volume, in contrast to their traditional roles as sources of linear counterpoint.

[1] It was Bertrand who was subsequently to construct the Dynaphone.

His philosophy of musical expression, to use his own term, was based on the concept of 'organized sound', with no *a priori* restrictions as to the choice or use of the component sound sources involved in the process of synthesis. Percussion instruments figured prominently in his works. *Ionisation* (1930–1), for example, is scored entirely for instruments of this family. With the aid of effects such as sirens, whips, a lion's roar, and sleigh-bells he struggled to develop a compositional art which integrated the natural sounds of the environment with more traditional sources of musical expression. This was not the somewhat crude Futurist 'Art of Noises' exploring the exotic, but an attempt to extract an artistic perspective from the universe of sound.

Varèse was not without his imitators. The American composer George Antheil required the use of car horns, aeroplane propellers, saws, and anvils in his *Ballet mécanique*, first performed in Paris in 1926, and again in New York in 1927. The work of Joseph Schillinger is also of interest in this context. Schillinger, a Russian by birth, travelled to America in 1928 in response to an invitation from the American Society for Cultural Relations with Russia, remaining there until his early death fifteen years later. Soon after his arrival he entered into a collaboration with his fellow-countryman Thérémin, designing a domestic version of his instrument for manufacture by RCA. As an aid to promotion Schillinger composed his *Airphonic Suite for RCA Thérémin and Orchestra*, conducting its first performance at Cleveland, Ohio, in November 1929, with Thérémin as soloist. His interest in fostering the creative application of science for musical ends is illustrated by the following extract from an article entitled 'Electricity, a Musical Liberator', which appeared in *Modern Music* in March 1931:

The growth of musical art in any age is determined by the technological progress which parallels it. Neither the composer nor performer can transcend the limits of the instruments of his time. On the other hand technical developments stimulate the creation of certain forms of composition and performance. Although it is true that musicians may have ideas which hurdle these technical barriers, yet, being forced to use existing instruments, their intentions remain unrealised until scientific progress comes to the rescue . . . If we admit that the creative imagination of the composer may form musical ideas which, under the specific conditions of a given epoch, cannot be translated into sounds, we acknowledge a great dependence of the artist upon the technical position of his era, for music attains reality only through the process of sound.

During the remaining years of his life he became increasingly preoccupied with aspects of music theory, producing a set of twelve books describing *The Schillinger System of Musical Composition* (1940), followed two years later by a monumental work, *The Mathematical Basis of the Arts*. Neither of these, unfortunately, was published until after his death. Despite some rather curious aspects, for example the use of statistical data as a basis for measuring the degree of stylistic consistency displayed by some of the major classical composers in their works, and the formulation of a set of compositional rules based on empirical analyses of musical structures, his theories do contain some features of particular interest. His attempt to analyse musical sounds in musico-acoustic terms, using such identifying features as melody, rhythm, timbre, harmony, dynamics, and density anticipated the type of methodology to be applied from many quarters in the search for a morphology of electronic music.

Varèse, unlike Schillinger, continued to press actively for practical facilities. Towards the end of 1927 he became restless to learn more about the possibilities of electronic instruments, and contacted Harvey Fletcher, the director of the acoustical research division of Bell Telephone Laboratories, with a view to acquiring a laboratory for research in this field. Fletcher took an interest in his proposals but could not offer the funds necessary for such a venture. In desperation Varèse departed for Paris in the autumn of 1928 to ascertain from Bertrand what technical developments had taken place in his absence. One product of his visit was the formulation of a project to develop what might have become the first sound synthesis studio, and associated school of composition. Although details were never officially published, his biographer, Fernand Ouellette, managed to obtain a copy of this document from Ernst Schoen, Varèse's first pupil. The proposal ran as follows:

Only students already in possession of a technical training will be accepted in the composition class. In this department, studies will concentrate upon all forms required by the new concepts existing today, as well as the new techniques and new acoustical factors which impose themselves as the logical means of realizing those concepts.

Also under Varèse's direction, with the assistance of a physicist, there will be a working laboratory in which sound will be studied scientifically, and in which the laws permitting the development of innumerable new means of expression will be established without any reference to empirical rules. All new discoveries and all inventions of instruments and their uses will be demonstrated and studied. The laboratory will possess as complete a collection of phonographic records as possible, including examples of the music of all races, all cultures, all periods, and all tendencies.

The scheme was not to materialize, for Varèse was unable to find an adequate source of finance. On 1 December 1932, while still in Paris, he wrote again to Fletcher requesting access to the facilities of the Bell Telephone Laboratories in return for his services to the company: 'I am looking to find a situation where my collaboration would have value and pecuniary return.' Varèse was so eager for laboratory facilities that he was even prepared to sacrifice his career as a composer, at least for a time. He also applied to the John Simon Guggenheim Memorial Foundation for a grant towards his work. In response to a request for more details he wrote again to the Foundation on 6 February 1933 offering the following proposal:

The acoustical work which I have undertaken and which I hope to continue in collaboration with René Bertrand consists of experiments which I have suggested on his invention, the Dynaphone. The Dynaphone (invented 1927–28) is a musical instrument of electrical oscillations somewhat similar to the Thérémin, Givelet and Martenot electrical instruments. But its principle and operation are entirely different, the resemblance being only superficial. The technical results I look for are as follows:

1 To obtain absolutely pure fundamentals.
2 By means of loading the fundamentals with certain series of harmonics to obtain timbres which will produce new sounds.
3 To speculate on the new sounds that the combination of two or more interfering Dynaphones would give if combined in a single instrument.
4 To increase the range of the instrument so as to obtain high frequencies which no other instrument can give, together with adequate intensity.

The practical result of our work will be a new instrument which will be adequate to the needs of the creative musician and musicologist. I have conceived a system by which the instrument may be used not only for the tempered and natural scales, but one which also allows for the accurate production of any number of frequencies and consequently is able to produce any interval or any subdivision required by the ancient or exotic modes.

This application, unlike his previous proposal, laid down for the first time the acoustical principles which would serve as the basis for a programme of research into the musical application of electronic sound synthesis. The Dynaphone, despite his assertions, did not differ significantly from its relatives. Its ability to generate timbres additively using harmonic stops was matched by a similar facility within the Ondes Martenot. Nevertheless, since Varèse was well acquainted with its designer, he was aware of the potential of developing its circuits to produce not merely an enhanced electronic instrument, but a versatile sound synthesis system serving a wide variety of compositional demands.

The Guggenheim Foundation, unfortunately, did not understand the purpose of Varèse's proposal, and despite repeated requests Varèse failed to win their support. Similarly, despite a certain degree of interest, and a willingness to support his Guggenheim applications, Harvey Fletcher was unable to grant him access to the Bell Telephone Laboratories. It is ironic to note that the latter institution, twenty years later, was to pioneer research into a revolutionary new area of sound generation, computer synthesis.

Despite these setbacks some progress was being made in other quarters. The 1900s had seen the birth of the commercial 78 r.p.m. gramophone record and the 1920s the development of electrical recording systems as a sequel to broadcasting, making generally available a technique not only for storing sound information, but also for effecting certain alterations to its reproduction. Darius Milhaud realized that changing the speed of a recording varies not only the pitch but also the intrinsic acoustical characteristics of the material, and during the period 1922 to 1927 carried out several experiments investigating vocal transformations. Percy Grainger performed similar experiments during the 1930s, paying particular attention to the use of piano sounds as source material.

During 1929–30 Paul Hindemith and Ernst Toch carried out rather more detailed operations on phonograph recordings at the Rundfunk-Versuchsstelle Hochschule für Musik in Berlin. Hindemith was primarily interested in testing his theories of acoustics and the analysis of harmonic structures, later outlined in his treatise *The Craft of Musical Composition* (1937). A by-product of this period of scientific investigation was a collaboration with the scientist Friedrich Trautwein, leading to the invention of the Trautonium, and the composition of his *Concerto for Solo Trautonium and Orchestra* (1931).

Hindemith did not choose to explore the creative possibilities of synthetic sound production beyond the boundary of instrumental imitation. The time was still not ripe for any general acceptance of processes of musical composition which extended beyond the traditional orchestra. Varèse, however, was not to remain so isolated in his endeavours, for the climate of musical opinion was slowly beginning to change. A prophetic address was given extemporaneously by the conductor Leopold Stokowski to a meeting of the Acoustical Society of America on 2 May 1932, entitled 'New Horizons in Music'. Stokowski, as a keen conductor of contemporary music, devoted much effort to bringing young composers into contact with as large a public as possible, and he appreciated the importance of establishing, even on a general level, a sustained dialogue between scientists and artists in an increasingly technological society. His address included not only a discussion of the artistic implications of the uses of technology as an aid to communication through the media of the radio and the phonograph, but also some interesting predictions regarding the future use of electronic synthesis devices as compositional tools.

Another vista that is opening out is for the composer, for the creator in music . . . Our musical notation is utterly inadequate. It cannot by any means express all the possibilities of sound, not half of them, not a quarter of them, not a tenth of them. We have possibilities in sound which no man knows how to write on paper. If we take an orchestral score and reproduce it, just mechanically perfect, it will sound mechanical. It won't have the human element in it. Also there would be so much that the composer was trying to express, that he conceived but couldn't write down because of the limitations of notation . . . One can see coming ahead a time when the musician who is a creator can create directly into TONE, not on paper. This is quite within the realm of possibility. That will come. Any frequency, any duration, any intensity he wants, any combinations of counterpoint, of harmony, of rhythm—anything can be done by that means and will be done.

Stokowski's predictions were based at least in part on a knowledge of some interesting technical developments which were taking place at the time. Hindemith's experiments with phonograph records had caught the attention of several members of the Bauhaus movement, including László Moholy-Nagy, Oskar Fischinger, and Paul Arma. These artists became absorbed with the physical shapes of recorded sound-waves and carried out their own investigations during the period 1930–2. Initially they attempted to alter the acoustical content by running the recordings backwards against the stylus to scratch new patterns. The results, however, were largely unsatisfactory, and their attention soon turned towards the more interesting possibilities of manipulating optical sound-tracks, a recording method developed for use with moving film.

Optical recording involves the transfer of sound information on to film in the form of patterns of varying densities, which may subsequently be detected and reproduced acoustically via a photocell detector. Physical alterations to the shaded contours will thus affect the sound reproduction. Research in this field was pioneered by the German inventor Rudolf Pfenninger, who discovered in 1932 that analysis of the shapes on an optical sound-track elicited sufficient information for the synthesis of a wide range of musical timbres in terms of hand-drawn patterns.

This work was important, for despite its practical limitations it resulted in the first really flexible system of communication between the composer and his synthesis tools. Investigations continued in Ottawa where Norman McLaren completed a series of films employing 'drawn' sound-tracks, and in Leningrad, where Yevgeny Sholpo developed four versions of his Variophone, a machine for graphically encoding sound information. The latter acted as models for the ANS (photoelectric optic sound synthesizer) developed at the Moscow Experimental Studio, later expanded into the Scriabin Museum Laboratory in 1961.

The relentless march of technology, nevertheless, was already signalling the demise of optical recording techniques in favour of another medium, magnetic tape. Magnetic recording systems had been in existence since 1898, when the Danish scientist Valdemar Poulsen invented his Telegraphone, a machine employing a steel wire which could be permanently magnetized by an electromagnet. The quality of reproduction, however, was very poor and the system as a whole decidedly cumbersome. Poulsen made some improvements to his machine during the early 1900s and launched a series of companies to market the device, but these soon ran into financial difficulties and collapsed.

The development of magnetic recording then remained almost dormant until a German, Dr Kurt Stille, began filing patents during the early 1920s. His work led to the development of a synchronized sound system for films using magnetized steel tape. Stille sold the rights of his machine to Ludwig Blattner, who marketed his first commercial machine, the Blattnerphone, in

1929. A model was bought by the British Broadcasting Corporation in 1931 and installed at their Savoy Hill studio. During the early 1930s the firm of Marconi bought the manufacturing rights and began marketing a less cumbersome machine, the Marconi–Stille recorder. Steel tape, however, was still employed as the recording medium and this created many practical difficulties. Erasure of previously recorded signals was now possible, but the tape was awkward to splice, requiring welded joints. It was also extremely heavy and liable to sheer dangerously when spooled at high speed.

A major breakthrough occurred in Germany in 1935 when the firm of AEG produced the Magnetophon, a machine which utilized a plastic tape coated with fine ferrous particles. This invention was a notable improvement on the steel tape recorder and heralded the start of a series of technological developments which led, by the end of the Second World War, to a compact and versatile recording system soon to rival the direct disc-cutting methods of the previous era. The primary advantages of the new medium were the facility to re-use the recording tape, the ease of editing, and the ability to record two or more discrete tracks of recorded information simultaneously on the same piece of tape. Magnetic recording soon displaced its optical rival, mainly as a result of its superior quality of reproduction. This process of change was inevitably self-perpetuating, for engineers were diverted from the task of improving the characteristics of optical sound transfer, and as a result one important recording technique, of considerable interest to electronic sound synthesis, lost the support of commercial development.

Magnetic tape systems supply no direct means of contact between the composer and the component characteristics of his recorded sounds, for the wave patterns are not visible to the eye, nor may they be usefully modified by any direct physical action. Little importance was attached to such a disadvantage for some considerable time, for very few of the studios which emerged during the 1950s and early 60s incorporated any visual means for specifying or altering material. For the most part designers concentrated on the keyboard, the slider, and the rotary knob as the primary control facilities for their systems. It is only in more recent years that the increasing importance of digital technology has encouraged renewed interest in the possibilities of communication through visual devices such as the computer graphics terminal.

Once again it was Varèse who prophesied the advent of such a synthesis facility well before it became accepted as a useful feature. During the late 1930s he entered a period of deep personal crisis regarding his whole language of composition. Having spent a considerable amount of time conducting his own experiments with phonograph records, becoming increasingly dissatisfied with the limitations of his equipment, he spent three years attempting a rationalization of his ideas for a new sound world. As a result of this effort he delivered one of his most important lectures to the University of Southern California during 1939. This included the following observations:

> When you listen to music do you ever stop to realize that you are being subjected to a physical phenomenon? Not until the air between the listener's ear and the instrument has been disturbed does music occur . . . In order to anticipate the result, a composer must understand the mechanics of the instruments and must know just as much as possible about acoustics . . . We composers are forced to use, in the realization of our works, instruments that have not changed for two centuries . . . Personally, for my conceptions, I need an entirely new medium of expression: a sound-producing machine (not a sound re-producing one) . . . Whatever I write, whatever my message, it will reach the listener unadulterated by 'interpretation'. It will work something like this: after a composer has set down his score on paper by means of a new graphic, similar in principle to a seismographic or oscillographic notation, he will then, with the collaboration of a sound engineer, transfer the score directly to this electric machine. After that anyone will be able to press a button to release the music exactly as the composer wrote it . . . And here are the advantages I anticipate from such a machine. Liberation from the arbitrary, paralyzing tempered system; the possibility of obtaining any number of cycles or if still desired subdivisions of the octave, consequently the formation of any desired scale; unsuspected range in low and high registers, new harmonic splendors obtainable from the use of sub-harmonic combinations now impossible, new dynamics far beyond the present human power orchestra; a sense of sound projection in space by means of the emission of sound in any part or in as many parts of the hall as may be required by the score.

Many of the more ambitious predictions could only be matters of speculation at that time, from both a technical and a musical viewpoint. Composers then, as today, faced major problems of specification, particularly in equating the subjective world of the creative musician to the highly objective characteristics of the new technology. By the end of the 1930s, nevertheless, scientific advance had produced the basic theories for the design of sound synthesis systems, and the imaginative and informed musician was thus in a position to make firm predictions as to possible lines of development.

The writings of both Stokowski and Varèse on the potential uses of electronics in musical composition at that time were endorsed by John Cage, a composer who in most other respects subscribed to a very different school of aesthetics. Speaking to a meeting of a Seattle Arts Society in 1937, he postulated:

I believe that the use of noise . . . to make noise . . . will continue and increase until we reach a music produced through the aid of electrical instruments . . . which will make available for musical purposes any and all sounds that can be heard. Photoelectric film and mechanical mediums for the synthetic production of music . . . will be explored. Whereas, in the past, the point of disagreement has been between dissonance and consonance, it will be, in the immediate future between noise and so-called musical sounds.

Wherever we are, what we hear is mostly noise . . . We want to capture and control these sounds, to use them not as studio effects but as musical instruments. Every film studio has a library of 'sound effects' recorded on film. With a film phonograph it is now possible to control the amplitude and frequency of any of these sounds and to give it rhythms within or beyond the reach of the imagination . . . Many inventors of electrical musical instruments have attempted to imitate eighteenth and nineteenth century instruments just as early automobile designers copied the carriage . . . When Thérémin provided an instrument with genuinely new possibilities Théréministes did their utmost to make the instrument sound like some old instrument giving it sickeningly sweet vibrato, and performing upon it, with difficulty, masterpieces of the past . . . The special function of electrical instruments will be to provide complete control of the overtone structures of tones (as opposed to noises) and to make these tones available in any frequency, amplitude and duration . . . The composer (organizer of sound) will be faced not only with the entire field of sound but also with the entire field of time. The 'frame' or fraction of a second, following established film technique, will probably be the basic unit in the measurement of time. No rhythm will be beyond the composer's earth.

In the event, these commentaries proved to be more than mere conjecture. Collectively they established artistic principles which were well in advance of the practical means for realizing them. Thus the subsequent birth of electronic music studios took place in a climate where the problems encountered in relating such technology to the language of music had already been identified, if not actually solved.

On 9 December 1939 Cage performed his *Imaginary Landscape No. 1* in Seattle, employing a muted piano, cymbal, and two variable-speed turntables playing RCA Victor test recordings of fixed and variable frequencies. In 1942 he produced *Imaginary Landscape No. 2* for percussion quintet and amplified coil of wire, and *Imaginary Landscape No. 3* for percussion sextet, tin cans, muted gong, audio frequency oscillators, variable-speed turntables, for the playing of frequency test recordings, buzzer, amplified coil of wire, and marimba, amplified by a contact microphone. Interest in the medium had thus extended to the use of live electronic techniques, and the stage was set for the first properly equipped studios, and their associated schools of composition.

# Developments from 1945 to 1960

# 2 Paris and *Musique Concrète*

The revival of the arts after the Second World War took place in an environment altogether more favourable for the development of electronic music. The rapid advances in technology as a result of the war, an upsurge of interest from many quarters in new sound techniques, and a generally expansionist economic climate provided sufficient incentives for institutions to provide support.

In Europe the initiative was taken by two broadcasting networks, Radiodiffusion Télévision Française (RTF) in Paris, and Westdeutscher Rundfunk (WDR)[1] in Cologne. Both of these established studios of considerable importance, in the first instance pursuing radically different objectives. Movements towards new paths in musical composition during the second half of this century have tended so far to polarize around select groups of activists with a strongly defended identity, and these studios were no exception. The Paris group, which will be considered first, became dedicated to the advancement of their self-styled *musique concrète*, whilst the Cologne group championed the cause of *elektronische Musik*. Intense disagreements developed between the studios and these were aired in public on a number of occasions, notably at the summer European festivals of contemporary music which were then at their zenith. The reasons for this overt hostility were not merely a matter of patriotism, although understandably this factor played a part. They lay more fundamentally in marked differences of outlook as regards the acceptable practices of electronic composition.

To talk of a group when considering the early years of the Paris studio is a little misleading, for the initiative and leadership for the project came from a single pioneer, Pierre Schaeffer. Schaeffer, an electronic engineer, served his apprenticeship with the RTF during the 1930s after initial training at the Paris Polytechnic. His technical skills led to rapid promotion, and by 1942, at the age of only thirty-two, he was able to persuade the corporation, then under the control of the German occupying forces, to initiate

---

[1] Renamed Nordwestdeutscher Rundfunk in 1955.

research into the science of musical acoustics with himself as director. From very modest beginnings as a Studio d'Essai this venture gradually gathered momentum, the more familiar name Club d'Essai being substituted in 1946. In the course of his research Schaeffer's attention was drawn towards the use of recording techniques as a means of isolating naturally produced sound events, and in 1948 he started to consider how such material might be used as a basis for composing.

Schaeffer's preliminary investigations, inspired to some degree by an interest in the Futurists, were concerned with an exploration of the properties of percussion sounds. His recording equipment was very basic, consisting of a simple direct disc-cutting lathe, with all its attendant limitations. Taping facilities were introduced in due course, but not before a considerable quantity of work had been carried out using the former facility. During the first four months of 1948 he studied the effect of striking a number of percussion instruments in different ways. This led him to observe that any single musical event is characterized not only by the timbre of the main body of the sound, but also by the nature of its attack and decay. On 21 April he carried out experiments recording bell tones on to disc, where by operating a volume control inserted between the microphone and the cutter he was able to eliminate the natural attack of each note. Two days later he speculated whether an instrument might be constructed to produce the sounds of an orchestral instrument by means of a bank of previously recorded events. This idea anticipated the Mellotron, an instrument utilizing pre-recorded loops of tape, and more recently the 'computer' organ, where digitally encoded note information derived from recordings of conventional organs is recovered via a performance console.

Having made a superficial study of the attack, body, and decay of isolated sound events, and also the effects of playing recordings backwards, Schaeffer turned his attention towards the task of re-synthesis. His first work, *Étude aux chemins de fer*, was constructed from recordings made at the depot for the Gare des Batignolles, Paris. These included the sounds of six steam locomotives whistling, trains accelerating, and wagons passing over joints in the rails. The piece was constructed for the most part from successive rather than overlaid extracts of material, and this drew particular attention to the repetitive characteristics of the sounds. Schaeffer quickly realized that major problems of association had been created by using sources which retained a significant proportion of their identifying characteristics after processing. As a result the piece was more an essay on the activities of an apparently schizophrenic goods yard than a creative study in sound to be appreciated on its own terms.

In an attempt to overcome this difficulty he reverted to more conventional sources of musical sounds, investigating the effects of playing recordings at different speeds. This led to the discovery that such alterations affected not only the pitch and overall duration of individual events, but also their amplitude envelope (attack–body–decay). Such interdependence made it impossible to vary one of these factors in this manner without affecting the others. A further study of the relationships between these intrinsic features led to a series of short *Études*, realized during the early summer of 1948.

The *Étude pour piano et orchestre* endeavoured to combine the sounds of an amateur orchestra tuning up with a spontaneous piano improvisation played by Jean-Jacques Grunenwald. The result was largely unsatisfactory, for there was no coherent dialogue between the areas of sound material, creating the impression that two apparently unconnected pieces had been crudely mixed together. This early discovery of the problems of integrating dissimilar sources was an important one, for it identified a major stumbling-block for composers of electronic music. Two of the studies, *Étude au piano I* and *Étude au piano II*, were based on sounds derived from the piano alone. Schaeffer had considered the possibility of a *piano à bruits* from a very early stage in his investigations, unaware at the time of similar experiments by John Cage in America. His provisional conclusions, however, led him to reject live performance on a modified piano as little more than a simple extension of the normal characteristics of the instrument, and these studies were created instead by manipulating disc recordings of traditionally produced sonorities. The source textures were performed by Pierre Boulez, the intention being to reflect different musical styles, for example classical, romantic, impressionistic, atonal. Schaeffer endeavoured to achieve a degree of continuity by careful juxtaposition of the selected material, but once again the fragmentary nature of the latter proved problematical.

The first public presentation of these pieces took the form of a broadcast entitled *Concert à bruits*, transmitted by the RTF on 5

October 1948. The reactions of the unsuspecting listeners were fiercely divided, developing into a spirited controversy both in musical circles and the general press. Further developments, however, had to wait for several months, for Schaeffer was posted abroad until the spring of 1949 as an official representative at a number of symposia on recording and broadcasting. On his return he approached the RTF with a view to gaining the funds necessary for supporting a team of assistants. In response they appointed the composer Pierre Henry as co-researcher, and seconded the sound engineer Jacques Poullin, who had already expressed an interest in Schaeffer's work, as studio technician. During the summer of 1949 Schaeffer began to reappraise the role of natural instruments as sound sources, carrying out experiments which retraced much of the ground covered by Varèse some twenty years previously. His next piece, *Suite pour quatorze instruments*, is of particular significance, for it provided the starting point for his work on a syntax for *musique concrète*.

His main preoccupation at this time was the possible parallels which might be drawn between the processes of conventional and *concret* composition. This led to the identification of two distinct methods of approach. On the one hand a composer may choose to start by developing a clear concept of the sound structures he wishes to achieve. Such a picture then requires rationalization and modification in terms of the available practical facilities, leading in the case of *concret* work to a precise set of studio routines which may then be executed. On the other hand a composer may wish to start with a selection of potential sound sources, offering a range of characteristics with which he may experiment, building up from the results of such investigations the elements for a complete composition.

These distinctions were to prove important not only for Schaeffer, but for the development of electronic music in general, for they highlighted important procedural difficulties encountered in relating the subjective world of musical creativity to the objective, scientific world of the sound studio. It will be seen in due course how the former approach requires provision of a versatile specification language, capable of translating a variety of musical ideas into equivalent studio procedures. The latter approach, by contrast, involves a less complex dialogue between the composer and the system, built around the functional characteristics offered by the devices themselves, or in the case of *concret* material the intrinsic characteristics of the chosen sources. Classical ideas of an 'orchestra' and a 'score' may thus be pursued, electronic devices, where appropriate, taking the place of traditional instruments.

In practice most composers have drawn upon aspects of both approaches and Schaeffer was quick to recognize the existence of a dichotomy. His earlier pieces had for the most part proceeded from a general idea of the desired result to an attempt at its realization by the selection of suitable material and processes. In the *Suite* he experimented with almost the reverse approach, studying the intrinsic characteristics of instrumental music and then applying suitable *concret* procedures to produce a new music. Each of the five movements highlighted one particular aspect of this compositional method. The Courante, for example, was a monody assembled from the juxtaposition of short extracts drawn from the entire library of source material. The Gavotte, in contrast, used interpretations of one short musical phrase on different instruments, juxtaposed to create a set of variations. Extensive use was made of pitch transposition, effected by playing the source recordings at different speeds.

Schaeffer was not happy with the musicality of the results, and not without cause. The latter movement suffered particularly badly from its reliance on a phrase which, despite many interpretations and transpositions, retained many of its original characteristics. As a result the primary impression gained was one of monotonous repetition with little sense of shape or direction. These difficulties provoked him to carry out closer analyses of the nature of sounds, leading to a preliminary definition of an *objet sonore*; a basic sound event, isolated from its original context and examined for its innate characteristics outside its normal time continuum. He asserted that the abstraction of such events from natural sound sources to provide components for the regeneration of musical material required processes compatible with the principles of post-Webern serialism. (This assertion was later to be challenged fiercely by the German school of *elektronische Musik*.) Schaeffer tried to establish why his transformation procedures failed to remove or alter significantly many of the distinctive characteristics of his sound sources. He concluded that techniques such as playing recordings at different speeds or in reverse, and the use of elementary montage, did not produce anything essentially new. The use of musical instruments, musical habits, and musical structures had conditioned the way in which he had carried out his processes of analysis and re-synthesis, and it thus seemed appropriate to return to his starting-point, the world of noises, as a more basic source of sound information. Such a move, however, did not remove the problems of association, as he had already discovered in preparing *Étude aux chemins de fer*, and it proved necessary not only to examine the nature of sounds in more detail but also to perfect an expanded range of transformation techniques.

Taking sound events of varying lengths and degrees of complexity as sources, Schaeffer began to study them not only on a 'macro' level as before, identifying the primary characteristics of the structures as a whole, but also on a 'micro' level, examining the inner detail of the characteristics themselves, for example the way in which an attack developed, or the changes in timbre occurring during the body of a note. Such exercises, however, did not offer any major solutions to the problems already posed. At one extreme the micro-elements were still of sufficient duration for the retention of distinctive characteristics which would survive processes of juxtaposition and transposition. At the other extreme the division of sound events into too short a series of extracts led all too quickly to the isolation of meaningless 'blips'.

Despite these setbacks Schaeffer decided that his investigations had reached a stage where he was ready to embark upon a major piece of *musique concrète*, and in collaboration with Henry commenced work on *Symphonie pour un homme seul*. During the early stages of formulation Schaeffer encountered considerable difficulty in selecting suitable sources of material. Two lines of development were uppermost in his mind at this time: (1) the extension of the possibilities of instrumental sources by means of new technical aids, and (2) the development of his principles of *objets sonores*, and their rules of composition.

His quest for an area of sound material which would prove sufficiently rich to sustain a major composition led him to select a source which in many respects offered connections with instrumental material and noises, the sounds of man. His initial idea was to select sound material from noises produced naturally by a man, for example breathing, walking, whistling, but this selection became extended to include sounds drawn from man's communication with the world via his actions, for example the production of percussive sounds, or the playing of orchestral instruments. The inclusion of a prepared piano in the latter category was inconsistent with his earlier views on such devices, and this element of ambivalence suggests that Schaeffer was still far from achieving a thorough consolidation of his ideas. In this instance the influence of Henry clearly served to widen his artistic outlook, resulting in a less dogmatic approach to the use of technology as a compositional tool. The final catalogue of sounds selected as sources was as follows:

| *Human sounds* | *Non-human sounds* |
| --- | --- |
| Various aspects of breathing | Footsteps, etc. |
| Vocal fragments | Knocking on doors |
| Shouting | Percussion |
| Humming | Prepared piano |
| Whistled tunes | Orchestral instruments |

The work is divided into eleven movements, some of which are modelled loosely on classical structures, for example Partita, Valse, Scherzo. The rhythmic pattern of the spoken word or phrase acts as the central theme, highlighted by the use of repeated loops and the juxtaposition of extracts with complementary fragments of instrumental and percussive patterns. The mood is light and humorous, contrasting sharply with the rigid structures of the early pieces of *elektronische Musik*.

During the winter of 1949–50 Schaeffer and Henry turned their attention towards staging the first public concert of *musique concrète*, finally presented in the hall of the École Normale de Musique, Paris, on 18 March, the *Symphonie* providing the centre-piece. Schaeffer was at last able to investigate how the characteristics of a concert auditorium might best be exploited, and accordingly designed and built a complete live performance system incorporating several sets of turntables, loudspeakers, and mixing units. The performance did not go as smoothly as expected, for the routines involved in mixing and projecting the sounds around the hall were under-rehearsed, and the complexities of creating live montages from unwieldy turntables proved at times overwhelming.

The concert, nevertheless, was favourably received by many of those who attended, and was followed by further public recitals on a more modest scale in the Club d'Essai, where the equipment of Schaeffer's studio could be utilized more conveniently *in situ*. The critic Roger Richard, writing in the magazine *Combat*, 19 July 1950, noted that

A public not especially prepared or warned to be on their guard readily accepts the impact of this extraordinary music . . . *Musique concrète* is ready to leave the laboratory. It is time musicians exploited it. When musicians and musicologists such as Roland Manuel, Olivier Messiaen and Serge Moreaux express interest in it we can trust in this departure.

After a short period of absence Schaeffer returned to his studio in the autumn of 1950 to find Henry working on two of his own compositions, *Concerto des ambiguïtés* and a *Suite*. Henry had encountered considerable difficulty in devising an acceptable method of notation for his construction score, and Schaeffer became preoccupied with the task of creating a syntax for *musique concrète*, using these two works as models. The characteristic source phrases in the *Concerto* had been notated traditionally whilst the material for the *Suite* consisted of a series of graphic drawings. The structure of the *Concerto*, however, rapidly rendered the use of conventional scoring unsatisfactory, for the principle sound source was a prepared piano, producing acoustic results which differed significantly from the note-events suggested by the original score.

After much thought he concluded that it was necessary to assemble a *solfège* for the *objets sonores* which would classify sounds in terms of hierarchies of tessitura, timbre, rhythm, and density. A provisional system of scoring was adopted, closely modelled on the classical system. Using conventional five-line staves for each sound element a page of the score was divided into four areas: (1) living elements such as voices, (2) noises, (3) prepared instruments, (4) conventional instruments. The time scale was linear, drawn along the bottom of the score in seconds, with a vertical dashed line every five seconds. For natural instruments and vocal sources normal clef and notational symbols were employed, excepting that the durational values of the individual pitches had to be modified to conform to the time axis. For *concret* sounds, elements of standard notation were combined with extra graphical symbols to give an approximate indication of the events' pitch characteristics with respect to time. Schaeffer appreciated that the method suffered from several disadvantages, for example the use of the vertical axis to represent pitch precluded any clear indication of timbre. This method of representation was nevertheless a distinct improvement.

The year 1951 was to prove extremely important from a technical point of view, for the RTF agreed to provide Schaeffer with a new, purpose-built studio. This development led to the introduction of the tape recorder as the principal recording medium in place of the ageing disc cutters. The effect was considerable, for the whole philosophy of *musique concrète* was centred on the simple manipulation of microphone recordings, the use of electronic sound sources and electronic processing devices being expressly forbidden. The initial reaction was singularly unenthusiastic, for the long and close association with the old equipment had fostered a methodology such that its limited facilities had become a major part of the musical process. Familiarization with the enhanced capabilities of tape gradually dispelled such prejudices, although it was some time before the disc cutters were totally abandoned.

In addition to a set of conventionally equipped recorders, including one capable of registering five independent tracks of sound, three special versions were installed. One of these, known as a Morphophone, was fitted with a row of twelve playback heads instead of the usual one. Sounds fed to the recording head would thus be reproduced by each head in turn, producing delayed echoes which could be mixed to create a pulsed type of reverberation.[1] The two other machines, known as Phonogènes, were designed to play pre-recorded tape loops via a single replay head at different speeds. One provided a continuously variable range whilst the other was controlled by a twelve-note keyboard with a two-position switch, providing twenty-four tempered pitch transpositions.

Poullin had been particularly concerned with the problems of sound distribution in an auditorium ever since the experience of the first public concert of *musique concrète*. The ability to record five sound channels on a single reel of tape provided the basis for a well-ordered system of multi-channel distribution, and this inspired him to develop a sound projection aid known as a *potentiomètre d'espace*. It is important to appreciate that very little was known about the practical applications of multiphonic recording in the early 1950s. The monophonic long-playing record was only just beginning to pose a serious challenge to the old 78s, and the stereophonic groove was yet to leave the laboratory. Poullin's

---

[1] A more detailed account of this principle, known as tape-head echo, will be given in the next chapter.

enhancement of a multi-channel playback system was thus quite remarkable for its time, offering composers the opportunity to explore spatial projection as an added dimension for *musique concrète*. Four loudspeakers were employed to reproduce discretely encoded sound information, recorded on four of the five available tracks. Two loudspeakers were positioned at the front of the auditorium on either side of the stage, a third in the centre of the ceiling, and the fourth half-way along the back wall. The effects of mispositioning arising from the impossibility of seating an entire audience at a point equidistant from all the loudspeakers were minimized by employing specially designed units which concentrated their energy in a 60° cone, thus increasing their power of projection. This arrangement had one major advantage over the present-day quadraphonic convention of a loudspeaker in each corner. The use of a ceiling loudspeaker made it possible to create illusions of vertical as well as horizontal movements, adding an extra dimension to the diffusion of sound. The fifth tape track supplied an additional channel of information, to be distributed between the four loudspeakers by a concert performer operating the *potentiomètre d'espace* itself. The latter consisted of a small hand-held transmitting coil, and four wire receiving loops arranged around the performer in a tetrahedron, representing in miniature the location of the loudspeakers in the auditorium. Moving the coil about within this receiving area induced signals of varying strengths in the loops, this information being applied to attenuators regulating the distribution of the fifth track between the four channels.

The new studio led to a considerable expansion of activities. Schaeffer and a growing number of associates adopted the title 'Groupe de Musique Concrète, Club d'Essai', renamed 'Groupe de Recherches Musicales' in 1958, and this body was formally adopted by the RTF as part of what became known as 'Service de la Recherche de l'ORTF' in 1960. During 1951 Schaeffer and Henry worked intensively on the first *opéra concret, Orphée*. Many practical problems arose in the construction of a score, and Schaeffer found his visions of a grand opera greatly tempered. After a less than satisfactory première in Paris the work was revised and considerably expanded for a performance at Donaueschingen in October 1953. (Henry was later to rework the piece yet again, producing a new version, *Le voile d'Orphée*, in 1966.)

The difficulties encountered in sketching *Orphée* forced Schaeffer to develop still further his ideas regarding a *solfège* for *musique concrète*. This led him to formulate the idea of an *orchestre concret*, based on the observation that certain sounds would continue to display specific characteristics whatever the degree of transformation effected, within the perceptual limitations of the human ear. The persistence of these characteristics resulted in these elements being treated as 'pseudo' instruments, notated in the realization score in a manner similar to that accorded to conventional instruments.

Schaeffer also felt it necessary to prepare two entirely different types of score: (1) *la partition opératoire*, concerned with notating the technical procedures invoked within the studio, and (2) *la partition d'effet*, concerned with indicating the development of musical ideas in terms of parallel staves, each associated with an element of the *orchestre concret*. To an outside observer an idea of the structure of the work would only be given by the second representation, taking the form of the provisional score discussed earlier. This notational system, however, was still far from adequate, and the problems of sound classification greatly retarded his progress throughout 1951. These frustrations precipitated a deep personal crisis, exacerbated by the discovery that his colleagues were more interested in developing musical ideas within the constraints of the existing studio than with the task of pioneering new techniques and an associated morphology. This conservatism disturbed him greatly, for he could foresee not merely disagreements but more serious conflicts arising between musicians and scientists over the future of the medium.

His morale was boosted considerably by the appointment of the scientist André Moles as a research member of the team during the summer. Moles was particularly interested in the study of perception and had already written a thesis on the physical structure of recorded sounds which closely concurred with the observations of Schaeffer. Investigation of the relationship between the composer and his sound world became the main subject of his work, and his analyses of psychoacoustic phenomena were to prove invaluable in the quest for a *solfège*. Moles was acutely aware of the problems of communication, and he advocated the design and development of machines which could record and display acoustical features in a graphic form.

It was during 1951 that the previously mentioned disagreements between the proponents of *musique concrète* and *elektronische Musik* began in earnest. Schaeffer and Henry's *Symphonie pour un homme seul*, broadcast on radios Cologne, Hamburg, Baden-Baden, and Munich, was received with considerable hostility by those favouring the German approach. The Summer School at Darmstadt, the Internationale Ferienkurse für neue Musik, took up the controversy by organizing a symposium on the subject of sound technology and music. The French and the Germans disagreed violently and the Swiss criticized both for describing their work as 'music'.

Schaeffer returned to his studio to spend several months in a further period of consolidation, determined to defend and expand the aesthetic principles in which he believed. His diary at this time reflects the conflicts which arose at Darmstadt. In particular he criticized the concepts of *elektronische Musik* for providing no obvious key to the problems of communication associated with contemporary music. He also denied the suggestion that *musique concrète* had no connection with the languages of Schoenberg and Stravinsky, saying that it had a middle role to play, between the poles represented by the two composers. In support of this view Schaeffer equated techniques of montage and tape looping with the polytonal and polyrhythmic structures of Stravinsky, and suggested that the *objet sonore* provided a basis for an extension of Schoenberg's *Klangfarbenmelodie*, reaching beyond the concept of a melody of timbres derived from a series of pitches to include more comprehensive structures derived from other acoustical features.

In 1952 Schaeffer finally published a definitive syntax for *musique concrète* in the form of a treatise entitled 'Esquisse d'un solfège concret'. This appeared as the last section of a book, *À la recherche d'une musique concrète*, which outlined the events of the previous four years. The treatise is divided into two main sections. The first consists of a set of twenty-five provisional definitions for use in the description of *objets sonores*, and the basic processes which might be applied to them, whilst the second is concerned with the application of these definitions to create an operational language for the synthesis of *musique concrète*.

The twenty-five provisional definitions may be summarized as follows:

(1) *Prélèvement*, the initial action of creating a sound and recording it on to disc or tape.

Any such sound event (*objet sonore*) is then classified in two ways, each associated with its own set of definitions:

A.  (2) *Classification matérielle des objets sonores*, the material classification of sounds prior to any aesthetic or technical analysis. This classification is based on the temporal length of each sound and its centre of interest. Three classes are identified:

    (3) *Échantillon*, a sound lasting several seconds or more with no clearly defined centre of interest.

    (4) *Fragment*, a sound lasting one or perhaps a few seconds with a clearly defined centre of interest.

    (5) *Éléments*, short extracts isolated from a sound, for example the attack, decay, or part of the main body of the event.

B.  (6) *Classification musicale des objets sonores*, value judgements on the nature of sounds, in particular their degree of complexity. Four classes are identified:

    (7) *Monophonie*, concomitant elements isolated by the ear from an accompanying texture. Schaeffer draws a parallel with the subjective ability to identify a melody within a polyphonic texture.

    (8) *Groupe*, a *monophonie* of some significance lasting many seconds which may be studied for its internal development or repetitions. A *groupe*, by definition, is constructed from *cellules* or *notes complexes*:

    (9) *Cellule*, thick sound complexes with no overall shape, involving rapid changes of rhythm, timbre, or pitch, or complex combinations of notes which cannot easily be discerned.

    (10) *Note complexe*, any element of a *monophonie* which displays a sufficiently clear envelope (attack, body, and decay) to be equated to a musical note. Schaeffer adds a rider to the effect that the element must also be of a simple nature.

    (11) *Grosse note*, a *note complexe* in which the attack, the body, or the decay is of a significant duration. Beyond certain limits a *grosse note* must be treated as a *groupe*.

    (12) *Structures*, the ensemble of material with which the composer starts his examination. This may consist not only of *cellules* or *notes complexes* but also of ordinary notes, prepared or not, obtained from classical, exotic, or experimental instruments.

The next group of definitions identifies the operations involved in processing the sound prior to the main task of composition,

(13) *Manipulations*. Three types are identified:

(14) *Transmutation*, any manipulaion of the material which leaves the form essentially unaltered.

(15) *Transformation*, any manipulation which alters the form rather than the material.

(16) *Modulation*, any manipulation which is not clearly a *transmutation* or a *transformation*, but a variation selectively applied to one of the three attributes of pitch, intensity, or timbre.

(17) *Paramètres caractérisant un son* leads on from definition (16) to propose parameters for the analysis of *concret* sounds. In place of the classical notions of pitch, intensity, and duration, Schaeffer substitutes the idea of

(18) three *plans de référence*, which describe the evolution of each of these quantities as a function of one of the others: pitch/intensity, pitch/duration, and intensity/duration.

The importance of these *plans* merits a close examination of their characteristics, and these will be returned to in due course.

The next group of definitions describes the primary processes involved in realizing a piece of *musique concrète*:

(19) *Procédés d'execution*. Six operations are identified, the last three being concerned with the spatial organization of the material in its final realization:

(20) *Préparations*, the use of classical, exotic, or modern musical instruments as sound sources, without any restriction as to the mode of their performance.

(21) *Montage*, the construction of *objets sonores* by simple juxtaposition of pre-recorded fragments.

(22) *Mixage*, in contrast to *montage*, involves the superimposition of *monophonies*, to create polyphonic textures.

(23) *Musique spatiale*, all music which is concerned with the projection of *objets sonores* in space during a public performance.

(24) *Spatialisation statique*, the projection of clearly identifiable *monophonies* from specific loctions. This feature arises from the use of different channels on the multitrack tape recorder for the distribution of information at the time of *mixage*.

(25) *Spatialisation cinématique*, the dynamic projection of *objets sonores* during performance using the *potentiomètre d'espace*.

These definitions by their very nature could only serve as generalizations of the processes involved in the earlier stages of *musique concrète*. The whole *solfège* was subject to substantial change as Schaeffer's work continued, to be consolidated in a formidable work, *Traité des objets musicaux*, which appeared in 1966. It nevertheless gives a useful insight into the philosophical principles applied during its gestation. The three *plans de référence* have a more lasting significance which extends well beyond the limited sphere of *concret* composition, for they are germane to any psychoacoustic study or synthesis of sound material.

Schaeffer defined his *plans* as follows:

(i) *Plan mélodique ou des tessitures*, the evolution of pitch parameters with respect to time.

(ii) *Plan dynamique ou des formes*, evolution of intensity parameters with respect to time.

(iii) *Plan harmonique ou des timbres*, the reciprocal relationship between the parameters of pitch and intensity represented as a spectrum analysis.

These three *plans* may be combined as follows:

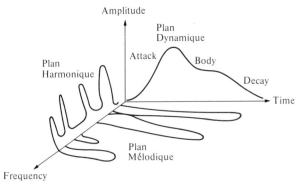

**Figure 1**

The result highlights the problems encountered in creating a visual representation of sonological events.[1] Although several attempts have been made to improve on this model over the years the impossibility of reducing such detail to a single two-dimensional graph has proved a major stumbling-block. The model cannot be expanded to embrace multiple *objets sonores*, and is in itself only

---

[1] The term 'sonology' has been proposed for the mental processes which operate upon received sound information for purposes of image retention, intelligibility, and contextual analysis.

capable of limited accuracy. The *plan harmonique*, for example, only provides an accurate indication of timbre at one selected instant during the course of the event. If this spectrum changes significantly several extra *plans harmoniques* might be required to represent the timbre at different stages in the evolution of the *objet sonore*.

Schaeffer was only too well aware of these difficulties. His solution was to construct a syntax based on a limited number of descriptive criteria for each *plan*. This involved a rationalization of the seemingly infinite range of sonological possibilities into categories which were neither too specific nor too vague. His approach was based on the following line of reasoning. In the strictest sense it is impossible to give a simple description of the evolution of pitch with respect to time unless the sound under examination is exceptionally pure. As noted above, a thorough description would demand the superimposition of the *plan harmonique* both on the *plan mélodique*, to obtain a frequency/time graph of partials, and also on the *plan dynamique*, to obtain an amplitude/time graph of partials, thus destroying the whole purpose of the simplified analytical model. Fortunately the psychology of perception offers a viable compromise, for the brain, when evaluating the quality of a sound at a selected instant, takes into account the acoustic phenomena which have immediately preceded. Indeed, there is a minimum sampling time necessary for the comprehension of any sonological event. Experiments have shown that sufficient information is contained in extracts of the order of about 1/20 sec for the brain to identify any centre or centres of pitch interest with some degree of certainty. Lengthening the analysis interval permits the ear to study the changes in these centres with respect to time.

Schaeffer's approach is of considerable significance, for it focuses attention on aspects of psychoacoustics which are an essential part of any study or manipulation of sound material, whether natural or electronic in origin. He made an important distinction between two very different elements regularly encountered in *objets sonores*: (i) the complex spectrum associated with a sharp attack or an abrupt change in content, (ii) the more ordered, slowly changing spectrum usually associated with the body and the decay. The latter characteristic is particularly clear if the *objet* is a note with a definite pitch centre. The former characteristic is often described as a transient response, an important feature in many natural musical sounds. One of the major problems of all-electronic synthesis even today is the difficulty encountered in creating satisfactory transients, and this aspect will be returned to in due course.

During attack transients the spectrum table is extremely complex, so much so that a *plan harmonique* drawn during this particular stage of a sound would be most misleading, for its content will be undergoing rapid changes only partially comprehended by the ear. The spectral elements are in many instances so disordered that the result is a semi-continuous spectrum of noise, indicated on the *plan mélodique* by a wide shaded band or bands of frequencies. The body and the decay, on the other hand, are often sufficiently stable for a much narrower band or bands to be drawn, in particular clear cases reducing to a line. Schaeffer thus proposed that a single *plan harmonique* for an *objet sonore* should be drawn during the body of a note, at the point where the spectrum reaches its greatest state of development. The diagram above (p. 33) illustrates the use of the three *plans* to identify the salient features of a sound of moderate density, displaying three predominant areas of partials after an initial transient. It also reveals that the decay is characterized by a more rapid attenuation of higher partials relative to their lower counterparts.

Five principal criteria were proposed for evaluating the *plan mélodique*, to be associated specifically with the pitch characteristics displayed during the body of the *objet sonore*: (a) *stable*, displaying a fixed pitch characteristic, (b) *cyclic*, displaying a pitch vibrato of about 5 to 6 Hertz (Hz), (c) *continuous ascent*, (d) *continuous descent*, and (e) *discontinuous*, where the pitch flickers in a complex fashion. (See fig. 2.)

Suggestions for subsidiary criteria included a variation on (b), *spinning*, to describe sounds which fluctuate more rapidly about a central pitch, and a variation on (e), *indistinct*, to describe the pitchless quality of uniform noise.

The principal criteria for the *plan dynamique* were divided into four groups, one for the attack, two for the body, and one for the decay. Three principal criteria are specified for the attack: (a) *plucked*, (b) *percussive*, and (c) *aeolian*. (See fig. 3.)

Two subsidiary criteria were suggested for use in describing the artificial types of attack encountered in the use of *concret* techniques: (a) *stepped*, to describe an attack which develops as a succession of terraced levels, and (b) *pulsed*, to describe an attack

**Figure** 2

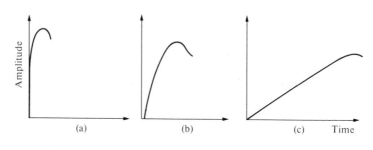

**Figure** 3

which develops in successive waves.

The decision to provide two complementary sets of principal criteria for the body of the sound requires some explanation. Schaeffer clearly felt it desirable to classify not only the nature of the body itself, but also the way in which it develops out of the attack. Under the latter heading six principal criteria were proposed: (a) *shock*, no sustaining into a body at all, (b) *natural resonance*, the sound sustained by a smooth natural reverberation, (c) *artificial resonance*, the same effect created by artificial overlaying, (d) *drubbing*, a beating continuation of the attack impetus, (e) *pulsation*, sustaining by repetition of the attack either sequentially or by partial overlaying, and (f) *artificial*, a synthetic sustaining characteristic produced by a montage of various elements.

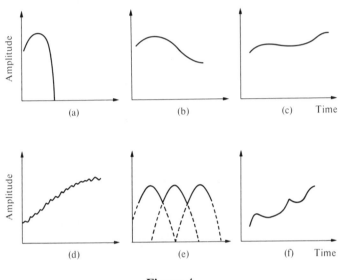

**Figure** 4

Five principal criteria were proposed for the body itself, with the intention that these should be treated as complementary to the criteria for the *plan mélodique*, discussed above: (a) *stable*, steady intensity, (b) *cyclic*, continuous amplitude vibrato of about 1 to 5 per cent, (c) *continuous crescendo*, (d) *continuous decrescendo*, and (e) *discontinuous*, for example stepped or pulsing. (See fig. 5.)

The decay of a sound, concerned with the reverberative dissipation of the accumulated energy, was accorded five principal criteria: (a) *cut dead*, rapid decay with almost no reverberation, (b) *normal reverberation*, a natural exponential decay, (c) *artificially extended reverberation*, generally involving a subsidiary peak of reverberant energy, (d) *artificially discontinuous reverberation*, sharp interruptions to the natural decay characteristic, and (e) *artificially cyclic reverberation*, superimposition of an amplitude vibrato on to the decay. (See fig. 6.)

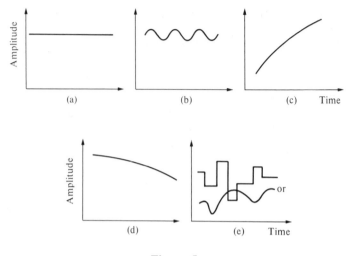

**Figure** 5

The *plan harmonique*, as already observed, provided an analysis of the timbral spectrum of an *objet sonore*, most suitably at the peak of its development. Schaeffer's approach was slightly different for this *plan*, for he divided his principal criteria into three complementary groups, concerned respectively with density, richness, and coloration. Four principal criteria of density were proposed: (a) *pure*, a single fundamental tone, (b) *blurred*, a less distinct fundamental, (c) *thick*, an identifiable primary area of frequency, but with no clear fundamental, and (d) *white*, no distinct frequency area. (See fig. 7.)

Two principal criteria of richness were identified: (a) *rich timbre*, displaying many partials, and (b) *poor timbre*, displaying few partials. (See fig. 8.)

Three principal criteria of coloration were identified. These were intended to provide a qualitative assessment, as a counterpart to the more quantitative assessment provided by the criteria of richness: (a) *dark*, few partials, rapidly falling in intensity up the spectrum, (b) *clear*, few partials, but with a more evenly distributed energy spectrum, (c) *brilliant*, a similar energy distribution to that shown in a clear sound, but with a greater number of upper partials forming more concentrated groups.

**Figure** 6

**Figure** 7

**Figure** 8

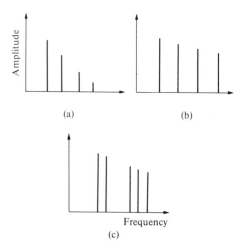

**Figure** 9

These thirty-three criteria, for all their generalities, provide for some 54,000 different combinations of sonological characteristics, a daunting indication of the scale of the task facing any prospective morphologist. The 'Esquisse d'un solfège concret' was only intended as a preliminary treatise, designed to serve the needs of a particular school evolving around the philosophy of *musique concrète*. It is pertinent, nevertheless, to note that this pioneering attempt to study the nature of sound in relation to the electronic studio has provided a major bench-mark for those who have sought to improve upon it.

The year of its publication could not have been more auspicious. During the rebirth of the arts after the Second World War, Paris had become increasingly important as a focal point for developments in new music. Composers who worked in the studio at this time included Jean Barraqué, Pierre Boulez, Michel Philippot, and Hermann Scherchen. Visits were also paid by Yves Baudrier, Marcel Delannoy, Henri Dutilleux, Karel Goeyvaerts, Jean-Jacques Grunenwald, André Jolivet, Olivier Messiaen, Darius Milhaud, and Karlheinz Stockhausen. The compositional ideas of the period influenced the way in which *concret* techniques were developed, particular interest being paid to the application of serial or similar determinate procedures for the specification of duration, pitch, dynamics, and timbre. Messiaen, for example, produced a short study, *Timbres-durées*, and Boulez employed a precise plan for both duration and pitch in his *Étude I sur un son*, using the Phonogènes to give chromatic intervals and octave transpositions of a single sound source. Neither of these composers, however, sustained more than a passing connection with Schaeffer's studio, discouraged perhaps by the inevitable lack of refinement at this time. Stockhausen's brief association with the studio arose during his year's study with Messiaen at the Paris Conservatoire. Goeyvaerts had drawn his attention to the synthesis possibilities of the sine-wave generator, and the recording facilities at the Club d'Essai attracted him for reasons which were distinctly counter to Schaeffer's ideas. Stockhausen nevertheless completed a short piece of *musique concrète* entitled *Étude* (Electronic Composition 1953 No. 1) before returning to Germany and a far more lasting and well-known association with developments at Cologne. In 1954 Milhaud produced a work entitled *La Rivière endormie* for mezzo soprano, two actors, orchestra, and tape, and Varèse visited the studio to produce the first version of the tape part for his piece *Déserts*, an event which will be returned to in a later chapter.

Towards the end of the decade the principles of *musique concrète* became far more catholic, electronic sound generation and processing techniques gaining gradual acceptance. Natural sound sources, however, remained the primary interest for many composers. During 1957–8 the Greek-born composer Iannis Xenakis produced his first major studio work, *Diamorphoses* (revised 1968), in which he applied principles of mathematical organization to the processes of composition with *concret* sounds. The mechanistic influence on the modern world is reflected in the choice of material, for example jets, bells, and the sounds of destruction. Over the same period Schaeffer began a major reorganization of both his methods of composition and also the studio itself, and the term *musique concrète* was replaced by the far more universal description *expériences musicales*. Schaeffer's two major compositions of 1958, *Étude aux allures* and *Étude aux sons animés*, demonstrated a significant change in his outlook. Instead of concentrating on the manipulation of material extracted from existing sound sources he placed considerable emphasis on the reverse technique of additive synthesis, building up rich timbres from simple components. This approach reflected the philosophies of the Cologne and Milan studios, to be discussed shortly. Henry departed to found his own studio Apsome elsewhere in Paris, and

Luc Ferrari and François-Bernard Mâche joined Schaeffer's team, the group renaming themselves 'Groupe de Recherches Musicales', as noted earlier.

Diversification of ideas and techniques was by then leading to very new pastures for some. Xenakis, for example, having worked with sounds of both natural and electronic origin, began to experiment with computers, first as normal data-processing machines and then as sources of synthetic sounds themselves. By the early 1960s work inspired by Schaeffer's studio was merging with other lines of development to create a rapidly expanding medium of electronic music; the age of isolated pioneering was coming to an end.

# 3  Cologne and *Elektronische Musik*

*Elektronische Musik*, unlike *musique concrète*, was pioneered not as the result of the endeavours of a single individual, but as the result of a collaboration between several interested parties drawn from both musical and technical backgrounds.

During 1948 Dr Werner Meyer-Eppler, at that time director of the Department of Phonetics at Bonn University, was visited by Homer Dudley, a research physicist at Bell Telephone Laboratories, New Jersey, USA. Dudley brought with him a newly developed machine called a Vocoder (Voice Operated reCOrDER) which could function both as a speech analyser and also as an artificial talker. In the former capacity the instrument operated by detecting the energy levels of successive sound samples measured over the entire audio frequency spectrum via a series of narrow band filters, the results being displayed graphically as functions of frequency energy against time. The relative levels detected by these filters thus produced a dynamic analysis of the changing timbres. Synthesis, the reverse process, was achieved by scanning graphs displaying shaded representations of selected timbres and supplying the characteristics to the feedback networks of the analytical filters, suitably energized from a noise generator to produce audible spectra.

Although the fidelity of the machine was distinctly limited, its purpose being primarily to process speech rather than music, Meyer-Eppler was considerably impressed. During 1949 he published an important account of the history and design of electronic musical instruments entitled *Elektrische Klangerzeugung*, which included a description of the Vocoder. In the same year he used tape recordings of sounds produced via the instrument to illustrate a lecture on electronic sound production, given at the North-West German Music Academy, Detmold. By good chance the audience included Robert Beyer from North-West German Radio. Beyer had already shown a keen interest in the musical uses of electronic technology. As early as 1928 he had published an article on 'The Problems of the Coming Music' in the periodical *Die Musik* which included a discussion on the use of electronic instruments in musical composition.

Both scientists felt the interest shown at Detmold warranted further public exposure, and they both presented lectures on 'The Sound World of Electronic Music' at the 1950 International Summer School for New Music at Darmstadt. Beyer concentrated on the design principles employed in the manufacture of electronic musical instruments and Meyer-Eppler outlined the state of research in the field of speech synthesis. The composer Herbert Eimert expressed particular enthusiasm and the three men agreed to enter into an informal association, with the object of furthering the development of *elektronische Musik*.

During the autumn of 1950 the design engineer Harald Bode delivered one of his Melochords, an electronic solo instrument not unlike the Trautonium, to Meyer-Eppler at Bonn. This was used to prepare a number of *Klangmodelle*, simple studies in the production of electronic sounds created by layering recordings of selected tones. The results of these preliminary investigations were presented by Meyer-Eppler at Darmstadt in July 1951 in a lecture entitled 'The Possibilities of Electronic Sound Production'. Beyer contributed a paper on 'Music and Technology' and Eimert discussed 'Music on the Borderline'. Schaeffer attended the Summer School that year and, as noted earlier, this public confrontation provided a sharp impetus to the growing differences between French and German philosophies of electronic music.

On 18 October 1951 the radio station at Cologne broadcast an evening programme entitled 'The Sound World of Electronic Music', which consisted of a forum held between Eimert, Beyer, and Meyer-Eppler, using the *Klangmodelle* as illustrations. On the same day a committee consisting of the three participants, the technical director of Cologne Radio, Fritz Enkel, and a number of his assistants, agreed to establish an electronic music studio 'to pursue the processes suggested by Meyer-Eppler and compose directly on to tape'. Work began on the studio that autumn, but it was to take nearly two years for the system to become fully operational, an occasion marked by the formal appointment of Eimert as artistic director.

Throughout the intervening period interest continued to grow. In December 1951 Meyer-Eppler lectured on 'New Methods of Electronic Tone Generation' to an audience of nearly a thousand at a meeting of technologists in Bonn. During the first half of 1952 the composer Bruno Maderna produced a piece entitled *Musica su due Dimensioni* in association with Meyer-Eppler at the Institute of Phonetics, Bonn. This was presented at the ensuing Darmstadt Summer School to an audience which included Goeyvaerts, Bengt Hambraeus, Giselher Klebe, Gottfried Michael Koenig, and Stockhausen, all of whom were subsequently to become involved in the composition of *elektronische Musik* at Cologne. Viewed in retrospect the scoring of Maderna's piece for flute, percussion, and a loudspeaker reproducing a tape of electronically generated material is of some interest stylistically. This integration of natural and electronic sounds conformed neither to the principles of *musique concrète* nor to the early manifestations of *elektronische Musik*, anticipating, perhaps unwittingly, a time when the application of electronic techniques to processes of musical composition would cease to be subjected to such rigid distinctions.

Beyer and Eimert, with technical assistance from Enkel, composed their first all-electronic compositions whilst the studio was still under construction: *Klang im unbegrenzten Raum* (1951–2), *Klangstudie I* (1952), and *Klangstudie II* (1952–3). Towards the end of 1952 the studio became partly operational as a self-contained system, permitting work to be transferred in stages from the laboratory bench to more congenial surroundings. During the first half of 1953 Beyer and Eimert composed *Ostinate Figuren und Rhythmen*, and Eimert alone composed *Struktur 8*. These pieces are characterized by the strict application·of serial procedures to the processes of tone selection and processing. *Struktur 8*, for example, is derived entirely from a restricted set of eight intervallically related tones.

In June of the same year these first complete pieces of *elektronische Musik* were premièred in Paris, ironically for Schaeffer, during the Festival of New Music organized by the Centre de Documentation de Musique Internationale in association with North-West German Radio, and a few weeks later extracts from this programme were presented by Eimert and Meyer-Eppler at the 1953 Darmstadt Summer School. During the autumn, work at the studio gathered momentum. Goeyvaerts composed *Compositie nr. 5 met Zuivere Tonen*, and Eimert composed *Glockenspiel*. The latter piece consisted of twice 60 sounds of a bell-like quality using calculation tables which arranged bell timbres derived from natural bells in series of increasing and decreasing density.

It was at this time that Stockhausen began his long and

influential association with the Cologne studio, realizing *Studie I* (Composition 1953 nr. 2), quickly followed by *Studie II* early in 1954. These last two pieces provide a useful focal point for an assessment of the musical characteristics of this early era, but first account must be taken of the technical and philosophical climate in which they were produced.

The early 1950s has already been identified as a time characterized by powerful cross-currents in the search for new horizons in musical composition. The Germans held the work of the Second Viennese School in high esteem, and many became avowed disciples of the cause of furthering the principles of serialism. An increasing desire to exercise control over every aspect of musical composition led to a keen interest in the possibilities of electronic synthesis, for such a domain eliminated not only the intermediate processes of performance but also the need to accept the innate characteristics of natural sound sources. The acquisition of such power, however, was to precipitate a major crisis in this movement towards total determinism, for it proved extremely difficult to create culturally acceptable alternatives for these essential characteristics of traditional music. *Musique concrète*, for all its limitations and shortcomings, retained a reassuring degree of familiarity by virtue of its derivation from the resources of the natural sound world. The early advocates of *elektronische Musik* not only restricted themselves to entirely synthetic means of sound production, they also were at pains to dissociate their work from the imitative qualities of electronic musical instruments. A continuing interest in phonetic research under the supervision of Meyer-Eppler, however, was to exert a major influence on this quest for a 'pure' electronic serialism, working entirely from first principles of sound synthesis. An initial captivation by the subtleties of formant synthesis was to lead to an integration of natural voice sounds with electronic sources and thence to other naturally produced material. Such a development is hardly reconcilable with the aims expressed during the early years.

Eimert's attitude was particularly pointed. In an article published in *Die Reihe*, vol. 1 (1955), he declared:

In electronic serial music . . . everything to the last element of the single note is subjected to serial permutation . . . Examination of the material invariably leads one to serially ordered composition. No choice exists but the ordering of sine tones within a note, and this cannot be done without the triple unit of the note. A note may be said to 'exist' where elements of time, pitch, and intensity meet; the fundamental process repeats itself at every level of the serial network which organizes the other partials related to it . . . Today the physical magnification of a sound is known, quite apart from any musical, expressionist psychology, as exact scientific data. It cannot, however, be the function of electronic music to make the sine tone the living parasite to feign similarity where disparity exists. Talk of 'humanized' electronic sound may be left to unimaginative instrument makers.

Such confidence in the potential of *elektronische Musik* did not escape contemporary criticism. In the same volume of *Die Reihe* H. H. Stuckenschmidt, writing on the aesthetics of electronic music, observed that

[Eimert] is opposed to all metaphorical synaesthetic interpretation—that is, he is opposed to the idea of composition and interpretation by association and reference.
Aesthetic understanding of the new art is not facilitated by this attitude. It cannot be denied that the associative effect, which the initiator denies as being of any relevance, has been the principal reaction of the majority of listeners faced for the first time with electronic music. There appears to be a considerable discrepancy between postulation and reception, a discrepancy which must be of the very nature of the new art form . . . in that nothing pertaining to electronic music is analogous to any natural existent phenomenon of traditional music, associations have to be evoked from elsewhere. Instead of being integrated, they remain an ever increasing conglomeration of mentally indigestible matter. Thus the listener's reaction in broad outline corresponds to his relationship to a humanly transfigured world.

One year previously, Eimert, writing in the technical handbook of Westdeutscher Rundfunk, had himself drawn attention to a major difficulty: 'A far reaching, still unsolved question is whether electronic music as a universal source of all sounds possesses any coherent form-sustaining force corresponding to tonality—a self-sustaining system of timbres.'

The desire to exercise total control over the processes of timbral specification led, after some deliberation, to the selection of the sine-wave oscillator as the most suitable source of electronic material. From the world of mathematics Fourier's principles of wave-form analysis established that periodic sound material could be broken up into basic sinusoidal components of different frequencies, amplitudes, and phases, and the key to complete flexibility in the reverse process of synthesis lay in the provision of facilities capable of generating each of these components separately. Each of these components is a geometric derivation of simple harmonic motion, a natural example of which is the oscillatory movements of a clock pendulum. The resultant function, if plotted on a sheet of graph paper or displayed electronically on a cathode ray oscilloscope, reveals the wave characteristic ⌒⌣ where the speed of repetition determines its frequency and the degree of oscillation its amplitude. Initially the Cologne studio was equipped with a single sine-wave oscillator. The original studio design, however, offered three other possible electronic sources. Two of these, despite Eimert's avowed dislike, were electronic musical instruments: a Melochord and an Electronic Monochord.

The Monochord was especially commissioned from Trautwein, taking the form of a modified concert Trautonium. Trautwein, however, failed to complete the instrument on time, and it was left to Enkel to finish its construction in the studio workshop. The Melochord, it will be recalled, had already been used for the construction of Meyer-Eppler's *Klangmodelle*.

Both instruments were equipped with a pair of keyboards, each providing an independent monophonic output. The Melochord generated pitches derived from the traditional equal-tempered twelve-note scale, octave transposition switches extending the range of the thirty-seven keys from three octaves to seven. A foot-pedal was employed to regulate the overall volume level. In addition an electronically operated attack and decay envelope characteristic could be triggered for each new key selection. The keyboard system for the Monochord was more flexible, for both the interval step size and also the general compass could be varied using separate controls. Again, a foot-pedal volume control was provided, but in place of an electronic enveloping facility both keyboards could be set to produce a dynamic response which varied according to the pressure exerted on each key.

The keyboard oscillator produced a sawtooth characteristic ∧∧∨, one of the three basic harmonic wave shapes offered by electronics, the other two being the triangle wave ∧∧∨ and the square wave ⊓⊔⊓. The harmonic structures of these waves are determined by simple mathematical algorithms. The sawtooth, or ramp, wave contains a complete series of harmonics such that the amplitude of each component relative to the fundamental is the reciprocal of its numerical position in the series. If the fundamental frequency, $F$, has an amplitude of $x$, the second harmonic, $2F$, will have an amplitude of $x/2$, the third harmonic, $3F$, an amplitude of $x/3$, and so forth. Both the triangle and the square waves are composed of odd harmonics only. In the case of the triangle wave the amplitude of each component decreases as the square of the reciprocal of its position in the harmonic series. The frequency components $F$, $3F$, $5F$, $7F$, etc. are thus associated with amplitudes in the proportions $x$, $x/9$, $x/25$, $x/49$, etc. In the case of the square wave the relative amplitude of each component is the simple reciprocal of its position in the series. The components $F$, $3F$, $5F$, $7F$, etc. are thus associated with amplitudes in the proportions $x$, $x/3$, $x/5$, $x/7$, etc.

In their raw state these three sources are quite disappointing, for they produce fixed timbres lacking in distinctive characteristics. Despite their mathematical differences, the very regularity of their overtone series makes it hard to distinguish between these sources subjectively. A square wave may be mistaken for a sawtooth, and a triangle wave would seem merely to be a less strident version of either. Their intrinsic characteristics only become significant when they are subjected to electronic processing. The most useful technique involves the application of filters to highlight certain harmonic components and attenuate others. Such shaping facilities were incorporated in both the Melochord and the Monochord, but their applications were limited to a general smoothing of the higher-order harmonics associated with the sawtooth generators, rounding rather than structuring the timbre. The result was a consistency of quality appropriate to a performance instrument but highly restrictive when applied to the compositional aims of *elektronische Musik*.

Attempts such as the above to provide simplified methods for creating synthetic sound lead all too readily to some sacrifice of flexibility. At Cologne, during the early 1950s, the only acceptable solution to this dilemma seemed to be the rejection of any technique imposing undesirable constraints in favour of more basic methods of synthesis, however arduous and time-consuming their application should prove to be.

One other source was available in the early Cologne studio, a white-noise generator. 'White' noise consists of a concentrated succession of random frequency elements evenly distributed throughout the audio spectrum to produce a bland 'hiss'. As the antithesis of the single sine wave such a source was of considerable interest, for it is possible by means of highly selective filters to isolate bands of frequencies so narrow that the results are to all intents and purposes single tones. Under these conditions, varying the tuning of each filter produces a result almost identical to that obtained by turning the frequency dial of a sine-wave oscillator. Progressive widening of the filter creates a gradually expanding timbre, for the single tone is transformed first into a cluster of closely adjoining frequencies either side of a central focus of interest, and then into a widening spectrum of 'coloured' noise, displaying an ever decreasing sensation of pitch centre.

Within limits imposed by the number of generators available, and the practicalities of overlaying a number of recordings, a similar effect may be achieved by mixing together a sufficient number of sine tones of suitable amplitudes to span the desired frequency band. Using this technique it is possible to manipulate the individual generators to produce interesting deviations from the gradual progression into noise spectra associated with the former method. Instead of increasing the number of sine tones to span an ever increasing bandwidth with a consistent density the existing components may be retuned to provide a more structured representation of the frequency spread, the individual elements becoming recognizable as individual spectral components. These so-called 'note mixtures' became a major feature of *elektronische Musik*, for they provided a useful basis for creating a continuum between noise-like spectra and pure tones.

The term 'note mixture' (a more accurate description would have been 'tone mixture') was reserved for combinations of sine tones where the constituent frequencies are not related harmonically to a fundamental pitch. This attempt to distinguish between harmonic and inharmonic spectra was not entirely successful, for the subtleties of transformation which are possible between these two types of timbre create a very grey boundary area. The pieces *Studie I* and *Studie II* provide very interesting illustrations of this morphological feature. Stockhausen considered all four possible sources in the Cologne studio before selecting the sine-wave generator as the sole source for both pieces. The possibilities of synthesizing noise-like spectra from sine tones, however, were to manifest themselves in *Studie II*, a prelude to a more thorough working-out of the tone/noise continuum in his more substantial composition *Gesang der Jünglinge* (1955–6).

The timbres for *Studie I* were derived from a table of frequencies, calculated in turn from a series of harmonic ratios. Taking the pitch of 1920 Hz as a starting-point he first obtained a series of six frequencies, successively dividing by the following proportions:

$$12/5 \qquad 4/5 \qquad 8/5 \qquad 5/12 \qquad 5/4.$$

This produced the following values:

$$1920 \text{ Hz} \quad 800 \text{ Hz} \quad 1000 \text{ Hz} \quad 625 \text{ Hz} \quad 1500 \text{ Hz} \quad 1200 \text{ Hz}.$$

Each of the five new frequencies was then subjected to the same sequence of proportional divisions, and the process repeated on each of the new values obtained until the frequency of 66 Hz was reached, this value being declared as the lower limit. A mirror process upwards from 1920 Hz was then applied to provide a complementary series. The selection of timbres was determined by first dividing the table vertically into groups of six frequencies and then marking off sequences of one to six elements in the following order, the columns being read off left to right:

$$4 \quad 5 \quad 3 \quad 6 \quad 2 \quad 1.$$

This technique can best be illustrated by reference to the first section of the lower half of the table:

|   |   |   |   |   |   |   |   |   |   |   |   |
|---|---|---|---|---|---|---|---|---|---|---|---|
|   | 1920 |   | 800 |   | 1000 |   | 625 |   | 1500 |   | 1200 |
| 4 | 800 | 5 | 333 |   | 417 | 2 | 260 |   | 625 | 3 | 500 |
|   | 1000 |   | 417 | 6 | 521 | 1 | 325 |   | 781 |   | 625 |
|   | 625 |   | 260 |   | 325 |   | 203 | 5 | 488 |   | 390 |
|   | 1500 | 3 | 625 |   | 781 | 4 | 488 |   | 1170 | 6 | 937 |
|   | 1200 |   | 500 |   | 625 |   | 390 |   | 937 |   | 750 |
|   | 800 |   | 333 |   | 417 |   | 260 |   | 625 |   | 500 |
|   | 333 |   | 138 |   | 173 |   | 108 |   | 260 |   | 208 |
|   | 417 |   | 173 |   | 217 |   | 135 |   | 325 |   | 260 |
|   | etc. |   | etc. |   | etc |   | etc. |   | etc. |   | etc. |

Without knowledge of the method of derivation, and an ability to recognize harmonic ratios calculated in inversion, the casual observer might be forgiven for deducing that the groupings just illustrated are composed of inharmonic partials, for there is no obvious fundamental to which all the elements in each compound timbre may be related. A normal harmonic series, for example derived from a fundamental of 100 Hz, would follow the sequence

100,    200,    300,    400,    500,    600,    700,    etc. HZ.

No such lowest common multiple exists for the sequence

325,    417,    521,    625,    781,    1000 Hz.

All the ratios, however, are in whole-number proportions (to facilitate study the above figures have been rounded to the present Hertz) by virtue of their method of calculation. Aurally the simpler ratios have a recognizable harmonic coherence. 325 to 781, for example, satisfies the ratio 5/12, perceived as a perfect (non-tempered) minor tenth. The more complex ones, however, focus attention on harmonic relationships which are not so familiar. 781 to 1000, for example, satisfies the ratio 25/32, a 'mistuned' fourth.

These sounds display remarkably bell-like qualities, particularly in the upper registers, and their closely structured relationships create an air of timbral stability. The uncertain boundary between these harmonic timbres and note mixtures may readily be demonstrated by tuning a bank of oscillators to any of the larger groupings and then mistuning them slightly to achieve indisputably inharmonic ratios. The effect is a subtle shift in timbre and the introduction of more pronounced beating between components, but there is no feeling that a major morphological transformation has occurred.

The selection of groupings and the specification of their durations and dynamics were all determined serially. During the piece the entire sequence of frequencies repeats six times. For each pass the members of each source group of frequencies were allocated unique amplitude values in the proportions $n$ decibels, $n-4$ dB, $n-8$ dB, $n-12$ dB, $n-16$ dB, and $n-20$ dB.[1] The value $n$

[1] The decibel, as a logarithmic measurement of relative sound intensity, is a much-maligned and misunderstood quantity, particularly when adopted to measure loudness, the subjective response of the human ear. For the purposes of the current discussion it might be usefully noted that a tone of 1000 Hz may be varied over a range of about 130 dB between the threshold of hearing, the point where a sound is just perceived, and the threshold of pain, the upper limit of the ear's tolerance. Each decibel step upwards involves a change of about 25 per cent in the sound energy level, and represents subjectively about the smallest detectable increase in volume. As a guide, increasing such a tone from a musical pianissimo to a musical mezzo forte would involve an increase of about 20 dB. A further increase of about 25 dB would raise the level to a fortissimo.

corresponded to the standard reference studio level, subjectively associated with a healthy fortissimo. After each pass the allocations within each group were rotated one step so that each frequency in turn became the strongest timbral element. For example:

| *First pass* | | *Second pass* | |
|---|---|---|---|
| 1920 Hz | n dB | 1920 Hz | $n-20$ dB |
| 800 Hz | $n-4$ dB | 800 Hz | n dB |
| 1000 Hz | $n-8$ dB | 1000 Hz | $n-4$ dB |
| 625 Hz | $n-12$ dB | 625 Hz | $n-8$ dB |
| 1500 Hz | $n-16$ dB | 1500 Hz | $n-12$ dB |
| 1200 Hz | $n-20$ dB | 1200 Hz | $n-16$ dB |

After these elements had been further partitioned into their timbral selections as outlined earlier the constant reference level *n* in each selection was modified by a further series of attenuation ratios to provide a greater degree of dynamic structuring. Finally one of six envelope patterns was superimposed on each selection according to yet another series of permutations. Three of these patterns involved the addition of a little coloration from an echo chamber, an interesting method of timbral modification to feature more prominently in *Studie II*.

The duration of events was determined by the strongest frequency in each selection. In the lower half of the table (1920 Hz down to 66 Hz) this value was divided by ten to produce a figure which served as the physical tape length of the recorded sound, measured in centimetres. Frequency and duration were thus directly proportional, the lower the predominant frequency the shorter the sound. Given a recording speed of 76.2 cm/sec (30 in/sec) this created a durational scale ranging from about 2½ sec at 1920 Hz to about 1/11 sec at 66 Hz.

For the upper half of the table a mirror characteristic was extrapolated, durations becoming progressively shorter with ascending frequency centres. Procedurally this was achieved by using pre-recorded complementary selections from the lower half of the table and subjecting them to variable speed transposition. A doubling of the tape speed, for example, led to a doubling of the component frequencies and a halving of their duration.

Three tape machines were available for the construction of this piece; one single-track recorder, one four-track recorder, and one variable-speed recorder. The first two machines provided the primary means for assembling the timbres by montage from the single sine-wave generator. The process was inevitably laborious. Up to four tones could be independently recorded on the multitrack machine, the result being mixed down on to the single-track machine and, where appropriate, copied back on to one track on the former machine, releasing the other three tracks for the recording of further tones. The variable-speed recorder was an old AEG model, one of the very first, specially converted to provide a continuous range from about 9 cm/sec to 120 cm/sec, allowing pitch transposition over about 3¾ octaves.

Variable-speed processing has provided a powerful tool for the composer of electronic music, and its potential was well appreciated by the schools of *elektronische Musik* and, as already noted, *musique concrète*. In the serially orientated sphere of the former the very consistency of the process in imposing proportional change on all the recorded characteristics provided the greatest attraction. In contrast it was this very degree of permanence which presented Schaeffer with some of his greatest compositional problems. Doubling the playback speed not only halves the overall duration of the recorded events, but also smaller-scale variations in amplitude and frequency characteristics such as vibrato, and the attack and decay. As Schaeffer was quick to discover, subjecting recordings of natural sounds to different playback speeds could produce some interesting effects. The sharp attack of a trumpet note, for example, will be perceived as a noisy and irregular succession of noise elements if played at a fraction of the original recording speed. The permanence arises from the impossibility of manipulating such features independently of all the other aspects of the sound. The apparent transformations are the result of our subjective reactions to a scientifically determined process which affects the material as a whole.

The techniques of electronic synthesis, by contrast, provide the composer with the option of avoiding these fixed relationships between envelope, pitch, and duration, at least during the first stages of material preparation. If dynamic shaping is applied to an electronic source prior to variable-speed processing the situation is no different from that which would apply to a natural source. If, however, a source offering a stable spectrum is first subjected to variable-speed processing and then dynamically shaped, any desired envelope characteristic may be specified for the transposed material.

The use of echo enhancement in *Studie I* was followed by a more

significant use of reverberation in *Studie II*. For this piece the
selected pitch series for the source tones resulted in true note
mixtures, for the frequencies were derived from a scale of 81 tones
employing the constant interval $25\sqrt{5}$. This provided steps of
approximately 1/10 of an octave, starting from a lowest frequency
of 100 Hz. Instead of being combined into sets of different sizes,
five element groupings were employed throughout. Once again
Stockhausen used a serial procedure for selecting the frequency
components for each source, a simple algorithm providing a
pattern of frequency spacings as follows:

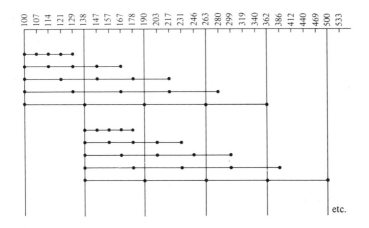

**Figure** 10

Unlike *Studie I* the amplitudes of the components for each
group were of equal volume. Instead of combining components to
produce a direct recording of each mixture, short extracts of each
tone were spliced in ascending frequency order and then joined
end to end to make a loop. Short bursts of these loops, which
produced rapid and repeating arpeggios of the constituent frequencies, were then fed into a reverberation chamber, and the
results were recorded on tape. This technique resulted in sounds
which were remarkably 'alive' by virtue of the overlapping effect
of the numerous reflections and the natural exponential decay of
the events from their initial sharp attack. The basic envelope of
each sound ⌐‿ could be lengthened or shortened by varying
the reverberation time. The mirror characteristic of an exponential

growth and a sharp decay ⌐ could then be created by the simple expedient of playing the recordings backwards.

Combinations and superimpositions of these shaped events provided the compositional building-blocks. The first section, for example, consists of successions of chords of similar density, based on pairs of events arranged to give smooth arched envelope shapes, ⌒. The second section, in contrast, highlights discontinuous montages of chord complexes, created by overlapping several forward or backward envelopes, for example: ⌒⌐.

The third section features rapid, staccato sounds, the fourth long chord complexes, and the fifth a fusion and transformation of the material presented in the earlier sections.

These two examples of *elektronische Musik* illustrate the type of processes involved in relating contemporary principles of structuralism to the early facilities for electronic synthesis at Cologne. So far, however, only passing reference has been made to the electronic processing facilities incorporated in the system, and an appreciation of their role demands an excursion into the realms of elementary electronic theory.

Filters have already been identified as devices which will attenuate specific frequencies in applied sound spectra, this subtraction serving to highlight those which remain. In general terms these devices may be divided into four distinct types: high-pass, low-pass, band-pass, and band-stop (notch). High-pass filters act to eliminate all applied frequencies below a specific point, known as the frequency cut-off. Low-pass filters, conversely, act to eliminate all applied frequencies above a specific point. Band-pass filters may be considered as, and indeed in some instances are physically constructed as combinations of high- and low-pass filters with overlapping ranges connected in series to eliminate frequencies either side of a selected region. Band-stop filters offer the inverse response characteristics to band-pass types, attenuating a specific region of frequencies but passing all others.

To the electronic engineer ideal filters should be capable, at an extreme setting, of providing a sharp transition between the two states of signal pass and signal reject. Such conditions would result in the following response diagrams for the four principal types (the shaded areas indicate the frequency regions permitted to pass by the units concerned):

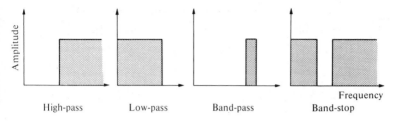

High-pass          Low-pass          Band-pass          Band-stop

**Figure** 11

In practice it is not possible to design filters which change so abruptly from a pass state to a reject state. Practical versions display a 'transfer' characteristic from one state to the other, taking the form of an attenuation curve which may be of varying steepness according to the filter design. In certain types this response may be varied by the user, in others it is fixed at the construction stage. The following examples illustrate the types of response which may be associated with a band-pass filter:

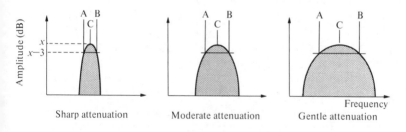

Sharp attenuation          Moderate attenuation          Gentle attenuation

**Figure** 12

The band-pass filter provides the most comprehensive range of characteristics for isolating frequency areas within a rich source spectrum. The following features are significant for the musical user:

(1) the centre frequency of the pass band ($C$ in the above diagrams);
(2) the effective width of the pass band, the limits being defined as the points at which the energy levels have fallen by 3 dB from the energy levels at the centre of the band ($A$ to $B$ in the above);
(3) the flatness of response within the pass band, and the associated rate of attenuation either side.

If such a filter is constructed from a pair of high-pass and low-pass units, as described above, the bandwidth and the rate of attenuation may be made independently adjustable:

Broad pass band, sharp
attenuation both sides

Narrow pass band, sharp lower limit,
gentle higher limit attenuation

**Figure** 13

If the filter is of an integrated type, however, the bandwidth and the response characteristics are usually interdependent, the steeper the response the smaller the effective bandwidth. The sharpness of such a filter's setting is described either in terms of decibels of attenuation per musical octave deviation from the centre frequency, for example 12 dB per octave, or as a '$Q$' factor, a measure of the curve's exponential characteristic with respect to the centre frequency. The penultimate set of diagrams above, representing $Q$s of about 2 to 80, is typical of the responses obtainable from this type of variable, band-pass filter. The effect of applying noise as an input signal to such a unit and increasing the $Q$ is thus the isolation of a progressively narrower band of frequencies. This process of increasing resolution is not infinite, however, for according to the quality of the design there comes a point when the filter circuitry cannot be prevented from becoming self-oscillatory, generating a sine wave at the centre frequency without any external excitation. In cheap modern synthezisers, often quite deliberately, band-pass filters are designed to resonate at relatively modest $Q$ values. High-quality designs, however, can be set to very high $Q$s, perhaps in the order of 200, before resonance occurs.

The Cologne studio was equipped with a variable centre frequency, centre $Q$, band-pass filter unit, offering as options a high-pass or a low-pass mode of operation according to the position of a selector switch. Such a facility was limited in its application, for only one simple shaping characteristic could be produced at a time. More elaborate manipulations of a number of areas of the applied spectrum requires the use of several band-pass units tuned to different frequencies, each receiving its own direct feed of the source and passing its processed output to a mixing unit. Such an arrangement of filters in parallel is commonly referred to as a filter bank. In the majority of modern designs the centre frequencies of the constituent units are fixed at the construction stage, the most commonly employed settings being in accordance with the frequency divisions associated with the tempered scale, for example octave, third-octave, or semitone spacings. To a musician it might seem appropriate to derive the tunings for such a bank from a suitable reference pitch such as concert A, 440 Hz. The electronics industry, however, has generally thought otherwise. The standard settings for a third-octave bank, for example, have been specified as 40, 50, 62.5, 80, 100, 125, 160, . . . etc. Hz, quite unrelated to any of the tempered pitches of the musical keyboard.

In a typical unit each filter is fitted with an attenuator allowing the overall gain at the centre of the pass band to be varied from zero to a suitable maximum, typically level in = level out.

INPUT

OUTPUT

Gain controls

Filter units tuned to a sequence of centre frequencies

**Figure** 14

The $Q$ response, like the centre frequency, is normally fixed so that two adjacent filters set to the same through gain will combine to produce a flat response over the enclosed frequency region.

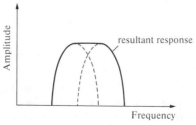

Amplitude

resultant response

Frequency

**Figure** 15

The reason for this becomes clearer when the effect of setting all the filters to the same through gain is considered. The result is an even response throughout the range of the bank, all components of the applied spectra being passed without undue alteration. Variations from this norm introduce elements of timbral shaping, the variety of choice being determined by the spectral nature of the source and the number of filters assigned to each octave. 'White' noise would appear to provide the most versatile source of input for such a bank in view of its uniform spectral density. A filter bank tuned to musical octaves or divisions thereof, however, does not divide the audio spectrum into equal frequency bands, for musical pitch follows a logarithmic characteristic, not a linear one. Octaves from a starting frequency of 55 Hz, for example, follow the series 110, 220, 440, 880, etc. Hz. The absolute bandwidth of each filter thus increases in proportion up the bank, doubling every octave. The use of 'white' noise, supplying constant energy per unit frequency division, will thus bias the output of any shaping characteristic selected via the bank towards the higher frequency regions. To overcome this drawback many studios have incorporated a 'pink' noise generator as an alternative source. This provides a constant density of spectral energy per musical interval, exactly matching the bandwidth characteristics of the above types of filter bank. Patterns of attenuation settings thus match the perceived result. For example:

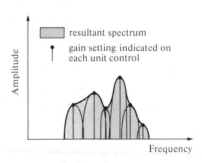

**Figure** 16

Lack of funds restricted the Cologne studio to a single, octave filter bank in the first instance. This consisted of eight filters tuned to centre frequencies of 75, 150, 300, 600, 1200, 2400, 4800, and 9600 Hz respectively. In due course, whilst expanding the range of studio facilities generally, some thought was given to the possible benefits of constructing non-standard filter banks where, instead of dividing the audio spectrum into octave or part-octave divisions, centre frequencies would be spaced to reflect the more linear distribution of partials commonly associated with conventional musical pitch sources. Harmonics, for example, as simple multiples of a fundamental frequency, become increasingly closer together intervallically as the series is ascended. A consistent measure of control over the selection of components from any such source would thus demand a bank of evenly spaced filters, perhaps every 100 Hz or so, depending on the frequency of the fundamental. The number of units required, however, makes such an approach totally impracticable. One of the engineers at Cologne radio, Karl-Heinz Adams, proposed the following compromise, incorporating a facility to switch the centre frequencies of the units to a number of different settings:

One filter with three switch settings, covering the range 25–100 Hz in 25 Hz steps.
Three filters with twelve switch settings, covering the range 100–1000 Hz in 75 Hz steps.
Three filters with thirteen switch settings, covering the range 1000–5000 Hz in 307 Hz steps.
Three filters with ten switch settings, covering the range 5000–15 000 Hz in 1000 Hz steps.

Despite the flexibility of operation suggested by the above arrangement such approaches to filter-bank design never became popular, and it is rare to find such a device in a modern studio.

One important area of sound processing which has so far received little explanation concerns the use of modulation techniques. Two of these processes, amplitude and frequency modulation, have become especially identified with the voltage-controlled synthesizer, commercial versions of which first appeared during the mid 1960s. Despite the less developed state of studio electronics during the previous decade, devices offering these characteristics were incorporated in the designs of early studios such as Cologne. One special type of modulator, known as a ring modulator, has survived the advances of technology virtually unaltered. This is a device which accepts two separate input signals, performs a mathematical operation on the constituent frequency components, and presents the results as a single output. The products of this modulation are known as sum and difference tones in view of the interaction of the applied signals: If a frequency, $F_1$, of 400 Hz is presented to one of the inputs and a frequency, $F_2$, of 300 Hz is presented to the other, the products are a sum tone $F_1+F_2$, and a difference tone $F_1-F_2$. (If the latter result is negative the sign may be ignored since it is the *difference* value which is required.) In the above instance the result is a sound consisting of two tones, one of 700 Hz, the other of 100 Hz. If one (or both) of the inputs is complex then each component is subjected to modulation. A sound consisting of the three harmonics 300, 600, and 900 Hz, modulated with a tone of 75 Hz, for example, will produce a spectrum consisting of the sum tones 375, 675, and 975 Hz, and the difference tones 225, 525, and 825 Hz.

The mathematical nature of the process results in a very distinctive range of timbres. The products obtained will be non-harmonic unless the source tones are related in specific whole-number ratios. By way of an illustration, a tone of frequency $F$ modulated with a tone of frequency $4F$ will generate products of $5F$ and $3F$. Further examples may be investigated by a few minutes' quick calculation with paper and pencil. The ability to transform harmonic spectra into non-harmonic spectra (consider the earlier example of a note consisting of the components 300, 600, and 900 Hz modulated with a tone of 75 Hz) provides an interesting studio procedure. The usefulness of the technique, however, is restricted by its very nature, for the ratios are fixed determinates. One may vary the sources, but not the way they interact. The process is particularly conducive to the production of bell-like sounds, amenable to further modification via devices such as filters.

With regard to other modulation devices available at Cologne, the basis for one type of amplitude modulator existed in the electronic enveloping facility attached to the Melochord. If such a circuit is made self-triggering the attack/decay characteristic will automatically recycle, setting up a regular modulation of amplitude. As an integral part of a much-disliked electronic musical instrument, however, this envelope shaper received little attention. Instead a technique was developed whereby a ring modulator could be transformed into an electronic 'gate', alternately blocking and passing an applied signal. This involved the following arrangement:

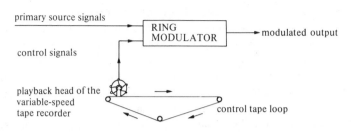

**Figure** 17

The tape loop consisted of a prepared pattern of impulses; short bursts of a signal alternating with short periods of silence. The ring modulator, it will be recalled, is a device which requires two input signals to operate. If one of these is removed the other cannot pass. The use of an audio frequency signal for the control impulses in the above arrangement would result in corresponding bursts of a ring-modulated sound at the output, assuming that the primary source was of a continuous nature. By using a control-impulse frequency well above the audio range, however, the normal functioning of the device was inhibited. Some generation of sum and difference tones would occur, safely above the upper limit of hearing, but the main effect was a leaking of the primary source signals directly to the output of the modulator whenever the control signal was also present.

The use of this technique required care, for variations in the playback speed affected the pitch of the recorded control signals. This problem was partly overcome by selecting a tone for the original recording which transposed to the required frequency on playback at the new speed. Little scope existed, however, for varying the speed of an existing control loop. Cologne set their standard control frequency at 30 kHz, right at the upper limit of the playback response of their machine. Any increase would have led to the disappearance of the control tone altogether, and any significant decrease would have resulted in the reappearance of difference tones at the upper end of the audio spectrum.

The studio incorporated another amplitude-processing facility which permitted the timbre of a sound to be varied dynamically via the octave filter bank. Each of the eight output lines could be switched on or off via an associated relay and level detector, driven in turn by a very narrow band-pass filter tuned to a unique centre frequency between 1000 and 5000 Hz. The inputs to these drivers were connected in parallel to create a frequency-operated control network, capable of decoding multiple patterns of activating tones, recorded individually and mixed down on to a single tape track.

One other device was available for dynamic shaping. This consisted of a photoresistor and a constant light source positioned either side of a moving strip of transparent film. By means of a paint brush and a quick drying opaque varnish, varying proportions of the strip width could be masked, leading to fluctuations in the light levels reaching the resistor. The corresponding changes in the value of the latter were then harnessed to control the gain of an amplifier, which could be inserted at any suitable point in the main synthesis chain.

Reference has already been made to the use of echo and reverberation in the preparation of Stockhausen's *Studie I* and *Studie II*. The differences between these two types of sound coloration are frequently a source of much confusion, and some clarification is appropriate before discussing the techniques involved in more detail. In examining the subjective response of the ear to sounds of different frequencies the lower limit of pitch recognition is identified as the point at which repetitions of a wave become individually perceived, about 10 to 15 Hz. Our ability to detect these repetitions, however, is influenced by the wave characteristic itself. If the shape is extremely smooth, for example a sine wave, the function is perceived as a gentle pulsing, felt rather than heard. If the contours are sharper, for example a sawtooth wave, the abrupt changes in shape are perceived as sharp, regular clicks. Increasing the repetition rate of the latter leads to a blurring of the clicks and an increasing sensation of pitch. What is happening neurologically is that new clicks are being detected before the brain has finished processing their predecessors, hence a growing sensation of continuity. This persistence factor is an important auditory feature, for as the above study has shown the ear displays a response time of the order of 100 milliseconds (1/10 sec) at the lowest boundary point.

Echo and reverberation both involve the generation of successive reiterations of a sound source. Echo enhancement is generally associated with either single or multiple repetitions such that each reflection may be distinguished as a distinct event. Unless the sound is extremely short, or the delay between repetitions particularly long, the sounds and their echoes will overlap to some degree. This feature will not mask the echo effect providing that the time between repetitions is no shorter than the boundary interval of 100 milliseconds (msec) and the envelopes of the individual sounds are sharply focused. Should the sounds display particularly smooth envelope characteristics, however, the value of this boundary as a discriminator between echo and reverberation becomes less certain, for repetitions spaced considerably further than 100 msec apart may become indistinguishable.

Reverberation is generally associated with successive reiterations occurring less than 100 msec apart, for the ear will be acting to blur the repetitions into a smooth extension of the original sound. At Cologne the facilities for this type of enhancement consisted initially of a room with highly reflectant surfaces equipped with a loudspeaker for relaying signals, and a microphone for capturing the resultant response. Acoustic chambers such as this provide by far the most natural type of reverberation. The complex reflections set up under such conditions ensure that multiple reiterations are generated at intervals considerably less than 100 msec. Furthermore, each new element of source information experiences a smooth exponential decay, caused by the steady loss of energy on each new reflection. The main disadvantages encountered are the physical space required, the cost of lining the surfaces with suitably non-absorbent materials, and the practical restrictions on alterations to the reverberation time, defined scientifically as the time taken for a sound to decay to one-millionth of its original intensity, a drop of 60 dB. The introduction of cushions or curtains will achieve a reduction in reverberation, but such a measure is hardly practicable as a regular means of variation.

Such limitations hampered the work of composers at Cologne, and attention was quickly turned towards other methods of producing reverberation, in particular the reverberation plate developed by the German firm EMT. This device, still widely used today throughout the recording industry, consists of a highly tensile sheet of metal carefully suspended in a long wooden box, and heavily screened from external noise and vibration. At one end an electromechanical transducer is attached, converting incoming electrical signals into equivalent mechanical vibrations which excite the plate. Shock waves are thus created which travel in various directions through the sheet, setting up reflections at the edges similar to those created in an acoustic chamber. These are detected by another transducer at the other end which converts the reflected waves back into an electrical form. The tensility of the medium permits the production of extremely long reverberation times, eight seconds or more in some versions. This characteristic may easily be reduced to as little as a fraction of a second by operating a variable damping system.

Such versatility and convenience are not achieved without some sacrifice, for all such reverberation devices introduce their own particular element of artificiality. Cheaper designs, usually based on a coiled spring rather than a plate, are particularly troublesome in this respect, often producing a pronounced and uneven coloration due to the existence of a number of resonances in the spring itself. Plates are far less prone to such distortions, but they nevertheless impart a distinctive quality to the treated sound. For all the early dogma over the use of totally specifiable synthesis techniques, many of the works to emerge from Cologne carry this trade mark. Reverberation provides a valuable tool for creating feelings of warmth and depth in the clinical world of electronic sounds, and the desire for such a tempering clearly outweighed the resultant compromise of principles.

Echo facilities were provided by a tape delay system. In its simplest form such a device may be created by modifying the operation of a conventional tape recorder. Professional machines are fitted with three independent tape heads. The first head, the erase head, carries a very high frequency signal acting to randomize the magnetic particles embedded in the tape coating. Any signals left on the tape as a result of a previous recording are thus removed in preparation for the new recording, imprinted by the second, record, head. The third, playback, head provides the reverse function to the record head, translating the magnetic imprint back into electrical signals. During the playback of a pre-recorded tape the first two heads are switched off. During a recording all three are active. Although the signal from the replay head may be ignored in this mode, listening to its output provides an immediate check of the quality of the recording just made. The significant feature in the present context is the delay which results between the magnetic imprint leaving the record head and its arrival at the replay head. This time interval is determined by the distance between the two heads and the speed of the tape. If the heads are ¾ in (1.9 cm) apart, and the tape is travelling at

7½ in/sec (19 cm/sec) the delay will be 1/10 sec (100 msec). Monitoring the source signal and the recorded signal simultaneously will thus produce a single repetition which may just be distinguished from its origin. Halving or quartering the tape speed will increase the delay to 200 or 400 msec, resulting in a clearly discernible echo. Multiple echoes may be generated by passing the output from the replay head back into the recording channel via a feedback level control:

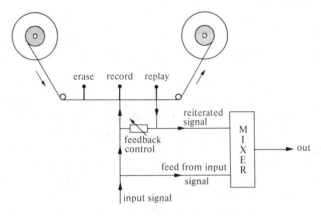

**Figure** 18

If this control is set to unity gain, the reiterations will recycle at a constant amplitude, continuing theoretically *ad infinitum*. In practice the increasing degradation of quality with each re-recording limits the useful life of the recycling process. It is more usual to set the feedback control to a less-than-unity gain, giving rise to an exponential decay in the amplitude of successive reiterations. This technique may be modified to provide a form of reverberation by shortening the tape delay to less than 100 msec. Subjectively, however, the quality of this enhancement leaves much to be desired, for in addition to a growing risk of spurious interference from the recording circuitry the constant repetition time results in a very rigid prolongation, lacking all the subleties of natural or even plate reverberation.

An extension of this technique was introduced into the Cologne studio. This took the form of a special tape recorder fitted with several replay heads, positioned in a row to provide successive reiterations of signals presented to the record head. In addition to separate gain controls for each output, the delay pattern could be varied by adjusting the spacing of the heads. The conventional reel-to-reel transport was replaced with a single recirculating loop, allowing the machine to operate without interruption for extended periods. This device was almost identical to Schaeffer's Morphophone, outlined earlier, and it is pertinent to note that the techniques of tape-head echo were already very familiar to composers of *musique concrète*, albeit in the world of natural, rather than electronic, sound sources.

A modification of the erase–record–replay head arrangement permitted the addition of reiteration to an existing recording on the same piece of tape. By adding an extra replay head prior to the erase head pre-recorded information could be recovered before the tape was wiped clear, the signals passing electrically to the record head for re-recording. Mixing of the output from the normal replay head with this feed could then be applied to provide the desired degree of enhancement. (Direct superimposition of echo/reverberation, achieved by switching off the erase head whilst leaving the record head live is a most unsatisfactory alternative, for the new magnetic field causes partial erasure of the original imprint.) The need for an extra replay head may be avoided by playing the source tape on one machine, and feeding the information to another. This approach, importantly, preserves the original tape for another attempt, should the first operation prove unsuccessful. With tape recorders at a premium in the early 1950s, however, the four-head arrangement on a single machine provided a significant saving on resources.

The play–erase–record section of the latter arrangement provided another synthesis technique explored in particular by Stockhausen in his later works such as *Kontakte* (1959–60). This involved disconnection of the normal replay head and the substitution of a tape loop of a suitable length for the conventional reel-to-reel arrangement, as described in connection with the multi-replay-head machine. Information transferred to this piece of tape from an external source would then recirculate to the replay head after a delay, determined by the length of the loop and the tape speed. Passing this information back electrically to the record line thus provided a powerful means of building up complex spectra with considerable flexibility over the reiteration time.

The spatial projection of sounds was an aspect that received increasing attention as the studio developed. In addition to versatile monitoring facilities within the studio itself, a multi-channel loudspeaker system was installed in the main recording studio for concert hall recitals. During the early years three-channel sound projection found favour, using eighteen loud-speakers arranged in three groups, two in the front corners, and the third in the middle at the back. Driving this system from the four-channel tape machine left one channel free to carry inform-ation which, if so desired, could be superimposed on any of the loudspeaker groups via a set of three frequency-controlled switches and an associated control tape loop or reel-to-reel recording. In a recital the latter facility could be employed to create some degree of live performance, though adherence to the compositional practices advocated by Eimert would have demanded strict control over its operation. This approach to spatial projection contrasted sharply with that associated with Poullin's *potentiomètre d'espace*, where the distribution of sound events was freely influenced by the physical movements of a visible performer.

Attention was drawn earlier to the sensation of depth associated with a reverberative sound. In the natural sound world the distances of sources from a listener are only partially deduced by their perceived amplitudes. The ratio of directly to indirectly radiated information is far more important, the greater the distance, the greater the degree of environmental coloration. In planning the projection of electronic sounds the addition of varying degrees of reverberation to selected elements is an important factor, for the inherently dry characteristics of electronic sources all too readily create a very shallow landscape of sound. Pierre Boulez, writing in the first volume of *Die Reihe*, made the following pertinent observations:

> A final obstacle linked with 'interpretation' is the continuity of projection of a work in space . . . We are here faced with definite limitations; the attraction of an 'objective' work is speedily dissolved, for the psychological reactions of an audience to which music is fed by loudspeakers can hardly be avoided where the audience is deprived of the possibility of associating a sound with a gesture. Thus the arrangement in space becomes a structural necessity and represents considerably more than an appropriate setting for a more or less spectacular exhibition.

The possibility of dynamic alterations to the location of sounds brought a new dimension to the compositional process, for hitherto ideas of utilizing space in musical performance had almost always been associated with static distributions of instruments. The movements of opera singers on stage might be considered an exception, but these are largely improvised as a visual characterization of the written drama, and have little bearing on the music itself. It is perhaps ironic that sudden movements in stereophonic recordings of such works can prove at times quite disconcerting for the listener, denied any visual contact with the dramatic action.

The position of images in a stereo- or multi-phonic system is determined by the relative distribution of energy between the channels. Stereophony permits the creation of a structured spread of sound between two loudspeakers, situated ideally a few feet away from the listener on axes radiating at 45° either side of centre. Wider angles are possible, but these lead to an increasing lack of spatial definition for more centralized images. If a sound is fed exclusively to one of the channels the image will be identified as coming from a bearing coincident with the position of the associated loudspeaker. Its distance, as already noted, will be determined by the degree of reverberative colouring and its perceived amplitude. Progressive redistribution of the signal from this channel to the other will cause the image to move across the listening area, a central position being established when the energy is shared equally between the two loudspeakers.

The generation of images fully surrounding a listener requires a minimum of three channels, the angles between the loudspeakers of necessity increasing from 90° to 120°. Image location, however, is considerably improved by increasing the number of channels to four, allowing retention of the 90° axes. The engineers at Cologne soon realized the desirability of the latter arrangement and quadraphony soon became established as the most useful extension of stereophony.

The decision to locate the fourth speaker in the ceiling for Poullin's system in Paris was notable for its introduction of vertical movement into the location of sound images. Such an arrangement, nevertheless, is rarely employed today, mainly as the result of pressure from the commercial recording industry which has favoured the former approach to surround-sound presentation, not least on the grounds of practicality in the domestic environment.

In a modern studio a variety of techniques are employed for moving sound sources between channels, both mechanical and electronic. A simple rotary control is all that is required to pan a single sound between two channels. Rotation between three or four channels is a more complicated task, involving the manipulation of several control functions simultaneously. One popular arrangement presents the user with a joystick which may be used to steer the sound image over the entire listening area. More sophisticated electronic techniques will be discussed in Chapter 6. One ingenious method for automated panning was devised at Cologne during the late 1950s. Four microphones were positioned at 90° intervals around a rotating table, the latter supporting a single loudspeaker with a particularly directional horn. Sounds fed to the latter could then be passed from one microphone to the next in either direction, the captured signals being distributed to the appropriate output channels.

The practical problems encountered in using a single sine-wave generator as the exclusive source of electronic material led to considerable frustration, especially amongst the younger composers at Cologne, less inclined to follow the strict doctrines of Eimert. Their resultant reappraisal of the potential of other sound sources generated the first major challenge to the establishment. It seemed clear to the new school that there were no a priori reasons for always resorting to first principles when embarking upon an electronic composition. Where existing spectra from harmonic generators could usefully serve particular synthesis routines there was little purpose in prolonging the technical process unnecessarily. Clearly the sheer diversity of compositional ideas precluded the possibility of a single unified aesthetic for electronic music. There was a marked tendency, however, to adopt hierarchical procedures in preparing and structuring sound material, such that the processes of composition became increasingly concerned with the manipulation of earlier defined complexes, or 'macros'. In traditonal music-writing individual instruments are in a sense treated as macros, for they offer a specific range of functional characteristics determined at the point of their construction. Eimert's doctrines are to be commended for their challenge to the assumption that the 'instrument' provided the only philosophical basis for musical composition. Few composers, however, were willing to reject the basic concept of a composite sound source, offering in itself a structured range of functional characteristics. The wind of change, thus, was directed towards a more flexible environment for studio working, where composers might be free to define their own terms of reference, freely drawing upon an expanded range of basic resources.

The electronic source which attracted the greatest interest was the square-wave generator, for it transpired that a simple development of its circuitry transformed the device into a powerful source of compound timbres. In essence a conventional square wave consists of an electronic timing circuit which switches a steady voltage supply on and off at regular intervals, the speed of switching determining the frequency of the resultant note:

**Figure** 19

By varying the proportions $t_1 : t_2$, such that the overall cycle time $T_c$ ($t_1 + t_2$) remains constant, a change in timbre may be produced without any alteration to the fundamental pitch of the note, for example an increase of $t_2$ at the expense of $t_1$ could lead to the following:

**Figure** 20

Aurally the effect on the raw sound is a squeezing out of the strong lower-order harmonics, to leave their weaker higher relatives increasingly exposed. At the extreme case of $t_2 = T_c$, and thus $t_1 = 0$ the sound disappears altogether. The timbral possibilities increase significantly if the generator provides control over groups of impulses, rather than single pulse cycles. A double-impulse generator provides the simplest example of this development:

**Figure** 21

$T_c$ (the first complete on/off cycle) no longer determines the fudamental pitch of the note, for there is a new master-cycle time $T_m$. $T_c$ thus becomes a secondary centre to $T_m$, with a complement $T_m - T_c$. Further, the timbres of these pitch components are determined by the ratios of $t_1 : t_2$, and $t_3 : t_4$. A facility to adjust $t_1$, $t_2$, $t_3$, and $t_4$ independently thus creates a versatile source of compound spectra. Triple- or multiple-impulse generators merely require the addition of further timing circuits into the oscillator loop. One version, favoured at Cologne, is known as a burst generator. This consists of an ordinary square-wave generator which may be interrupted at regular intervals to create pulse trains, for example:

**Figure** 22

One feature associated with square waves and their derivatives has so far escaped attention. All the other electronic wave shapes discussed produce functions which are constantly changing in value with respect to time. When these are transformed into acoustical waves via a loudspeaker the cone of the latter is continuously moving in or out, pushing or pulling the surrounding air to set up pressure patterns which radiate to the ears of the listener. In the case of a square wave the function is merely an alternation between two steady voltage states. This causes the louspeaker cone to jump in and out between two static points of displacement. The air is thus energized by the transient act of switching, no information being transmitted during the intervening time intervals.

If the repetition rate is sufficiently fast the static periods are of little consequence. At lower speeds, extending down into the sub-audio range, however, an interesting possibility arises. Instead of alternating between fixed voltage levels and applying these directly to the loudspeaker, the switching process itself may be used as a treatment for other signals. The alternate blocking and passing of a signal is an important studio technique, as already demonstrated in discussing the tape-controlled ring and timbre modulators installed at Cologne. Direct electronic switching merely awaited development of the appropriate technology. Although this may be classified under the general heading of amplitude modulation its special characteristics have merited the descriptive term 'gating'. At sub-audio speeds the ear will follow the periodicity of the gating function as a rhythmic articulation. As the speed is increased the transient characteristics become progressively more significant, first merging with, and then masking, the source signal.

The significance of these processes was discovered during the middle and late 1950s, powerfully enhancing the range of synthesis techniques. In addition to electronic impulse generation and signal gating, parallel procedures involving the manipulation of magnetic tape were explored in earnest. A continuous source recording of sound material may be physically gated by cutting out appropriate sections and substituting equivalent lengths of blank tape. Playing the modified versions at different speeds will then vary both the rate of gating and the pitch of the processed material. Alternating between fragments of two different sounds, or juxtaposing extracts of several sounds, spliced into a loop, opens up further possibilities, for the resultant timbres are influenced both by the merging of the components and also by the pulse characteristic produced by the transition from one sound to another. Such a technique, it will be recalled, was used for generating the source material for Stockhausen's *Studie II*, and was subsequently the object of much experimentation. The primary drawbacks were very practical ones: the considerable time required in preparation and the impossibility of changing the gating characteristics dynamically. Nevertheless the process could be serially organized, if so desired, and the loops once prepared proved powerful sources of material.

The increasing desire for compositional flexibility eventually forced a move away from 'cut and stick' techniques for material preparation. The play–erase–record head arrangement for building up sound complexes on tape loops was a significant break with this tradition, for such a technique of necessity involved a human performance element, reacting to and controlling the aggregation of events. Stockhausen's *Gesang der Jünglinge* (1955–6) provided a major turning-point in the artistic development of the studio, for against all the teachings of the establishment the piece was structured around recordings of a boy's voice, treated and integrated with electronic sounds. Stockhausen's interest in phonetics stemmed from his earlier contacts with Meyer-Eppler, who, as noted earlier, had continued to research into the characteristics of speech and aural perception. The innate characteristics of such material inspired a fascination with its potential as compositional material, and he accordingly set to work to create a continuum between electronic imitations of phonemes and naturally recorded speech. Cutting up progressively shorter extracts of the latter produced most interesting results, for the events thus isolated displayed remarkably stable spectral features, some approximating to tones, others to noise. Such elements provided a meeting-point with electronically produced sounds, and the possibility of synthesizing speech characteristics or developing new structures around specific elements.

The electronic sources were no longer treated as static, totally determined quantities, for the need to inspire living qualities into the material demanded the use of techniques which produced dynamically variable and conveniently malleable spectra. Macro-generating procedures such as impulse generation and modulation were thus of primary importance. The use of naturally produced source material was taken a stage further in Ernst Křenek's *Pfingstoratorium—Spiritus Intelligentiae, Sanctus* (1955–6). This piece freely combined electronic note mixtures and noise spectra with both spoken and sung material, the latter clearly echoing the era of plainsong and modal polyphony. It was Stockhausen's *Kontakte* (1959–60), however, which provided the most important turning-point in the studio's development, for the piece combined an all-electronic tape with live parts for piano and percussion. Musically and technically it remains to this day one of the finest achievements in the repertoire of electronic music.

Stockhausen was at pains to develop a strong sense of integration between the electronic sounds and the resonant qualities of the live instruments. This demanded the infusion of an even greater feeling of naturalism into his synthetic textures, to an extent where the intrinsic barrier between the two spheres became essentially transparent. Such an objective was not achieved by resorting to the crude technique of electronic imitation so detested by Eimert. On the contrary the integrity of the tape part is such that it functions, and may indeed be performed, on its own without any obvious exposure of its links with the chosen instruments. The points of 'contact' are far more subtle, built on common acoustical features which act to unify the dissimilar elements when they become integrated as a single aural experience.

Impulse techniques figure prominently in this piece. In an apparent contradiction to the trend suggested earlier in a piece such as *Gesang de Jünglinge* the synthesis procedures were meticulously specified throughout, little being left to chance interactions of electronic devices. A closer examination of the construction score (no such document exists for *Gesang der Jünglinge*), however, reveals that considerable experimentation took place during the early stages of composition, subjective assessment thus playing a primary role in determining the generative routines. Further, the application of his concepts of 'moment form' led to a self-regulated freedom of material within the overall ordered structure. Sounds thus could evolve as if part of a separate existence, evaluated for their instantaneous value rather than as consequents of and antecedents to surrounding events.

From the philosophical angle *Kontakte* illustrates *par excellence* the powerful continuum which may be created between the durational structure of events and the timbre of the events themselves. In discussing impulse generation a little earlier a basic relationship was established between the timing of components in a cyclic pattern and the resultant quality of the sound produced. At sub-audio speeds the components become events in their own right, the 'atomic' structure thus being revealed as a rhythmic force. About seventeen minutes into the piece a passage occurs in which the interdependence of these two aspects is dramatically demonstrated: both piano and percussion fall silent, heralding the appearance, like an aeroplane falling out of the sky, of a rasping, twisting stream of sound. This strident intruder spirals down until its pitch characteristic becomes transformed into an ever-slowing succession of sharp clicks, the very components of the original sound. Initially these clicks are very dry, similar to the sound obtained from a wood-block when struck with a hard object. By the gradual addition of reverberation these clicks then become smoothed and extended, with a growing sense of a pitch centre on

E below middle C. This pitch is then echoed by the piano and the xylophone, the resultant merging of timbres providing perhaps the most poignant point of contact in the whole work. This process of gradual transformation is not yet finished, however, for as the pulses blur into one another a fresh stream of sound is heard emerging from the background, echoing the higher resonances of the former like a ringing cluster of finely filtered noise components.

Such a thorough mastery of creative sound synthesis as displayed by *Kontakte* has rarely been approached by other composers. The dangers of allowing technology to dominate creativity rather than the reverse have already been hinted at, and this piece provides a useful point of reference when evaluating the benefits of the increasingly automated studios which were to follow.

By the early 1960s several composers had contributed to the artistic output of the Cologne studio. In addition to the works already discussed the following are of note from the first decade of operation: Herbert Brün, *Anepigraphe* (1958); Eimert, *Etüde über Tongemische* (1953–4), *Fünf Stücke* (1955–6), *Zu Ehren von Igor Stravinsky* (1957), *Variante einer Variation von Anton Webern* (1958), *Selektion I* (1959–60), *Epitaph für Aikichi Kuboyama* (1960–2), and *Sechs Studien* (1962); Bengt Hambraeus, *Doppelrohr II* (1955); Hermann Heiss, *Elektronische Komposition I* (1954); Mauricio Kagel, *Transición I* (1958–60); Gottfried Michael Koenig, *Klangfiguren I* (1955), *Klangfiguren II* (1955–6), *Essay* (1957–8), *Suite* (1961), and *Terminus I* (1961–2); György Ligeti, *Glissandi* (1957) and *Artikulation* (1958), and Henri Pousseur, *Seismogramme I und II* (1954).

The very titles of these pieces give an indication of the strong interest in serially ordered procedures in sound synthesis. The desire to adopt more flexible approaches to compositional procedure, however, fuelled the earlier-noted move away from the strict dogma of the earliest years. Eimert was not unmoved by this pressure, his *Epitaph für Aikichi Kuboyama*, for example, followed the vogue for exploring the use of phonetics by including a part for a speaker, complementing the use of speech sounds for the tape itself. More radical changes in outlook, nevertheless, heralded the time for a change in directorship, and in 1963 Stockhausen replaced Eimert as head of the Cologne studio. Work began immediately on a long-overdue reconstruction of the studio, the most major change being the expansion of facilities into two interlinked production rooms, one equipped with the sound-generation and processing devices and the other with a comprehensive range of recording and playback facilities. The latter arrangement permitted live material to be recorded in suitable surroundings without recourse to one of the main production studios, otherwise heavily committed to tasks of day-to-day broadcasting. In practical terms, at least, the techniques of *musique concrète* and *elektronische Musik* thus became formally recognized as complementary facets of electronic music.

# 4 Milan and Elsewhere in Europe

The breaking down of the dogmatic barriers between the Cologne and the Paris studios had been influenced by the establishment of another important studio at Milan in 1955 by Radio Audizioni Italiane (RAI), with Luciano Berio as director. This centre, although clearly influenced by the design of the Cologne studio, was created to serve the needs of the Italian schools of composition, reflecting far more catholic tastes than those associated with either of its forebears. The majority of composers thus paid little attention to the philosophical implications of using or avoiding the use of microphones in the production of material, for they were far more interested in the perceived characteristics of sound structures than the formalistic principles by which they were obtained.

Berio, writing in the periodical *Score* (March 1956), noted that

> Thus far the pursuit of the other Studios has been classified in terms of *musique concrète* and 'electronic music' which have become debatable definitions from today's armchair perspective since they seem to have been coined partly from retarded-futuristic pioneerism, partly to be 'dissociated from the rabble' and partly from a simple and legitimate desire to identify the objects of our daily discourse. In the long run, what really counts is the approach itself in its purest conception: it establishes an element of continuity in the general picture of our musical culture and is not to be identified only with its technical means but also with the inner motivation of our musical evolution.

The pieces to be produced in this studio during the late 1950s and early 60s included Berio, *Mutazioni* (1955), *Perspectives* (1957), *Thema—Omaggio a Joyce* (1958), *Différences* (1958–60), *Momenti* (1960), and *Visage* (1961); Bruno Maderna, *Notturno* (1956), *Syntaxis* (1957), and *Continuo* (1958); Luigi Nono, *Omaggio a Emilio Vedova* (1960); André Boucourechliev, *Etude I* (1956) and *Texte I* (1958); Pousseur, *Scambi* (versions I and II) (1957); and John Cage, *Fontana Mix* (1958–9). A predominant feature in these works is an overriding preoccupation with texture and sonority, where in an almost surreal manner sound clusters built both from conglomerations of sine tones and also streams of filtered noise become the very life force of the pieces, defining their own structures and relationships to one another.

The very freedom of expression provided a powerful connection with contemporary styles of Italian instrumental composition, concerned likewise with the exploitation of colour and sonority. The Milan school provided cogent answers to the problems of the early Cologne works and the naïvety of the first excursions into *musique concrète*. Berio's *Différences* illustrates how the natural sound world can be subtly enlarged by the skilful use of electronic processing. The piece is a quintet for flute, clarinet, harp, viola, and cello, to which is added a part for tape, consisting of a manipulation of the instrumental material, previously recorded. The latter appears after an exposition by the instruments alone, acting as a powerful force in the development of sonorities as the piece unfolds. Speed transposition, filtering to make textures more remote, and modulation to multiply them become primary features of the electronic process.

Speech, too, became a primary source of interest to composers, particular attention being paid to the continuum which may be established between the rich but unintelligible timbres obtainable from treated phonemes (the smallest units of speech) and the sharply structured and meaningful groupings of untreated phonemes which create recognizable words and phrases. The ability to play upon the processes of human understanding by regulating the degree of perceptive consciousness provided a primary means of sharpening the ear of the listener to explore and evaluate the stranger world of electronic sound. The immediacy of this approach broke free from the structuralism of the Cologne school in a manner which was most appealing.

Berio's *Thema* is based entirely on such a manipulation of a short text taken from James Joyce's *Ulysses*. After an unaltered reading of the entire passage lasting just under two minutes, the piece develops as a growing dissolution of the original text by fragmentation, overlaying, and variations of the vocal timbre via processes of filtering. The text readily lent itself to a manipulation of onomatopoeic elements such as 'chips', 'smack', 'trilling', and 'hiss', considerable play being made upon the noise quality associated with 's' sounds. Alliterative elements, too, provided a tantalizing focus of attention: for example, 'a veil awave', 'blew, blue, bloom', and 'jingle, jaunted, jingling'. His *Visage* went several stages further, technically, integrating phonemes with streams of filtered noise and amalgams of oscillator tones, enhanced by the application of modulatory processes. Here the play on our perceptive skills is all the more tantalizing, for with the exception of the Italian word 'parole' (word), which emerges from ghostly mutations only on the rarest of occasions, no semantically meaningful combinations of phonemes are used. Syllables such as DA, ST, FER, and SA abound, combining to produce nonsense speech which merges with non-verbal sounds of human communication such as gabbles, laughs, moans, and sobs. Such constant inferences of human emotions form a powerful central theme. The work contrasts sharply with Schaeffer and Henry's *Symphonie pour un homme seul*, where the expression of such quantities is for the most part masked by the immediacy of the described actions. In the stage version of *Visage* the original vocalist, Cathy Berberian, added a visual aspect by dressing as an old woman in grey rags, initially huddled in a heap in almost total darkness. As the piece unfolds a cold light grows around her, and, as if in the guise of a supernatural apparition, the body untwists until the face is revealed for an instant before descending to the gloom from whence it came.

Pousseur's *Scambi* is an example of an electronic work which may be varied in performance. The tape is split up into sections which may be freely permuted. The sole source of material is white noise, treated subtractively via filters to provide frequency bands which are gated and montaged to provide agitated mobiles of sound.

The technical facilities at Milan were extensive for this time, and for a short period this studio was to be the most comprehensively equipped in Europe. It was clear both to Berio and the system designer, Alfredo Lietti, that commercial electronic equipment was not always ideally suited to musical applications, and as a consequence the majority of the devices were built to their own specifications. Lietti, writing in the periodical *Elettronica* in 1956, noted that

The engineer who is to design the equipment must first of all consult with the musician so as to obtain a clear picture of the various requirements. Here certain characteristics must be overcome which arise from the different trainings received by engineers and musicians respectively, and the different terms they normally employ.

Consider electronic music, for example. The musician may have a clear idea of the sound he desires to obtain, but, of course, it is a musical idea.

The engineer, however, is interested in the physical data of the sound and whether it can be produced electronically. Obviously the difficulty can only be resolved by an effort at mutual understanding.

The electronic sound sources consisted of nine very stable sine-wave generators, a white-noise generator, an impulse generator, and a modified Ondes Martenot. The provision of nine good-quality sine generators was a considerable improvement over the single master generator offered at Cologne, for it permitted live manipulation of frequency complexes, a facility very much to the advantage of the composer. Special fine-tuning controls were fitted to facilitate accurate frequency selection, and the amplitude of each generator could be adjusted from a central control panel. A cathode ray oscilloscope was also available to provide a visual display of the synthesized material.

The manipulation of material was greatly enhanced by the provision of a generous array of mono, stereo, and four-track recorders. The treatment devices consisted of ring modulators, amplitude modulators, a reverberation chamber, a tape-head echo unit, two oscillator-controlled variable-speed tape recorders, various high-pass/low-pass/band-pass filters, and an octave filter bank connected to a wave analyser. The latter device not only provided a visual display of the frequency components present at the output, it also could be employed as an extremely powerful band-pass filter in its own right, reducing octave filtered sound material to bandwidths as narrow as 2 Hz.

The two variable-speed tape recorders were each fitted with special devices which permitted not only normal pitch/duration transpositions but also, within certain limits, the variation of either of these basic characteristics independently. This modification was developed by Springer at the firm Telefonbau und Normalzeit and later became commercially available as the Springer Machine or Tempophon. The basis for this system was a rotating arrangement of four playback heads set at 90° to each other, forming the periphery of a special capstan. (See fig. 23.)

If the drive capstan and the head capstan are both rotated, information from the original material will be reproduced as a series of consecutive samples drawn from each of the playback heads in turn. For the output to appear continuous a certain degree of overlapping between samples is required, and as may be seen from the diagram opposite the transport is arranged so that at

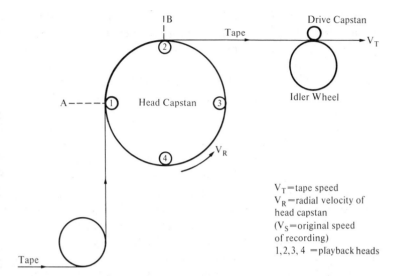

**Figure** 23

the point of change-over the succeeding head makes contact with the tape just before the preceding head drops out.

It is possible to arrange for the head capstan to remain stationary, that is, $V_R = 0$. If $V_T$ is thus set equal to $V_S$, the pitch and duration content of the original material will be reproduced exactly. If the drive capstan and the head capstan are varied such that $V_T + V_R = V_S$, the speed of the heads relative to the tape will remain constant whilst the absolute speed of the tape itself and the duration of the recorded material will be altered. The rotating heads thus extract 'snapshot' samples of sound from the travelling tape and reproduce these at their correct pitches. The machine may also be employed in a more extreme fashion by varying the speeds of both drives quite independently, changing both pitch and duration. If the tape is stationary and the heads rotated, for example, the information recorded on a small section of tape—between *A* and *B* in the diagram—may be frozen as a continuous sound, varying in pitch as a direct function of the capstan speed.

The fidelity of sound produced from this device is unfortunately rather poor, for the head design limits the frequency response and the process of breaking up analogue sound into discrete samples often results in considerable distortion at the point of change-over from one head to the next. The machine, nevertheless, has usefully served the requirements of a number of composers over the years, anticipating more sophisticated approaches offered today by digital technology. The Cologne studio, amongst others, purchased a Springer machine in the late 1950s, and Eimert used the instrument extensively in preparing his composition *Epitaph für Aikichi Kuboyama*.

The Milan studio, like those at Paris and Cologne, continued to exert a major influence on the artistic development of the medium throughout the 1960s. The veritable explosion of activity during this decade, however, was to divert attention from the uniqueness of these institutions and encourage a cross-fertilization of ideas, both compositional and technical. Already by the beginning of this period a number of centres had been established, not only in Europe, but also in Russia and Japan. Developments in America and Canada, too, were well under way, and these will be discussed at some length in the next chapter. Some of the studios had only a short or an intermittent life, for example Geneva (1959–62), Eindhoven (1957–60), Munich (1957–66). The majority, however, were to survive throughout the decade and into the next, to become major centres in the 1970s, for example APELAC, Brussels (1958–   ), Berlin (1962–   ), Gent (1962–   ), Stockholm (1964–   ), Tokyo (1956–   ), Warsaw (1957–   ), Utrecht (1961–   ).

Developments were few and far between in Great Britain during the 1950s and early 1960s. The establishment of a Radiophonic Workshop by the British Broadcasting Corporation in London in 1958 should have provided a major focal point for British electronic music. The artistic policy of the Corporation, however, was to direct otherwise, for the studio was expressly required to serve the day-to-day needs of the radio and television drama groups, leaving little time for serious composition. The principal composing members of the studio staff, Daphne Oram, Desmond Briscoe, and Delia Derbyshire, thus experienced a working environment quite different from that enjoyed by their Continental counterparts, and with the notable exception of Roberto Gerhard few other composers were granted access to the facilities. Artistic advance was thus left largely in the hands of a few spirited pioneers such as Tristram Cary, struggling with little or no financial help to establish private studios of their own.

This situation was to change with the advent of voltage control technology, a revolution in which Britain was to play an important part. The initiative, however, was to come from America, and it is to developments on that side of the Atlantic that attention must now be turned.

# 5 America

Events in America after the Second World War followed quite different paths from those in Europe, owing primarily to a lack of institutional support during the early years. Indeed, until the mid 1950s no major systems of interest were constructed, many of the so-called studios consisting merely of a collection of tape recorders and interconnecting wires assembled in a back room or, at best, commercial recording systems leased for experimentation. Despite this lack of dedicated systems, several composers managed to investigate the possibilities of manipulating sounds recorded on tape, preparing the way for more suitably equipped electronic studios which were eventually to follow.

In 1948 two recording engineers working in New York, Louis and Bebe Barron, began to experiment with the musical possibilities of magnetic tape, playing recordings of instruments backwards and forwards and investigating the effects of splicing out selected elements and juxtaposing others. John Cage became interested in their work and in 1951 gathered together a group of musicians and technical advisers for the purpose of making music directly on to tape. The composing members of the group consisted of Cage, the Barrons, Earle Brown, Morton Feldman, David Tudor, and Christian Wolff, and for the next two years they worked in the Barrons' studio developing a project which became known as 'Music for Magnetic Tape'.

The only complete pieces produced in the studio during this period, apart from *Heavenly Menagerie* (1951), *For an Electronic Nervous System No. 1* (1953), and some background music for films prepared by the Barrons themselves, were: Cage, *Imaginary Landscape No. 5* (1951–2) and *Williams Mix* (1952), and Wolff, *For Magnetic Tape* (1952–3). These compositions explored many of the techniques associated with *musique concrète* and to a certain extent *elektronische Musik*, but musically they were motivated by rather different aims. Cage in particular was concerned with exploring principles of indeterminacy: *Williams Mix* and *Imaginary Landscape No. 5* were based on 'I Ching' chance operations, involving an elaborate series of tape-splicing and looping routines.

The source material for the former work consisted of about 600 recordings prepared from six categories of sounds: basic electronic sounds, manually produced sounds including instrumental sources, wind-produced sounds including singing, city sounds, country sounds, and quiet sounds amplified to levels comparable with the rest of the material. The resultant succession of haphazard events creates a powerful impact on the ear of the unsuspecting listener. The intention was to provoke a positive reaction to such a kaleidoscope of disorder, shaking the protective assuredness of traditional musical tastes and expectations and impelling the listener to search actively for plausible associations amongst the diverse events. In complete contrast to the early Cologne works, *Williams Mix* forces a level of communication by its very assault on traditional values, without any pretence to provide an alternative aesthetic which may be safely assessed from a distance. This challenge to the normal detachment of audiences is made all the more pointed by the inclusion of cheers, jeers, and applause towards the end of the piece, as if the composer is assessing the performance of the listener, rather than vice versa.

The project terminated in 1953 and the composers went their separate ways. Brown and Feldman continued their investigations for a time at the Rangertone Studios, Newark, New Jersey, producing *Octet* 1 (for eight loudspeakers) and *Intersection* respectively in the same year. Only Tudor failed to produce a work at this time. Brown subsequently travelled to Paris and continued his work there. Cage continued to work at various private studios in New York, travelling to Milan and producing *Fontana Mix* in 1959 before settling down to work both at Brandeis University and at Stony Point, New York, where in collaboration with David Tudor he became preoccupied with the use of electronic equipment in live performance.

*Fontana Mix* in many respects was a direct consequent of *Williams Mix*, the elements of indeterminacy being derived from graphic designs rather than detailed computations of chance routines. Speech sounds played an important part in the compositional process, and the technical sophistication of the Milan studio facilitated an altogether more compelling piece. Two subsequent works were based on this tape, both signifying Cage's progression towards live improvisatory techniques and away from the permanence of studio composition. *Aria with Fontana Mix* completed at Milan in the same year adds a part for a live vocalist. The score for the latter consists of indeterminate arrangements of phonemes from five languages—English, French, Italian, Armenian, and Russian—with the addition of several extra-musical sounds such as cheek-slapping and finger-clicking. Ten different vocal styles are demanded, indicated in the score by colours. The choice of these styles is left to the performer, adding further to the indeterminacy of the result. *Fontana Mix-Feed* (New York, 1964) belongs more properly to a discussion of live electronic music, for it uses a group of percussion instruments fitted with contact microphones, the signals from the latter being amplified to such an extent that they feed back from the loudspeakers to the microphones via the instruments with an effect similar to the 'howl around' of a badly adjusted public address system.

Music for Magnetic Tape thus existed for only a limited period as a movement before diversifying into a series of individual objectives beholden to no particular studio philosophy, but freely drawing from, and contributing to, the increasing ferment of ideas.

While Cage and his associates were experimenting in the Barrons' studio another line of investigation was being pursued by Vladimir Ussachevsky, shortly to be joined by Otto Luening. Superficially their experiments, which became generally known as 'Tape Music', closely related to those of Music for Magnetic Tape, for both approaches were based on the use of the tape recorder as a tool for registering and manipulating sound material. Closer examination reveals a marked difference in musical outlook, for both Luening and Ussachevsky were far more conservative in their attitude towards composition. In particular they saw the tape recorder as a means of extending traditional ideas of tonality and instrumentation, rather than as a tool for creating a totally new sound world.

During 1951–2 Ussachevsky carried out a series of experiments, preparing five studies entitled *Transposition, Reverberation, Experiment, Composition,* and *Underwater Valse.* These were presented at a Composers' Forum given on 9 May 1952 in the McMillin Theater, Columbia University. *Transposition* was simply a study in octave transposition using piano notes as sources. *Reverberation* was based on the application of tape-head echo, and the other pieces were arrangements of instrumental material, subjected to similar simple processes of modification. Their performance attracted considerable attention, and the composer

Henry Cowell wrote an encouraging review in the *Musical Quarterly* (October 1952):

> People who work experimentally with new sounds seem to have trouble in distinguishing between the material of musical composition and the compositions themselves. They are apt to rush their new sounds prematurely into pieces that are hardly creative work in the generally accepted sense, and that are easily identified as vehicles for new sounds rather than works in which these sounds form an integral part. . . . It is therefore refreshing when a composer offers his experiments frankly by that name, without confusion. Vladimir Ussachevsky did just this . . . These were not compositions and no attempt was made to call them so. But the sounds are certainly a possible resource for composers.

Luening attended the Forum and invited Ussachevsky to present his experiments at a composers' conference in Bennington, Vermont, during August 1952. Luening had studied with Busoni in Zurich, Switzerland, from 1918 until 1920 and had been interested for many years in the study of musical acoustics and instrumental design. At Bennington Ussachevsky experimented with violin, clarinet, piano, and vocal sounds using an Ampex tape recorder, and Luening began to prepare a tape composition using a flute as the source of material. News of their work came to the attention of Oliver Daniel, who invited them to prepare a group of short compositions for inclusion in a concert to be promoted by the American Composers' Alliance at the Museum of Modern Art, New York, under the direction of Leopold Stokowski. The invitation was accepted, and Luening and Ussachevsky departed for the home of Henry Cowell at Woodstock, New York, where, using borrowed tape recorders, they prepared pieces for the first public concert of Tape Music on 28 October 1952. Four pieces were performed: Ussachevsky, *Sonic Contours*; Luening, *Invention in 12 Notes*, *Low Speed*, and *Fantasy in Space*, the last work being the product of his earlier experiments with flute sounds at Bennington.

Again the critics were encouraging in their accounts. The audience included Luciano Berio, who was especially impressed with *Sonic Contours*. These pieces made considerable use of tape techniques such as overlays (montage), tape-head echo, extreme changes of speed, and splicing, but their structures retained many recognizable tonal characteristics such as simple chords, scales, and arpeggios. The attention accorded to this recital overshadowed the work of Cage and his associates. *Williams Mix*, for example, had to wait for two years before receiving its first public performance before an unsympathetic audience at the 1954 Donaueschingen Festival, Germany. Examples of Tape Music had already been presented in Europe alongside *musique concrète* during the festival promoted by Radiodiffusion Télévision Française in Paris in April 1953. Other potential developments at this time also passed unnoticed: Milton Babbitt at Princeton University, for example, had been interested in electronic sound production for many years, and he was instrumental in instigating a series of experiments into the possibilities of hand-drawn sound. Lack of support, however, led to the initiative in this field passing to Norman McLaren at Ottawa.

After their early successes Luening and Ussachevsky began exploring the possibilities of using prepared tapes in conjunction with performing instruments. Late in 1953 Luening received a commission from the Louisville Orchestra to write a work for them, and this he accepted on the condition that he could share the venture with Ussachevsky. Permanent studio facilities were still not available, and the equipment had to be gathered together from a variety of sources. A small grant from the Rockefeller Foundation facilitated the purchase of one tape recorder, but the others had to be borrowed or purchased privately. After a trial performance at the Bennington Composers' Conference the work, *Rhapsodic Variations*, for tape recorder and orchestra, was publicly performed by the Louisville Orchestra on 20 March 1954 under the direction of Robert Whitney. Another commission soon followed, this time for the Los Angeles Orchestra. The work, *A Poem in Cycles and Bells*, took the form of a paraphrase of their earlier works *Fantasy in Space* and *Sonic Contours*, and was altogether more successful, a better sense of integration being achieved between the instrumental parts and the prepared tape. The publicity accorded to Tape Music inspired several private studios to begin experimenting with the medium, but for the most part their activities were directed towards commercial ends, providing the background effects for films, radio, and television.

So far no mention has been made of Varèse's role in these developments. After his determined, but unsuccessful, agitations for studio facilities in the inter-war period it might have been expected that the changing climate of the 1950s would have placed him at the forefront of advances in this field. Unfortunately this did not prove to be the case. The late 1930s and the whole of the 1940s found Varèse involved in the deepest personal struggles with his music. After *Densité 21.5* for solo flute (1936) no works were produced for eighteen years, with the single exception of *Étude*, scored for two pianos, percussion, and mixed chorus. This was intended to form part of *Espace*, a project of immense proportions involving simultaneous performances from all the capitals of the world, mixed and co-ordinated via a specially arranged link-up of broadcasting stations. Sadly this vision of a universal hymn to humanity was not to become a reality despite several attempts to attract support. The post-war upsurge of interest in electronic music occurred well towards the end of his life. In 1950, for example, when he started composing again in earnest, he was already 67. It is thus hardly surprising that at such a late stage in a career characterized by continual disappointment and disillusion-ment with the Establishment, he should now leave others to carry on the crusade for studio facilities and concentrate only on the realization of his own compositional ambitions. In a modest way, nevertheless, his explorations into the possibilities of electronics made a contribution which was far more significant musically than the much-publicized early efforts of Luening and Ussachevsky.

During the late 1940s Varèse had been formulating an idea for a piece which would interpolate passages of sound material organized on magnetic tape with live instrumental performance, and by the beginning of 1950 an outline of the work, *Déserts*, had been prepared. In the summer he began composing the instrumental parts, completing them towards the end of 1952. During 1953, with the aid of a technical assistant, he began gathering together recordings of iron mills, saw mills, and various other factories in Philadelphia with the object of assembling material for use in the taped sections. Gradually he built up a comprehensive library of sound material, in his own private way carrying out investigations just as detailed as those of Schaeffer, working unaided with a very modest collection of taping equipment in his house in Greenwich, New York.

Boulez visited America in the winter of 1952–3, presenting *musique concrète* to New York for the first time at a special concert for the Composers' Forum, Columbia University. During his stay the two composers met for the first time, and Boulez was thus able to give an informed account of his work on *Déserts* on return to Paris. Rumours of Varèse's work had spread to Paris some time previously, and Schaeffer himself made a rather inaccurate reference to him in *A la recherche d'une musique concrète* (1952):

> Varèse has dedicated himself to that poor relation of the orchestra, the percussion section. He has promoted it to orchestral status. He has added to it various effects supplied by American studios. I do not know the details: more or less electronic 'Varinettes', produced I know not how, but occasionally similar to ours. Varèse crosses France without stopping. This Frenchman has not had our misfortune to be a prophet in his own country. He is listened to and revered in Germany. Soon he will return to New York where he is considered Maestro.

The reference to Germany concerns a series of lectures Varèse presented to the 1950 Darmstadt Summer School at the invitation of Wolfgang Steinnecke, and *Déserts* would naturally have been uppermost in his mind at this time. The association of this work with *musique concrète* is not particularly appropriate, for his approach to organized sound was far more liberal including elements which might equally be attributed to *elektronische Musik*, or Music for Magnetic Tape, or Tape Music; common to all, yet restricted by none.

In 1954 Varèse received an invitation from Schaeffer to complete the tape parts for *Déserts* in his Paris studio. In the absence of any comparable opportunities in America this was accepted, and he departed for France in late September. At the Club d'Essai he worked remarkably quickly, completing the work in barely two months. His enlightened approach to principles of sound organization took Schaeffer by surprise, for Varèse would frequently indulge in elaborate transformations, investigating whatever electronic techniques the engineers could devise. The studio was naturally ill equipped for such operations; the use of extensive filtering or ring modulation, for example, was foreign to the still-strict doctrines of *musique concrète*.

The results were not wholly satisfactory, a combination perhaps of three factors: the relatively short period spent in preparation, the limitations of the equipment, and the immense practical problems which confront any composer encountering a complex studio system for the first time. Varèse, indeed, was to spend the next eight years trying to improve the tape, creating no fewer than four different versions. The first performance of *Déserts* took place in the Théâtre des Champs-Elysées on 2 December 1954, conducted by Hermann Scherchen. Forty years previously this hall had been the venue for the riotous first performance of Stravinsky's

*Rite of Spring*, and the audience for *Déserts* was quite ready to demonstrate that noisy public disapproval was not quite a phenomenon of the past. Matters were made worse by the fact that the RTF were making a live transmission of the concert, which also included works by Mozart and Tchaikovsky. The considerable adverse publicity which followed was positive in at least one respect: the use of electronics in music was now attracting the attention of a wide if often unsympathetic audience.

After two rather more successful performances in Hamburg and Stockholm conducted by Bruno Maderna, Varèse remained in Paris for a while, returning to the United States in the spring of 1955. During May of the same year he attended an arts conference at Bennington, Vermont, presenting a lecture on his work on the 16th, and supervising the first American performance of *Déserts*, given in the National Guard Armoury the following day. The first major presentation of the work took place on 30 November 1955 in the Town Hall, New York, and on the whole was favourably received. This performance could not have occurred at a more appropriate time, for the interest of institutions in supporting electronic music was just being kindled.

In June 1955 Luening and Ussachevsky had obtained a generous grant of nearly $10 000 from the Rockefeller Foundation, funded through Barnard College, to investigate the state of studio facilities both at home and abroad. During a six-week tour of Europe they visited Schaeffer in Paris, Meyer-Eppler in Bonn, Eimert in Cologne, and Berio and Maderna in Milan. They were thus able to piece together a very thorough account of the work being carried out at these major centres. In Canada they discovered that developments were also well advanced, for Hugh le Caine, working with the support of the Canada Research Council, had established a studio at Ottawa University in 1954, and, as mentioned earlier, Norman McLaren was making useful advances in the use of optical sound-generation techniques.

By comparison, only limited progress had been made in America. One or two universities were willing to consider giving some support to suitable ventures, but none had yet made a commitment to a major, long-term programme. At Illinois, however, they learnt of a project which was to hold a particular significance for the future, for an investigation had been started into the possible uses of computers in musical composition. This research, headed by Lejaren Hiller and Leonard Isaacson, was concerned in the first instance with the use of calculative procedures to generate data for conventionally notated instrumental scores, but this was to herald the use of the computer itself as a means for generating sound. In the latter context Luening and Ussachevsky discovered that one of the research programmes at the Bell Telephone Laboratories, New Jersey, was directed towards the development of techniques for both the analysis and the synthesis of sound. These investigations were concerned not only with conventional analogue approaches but also with the possibility of developing computer-based methods. This organization, as will be seen in a later chapter, was subsequently to pioneer digital sound synthesis under the direction of Max Mathews.

The work at Bell Telephone Laboratories proved to be unique. Apart from Ampex, who were involved in the design and manufacture of recording and amplification equipment, most industrial concerns were not willing even to consider supporting research and development in this field unless they could expect to benefit commercially from the results within a matter of months.

Luening and Ussachevsky decided to take the initiative and make a formal approach to the authorities of Columbia University, with a view to establishing an electronic music studio within the Department of Music. The idea was favourably received, and a small grant made for an experimental laboratory. By this stage their approaches to electronic composition were beginning to extend beyond the restrictions of the tape recorder and microphone. Ussachevsky's *Piece for Tape Recorder*, produced early in 1956, for example, integrates both electronic and natural sound sources, although only limited use is made of the former. The piece incorporates, interestingly, two extracts from his earlier work *Sonic Contours*.

In fulfilment of their Rockefeller grant requirements they prepared a report on the state of electronic music in Europe and America, expressing a view that the development of electronic music in their country could best be assisted by channelling financial support into the universities, where research and development could be fostered in an environment free from commercial pressures. Their recommendations were accepted in principle, and protracted discussions commenced over the most suitable course of action. Developments were to take an unexpected turn, however, for on 31 January 1956 the Radio Corporation of

America demonstrated a fully self-contained sound synthesizer to a meeting of the American Institute of Electrical Engineers in New York. RCA's interest in the medium was, of course, not new, for it was they who had marketed a commercial version of the Thérémin during the 1930s. The sudden appearance of such an advanced machine was nevertheless a complete surprise, the product of rather a curious line of development which will be examined shortly.

The RCA synthesizer was quite different from any of the systems so far discussed, for it offered a programmable means of controlling the functions of the various devices. Ussachevsky, in particular, was keen to acquire the synthesizer for use as the basis of a studio at Columbia University, and preliminary approaches were made to several RCA executives. It soon transpired that Milton Babbitt, at Princeton University, was also interested in gaining access to the machine and they agreed to collaborate by preparing a joint application. RCA responded by granting access to the machine which was, for Babbitt, conveniently situated at their Princeton Laboratories.

The stage, meanwhile, was being set for an electronic composition which was to be of the greatest musical significance, Varèse's *Poème électronique*. In 1956 the electronics firm of Philips, based at Eindhoven, Holland, began to consider their plans for the World Fair to be held in Brussels in 1958. They decided to construct a special pavilion and invited the distinguished architect Le Corbusier to prepare the design. Le Corbusier immediately seized upon the idea of combining technology and the arts by creating not merely a building, but an environment of sound, colour, and structure, reflecting the creative role that electronics and associated sciences could play in contemporary society. He collaborated with Xenakis over the preparation of mathematical models for the construction of the building itself and invited Varèse to provide the music in the form of a prepared tape, leaving the composer totally free to approach the world of sound in whatever manner he should choose.

It was thus that Varèse was finally rewarded for his years of struggle, with an opportunity to compose an electronic work which explored the projection of sound in space, an area of investigation which had inspired his ill-fated project *Espace* twenty years previously.

Like *Déserts*, the realization of this piece was to take Varèse to

Europe, on this occasion to the Philips Laboratories at Eindhoven. Here he enjoyed a range of facilities which were without precedent at that time, for a complex studio system was especially assembled for this composition, backed by a team of highly skilled electronic engineers and advisers. The work which resulted reflected a style of electronic composition unique to the composer, tied in no way to any established studio conventions. The source material included machine noises, the sound of aircraft, bells, electronically generated sounds, singers, and piano and organ sounds, subjected to elaborate processes of pitch transformation, filtering, and modification of their attack and decay characteristics. The projection of sound was achieved by employing a three-channel tape system, fed to elaborate arrays of loudspeakers positioned in the ceiling alcoves and the walls. Visual effects, associated with the movement of sounds, were created by means of a comprehensive lighting system which produced changing patterns of coloured images.

The World Fair opened to the public on 2 May 1958 and by the time it finally closed its doors at the end of the year over two million people had visited it. *Poème électronique* was thus accorded a vast audience drawn from all over the world. News of this achievement naturally spread back to the United States, and shortly after his return to New York in the autumn of the same year a performance of the work was given in his honour in Greenwich Village. This concert, unfortunately, fell short of expectations, for when relayed in a small theatre over single loudspeakers, devoid of any lighting effects, the work lost a considerable proportion of its original splendour. This occasion was also to result in yet another disappointment. The concert was preceded by a lecture at the end of which Varèse proudly announced that the firm of Bogen-Presto, a division of the Seigler Corporation, had offered to provide him with a studio so that he could continue with his work. News of this received widespread coverage the next day in both the local and the national press, but the firm changed its mind and the offer was withdrawn.

Luening and Ussachevsky's quest for a fully equipped studio proved more successful. During 1957–8 concrete proposals drawn up jointly with Babbitt were submitted to the Rockefeller Foundation requesting financial support for the establishment of a permanent centre for electronic music. Initially they suggested that a University Council for Electronic Music should be established, consisting of representatives drawn from all the institutions which were already interested or involved in working in this field. The Foundation, however, did not wish to create a situation where it might find itself faced with the prospect of sponsoring a large number of different projects, each consequently being eligible for only a small share of the total grant. The final application thus drew up a plan for a single electronic music studio to be set up between the Universities of Columbia and Princeton only, outlining in detail equipment and staffing requirements for a five-year initial period, after which the universities would be expected to meet recurrent expenses.

The proposal was accepted, and a grant of $175 000 was advanced in January 1959 for a Columbia–Princeton Electronic Music Center, to be situated at Columbia University, and based upon the RCA synthesizer, which was to be purchased from the manufacturers. Delivery of the original Mark 1 version was soon arranged, pending its replacement by an improved Mark 2 version, delivered later in the year.

The origins of the RCA synthesizers may be traced back over a decade to the late 1940s. At this time two electronic engineers, Harry F. Olson and Herbert Belar, both employed by the company at their Princeton laboratories, became interested in the possibility of developing technological systems for both the composition and the realization of musical works. The company was sufficiently far-sighted to realize that such investigations might lead to useful advances not only in communication theory but also in areas of acoustical research, and accordingly gave them official support for their ventures.

The publication of the *Mathematical Theory of Communication* by Shannon and Weaver in 1949 inspired them to embark upon an elaborate project to construct a machine for musical composition, based on a system of random probability. Although the acoustical output of the device was limited to the production of a monophonic progression of tones, the operating system is of some interest for it attempted to rationalize some of the creative principles involved in the processes of musical composition into a programmed series of electromechanical functions.

The basis for the composing system lay in a statistical study of the characteristics of twelve Stephen Foster folk-songs. In the first instance the occurrences of two- and three-note pitch sequences were tabulated to provide a probability table. By providing random selection routines, weighted in accordance with the probability table, pitch sequences could then be generated as the basis for synthesized tunes. Seemingly unaware of the limitations of their analytical procedures and the inadequacies of such a limited sample of data the authors surmised that a composing machine might be developed which would produce new music similar to that of Stephen Foster songs, and proceeded to build it.

Doubts about the soundness of their theories are strengthened by the superficial consideration afforded to the rhythmic structure of the songs. Olson and Belar regarded this characteristic to be of secondary importance, merely incorporated into a succession of notes to make a 'satisfactory' melody, and accordingly provided their own probability table for bars in 3/4 and 4/4 metre offering just seven variations each. In an age when the computer had yet to make its mark the implementation of the system demanded the construction of an elaborate network of relays and associated valve electronics capable of assessing and interpreting logic states. The block diagram of the machine was as follows:

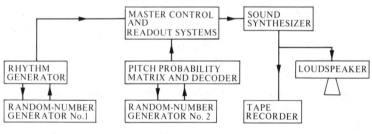

**Figure** 24

The output from each of the random-number generators consisted of four control lines. Each line could be set either to an 'on' state (a steady voltage present) or an 'off' state (no voltage present). As the truth table given below shows, a total of sixteen patterns may be generated from a group of four such lines, and providing a means of decoding is available these may be used to select sixteen different functions elsewhere in the system. This technique illustrates a simple application of binary logic, the basis of all digital computer systems:

| *Function Selection* | *Binary State of the Lines (0 = off, 1 = on)* | | | |
| :---: | :---: | :---: | :---: | :---: |
| | 1 | 2 | 3 | 4 |
| 1 | 0 | 0 | 0 | 0 |
| 2 | 0 | 0 | 0 | 1 |
| 3 | 0 | 0 | 1 | 0 |
| 4 | 0 | 0 | 1 | 1 |
| 5 | 0 | 1 | 0 | 0 |
| 6 | 0 | 1 | 0 | 1 |
| 7 | 0 | 1 | 1 | 0 |
| 8 | 0 | 1 | 1 | 1 |
| 9 | 1 | 0 | 0 | 0 |
| 10 | 1 | 0 | 0 | 1 |
| 11 | 1 | 0 | 1 | 0 |
| 12 | 1 | 0 | 1 | 1 |
| 13 | 1 | 1 | 0 | 0 |
| 14 | 1 | 1 | 0 | 1 |
| 15 | 1 | 1 | 1 | 0 |
| 16 | 1 | 1 | 1 | 1 |

The decoding system consisted of a four-element relay tree arranged as in fig. 25. This diagram shows all four relays in the off position, providing a through connection between input no. 1 and the output. Turning any relay on causes all the switches on the associated relay line to change over to their alternative setting. Only one through path, however, will still be available, selected according to the logic table given above.

Two such trees were required to operate the composing machine, one controlling selections from the rhythm generator, the other operating the probability matrix and decoder. In the case of the rhythm generator a preliminary choice had to be made between 3/4 and 4/4 time. For each metre seven different patterns were available for selection. Matching up the seven associated control lines with the sixteen available function selections was achieved by connecting two or more selections to certain pattern generators, biasing the probability of choice. Assigning two selection lines to the same pattern, for example, would double the chances of that pattern being selected to 2 in 16.

Operation of the probability matrix and decoder was altogether more complicated, for the selection of pitches required a dynamically changing bias in accordance with the earlier mentioned analyses of two- and three-note sequences in the source songs. As

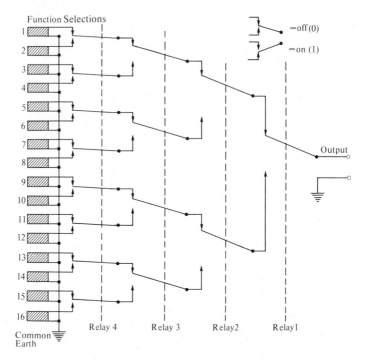

**Figure** 25

a matter of convenience all of the latter were transposed to D
major before examination. This rationalization reduced the
number of possible pitches to twelve, ranging diatonically from

to with the addition of G♯ to accommodate

the occasional modulation to the dominant.

All the possible two-note sequences were first identified, and
recorded as key entries in a table, fifty in all. Treating each entry
as the first two elements of a three-note sequence, an analysis was
then made of the pitches completing the sequence on every
occurrence in the source material. The statistics thus derived were
tabulated as a list of pitch alternatives, along with the proportional
frequency of their choice expressed in sixteenths.

Application of this table was implemented via a fifty-position
stepper switch, each position being uniquely assigned to one of the
fifty possible two-note sequences. On arriving at a new setting in

response to the preceding cycle the hard-wired matrix would route the sixteen function-selection lines to appropriate pitch generators in accordance with the probability data. Random-number generator no. 2 would then be permitted to activate one of the lines, the pitch selection thus made being output for a duration determined by the rhythm generator. The cycle would finish by changing the two-note reference setting to the note just generated and its predecessor, ready for the next cycle. By way of an example, if the current two-note sequence happened to be ♪ the probability matrix would route all the selection lines to one pitch generator, ♪ , making its choice a certainty, that is, a 16/16 chance. For the next cycle the new two-note reference would be ♪ . For this setting of the stepper switch the matrix would assign two lines to the generator of the pitch ♪ , two to ♪ , nine to ♪ , two to ♪ , and one to ♪ , weighting the chances of selection as 2/16, 2/16, 9/16, 2/16, and 1/16 respectively.

Such a machine offered considerable potential as a tool for experimenting with statistically based compositional procedures. Today the much faster and far more powerful processing facilities of advanced digital computers are readily available for such exercises. At the beginning of the 1950s the computer revolution had barely begun, and in its time the Olson and Belar machine offered a unique system for creating pitch sequences. The premises on which the whole project was based cannot be allowed to pass without further comment, however, for they provide a clear example of the consequences of a breakdown in communication between scientists and artists concerning the essential characteristics of each others' disciplines.

Olson and Belar misunderstood the creative processes of musical composition in one important respect, for they assumed that objectively expressed characteristics derived from an analysis of a selection of a composer's output of scores could supply the information necessary for a simulation of the intuitive processes which inspired them. Disciples of compositional theory will recognize that the machine would have been of interest to composers wishing to explore aspects of probability theory as part of their musical language, providing, of course, it could have been modified to allow easy reprogramming of the probability matrices. Such an application is quite different from that intended by Olson and Belar, for it does not presuppose the machine's capabilities to act as a substitute for the composer himself.

Coincidentally, the completion of the machine in late 1950 neatly bisects the time which elapsed between the completion of Schillinger's *The Mathematical Basis for the Arts* and the appearance of the first few chapters of *Musiques formelles* by Xenakis in the latter part of the decade, expounding the principles and virtues of stochastics as a basis for a compositional philosophy. The misjudgements of Olson and Belar, however, provide a salutary warning as to the dangers which can befall the unwary experimenter in applying probability theory to the art of musical composition. Leonard Meyer, writing 'on the nature and limits of critical analysis' in his book *Explaining Music*, succinctly pin-points the primary reasons for the failure of the machine to synthesize 'typical' melodies by Stephen Foster:

> To understand a composer's choices is to envisage the psychological-stylistic alternatives open to him at a particular point in the composition . . . Even in the long run our most confident surmises about routes and goals may prove wrong. This is because given the particular style within which he works the composer is a *free agent*. He invents and shapes his initial musical substance—his themes, harmonic progressions, textures and the like. These have implications for subsequent events. But they do not *determine* them . . . Determinism is a mistaken notion applied to works of art not only because implications are plural, but also because, within the style he employs, the composer may at any particular point in a piece be absolutely arbitrary. That is, he may invent and use a musical idea or relationship which has nothing to do with—was in no way implied by or dependent upon—preceding events in the piece.

On the very simplest plane it must be clear that the composing machine was incapable of synthesizing even a song-like structure, let alone a song in the style of a particular composer. The probability mechanism, working from note to note, could not accommodate such basic considerations as tonality and the strophic structure of phrases. These problems, fortunately, did not afflict their next venture, the first RCA synthesizer. Although the machine was not presented to the public until 1956, work on its construction began in early 1951, and there is evidence to suggest that the synthesizer was at least partly operational in 1952. The overall design of the completed Mark 1 version was as follows in fig. 26.

Two identical but functionally independent synthesis channels were provided, each sharing a common bank of sound sources. The latter consisted of a white-noise generator and twelve electrically driven tuning-fork oscillators, designed to generate the twelve tempered pitches of the musical scale between F♯/G♭:

 and F: in the form of sine tones. Selection of

these sources and control of subsequent operations was achieved via a set of relay trees of identical design to those used in the composing machine. Instead of random-number generators, however, the source of control lay in a pre-punched paper tape, and an associated group of brush sensors.

The first programmable function in each synthesis channel involved the selection of a sound-source generator via a sixteen-element relay tree, decoding the patterns contained in four punched tape columns. The three spare relay tree connections were available for the selection of additional external sources, should these be required. The diagram of the frequency-selection network for one channel shows clearly how the control system was derived from its ancestor. (See fig. 27.)

The next stage in the synthesis process involved the use of an octaver, bypassed only when the white-noise generator or the external inputs were selected. This device, operated by an eight-element relay tree and an associated three-column punched tape record, accepted a frequency from the oscillator bank, converted the sine wave electronically into a square wave, and passed it on to a set of octave multipliers and dividers. The latter, in a manner similar to that employed in electronic organs, acted to transpose the pitches to any one of eight octave ranges in accordance with the control code, extending the range of the synthesizer

from F♯/G♭:     to F:     . The wave was finally

**Figure 26**

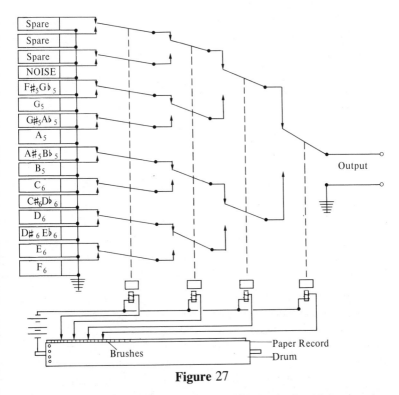

**Figure** 27

converted from a square function—composed of odd harmonics only—to a sawtooth function—composed of both odd and even harmonics.

The output of the source bank/octaver could, optionally, be connected to another device, a frequency glider, which permitted a smooth transition to be made from one pitch selection to another. Although to the user this unit appeared to act directly on the incoming sawtooth wave it actually consisted of another self-contained sawtooth generator, directly controlled by the incoming wave through a feedback network, which could be adjusted to respond to the changes in applied frequency in different ways. Normally the glider was not connected to the punched tape control system, and a single characteristic set manually via pre-set controls on the device for the duration of a synthesis run. By disconnecting one of the other control functions, however, a total of eight different types of glide could be programmed via a relay tree and three punched tape columns. The following are typical of the types

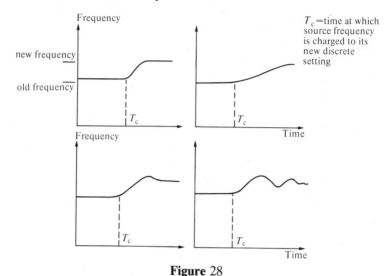

Figure 28

of frequency glide obtainable, ranging from a progressive pitch change to a damped oscillatory pattern. (See fig. 28.)

The frequency glider functioned as the last device in the generation section of the synthesis chain, all signals then passing to the processing stages. The first device in the latter chain consisted of an envelope shaper, triggered and controlled via the control tape. Up to eight different attack and decay patterns could be selected via a relay tree and three punched tape columns. Each selection involved a different set of time constants, creating attack times which varied from 1 msec to 2 sec, and decay times ranging from 4 msec to 19 sec.

In addition to simple attack and decay functions based on exponential characteristics, for example:

Figure 29

functions of a more artificial nature could be specified. Furthermore, by changing the punched tape code during the course of an envelope the functions could be combined to produce hybrid responses:

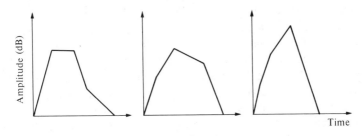

**Figure** 30

The next device in the processing chain consisted of a pair of filters supplying high-pass, low-pass, or in combination band-pass characteristics according to the position of a manually operated selector switch. These suffered from one particular disadvantage, for they could not be made to track the incoming signal automatically. Consequently it was not possible to provide a consistent shaping for a sequence of different pitches.

The output from these filters passed to a programmable, general amplitude control system. This device provided a total of sixteen different degrees of attenuation via a relay tree and four punched tape columns. Pre-sets regulated the attenuation range over which the device operated, and the circuits were designed to produce equal steps of intensity between the two selected limits.

The next stage in the processing chain provided a facility for the production of low-speed modulation. The device consisted of an amplitude modulator operating at a frequency of between six and seven Hertz with a shallow modulation pattern approximating to a square wave. The use of such techniques to 'humanize' electronic sounds has been referred to before, and the inclusion of a vibrato generator in the RCA synthesizer is indicative of Olson and Belar's original intention—to provide a machine capable of imitating conventional instrumental sounds, rather than a flexible system for the exploration of new timbres.

The last device in the processing chain consisted of a bank of eight resonators, employed to augment the timbre-shaping facility offered by the earlier described pair of filters. Each resonator comprised an amplifier fitted with a regulated feedback loop which could be tuned via a resistive/capacitive network to respond to excitation at a particular frequency. The effect on any applied signal was to boost any frequency components at or very close to the point of resonance, creating a band-pass type of response. By reducing the overall gain of the amplifier so that the output emerged at a more normal system level the circuit acted as an attenuator for frequencies outside the resonance area, the sharpness of the response being determined by the degree of feedback. By means of a toggle switch the resonator response could be inverted to produce a band-reject characteristic, attenuating instead of boosting the frequency band. The frequency of resonance itself for each unit could be set manually to a range of settings in steps of approximately one-third of an octave. Selection of the units was programmed via a relay tree and four punched tape columns, permitting the manipulation of up to sixteen different pre-set combinations.

The master control system provided the primary means of communication between the composer and the synthesizer in the realization of a work. It is clear from the preceding description that manual adjustments to device controls were necessary at several strategic points in the processing chain. These, however, were essentially pre-operative functions, determining the range of functional characteristics upon which the programmed sequence of instructions would draw.

The punched tape was fifteen inches wide, carrying device control information coded in thirty-six columns, eighteen for each channel, as follows:

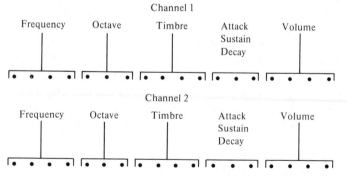

**Figure** 31

The tape was sprocketed on both edges to engage with matching teeth on a circular drum, the latter being linked to a motor with a variable-speed drive which transported the tape at speeds ranging from two to eight inches per second. A key-punching system permitted the composer to enter his instructions as a sequence of punched-hole patterns. Duration thus became a function of distance measured along the paper tape, according to the speed at which it was played. The punching system ensured that the holes were spaced equidistantly, the tape advancing a fixed distance after each complete row of punches had been entered.

The tape-reading system consisted of a set of spring-loaded brushes which pressed down on to the surface of the paper. When a hole passed under a brush, the latter made electrical contact with the drum beneath, activating the relay line assigned to that particular column. Several springs were connected to each brush to ensure that electrical contact was maintained until the tape had moved to the position for the next punched row. If a new hole was detected the circuit remained complete. If no hole was encountered, however, electrical contact was broken and the associated relay returned to its 'off' state.

The output from the two synthesis channels could be monitored via a pair of loudspeakers and also recorded directly on to disc. The choice of such a cumbersome recording medium, where a groove once cut could not be re-used contrasts sharply with the programming flexibility of the punched tape input system. The Radio Corporation of America, however, as a company with an extensive investment in the gramophone industry, was naturally interested in the development of specially designed disc-cutting equipment for the synthesizer. It should also be appreciated that the use of taping equipment was undervalued in many branches of the recording industry at this time, and there was a tendency to cling to and seek improvements in traditional techniques rather than explore new ones. Another factor may also have influenced this choice: the use of a gramophone turntable, with its comparatively low speed of rotation and high inertia, facilitated the use of a direct-drive system, powered via a flexible cable from the motor employed to transport the punched tape. This simple linkage between the control and the recording systems ensured accurate mechanical synchronization between the sequential instructions supplied by the former and the acoustical product registered by the latter.

The cutting lathe employed a sixteen-inch lacquer rotated at 33⅓ revolutions per minute. Instead of a single groove, six concentric tracks could be cut, each providing a maximum of about three minutes' recording time. A second cutting lathe, driven by the same motor, provided a means of blending the six channels together as a single track on a new lacquer, using a set of six playback pick-ups and a mixing system. By repeating this process this secondary lacquer could be used to record thirty-six channels of information, supplied from six primary lacquers. Similarly, six secondary lacquers could be employed to provide an aggregate of 216 channels on a single tertiary lacquer.

The three minutes of recording time per channel available on each disc compared slightly unfavourably with a maximum control tape time of about four minutes when the latter was run at its slowest speed. The assembly of complete pieces involved the playing of a sequence of completed lacquers alternately on the two drives, considerable manual dexterity being required to ensure smooth joins between sections.

Despite the mechanical ingenuity of the RCA engineers the lathe cutting system remained wasteful on lacquers and extremely cumbersome for the user. It is thus surprising that the Mark 2 version of the synthesizer delivered to the Columbia–Princeton Electronic Music Center in 1959 was equipped with the same system of recording. By this time multitrack tape recorders were widely accepted as standard items of studio equipment, and the engineers at Colombia soon replaced the direct-drive disc cutter with an electronically synchronized four-channel Ampex tape recorder.

The design of the Mark 2 version was clearly influenced by the experience gained in using its predecessor for serious musical composition, rather than the synthesis of popular tunes. Four channels were provided, doubling the output capabilities of the machine. The sound-source bank was also considerably enlarged. In addition to a set of twelve tuning-fork oscillators producing a master octave of tempered pitches, and a noise generator, two sets of twelve variable-frequency oscillators were provided, each of which could be tuned to any desired frequency setting between 8130 and 16 180 Hz, a range slightly larger than the revised master

octave tunings of C = 8372 Hz: and B = 15 804 Hz:

16ve

. Used together, these sources could be used to provide an octave scale with thirty-six divisions. An enlarged octaver, required now only to act as a divider, provided a ten-octave range of pitches extending down to C = 16.3 Hz: . Two relay trees were provided to control generator and octave selection routines for each channel as before. The availability of a ten-octave dividing network, however, necessitated the provision of a four-bit coding system, leaving four selections completely unused. Despite the provision of twenty-four extra oscillators no change was made to the size of the relay system controlling the selection of the generators. Each synthesis channel could thus only call upon sixteen of the sources at any one time, the selection being allocated manually via a special switchboard.

The frequency glider, envelope, and volume control systems were retained without major alteration. The low-frequency modulators, however, offered a slightly wider range of amplitude modulation speeds, ranging from 5 to 10 Hz. The facilities for shaping timbre, too, were rearranged to achieve greater flexibility. Two sets of resonators were included for each channel, and the high- and low-pass filters were fitted with relay control facilities. Selection of all these options was centralized via a comprehensive patch panel.

One general feature is particularly notable. The layout of the Mark 2 version took full account of the need to provide a system which is essentially modular in construction, for no restrictions were imposed regarding the way, or the order, in which the individual devices are used. In any one of the synthesis channels the routing of signals from the source bank to the output thus become entirely a matter for the composer concerned. Problems of mismatching were minimized by adding buffer amplifiers to the input and output of every device.

Two mechanically linked paper tape drives are used for control, each providing information for a pair of synthesis channels. The standard designation of punched columns to relays, with the addition of an extra column for the octaver, was identical to that used in the Mark 1 model. It was the clear intention, however, that these designations could be freely altered by interchanging the plug connections to the sensors. Furthermore, the destinations of the individual lines activated by the relay trees may be interchanged or even paralleled, in the latter case weighting particular device functions, and bypassing others. An alternative input system using continuous lines in place of punched holes, drawn with a felt-tip pen and read by an optical scanner, was introduced during the 1960s.

The use of a punched tape control system for the RCA synthesizers created a landmark in the development of systems for the production of electronic music. Despite the inevitable short-comings of an all-mechanical approach, the ability to programme a whole sequence of operations opened up modes of operation hitherto time-consuming at best and impracticable at worst. The construction of a sequence of enveloped and timbrally rich pitches from the single sine-wave generator at Cologne, for example, required extensive manual activity, turning knobs and cutting and splicing tape. Punching a control tape for the RCA synthesizers for similar ends took a mere fraction of the same time. The availability of such a facility, however, did not eliminate all the problems encountered in specifying sounds, and indeed created many of its own.

Olson and Belar, as in the case of their random probability machine, overestimated the potential of the synthesizers. In particular they failed to realize that despite the sophistication of their source bank and control systems, the devices themselves could not be programmed to synthesize many important character-istics of natural sound production, let alone supply satisfactory alternatives. It has already been seen how filter and resonator networks acting upon a sawtooth wave source may be used to produce a number of different timbres. The discussion of wave-form synthesis in connection with the Cologne studio however, has shown how such general shaping procedures cannot be compared to the totally controllable techniques of additive synthesis from individual sinusoidal sources. In claiming that the machine could simulate instruments such as the clarinet, saxophone, oboe, or violin the designers also overlooked the problem of generating realistic attack transients. The availability of a single envelope shaper for each channel, operating on a fixed source spectrum, was quite inadequate for such a purpose. As a precursor of 'Switched-on Bach' type of applications, however, the machine was handsomely capable of providing novel renditions of tunes such as *Obelin, Sweet and Low*, and the *Old Folks at Home*. Olson and Belar even ventured into the classical repertoire, reproducing such works as Brahms's *Hungarian Dance No. 1* 'in the gypsy style' and Bach's Fugue No. 2 from Book 1 of the *Well-Tempered Clavier*.

Despite these practical drawbacks and the narrowness of musical vision displayed by the designers, the removal of the RCA synthesizers to Columbia University ensured that considered attention could be paid to their true musical potential. The 'note/event' orientation of the programming system naturally imposed a considerable influence over the way in which the machines were employed; hence the common interest both of Luening and Ussachevsky, and also of Babbitt. The Electronic Music Center provided a major focus for composers both at home and from abroad. The level of activity was intense right from the start. Two inaugural concerts were given in the McMillin Theater, Columbia, on 9 and 10 May 1961 before an invited audience, in a blaze of publicity. The programmes included Bülent Arel, *Stereo Electronic Music No. 1*; Babbitt, *Composition for Synthesizer*; Mario Davidovsky, *Electronic Study No. I*; Halim El-Dabh, *Leiyla and the Poet*; Luening, *Gargoyles*, for violin solo and synthesized sounds; and Ussachevsky, *Creation: Prologue*.

Babbitt's *Composition* was the fruit of a seemingly effortless transition from his strictly ordered style of instrumental writing to an electronic equivalent. The piece is made all the more approachable by its particularly clear pitch and rhythmic articulation, allowing considerable emphasis to be placed on elements of repetition and symmetry. Ussachevsky's *Creation: Prologue* consisted of a choral setting of Latin and Babylonian texts, punctuated by the occasional passage of electronic sounds, again for the most part used orchestrally. There is a certain unease between the forces, the inevitably clinical nature of the electronic outbursts contrasting sharply with the nuances of human voices. The same unease permeates Luening's *Gargoyles* for much the same reason: the lack of a satisfactory continuum between two sharply contrasting sources of sound material. El-Dabh's *Leiyla* explored the potential of spoken texts in a manner not unlike that adopted by Berio for his *Visage*. Passages for two male voices are integrated with simple oscillator sounds from the synthesizer, and examples of mid-Eastern music performed on flute, string, and percussion instruments. The works by Davidovsky and Arel were the only ones to break away from the traditions of instrumental writing. Of the two, the Davidovsky *Study* makes the deepest excursion into the subtleties of textural manipulation, in a manner reminiscent of that adopted by the Milan school of electronic music.

The publicity accorded to Columbia/Princeton at this time overshadowed several other important developments which were taking place elsewhere in America, and over the border in Canada. The pioneering work of Le Caine at Ottawa, for example, was attracting national interest through a series of short pieces starting with *Dripsody* (1955), a study based on the sound of water drops. In 1958 the composers Gordon Mumma and Robert Ashley had established a private studio at Ann Arbor, Michigan, followed the next year by studios at the University of Illinois under the direction of Lejaren Hiller and the University of Toronto under the direction of Arnold Walter. 1959 also saw the establishment of another private venture, the San Francisco Tape Music Center, under the direction of Ramon Sender and Morton Subotnick. With the turn of the decade the medium entered an era of escalating activity, with a proliferation of studios throughout the world.

The scale of this expansion was greatly influenced by an important development during the mid 1960s: the introduction of the commercially marketed voltage-controlled synthesizer. Overnight, facilities for electronic music became available in the form of neat self-contained packages, operational from the moment of being switched on. The effect was truly dramatic. On the one hand, many thousands of composers of all abilities were able to experiment with the medium for the first time. On the other, questions of aesthetics and compositional philosophy were all but buried by the surfeit of mediocre works which poured forth from many of the newer studios.

Extracting and highlighting the more notable developments is no easy task, for the sheer diversity of activities demands the adoption of an increasingly selective approach, with the division of the medium into a number of different genres. Before consideration is given to the musical output of the 1960s and beyond, however, attention must first be turned to the new technology itself, the subject of the next chapter.

# New Horizons in Electronic Design

# 6 The Voltage-Controlled Synthesizer

The birth of the transistor in the late 1950s heralded a major turning-point in the development of facilities for electronic music. Hitherto the evolution of devices had been governed by the characteristics of thermionic valves. Problems of heat dissipation, fragility, and the sheer size of these components thwarted efforts to design systems which were both versatile and compact. The new technology suffered from none of these disadvantages and generated remarkably few of its own.

One of the first engineers to grasp the significance of this technological revolution for electronic sound synthesis was Harald Bode, the inventor of the Melochord. In 1961 he published an article on transistor-based devices, drawing particular attention to the advantages of modular design. Such a concept was new indeed, for with the advent of miniaturization it had become possible to envisage the production of easily transportable system packages, containing customized selections of self-contained and mutually compatible units such as oscillators, filters, and modulators.

The new designs were to prove revolutionary in another respect. Hitherto the functional characteristics of most studio devices had been controlled by uniquely assigned knobs or sliders. Connections between these units were thus concerned solely with the passing of audio signals from one stage in the synthesis chain to another. The versatility of transistor-based electronics made it possible to design any number of devices which could be controlled by a common set of voltage characteristics. These could be supplied either internally via manually operated regulators, or externally, from any suitable voltage source. The former mode of operation differed little from that employed for traditional studio equipment. The latter, however, introduced an entirely new dimension: the passing of control information from device to device via a secondary chain of interconnections.

Despite Bode's interest, the primary initiative passed elsewhere. In 1964 Robert Moog, an American engineer working in New

York, constructed a transistor voltage-controlled oscillator and amplifier for the composer Herbert Deutsch. This led to the presentation of a paper entitled 'Voltage-Controlled Electronic Music Modules' at the sixteenth annual convention of the Audio Engineering Society in the autumn of the same year, which stimulated widespread interest.

Similar developments were taking place on the West Coast. Sender and Subotnick had become increasingly dissatisfied with the limitations of traditional equipment at the San Francisco Tape Music Center, and their quest for new devices led to an association with another engineer, Donald Buchla. Buchla, like Moog, appreciated the musical possibilities of transistor voltage-control technology, and proceeded to develop his own prototype modules. On the strength of their early successes both engineers, quite independently, decided to establish their own manufacturing companies, launching the first commercial versions of the Moog Synthesizer and the Buchla Electronic Music System almost simultaneously in 1966.

During 1964–5 a third engineer, Paul Ketoff, designed and built a portable voltage-controlled synthesizer, known as the Synket, for the composer John Eaton. Although interest in its capabilities, especially as a live performance instrument, led to the construction of a number of copies, the synthesizer was not marketed commercially. By the end of the decade other manufacturers were entering the market. Two became major rivals for Moog and Buchla: Tonus, marketing under the trade name ARP in America, and EMS Ltd., pioneered by Peter Zinovieff in England. For several years synthesizer production was dominated by these four firms, each struggling for a major share of a highly lucrative and rapidly expanding market.

The effects of such commercialism have already been alluded to at the end of the previous chapter, in particular the rapid proliferation of studios, both private and institutional. The growing accessibility of system packages was to prove a mixed blessing, for in many instances the ease of device interaction led to a fascination with the technology for its own sake, rather than the musical premises for its use. Manufacturers were naturally keen to publicize the more novel features of their wares, leaving un-suspecting composers to discover for themselves the practicalities of utilizing such equipment. Several of the smaller models offered only the most basic facilities, dissuading a number of potential electronic composers from investigating the possible merits of the medium any further.

In order to evaluate the musical characteristics of voltage-controlled systems it is advantageous to understand the general principles upon which they operate. Except in the rarest of circumstances every studio device offers one or more adjustable characteristics. Oscillators, for example, are usually controllable in terms of both frequency and amplitude. Even a ring modulator, which is essentially of a fixed design, usually incorporates an amplifier to regulate the level of signals appearing at its output. If the system is voltage controlled, manually operated knobs or sliders fitted on the front of each device act as potentiometers, regulating the level of voltage supplied to the associated internal circuitry from a common power supply, typically +5 volts (V). Despite their integral construction it is helpful in the initial stages of study to view these potentiometers as separate from the devices themselves. The frequency and amplitude controls for an oscillator may be represented thus:

**Figure** 32

Such an arrangement may be usefully modified by inserting optional break-points in each control line, across which an additional voltage from another source may be applied. If the internal potentiometer for a device function is set to supply +2 V along its control line, and an external source supplies an extra +1 V across the break-point, a potential of +3 V will be delivered to the device. (See fig. 33.)

At this point the concept of *negative* voltage must be introduced. If the external voltage source is of a unipolar type, only capable of

**Figure** 33

generating positive potentials, it will always add to the internally supplied value. If the source is bipolar, however, capable of delivering both positive and negative potentials, the internally supplied voltage may be treated as a reference level, which may be increased or decreased as required. A supply of −1 V from the external voltage source in the above illustration, for example, will reduce the voltage arriving at the device from +2 to +1 V.

The response characteristics of the device functions themselves vary from one design to another. In the majority of cases, however, both frequency- and amplitude-control circuits are designed to operate logarithmically rather than linearly. Equal steps in voltage are thus conveniently associated with equal changes in musical interval or sound intensity throughout the operating range. Typical response values are 0.3 or 0.5 V per octave, and 0.3 or 0.5 V per 10 dB.

Keyboards have proved especially popular as control devices, easily attached to any device function across its associated control line break-point. Their voltage outputs are usually bipolar, the null point of 0 V being associated with a specific key at or near the middle of the range. Playing a succession of keys upwards from this point thus generates a stepped series of voltages which increase in positive potential. Playing a scale downwards generates the reverse, a stepped series of voltages which increase in negative potential. The step size itself is usually adjustable by means of a sensitivity control, expanding or contracting the voltage range of the keyboard either side of the null point.

The most obvious, and in practice the commonest, use of a keyboard is to control the frequency of an oscillator, the two devices combining to form a monophonic melody generator. Tuning involves two adjustments, one to the internal potentiometer of the oscillator to link the null key on the keyboard to the required pitch, the other to the keyboard sensitivity control to ensure that the voltage step size generates tempered semitones between adjacent keys. The ability to transpose the keyboard range upwards or downwards by means of the former control helps to overcome the practical limitations of short, three- or four-octave, keyboards favoured by several manufacturers. Non-standard tempered pitches are obtainable by resetting the voltage step size. Halving the sensitivity, for example, will result in quarter-tones between adjacent keys. Reducing this factor further permits the production of tempered microtones.

Chords or more complex aggregations of pitches may be manipulated by connecting a keyboard across the break-points of several oscillators, the latter being first tuned to the desired pitch intervals relative to one another via their internal potentiometers. The logarithmic response of the frequency circuits will ensure that the oscillators will track together upwards or downwards in response to applied keyboard voltage steps, preserving the intervallic relationships.

The use of a keyboard control for parallel tracking need not be limited to signal sources. If the audio output from a square, ramp, or triangle oscillator is passed for modification to a tuneable low-pass filter, the latter device may be made to track the former by connecting the keyboard output across both frequency control break-points. The advantage of this arrangement is a consistent modification of timbre no matter which pitch is selected.

Some keyboards provide two output voltage functions with individually adjustable sensitivities. In the example just given, applying one such function to the oscillator and the other to the filter with different sensitivity settings will cause the two devices to track key selections with different results. If the filter-control steps are larger than those applied to the oscillator the frequency settings of the former will increase more rapidly as ascending keys are selected. As a result the tonal quality will steadily brighten as fewer oscillator harmonics are subject to attenuation. If the filter steps are smaller the reverse effect will occur, the effects of attenuation increasing with higher key selections.

The idea of using keyboard voltage control for functions other than those associated with frequency may seem a little unusual. There are many instances, however, where a facility for generating a range of easily selectable steps for any number of device characteristics proves an invaluable aid to synthesis operations. As a regulator of amplitude, for example, the keyboard provides a useful means of controlling sound levels as a series of accurately specified gradations of intensity. In essence a keyboard provides a manually operated facility for sequential control.

Some designs of voltage-control keyboards incorporate circuits to provide yet another output characteristic, by making the keys touch-sensitive. A similar facility, it will be recalled, was incorporated in the Monochord supplied to the Cologne studio in the early 1950s. In some versions the keys generate a voltage proportional to the pressure exerted upon them. In others the time taken for each key to be depressed is measured electronically and converted into a corresponding voltage, which is sustained until the next key is struck. The faster the key action, the greater the voltage generated. If the touch characteristic is fed to the amplitude-control line of an oscillator whilst the normal keyboard output is fed to the frequency-control line, both dynamics and pitch may be directly controlled by the performer.

One further output facility is normally provided: a trigger voltage generated each time a key is depressed. This, as will be seen shortly, may be used to 'fire' the timing circuits of an associated signal-processing device such as an envelope shaper.

Keyboards were not the only manual control aids to find favour with designers of voltage-controlled systems. The joystick proved to be a popular alternative, permitting the operator to manipulate two functions simultaneously with one hand. The device consists of a lever protruding upwards from a central bearing, which may be freely moved in any direction within a circular outer limit determined by the mechanics of the bearing mounting. The spatial positioning of the lever end is decoded by a series of linkages under the unit into two coordinates: $x_1$–$x_2$, and $y_1$–$y_2$:

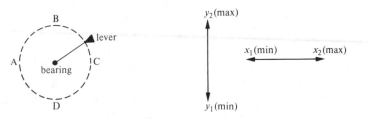

**Figure** 34

The movements from one lever position to another, measured in terms of these coordinates, are used to change the voltage outputs of two associated potentiometers. Moving the lever from position *A* to position *C*, for example, varies the output from the *x* potentiometer from its minimum setting to its maximum. Since the joystick maintains a mid-point position along the axis $y_1$–$y_2$, the output from the *y* potentiometer remains constant at its median voltage value. Moving the lever from position *D* to position *B* produces the converse response: the *x* potentiometer delivers a constant median voltage, whilst the output from the *y* potentiometer increases from minimum to maximum. All other joystick trajectories will involve simultaneous adjustments to both potentiometers.

Unlike keyboards, joysticks are not suitable for specifying accurately predetermined sequences of control voltage steps. As interactive, continuously variable performance aids, however, they provide the composer with a flexible tool for intuitive control over selected device functions. One or two designers have attempted to extend the versatility of the joystick control still further by suspending the bearing itself in a flexible mounting, permitting a third voltage output to be generated by movements in the vertical plane. Considerable skill, however, is required to achieve even generally predetermined changes in all three functions simultaneously.

Most joysticks are constructed to provide a bipolar output, 0 V being associated with a dead-centre position. Sensitivity controls regulate the degree of voltage variation obtained when the joystick is moved to the extremes of its travel in each plane. Variations on the joystick principle include a touch sensitive pad which decodes the position of a finger on a grid to similar effect.

Despite such improvements in manually operated facilities for device control, the primary fascination with voltage-control technology arose from the ability to utilize the dynamically varying outputs of devices such as oscillators as control inputs for others. A sine-wave oscillator, for example, generates a constantly recycling voltage function. The range of voltage variation within each cycle determines its amplitude, and the number of complete cycle repetitions per second determines its frequency. In a synthesizer, oscillator circuits are frequently designed to give bipolar characteristics, the associated function fluctuating either side of a zero voltage reference:

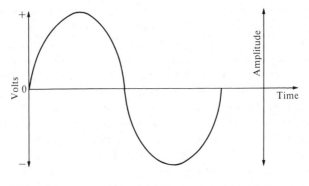

**Figure** 35

If such a voltage source is applied across one of the control break-points for another oscillator, its fluctuating output will modulate the selected function about the voltage level set via the internal potentiometer.

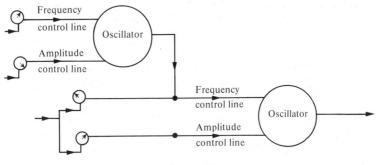

**Figure** 36

The first oscillator thus adopts the role of a frequency control voltage source for the second, the output of the latter providing the audio product. Once again numerous permutations and combinations of control connections are possible. Feeding the output of one oscillator to both the frequency and the amplitude control lines of a second, for example, will produce a linked modulation of both characteristics. Alternatively, separate oscillators may be connected to each control line to generate an altogether more involved, asynchronous modulation of frequency and amplitude. Even more elaborate characteristics may be produced by chaining several oscillators in series. Sheer complexity, however, in no way guarantees musical value, and over-enthusiastic experimentation will frequently prove counter-productive. Even the simplest arrangement illustrated above is capable of producing a multiplicity of timbres which demand some understanding of the procedures involved.

The novice electronic composer, experimenting with such device arrangements for the first time, is often impressed by the ease with which a single audio oscillator is transformed into a rich sound source. Such a reaction, however, is usually tempered by the discovery that the relationships between parameter settings and the perceived results are far from straightforward.

The acoustical products of both frequency and amplitude modulation are governed by mathematical considerations concerning the characteristics of both the modulated and the modulating waves. The wave shapes themselves are important elements in these equations, for each harmonic component gives rise to its own set of characteristics. In the interests of clarity, consideration is thus restricted in the first instance to the modulation of one sine-wave oscillator by another.

If the output of one such oscillator, delivering a low-frequency wave of small amplitude, is connected across the frequency control break-point of a second, the output of the latter will be subject to gentle pitch vibrato. The speed of this vibrato will be determined by the frequency of the control wave, and the depth of vibrato by the amplitude. Increasing the output level of the control oscillator will thus increase the depth of the vibrato without altering its speed. If both the speed and the depth are sufficiently gentle the ear will be able to follow the changes in frequency without difficulty. If the depth of modulation is particularly pronounced, or the speed exceeds about 11 to 12 Hz, however, it becomes impossible to track the changes as a function of time. The persistence factor of the human ear ensures that modulating speeds greater than the above boundary figure result in a blurring of these frequency changes, the sound becoming transformed into a seemingly stable complex of timbres.

This transformation may be analysed in terms of three determining components: (1) $c$, the carrier (= original) frequency of the second, audio oscillator; (2) $m$, the modulating frequency of the control oscillator; and (3) $d$, the depth of modulation created, measured in terms of the maximum frequency deviation obtained either side of the carrier. Two series of side bands will be introduced either side of the carrier frequency, drawn from the progressions $c-m$, $c-2m$, $c-3m$, . . . and $c+m$, $c+2m$, $c+3m$, . . . If the audio oscillator is generating a carrier frequency of 1000 Hz and the control oscillator a modulating frequency of 150 Hz, for example, side bands at 850 Hz, 700 Hz, 550 Hz, etc. and 1150 Hz, 1300 Hz, 1450 Hz, etc. may be generated in addition to the carrier.

The outer limits of side-band generation and the relative amplitudes of each component between these extremes, including the carrier, are determined in the first instance by a factor known as the modulation index, $I$. This is calculated by dividing the frequency of deviation by the frequency of modulation: $d/m$.[1] In the above illustration, if the modulating wave produces a deviation of 300 Hz either side of the carrier frequency, $I = 300/150 = 2.0$. The distribution of energy for different values of $I$ may be calculated from mathematical tables, known as Bessel functions, one for each matching pair of side bands. The carrier itself enters into the distribution equations, responding to its own zero order function. The functions themselves are complex, creating wave-like patterns for each order of side band. In essence, as $I$ increases, a fluctuating quantity of energy is 'stolen' from the fundamental and distributed amongst an increasing number of side bands. The following diagrams give an approximate indication of the characteristics of some representative modulation indices. (See fig. 37.)

Viewed as diagrammatic representations these characteristics reveal some fascinating responses for different degrees of modulation. Their musical significance, however, is far from straightforward, for there are no easily definable relationships between the perceived nature of frequency-modulated sounds and their scientific determinates. Modifications to $c$, $m$, or $d$ will indeed result in elaborate transformations which may be readily analysed. These characteristics, nevertheless, are determined by the process itself which may only be regulated in terms of three interdependent variables. The composer thus has limited scope for tailoring the

[1] In modulation theory it is always assumed that the deviation characteristic is symmetrical about the carrier frequency. In view of the preference for logarithmic response characteristics in voltage-controlled systems, it should be appreciated that the frequency asymmetry that results from equal control voltage swings will modify the effects of the modulation index to some degree. A similar situation will arise in the case of logarithmic amplitude modulations.

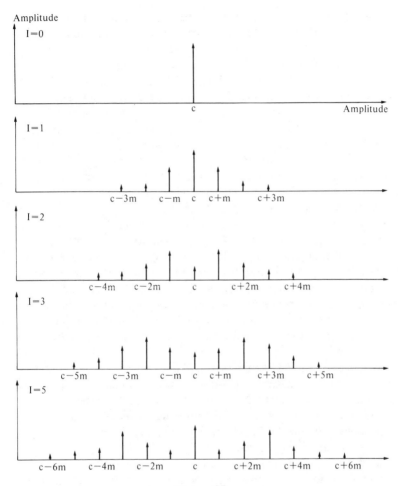

**Figure** 37

resultant range of sounds to his particular needs. Instead he must accept or reject a predetermined morphology, relying on subsequent signal-processing techniques such as filtering to produce any modifications to these mathematically ordered timbral characteristics. Further consideration of the characteristics of frequency modulation will be given in Chapter 10.

Amplitude modulation results in an altogether simpler set of side-band characteristics, providing once again the process is restricted to the modulation of one sine-wave oscillator by another. When the output of one such generator is applied across the amplitude-control break-point of a second, the amplitude of the former wave determines the degree of amplitude variation generated in the output of the latter, and its frequency the speed of modulation. At low modulation speeds, less than about 11–12 Hz, the modulating function will be clearly perceived as a variation of amplitude with respect to time. This effect may be varied from a gentle pulsing to a complete cyclic enveloping of the sound. The latter effect will be produced if the amplitude of the control wave is increased sufficiently to ensure that the greatest negative voltage swing generated during each cycle is sufficient to cancel out entirely the steady 'carrier' level supplied by the internal amplitude potentiometer of the second oscillator.

At higher modulation speeds, above the 11–12 Hz boundary, the variations in amplitude blur into a continuous spectrum. The resultant timbre is composed of three frequency components: the carrier frequency $c$ and two complementary side bands, one a summation of the carrier and the modulating frequency, $c+m$, the other the difference frequency, $c-m$. The amplitude of the modulating wave determines the strengths of the pair of side bands to the carrier: the greater the depth of modulation the stronger the side bands.

A distinct similarity may be noted between the characteristics of amplitude modulation and those of ring modulation. The latter process, it will be recalled, involves the use of a special circuit which acts upon two separate frequency sources, $F_1$ and $F_2$, to produce a summation frequency $F_1 + F_2$ and a difference frequency $F_1 - F_2$. If $F_1$ is viewed as a carrier frequency and $F_2$ as a modulating frequency the products of ring modulation may be seen to be identical with those generated by amplitude modulation. In the latter case, however, the carrier frequency is always present in the output, whereas in the former both input frequencies are firmly suppressed. Ring modulation may thus be considered a rather special form of amplitude modulation, although the electronic processes involved are distinctly different.

Frequency and amplitude modulation of complex signals involves similar multiplicative processes to those encountered in ring modulation of such sources. Each frequency component in the carrier wave is subject to modulation by each frequency component in the modulating wave, the amplitude of these elements affecting the characteristics of each set of side bands.

Voltage-control technology has facilitated a further type of signal modulation known generally as spatial or location modulation. It will be recalled that the left-to-right positioning of a stereo sound image is determined by the proportional distribution of its signal elements between two playback channels. Movement of the image in response to a single control voltage function demands a circuit arrangement which is capable of adjusting the amplitude of both channels simultaneously, a gain on one channel being automatically matched by an equivalent loss on the other. Such a function may be derived from a pair of voltage-controlled amplifiers (VCA), an inverter to reverse the polarity of the applied voltage being inserted in the control line of one of the units:

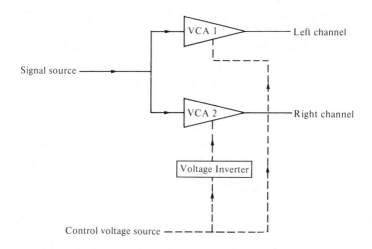

**Figure** 38

When the control voltage supply is set to its maximum value VCA 1 will be set fully on, and VCA 2 fully off. As the voltage is reduced, the resultant fall in the output of VCA 1 will be matched by a corresponding rise in the output of VCA 2, the former level falling to zero and the latter rising to a maximum at the other extreme.

Application of a control wave from an oscillator will result in a modulation of incoming audio signals between the two channels. The spatial movements become increasingly blurred as the oscillator speed is increased, leading to the production of amplitude-modulation side bands. Alternatively, a joystick may be employed as a manual panning control by applying the single voltage output associated with movements of the lever along one of its axes.

A simple extension of this principle allows the use of both voltage outputs to control the distribution of a sound image between the four output channels of a quadraphonic playback system. The composer may then 'steer' the sound image freely about the listening area, the joystick movements manipulating all four playback gains simultaneously. The capacitive detectors used for the Thérémin and the *potentiomètre d'espace* provide interesting precedents for the latter method of spatial control.

A number of other device characteristics are particularly amenable to external voltage control. Reference has already been made to the control of filter tunings via a keyboard. Most synthesizer manufacturers have also developed voltage-controlled reverberation units, usually of the simpler and more portable spring type, where an applied voltage may be used to control the depth of enhancement.

Envelope-shapers figure prominently in voltage-controlled systems, offering several functions which may be manipulated by other devices. These amplitude processors have proved especially popular in view of their ability to provide a semi-automatic dynamic shaping of events. Simpler versions provide three basic variables: an attack time, during which an applied sound is allowed to grow from zero intensity to a pre-set amplitude; a sustain or 'on' time during which this amplitude is maintained; and a decay time during which the signal level fades away to zero. The attack and decay functions are often fixed features, providing exponential amplitude curves.

Although the duration of all three segments may normally be varied manually, several manufacturers have restricted the provision of an external voltage-control break-point to the decay characteristic only. More comprehensive designs, however, provide control break-points for all three segments. The range of durations which may be specified for each segment varies considerably from design to design, but the following characteristics are typical: attack time 2 msec to 1 sec, sustain time 0 sec (= no sustain) to 2.5 sec, and decay time 3 msec to 15 sec. As these specifications suggest, a wide variety of envelope-shapers may be created by different combinations of segment settings, for example:

**Figure** 39

Many designs offer, in addition, an 'off'-delay function which may be switched in to allow automatic recycling of the shaper after a specified interval. This segment provides a timed period of silence between the end of each decay and start of the next attack, which may be varied typically from 0 sec (= immediate attack) to about 5 sec. If this recycling facility is switched out the envelope-shaper must be activated by a trigger voltage pulse supplied either internally via a manual push-button or externally from a device such as a keyboard. If the duration of this pulse is extended by holding down the button or a key it is normal for the sustain segment to be prolonged until the point of release, the chosen decay characteristic then completing the envelope. Similarly, interrupting an envelope with a fresh trigger pulse will reactivate the attack–sustain–decay characteristic, the attack segment being truncated to the portion necessary to restore the amplitude to its maximum level. In the extreme case of one key selection being immediately followed by another a constant amplitude will be maintained. The following connections between a keyboard, oscillator, and envelope-shaper will create a monophonic organ, responding to key selections with a succession of dynamically shaped pitches:

**Figure** 40

Some versions offer a level-detection facility which may be used to trigger the envelope function as soon as the incoming audio signal reaches a selected amplitude. The electronic circuit employed for this purpose is known as a threshold detector or Schmitt trigger. This consists of an amplitude-sensitive switch which closes to create an 'on' state only when an applied signal exceeds a pre-set value. This state is then maintained until the signal falls back below the threshold level, whereupon the switch opens again.

**Figure** 41

In this particular application of threshold detection only the 'off' to 'on' trigger pulse is required to activate the envelope-shaper, the reopening of the switch being ignored. More complex applications will be discussed in due course.

External voltage control of segment timings is restricted, in practice, to low-frequency control waves, or the output of manual devices such as joysticks. Modulating the decay time, for example, will only produce a detectable ripple in the decay characteristic if the modulation speed is significantly less than 11 Hz, and the internally pre-set 'carrier' decay time is sufficiently long to allow several repetitions of the control wave before the signal dies away, for example:

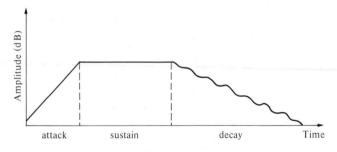

**Figure** 42

Very slow control waves with cycle times of the order of seconds may be used to produce sequences of dynamically changing envelopes, with the shaper set to recycle automatically. The following illustrates the effects of slowly modulating the decay time under these conditions:

**Figure** 43

One popular application of envelope-shapers set in a recycling mode is the extraction of 'snapshot' samples of sound from a source which is dynamically changing in frequency or timbre. If the attack and decay segments are set to their minimum values, adjustments to the sustain and recycle delay segments will regulate the on/off characteristics of what has now become a simple electronic 'gate'. Enveloping of a slowly oscillating frequency in this manner will extract a pattern of pitches which is a permutation of the gating speed and the cycle time of the source signal. More sophisticated designs of envelope-shapers provide an extra feature in the form of an initial decay characteristic, inserted between the attack and sustain segments. This addition permits an extra emphasis to be placed on the attack itself, in a manner much more akin to the transients of many naturally generated sounds. Various electronic techniques have been employed to achieve such a response. One of the commonest involves the use of two envelope-shaper circuits connected in parallel. One supplies the primary three-segment attack–sustain–decay envelope. The other supplies a secondary two-segment attack–decay envelope which fires simultaneously with the first. Providing the attack times of both circuits are set equal different initial peaks and decays may be produced by regulating the maximum gain and the decay time of the secondary shaper. (See fig. 44.)

Voltage-controlled envelope-shapers, despite such enhancements, are still limited in their processing capabilities. In particular, as individual units they are only capable of shaping the dynamics

**Figure** 44

of the entire sound applied to their inputs, and not the individual spectral elements. Most natural sounds exhibit extremely complex envelope characteristics with numerous independently evolving components. In addition, the usual restriction of fixed exponential attack and decay characteristics precludes the possibility of generating envelopes with more flexible shapes, for example an attack which tails off rapidly in its sharpness, or a decay which begins quickly and ends gently:

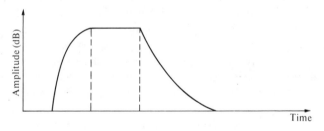

**Figure** 45

In an analogue, as opposed to a digital, domain the opportunities for refining techniques of envelope-shaping are extremely limited. Two solutions exist for the problem of generating a dynamic variation in timbre during the course of each shaped event. The first, applicable specifically to the synthesis of material from a bank of sine-wave oscillators, involves the provision of an envelope-shaper for each generator, shaping each frequency component before any subsequent Fourier addition. Synthesizers, however, do not in general provide sufficient oscillators or sufficient envelope-shapers for any useful application of this technique.

An orientation towards frequency and amplitude modulation as primary techniques of timbre generation in voltage-controlled systems has tended to produce designs restricted to a handful of oscillators and the most basic range of electronic wave forms: sine, square, ramp, and triangle. Further, any prospect of accurate Fourier synthesis by combining generators is overshadowed by problems of frequency stability in many of the cheaper synthesizers. Standards of reliability and accuracy have all too frequently been sacrificed in favour of commercial design economies, which have not always been in the interests of more serious composers.

The second solution to the problem of timbre variation during enveloping involves using the envelope-shaper itself as a control voltage source. In generating the segments of an envelope a composite electronic voltage function is produced to operate an internal amplifier. If this voltage, described by some manufacturers as a trapezoid function, is made available externally, it may be applied to other devices in a synthesis chain, for example a tuneable low-pass filter. The latter will then track the envelope function, the frequency of cut-off rising with the attack and falling with the decay. Suitable settings of both filter and envelope-shaper will then allow applied sounds to grow in brightness as their intensity increases, a feature associated with many instrumental sounds.

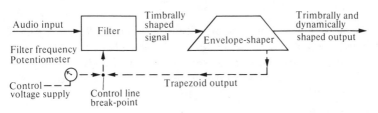

**Figure** 46

Larger synthesizers provide a number of ancillary amplitude-processing devices based specifically on the properties of the Schmitt trigger. Similarities may be noted between some of these and the standard envelope-shaper. The differences arise in the greater degree of versatility afforded. The simplest application is that of an electronic 'gate' which acts directly to block or pass applied audio signals depending on the state of the associated trigger. The latter may be activated either by the incoming signal itself or by any other suitable external voltage source. If the gating circuit responds instantaneously to trigger signals the resultant abrupt switching of the audio level may result in shocks to the human auditory mechanism which are perceived as clicks. These become particularly noticeable if the voltage of the gate control signal fluctuates rapidly about the threshold setting. Such unwanted side effects may be minimized by introducing special attack and decay circuits to slew the switching response slightly:

**Figure** 47

Comprehensive designs offer both a variable trigger threshold control and also adjustable slew rates. The characteristics of one audio signal may be used to shape another directly by using two gate circuits. The first is set in a self-triggering mode, the trigger response being additionally output as a control signal for the second unit.

**Figure** 48

In the above arrangement audio signal 2 will only pass when audio signal 1 is activating its own gate. A useful variation of this technique involves the insertion of a voltage inverter in the control line between the two gates. This reverses the response of the second gate such than an 'on' state in gate 1 generates an 'off' state in gate 2, and vice versa. Using this arrangement the audio signal fed to gate 2 will pass unhindered except when the audio signal fed to gate 1 triggers itself, whereupon the former is suppressed.

The Schmitt trigger provides the basis for another signal processor known as a limiter. Although originally intended as a recording and broadcasting aid to remove unwanted peaks from applied signals this device is of special value in an electronic music system, where the opportunities for generating unexpected overloads in signal lines abound. Further, the resultant modifications of attack transients can lead to marked transformations of the sound events themselves. The threshold setting determines the maximum level at which an applied signal passes through the unit unaltered. As soon as a signal exceeds this setting the trigger fires, switching in attenuation circuits which flatten out the overshoot. This effect may best be explained in the form of a diagram, comparing a steadily increasing input level with the regulated output:

**Figure** 49

As in the case of the gate, useful modifications to the trigger response may be introduced by adding attack and decay slew circuits, acting to delay the reaction of the attenuator to changes in the trigger state. Rapidly increasing input amplitudes, for example, may be allowed to overshoot the threshold level for an instant before the attenuator comes fully into operation:

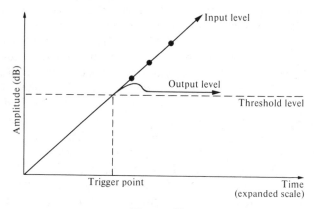

**Figure** 50

This modification generates artificial transients, the shorter the rise time of the input signal, or the longer the delaying effect of the attack slew circuit, the more pronounced the initial overshoot. The decay setting provides a matching effect when the input signal falls back again below the threshold level.

A useful development of the limiter, sometimes known as a sustain unit, incorporates amplifying circuits which act upon signals below the threshold setting. In this mode the latter acts as a reference level to which incoming signals are automatically adjusted. Such a facility is often used to highlight subtleties of timbre otherwise masked by fluctuations in amplitude.

The Schmitt trigger is also incorporated in several versions of a complementary pair of amplitude processors known as compressor/ expanders or companders. A trigger-based compressor differs from a limiter in the behaviour of the attenuation circuits to signals which exceed the threshold setting. Instead of flattening the overshoot, the characteristic is merely rounded, the degree of compression being fixed or variable according to the design. (See fig. 51.)

Expanders behave in exactly the opposite manner, increasing the gain of signals which exceed the threshold setting. (See fig. 52.)

In both cases the introduction of attack and decay circuits

**Figure** 51

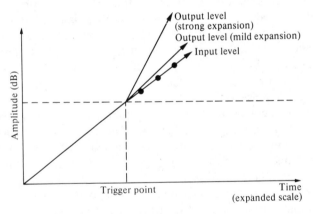

**Figure** 52

modifies the response to signals which cross the threshold by delaying the reaction of the amplitude processors.

In outlining the basic features of voltage-controlled systems it has become apparent that the potential advantages of such facilities for the composer are tempered by their very elementary provisions for programming the operation of the control networks. The need for some form of electronic storage mechanism for registering sequences of device control values was quickly appreciated, and by the end of the 1960s most manufacturers were incorporating such a facility in their more sophisticated system packages.

The basis for a link between digitally orientated control facilities and analogue devices arose in the first instance from the on/off voltage patterns created by pulse generators. These devices, it will be recalled, were commonly employed in 'classical' studios such as Cologne as direct sources of audio material. The transistor versions developed for synthesizers operate on very similar principles.

One special type of multiple-pulse generator developed for voltage-controlled systems incorporates a modified Schmitt trigger, the pulse patterns being made dependent on the characteristics of an external voltage source. The threshold detector functions in the normal way, firing the trigger whenever the input voltage reaches its pre-set value. Instead of the trigger signal being applied internally it is fed directly to the output of the unit, producing a positive voltage pulse. Two options are available at this stage, depending on the particular design. The trigger either remains on, or switches on and off repeatedly at an adjustable rate until the input voltage falls back again below the threshold level. Application of a fluctuating voltage to the input results in the generation of asymmetric pulse patterns.

A refinement of this triggering system is employed in a device known as a timing pulse generator. Three operating modes are normally provided: (1) 'single shot' manual firing via a push-button, one pulse only being produced each time the button is depressed; (2) repetitive mode firing, where the trigger fires repeatedly at a rate proportional to an applied voltage; and (3) pulse burst firing, where the trigger starts and stops firing at a selected rate in response to externally applied pulses. If the pulse patterns are generated at audio speeds, highly complex timbres may be produced.

The use of two fixed-voltage levels to determine the information content of an audio or control signal forms a useful parallel with the techniques employed in digital information processing, where all the operational instructions and data are specified in terms of binary number patterns, the digit 0 being used to indicate an 'off' state and the digit 1 to indicate an 'on' state. The digital equivalents of gating circuits are derived from a series of four basic logic functions known mnemonically as AND, NAND, OR, and

NOR. Each of these functions examines the states of two digital inputs, and generates an output pulse if particular on/off logic conditions are detected. An AND gate will switch on if both inputs are activated simultaneously. A NOR gate, conversely, will switch on if neither input is activated. The other gates are essentially extensions of the above, responding additionally to the possibility of just one input line being activated. Thus an OR gate will switch on if either one or both inputs are activated, and a NAND gate will switch on if neither or just one of the inputs is activated, but not both. These characteristics may best be illustrated diagrammatically as a truth table:

| Inputs | | | Logic gate type | | | |
|:---:|:---:|---|:---:|:---:|:---:|:---:|
| A | B | | AND | OR | NAND | NOR |
| | | | | | ✕ | ✕ |
| | # | | | ✕ | ✕ | |
| # | | | | ✕ | ✕ | |
| # | # | | ✕ | ✕ | | |

\# = Input active

✕ = Output active

**Figure** 53

Pulses, by their very nature, cannot directly supply variable control voltage characteristics. They may, however, be usefully employed for controlling the operation of special voltage-generating systems known as sequencers. The latter title is a little misleading, for it may generally be applied to a number of studio devices. A keyboard, for example, is a manually operated sequencer since its output consists of a series of voltage steps which may be used to control the production of a continuous progression of discrete events. In larger studios, however, the term is normally reserved for devices which produce a sequential output of voltage levels under electronic control.

The basic sequencer consists of a set of constant voltage supplies, each of which may be individually regulated, and a switching system which connects each supply in turn to an output line. Many designs offer a unipolar range of output voltage steps, typically from 0 V to +5 or +10 V. Bipolar responses are obtained in such cases by applying a negative voltage bias to the entire output, typically half the maximum output value, to make the overall range symmetrical about zero volts. The earliest prototypes used an electromechanical switching system consisting of a relay-activated rotary switch. This was quickly superseded by electronic switching techniques which are not only less cumbersome in terms of physical design but also capable of much faster speeds of operation.

The total number of individual voltage steps which may be produced varies from one design to another. Some smaller models provide as few as eight elements. More comprehensive designs are capable of sequencing fifty or even upwards of a hundred successive events. Three modes of operation are normally provided: (1) single step, where the switching system may be manually advanced one position at a time; (2) single run, where in response to suitable clock control pulses the sequencer will step itself through the bank of voltages once only; (3) repetitive mode, an extension of mode (2), where, on encountering the last position in the bank, the sequencer will automatically loop back to the beginning and continue to recycle until the source of control pulses is switched off. Good designs permit the operating length of the sequencer to be truncated via an adjustable last location marker. This allows the composer the freedom to programme any specified number of voltage steps up to the maximum available before termination or repetition.

Modern switching systems are usually all-digital, based on the characteristics of the switch register. This device is a digital counter, operating on a bank of binary storage locations wired in series:

**Figure** 54

Each location may either be de-energized 'off' (indicated below by the figure 0) or energized 'on' (indicated by the figure 1).

Initially the register is cleared so that all locations are de-energized. At the start of a sequence the register accepts an 'on' pulse from the input, which energizes the first location. This results in a switching pulse at the output, which is used in turn to effect a connection from the first position in the voltage bank to the output of the sequencer.

**Figure** 55

Subsequent pulses fed to the input will have the effect of displacing the start pulse location by location along the register. Since the object is to step through the sequencer bank one voltage location at a time these stepping pulses must be of a de-energized (= 'off') type, otherwise two or more locations will be switched on simultaneously.

**Figure** 56

On reaching the last location the 'on' pulse will either halt the sequencer automatically or recycle to the first location depending on the operational mode selected.

Sequencers need not be restricted to the production of single voltage functions. Some models provide two or even three parallel banks with independent outputs. Normally, however, a common switching system is employed, ensuring that the step-by-step changes in each bank occur simultaneously. This facilitates synchronous control of two or more device functions, for example frequency from one bank and amplitude from another. The stepping operation itself, as noted earlier, may be controlled manually, or by a clock pulse generator. For maximum flexibility the latter must be capable of offering a wide and continuously variable range of pulse rates. Some sequencers include a provision for manipulating the clock speed electronically via an external control voltage. A slowly repeating wave from a sine oscillator, for example, may be employed to vary the step rate continuously between two selected speeds. A more involved step-rate pattern may be produced from a sequencer with two or more output channels by connecting the voltage output from one of the banks directly to the clock input. Under these conditions the time of each successive step may be individually programmed.

From a musical standpoint the primary value of a sequencer is its ability to realize a programmed series of instructions. Sequencers of the type just described suffer from one important limitation, however, for they cannot provide a continuous variation in voltage. If, for example, an attempt is made to create a smooth glissando using a sequencer to control the frequency-control unit of an oscillator over an octave range, almost the entire resources of a hundred-element bank may be required to ensure that the individual frequency steps are too small to be detected. Further, each voltage level will have to be set painstakingly by hand. Such an operation proves extremely time-consuming for an effect which could, with care, be achieved by a single sweep of a manual joystick control.

The above illustration is an extreme one, but it highlights the problem of using discrete steps to create a gentle progression of parameter changes, particularly where these concern pitch information. A solution to this difficulty might be to enlarge the size of the sequencer bank to 250 or even 500 elements, increasing the number of voltage steps available for specifying changes of events. Such an improved accuracy, however, can only be utilized if the composer is prepared to spend considerable time and effort converting his or her musical ideas into formidable strings of individual voltage settings. It will be seen in due course that the use of a computer as a means of analogue studio control involves a very similar process, the specification of procedures entirely in terms of discrete steps, expressed in the first instance as numbers, which are then converted into corresponding control voltages. The added facility of arithmetic and logic programming facilities, however, makes it possible for the composer to express his ideas in terms of general functional descriptions with which he is far more familiar, delegating the task of calculating the necessary sequences of values to the machine itself.

The ability to program step functions is of particular value when the object is to generate sequences of discrete 'note/events', for these involve simple and precise specifications of pitch, duration, envelope, and timbre. This approach to electronic synthesis has already been highlighted in discussing the characteristics of the RCA synthesizers, and it may be appreciated that the elementary sequencer is well suited to such applications as the provision of control data for imitative instrumental textures, and the realization of serially based ideas.

One other application of this type of sequencer meriting attention is its use as an audio wave generator in its own right. If the bank, set in repetitive mode, is clocked at a sufficiently high speed the output voltages may be applied directly as a signal source. Varying the voltage levels of the individual bank elements will thus directly affect the timbre of the wave produced. Twenty-four elements' output in a bipolar mode might be set to create the following approximation to a sine wave:

**Figure** 57

The general characteristic of this wave, as may be seen from the above diagram, is approximately sinusoidal, and will be perceived aurally as a note with a clearly defined fundamental frequency. The stepped irregularities, however, introduce a considerable amount of harmonic distortion which will result in a harsh 'buzz'. If the number of steps per cycle is increased the outline of the wave will become progressively smoother, with an associated reduction in its impurity. The ear, unfortunately, is extremely sensitive to any such discontinuities, and for the production of frequencies towards the lower end of the audio spectrum up to 500 or more accurately set voltage steps per cycle may be required to achieve an acceptable degree of purity.[1]

Practical considerations thus temper the potential advantages. Some designers have reduced the problem of step distortion by incorporating a special circuit known as an integrator, which will electronically interpolate between steps to produce a gradient. This extra facility enables the composer to achieve more accurate approximations to continuous curves with far fewer elements. Contrast a sine wave constructed out of twelve voltage steps with one constructed out of twelve gradients:

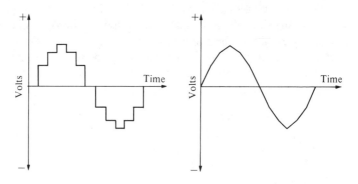

**Figure** 58

The gradient technique clearly produces a better approximation. Using this method as few as twenty-four elements are required to achieve a sine function of sufficient purity for many studio applications. Such a facility also enhances the use of the sequencer as a source of continuously varying control voltages.

Earlier discussions have drawn attention to the problems

[1] The problems of stepped wave-form approximations will be studied further in Chapter 10, in connection with digital sound-synthesis techniques.

encountered in attempting additive syntheses in an electronic music studio, in particular the number of individual sine-wave generators required, and the high degree of tuning accuracy and frequency stability demanded of each unit. The direct specification of wave shapes, by contrast, provides a powerful degree of freedom in the construction of stable harmonic spectra, within the practical constraints referred to above. Altering the clock rate will shift the entire spectrum upwards or downwards in frequency, preserving the wave shape exactly. If the object is to achieve dynamic changes in timbre, however, the composer is better advised to return to the technique of additive synthesis, for it is not practicable to restructure a sequencer wave shape dynamically by hand whilst the unit is in use. Even a simple idea such as progressively adding a second harmonic component to a pure sine wave would require adjustments to be made to all the voltage-bank settings simultaneously.

One feature which has been lacking in the types of sequencer so far described is a facility for registering and storing control voltage functions produced elsewhere in the system. The basis for such a device is known as a sample-and-hold processor. In its simplest form this consists of an analogue voltage-detection circuit which will sample the instantaneous value of an applied voltage function, the timing of this action being determined by a control pulse. The information thus obtained is retained as a steady voltage until replaced by a new value, sampled in response to the next control pulse. Providing a regular succession of pulses is applied, the device will produce a step pattern approximation to the applied voltage function, translating the characteristic into a succession of discrete values.

Storage of these values demands the addition of a memory facility. Some early designs incorporated arrays of analogue storage circuits capable of directly recording voltage steps in the form of electrical charges. Digital memories, however, proved generally more versatile, and as the years progressed the technology became not only more reliable but also cheaper. The conversion of analogue voltages into binary numerical equivalents, and the reverse procedure, the generation of analogue voltages from binary data, are subjects which merit close attention for such operations are axiomatic not only to control voltage registration and recovery, but also to all computer-based techniques of sound synthesis.

The principles of binary number coding have already been outlined in considering the control systems for the RCA synthesizers. Their application in digital electronics is similar, each possible permutation of 'on' and 'off' states in a given group of binary elements being associated with a unique numerical value. In a digital memory the organization of binary locations or 'bits' into groups or 'words' involves two considerations, the total number of words available, and the number of bits constituting each word. The former factor determines the total number of voltage samples which may be stored, and the latter the accuracy of their representation.

Each word in a digital memory is assigned a unique address by which it may be referenced via a pointer, the latter being manipulated by the control system. In a computer the associated memory may be randomly accessed via a pointer which may be freely moved from one location to any other. A memory sequencer, however, lacks the logical programming capability of the computer, and is usually restricted to serial access only—the pointer may merely be incremented via a counter to move sequentially along the memory from word to word.

Parallels may now be drawn with the control system for a conventional sequencer, offering manually-set voltage steps. A re-set button is normally provided to initialize the pointer to the first location in the memory. The effective working length of the memory is usually adjustable via a special 'last location' flag. Incrementing of the pointer itself is controlled via a variable rate clock pulse generator, the last location marker either terminating the operation or looping the pointer back to the first location, to repeat its progression.

Two modes of operation are possible. The sequencer may be set either to store new values, obtained via the sample-and-hold processor and an associated analogue-to-digital converter, or to reproduce previously stored values, via a matching digital-to-analogue converter.

In the former mode the process proceeds as follows: at the first clock pulse the instantaneous value of an applied voltage is sampled and temporarily registered as a steady voltage. The analogue-to-digital converter reads this value and generates an equivalent binary bit pattern. The control system then 'writes' this pattern into the word location addressed by the pointer. The sequencer then waits for the next clock pulse, which increments the location pointer and reactivates the sample-and-hold processor to obtain a new value for the next conversion and storage operation.

The alternative mode, used to recover previously stored voltage step values, is a reversal of this process, with two important differences. At the first clock pulse the control system 'reads' the contents of the location currently addressed by the pointer and passes this information to the digital-to-analogue converter. The location itself, however, is unaffected by this procedure, for only an image of its contents is transferred. This permits the stored value to be reproduced any number of times, as a result of either memory looping or a succession of separate scans. The digital-to-analogue converter translates the pattern image into an equivalent voltage level which is sustained until it receives a new pattern as a consequence of the next control pulse, which automatically moves the pointer to the next memory location. No sample-and-hold processor is thus required in this mode, the system clock providing a timed sequence of voltage steps. In both cases coordination of the various processing stages is synchronized by deriving all control pulses from the single clock.

If the system clock speed is freely adjustable, different sampling rates may be employed according to the nature of the voltage function to be registered. Too low a sampling rate for a rapidly fluctuating voltage will result in step approximations which are too crude. Increasing the sampling rate will improve the sampling accuracy but reduce the period over which the sequencer may be operated, for the end of the memory bank will be reached more quickly. As in the case of conventional sequencers a compromise has to be struck between these two limiting considerations. Over the years the cost of memory has fallen dramatically, however, facilitating the construction of larger-capacity memory sequencers at a relatively modest cost.

Sampling a voltage function at one clock speed and reproducing it at another allows the step rate to be freely varied without altering the step values themselves. Studio control characteristics may thus be speeded up or slowed down without affecting their content. The interdependence of frequency and durational characteristics when sounds are subjected to variable-speed tape processing is a limitation which has been discussed before. Using a memory sequencer in the manner just described to control the generation of frequency functions allows such features to be manipulated separately, providing all the material is generated within the confines of the voltage-control system itself.

The accuracy of step approximation depends not only on the frequency of their occurrence, referred to as the sampling rate, but also, when digitized, on the resolution of the numerical equivalents, referred to as the quantizing accuracy. As noted earlier, the total number of values available for encoding voltages between the operating limits of the system is determined by the word size itself. Memory sequencers generally employ word lengths of between eight and twelve bits. Thirteen-, fourteen-, or even sixteen-bit words are occasionally employed, but a practical restriction is encountered in the D-to-A and A-to-D converters themselves. Although the cost of these items has fallen considerably over the years each extra bit of resolution results in a major increase in price. Further, sixteen bits, to all intents and purposes, has marked the limit of attainable conversion accuracy. It will be seen in due course, however, that such a resolution is adequate even for high-quality digital sound synthesis, an application which imposes the most stringent demands on both sampling and quantizing.

It will be recalled that a three-row punched code in the RCA synthesizers permitted a total of $2^3 = 8$ different binary patterns to be created. Similarly, a four-row code permitted $2^4 = 16$ different patterns. A memory sequencer employing an eight-bit word length will permit coding of $2^8 = 256$ different numerical values. Assuming, as is more usual, that the A-to-D and D-to-A converters are linear, and that the synthesizer operates over a total control voltage range of 6 V, each digital increment will correspond to a voltage change of 6/256 = approximately 0.023 V.

The acceptability of such a minimum voltage step size will depend on the studio function to which it is applied. As a control of amplitude levels, or the duration characteristics of an envelope-shaper, for example, such a resolution will normally prove satisfactory. As a control of frequency, however, such a step size will generally prove too large. If the voltage response characteristic is 0.3 V per octave, for example, a rather unusual tempered scale with almost thirteen divisions to the octave will result. Although it is possible, with the addition of an analogue sensitivity regulator, to increase the basic step size in such a situation to a more useful semitone, the device will be restricted to the registration of conventionally tempered pitches. Any attempt to register and reproduce a smooth glissando will result merely in the production of a chromatic scale.

It may thus be appreciated that the simulation of acceptably smooth slides in frequency demands a much higher degree of step resolution. Ten-bit sequences will allow division of the voltage into $2^{10} = 1024$ discrete steps. Twelve-bit designs will provide $2^{12} = 4096$ different steps. In the situation discussed above the latter degree of resolution will provide voltage gradations sixteen times finer than those obtainable from an eight-bit converter. Pitch may thus be manipulated in steps of 1/208 of an octave, an interval size sufficiently small to provide an apparently continuous change of frequency.

Details such as the above are primarily the concern of sequencer design engineers. The consequences of their decisions as regards word length and memory size, however, are of the greatest importance to the composer when faced with the prospect of using such a device. Some small synthesizers have been equipped with exceedingly basic memory sequencers, offering as few as sixty-four words of eight-bit resolution. More comprehensive designs, however, offer 512 or even more memory locations of higher resolution, sometimes organized into parallel banks to provide simultaneous registration and control of several voltage functions.

Even these larger designs, however, lack one highly desirable facility: the ability to programme the memory locations directly. The introduction of such a capability heralds a major transition into the sphere of computer-controlled synthesis.

Voltage-control technology unquestionably provided the primary driving force behind developments in studio design during the late 1960s and most of the 1970s. It would be misleading, however, to suggest that all the major advances in electronic music during this period were intimately connected with the activities of commercial companies, or that the compositional philosophies built up around the more traditional technology of the 1950s became irrelevant in the new era of studio design. Indeed, several of the works to be discussed in the succeeding chapter were produced in studios which at the time offered relatively few voltage-controlled devices.

The impact of mass marketing, nevertheless, was without precedent, leading to artistic trends which were not entirely advantageous to the medium as a whole. It has been noted that the operational characteristics of a particular studio design exert a considerable influence on the range and type of compositional operations which may be satisfactorily executed. A proliferation of studios equipped with identical synthesizers dictates a single design philosophy to all potential users. Whilst modularity in some, though by no means all, commercial designs permits an element of choice, in most instances no opportunity exists for developing systems in direct response to artistic demand.

Such an environment contrasts sharply with the continuous dialogue which was sustained between the engineers and the composers in centres such as Paris, Cologne, and Milan during the pre-voltage-control era. Studios such as these took only a modest interest in commercial equipment, choosing for the most part to research those aspects of the new technology which were of particular relevance to their needs and develop their own items of equipment. The studio founded at the Institute of Sonology, Utrecht, in 1961 provides a striking example of a major centre which over the years has chosen to develop its own extensive and unique voltage-controlled system entirely to its own requirements, taking the utmost care to retain adequate provisions for expansion and alterations in the light of changing artistic needs.

Some useful contributions were made by individual design pioneers, often working with extremely limited resources. Reference has already been made to the work of Paul Ketoff in developing his voltage controlled Synket. His interest in live rather than studio synthesis focused attention sharply on the problems of immediate and effective communication between a composer and his tools. It was the latter problem, perhaps the greatest stumbling block throughout the evolution of the medium, which inspired a most remarkable private enterprise, Oramics, developed by Daphne Oram in England at Fairseat, Kent, from 1959 onwards.

As noted in the previous chapter, developments in England during the 1950s outside the closed doors of the BBC Radiophonic Workshop were few and far between. Miss Oram's association with this institution during its formative years provided a major inspiration for her own ideas, which were to bear fruit in her own studio.

The attraction of Oramics lies in its use of visual communication as the basis for sound specification. 'Drawn sound' techniques were by no means new to the medium. Reference has already been

1. Ondes Martenot, 1977 concert version

2. Thérémin, original concert version

3. Pierre Schaeffer at work in his studio in the early 1960s

4. Stockhausen at work in the Cologne studio, c.1960

5. The Milan studio, c.1960

6. The Philips Pavilion at the 1958 Brussels World Fair

7. The RCA synthesizer, as installed at the Columbia–Princeton
Electronic Music Center

8. The Moog Mk 3C synthesizer

9. The Tonus ARP 2000

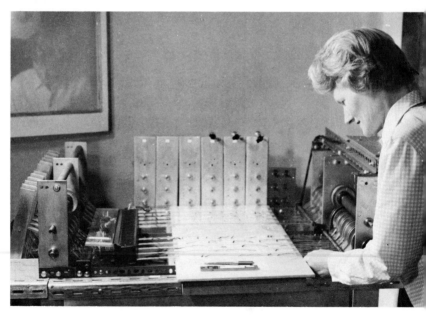

10. Miss Oram in her Oramics studio

11. The main voltage-controlled studio at the Institute of Sonology, Utrecht

12. The electronic music studio, University of Toronto, featuring the Hamograph

13. Performance of *Variations V* (1965) by the Merce Cunningham Dance Company. In the foreground John Cage (left), David Tudor (right)

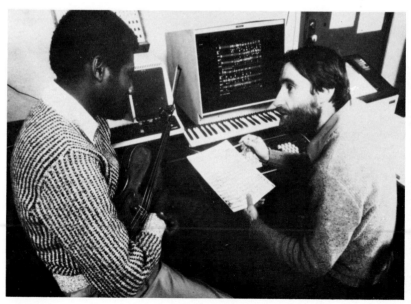

14. MIT experimental music studio, running music 11. Barry Vercoe (right) discusses the performance of his work *Synapse* (1976) for viola and computer-processed sound with Marcus Thomson

15. The IRCAM Musical Workstation

16. GROOVE system, Bell Telephone Laboratories, *c*.1970

17. The MUSYS studio of Peter Zinovieff, *c*.1970

18. The Yamaha SY99 synthesizer

19. The Synclavier II synthesizer

20. The Fairlight CMI synthesizer

made to Norman McLaren's manipulation of optical sound tracks in Ottawa, and the work of Yevgeny Sholpo in Leningrad. Projects such as these, nevertheless, remained isolated from the mainstream of technical advance, not least as a result of their geographical remoteness.

In Oramics a rationalized system of drawn shapes and neumes is employed to control sound production in terms of the primary characteristics of frequency, timbre, amplitude, and duration. The specification medium consists of ten sprocketed 35 mm clear plastic film-strips, mounted in parallel and transported synchronously by a central drive system from right to left over an array of photocells. Each of the latter is illuminated from above by a steady light source. The composer operates the system by adding shadow masks or neume patterns to the film-strips, which modulate the light intensity as they pass over the photocells. The latter translate these fluctuations into voltage functions which are used to control associated studio devices.

Time thus becomes a linear function of distance measured along the strips according to their speed of transport, normally set at 10 cm/sec. The strips are divided into two banks of five, the upper bank being employed for discrete control specifications, and the lower bank for continuously variable characteristics. This distinction is reflected in the construction of the photocell system. In the case of the lower bank one photocell is provided for each strip, measuring the overall contour of the shadow masks. For the upper bank, four narrow-aperture photocells are mounted in parallel under each strip, their positions being indicated by a faint four-line stave engraved on the film. These act as light-sensitive switches activated by rectangular neume patterns drawn on the stave lines. Although the coding system does not follow normal binary conventions a clear parallel may be drawn with the punched tape control systems of the RCA synthesizers.

The main purpose of the upper bank is to provide pitch control information, entered across three of the film-strips. A fourth strip may be used to operate switches within the system, and the remaining strip is available as a control facility for switching functions associated with any ancillary equipment which might be attached to the system from time to time.

In its normal mode of operation the pitch control system may be used to generate a tempered chromatic scale from  to

. The whole range, however, may be externally transposed via a master regulator downwards to start as low as  and upwards to finish as high as . Continuously variable adjustment on this control allows accurate fine tuning. Neumes on each line on the three pitch tracks are associated with a specific element of the coding system. In normal mode the lower two tracks provide coarse divisions of the frequency range tuned in fifths as follows:

**Figure** 59

The lines on the top pitch track are used in combination with these primary tunings to provide tempered semitones by means of a frequency addition process. For example:

**Figure** 60

Pitches above require more complicated combinations of neumes across the pitch tracks. The pitch generators themselves consist of a bank of four synchronized photo-multipliers which continuously scan shadow masks of hand-drawn wave forms, the pitch control system determining the rate of repetition. Up to four different source timbres may thus be specified and blended in amplitude using the lower optical tracks, the fifth track in this bank being normally reserved for the control of a reverberation facility.

The ability to draw the dynamic shaping of pitched events not only allows a readily assimilated audio-visual correlation of specifications, it also overcomes the rigid attack and decay characteristics of electronic envelope-shapers. One further shaping facility is offered: hand-drawn control over pitch vibrato, achieved by reassigning one of the lower optical control tracks to the time-base generator for the photo-multipliers. A fluctuating mask characteristic will then gently modulate the repetition speeds specified via the pitch-control system.

Oramics is only capable of generating a monophonic output. Polyphonic textures must thus be generated one strand at a time, the individual layers being built up through the processes of tape multitracking. Despite this procedural drawback, the flexibility afforded over the nuances of sound production provides the composer with a specification facility unparalleled in all but the most sophisticated voltage-controlled systems.

Analogue designs reached their zenith during the mid 1970s. As the decade drew to a close, the prospect of their demise during the 1980s became increasingly clear with the advent of a totally new design concept, based on the characteristics of the microprocessor. This product of the digital revolution has brought the power of the computer to even the smallest synthesis systems in a form which is both cheap and versatile.

Such a development is of the utmost significance to the future of the medium. An appreciation of its potential, however, must wait until the important genre of computer music, which stems as far back as the 1950s, has been studied in some detail.

# The Electronic Repertory from 1960

# 7   Works for Tape

The continuing work of the established studios provides a useful starting-point for a general perspective of the more significant electronic works to emerge during the 1960s and 1970s. Major centres such as Cologne, Paris, Milan, and Columbia/Princeton remained primarily concerned with the production of tape works. A growing interest in live electronics, however, foreshadowed by the activities of Cage and his associates, gave rise to a sphere of activity which is sufficiently distinctive to demand consideration in its own right in the next chapter.

Yet a third category must be added to take account of the birth and development of electronic techniques in the fields of rock and popular music during this period, for it is in this sphere that the characteristics of sound synthesis have attracted the greatest public attention.

The studio at Milan was to suffer mixed fortunes as the years advanced, leading to a major decline in its importance during the 1970s. After *Visage* Berio lost interest in the studio, moving away to work first at Columbia/Princeton and then at the RTF studio in Paris. With his departure attention focused on the work of his contemporary, Luigi Nono.

Nono was highly motivated by the principles of socialism, and this conviction is strongly reflected in his compositions. His first excursion into the electronic medium, *Omaggio a Emilio Vedova* (1960), shows an unexpected familiarity with electronic techniques, arising from his preoccupation with texture in his instrumental works. *La fabbrica illuminata* (1964) for soprano and tape is an aggressive commentary on the plight of the industrial worker, constructed from electronically treated recordings of factory sounds and choral singing. Over this scenario the soprano sings an impassioned protest against the tyranny of human exploitation. *Ricorda cosa ti hanno fatto in Auschwitz* (1965) is a harrowing recollection of the horror of the concentration camp. Nono treats this emotive subject with a directness and an integrity which is compelling. The effect is that of a terrible dream remaining throughout one step removed from the rational, controllable state of human consciousness.

*A floresta é jovem e cheia de vida* (1966), a work for four actors, soprano, clarinet, copperplates, and tape, is dedicated to the National Front for the liberation of Vietnam. The texts, compiled by Giovanni Pirelli, consist of eleven extracts from speeches and writings made by activists during the course of the anti-imperialist struggle. Nono concentrates here on an analysis and re-synthesis of their meaning rather than the linguistic components, thus differing noticeably from the approach adopted by Berio in works such as *Thema* and *Visage*.

*Contrappunto dialettico alla mente* (1967–8) by contrast shows a much closer indebtedness both to Berio and also to Stockhausen, a much-valued mentor during the 1950s. The piece consists of a rich interplay between vocal fragments and electronic sounds, highly reminiscent of Stockhausen's *Gesang der Jünglinge*. *Non consumiamo Marx* (1969) and *Y entonces comprendió* (1969–70) are both strongly expressed reflections on the political unrest inspired in part by the Paris student riots in 1968. Recordings of Fidel Castro and the sounds of street demonstrations permeate *Y entonces comprendió*, creating a powerful eulogy for those who perished in the cause. One of his last major works to have been composed at Milan, *Como una ola de fuerza y luz* (1971–2), explored the potential of electronic tape as a resource for use in conjunction with large orchestral forces. Here rich electronic textures are integrated with fluid mobiles of instrumental sound to create a work of considerable stature.

Work at the RTF studio in Paris polarized around the principal members of the Groupe de Recherches Musicales, in particular François Bayle (later to become its director), Luc Ferrari, Ivo Malec, and Iannis Xenakis. Schaeffer devoted his time increasingly to theoretical matters, culminating in an exhaustively researched book *Traité des objets musicaux* (1966). His only studio works of note consisted of a reworking of *Symphonie pour un homme seul* (1966) and *Étude aux objets* (1959, revised 1967).

Bayle, although firmly committed to the principles of *musique concrète*, gradually introduced electronic elements into his works, writing both for tape and for tape plus instruments. One of his first major studio pieces, *Vapeur* (1963), developed from an earlier study, *Lignes et points* (1961, in turn revised 1966), is based on the sounds of a bass clarinet, double bass, harp, and cymbals. As the work evolves, initially unaltered recordings of these sources undergo progressive electronic transformations, extending the compass and the timbral variety of the instrumental material. Another all-tape work, *L'Oiseau-Chanteur* (1964), combines electronic sources with recordings of a French horn, oboe, and harpsichord. In this instance the instrumental material remains unmodified, the processing of the other sounds serving to highlight and extend the timbral characteristics of the former.

Ferrari showed a particular disposition towards methods of rhythmic organization in his electronic works. After a series of preliminary studies, he produced a series of more substantial works including *Tautologos I* and *II* (1961) and *Presque rien No. 1* (1970). In both *Tautologos I* and *Tautologos II* the underlying structural principle is the regulation of timbre in terms of the frequency and density of the component events, organized into complex rhythmic patterns. *Presque rien No. 1* is an excursion into the sphere of organized collage using a wide variety of natural environmental sources such as birds, footsteps, seaside sounds, and children's voices. As the work progresses, the source elements, which remain largely untreated in themselves, become submerged under a growing stream of noise components which grow in density, eventually masking the environmental elements completely.

Malec pursued a compositional philosophy closely allied to that of Ferrari, structuring his work in terms of articulated changes of density and timbre. His works, however, were especially short in duration, typically between two and seven minutes. Such brevity demanded meticulous attention to detail so that the processes of sound manipulation could be adequately articulated as a structural feature. *Reflets* (1961) 2' 40" and *Dahovi* (1961) 6' 00", for example, both highlight the evolving timbres of a succession of individually articulated sounds, prolonged where appropriate by the judicious addition of reverberation.

Xenakis stands out as the most unusual member of the original Groupe de Recherches Musicales. His early association with the Paris studio dates back to the mid 1950s, and a continuing development of his mathematical theories of musical organization placed his electronic compositions in a class of their own. Rejecting any allegiance whatsoever to established schools of composition, he furthered the principles of stochastics, a self-styled description of an original and highly involved approach to probability calculus. Mathematical organization of this order quickly led him to the computer, in the first instance generating numerical data for use as the basis for both instrumental and electronic compositions. Computer-assisted sound synthesis was thus but a step away. Other aspects of technology were also to become part of his creative art. His training as an architect inspired the use of visual as well as aural means of communication in his works, for example holography and the projection of laser light beams. Such excursions into wider spheres of scientific development were motivated by a desire to develop an art of the universe in all its cosmic manifestations, thus pursuing in a highly individual way ideas very close to the heart of Varèse.

Such an integration of very different facets of the medium defies any attempt to divide his electronic works into categories. A mature tape piece such as *Persepolis* (1971), for example, owes as much to the computer as to the electronic studio in its conception. His most concentrated period of activity, 1957–62, nevertheless resulted in a group of pieces which are clearly identifiable with the *modus vivendi* of the Paris studio at that time. *Concret P.H.* (1958, revised 1968), realized directly after *Diamorphoses*, was produced for the Philips pavilion at the Brussels exhibition as a counterpart to Varèse's *Poème électronique*. The entire piece was realized from a single *concret* source, the sounds of burning charcoal, montaged to produce expansive sweeps of sound which reflected the curved construction of the auditorium.

*Orient-Occident* (1960, revised 1968) is characterized by rich expansive sonorities derived from both *concret* and electronic sources. The former material consisted of resonances produced by drawing a cello bow across the edges of metal rods, tam-tams, and cardboard boxes. The electronic sounds were derived from radio signals, demodulated into an audio form and transposed to produce high- and low-frequency tone clusters, linked by glissandi. Articulation is enhanced by using percussive material from a recording of an earlier orchestral work, *Pithoprakta* (1956), played at a reduced speed.

*Bohor* (1962) is perhaps Xenakis's most notable contribution to the Paris school of composition. His choice of source material, a Laotian wind instrument and some items of oriental jewellery, recalls the early studies of Schaeffer. The methods of manipulation, however, are far more subtle, involving slow transformations of repeating sounds, the resultant ostinati acting to sharpen the ear to the inner changes of detail.

The continuing reputation of the RTF studio attracted other composers during the 1960s, notably Earle Brown and Luciano Berio. Despite his earlier association with Cage's 'Music for Magnetic Tape', Brown's later works show a stronger affinity with developments in Europe, not least the mature manifestations of *musique concrète*. His *Times Five* (1963), for example, for flute, violin, cello, trombone, harp, and tape, uses recordings of instruments to extend both the apparent size of the live ensemble and also the range and variety of instrumental characteristics.

Berio's work at the studio culminated in *Laborintus II* (1965) for two sopranos, contralto, speaker, chorus, chamber ensemble, and tape, produced in response to a commission to commemorate the 700th anniversary of Dante's death. The origins of this work may be traced back to an earlier sketch, *Esposizione*, realized at Milan in 1962 just before his departure for the United States. Although further work at the Columbia/Princeton Center during the same year led to a preliminary version of *Laborintus II*, the final version owes a great deal to the major reworkings he carried out in Paris. The texts for the piece, compiled by Edoardo Sanguineti, are drawn from Dante's *Divine Comedy*, *Convicio*, and *Vitta Nuova*, biblical sources, and extracts from the writings of Eliot, Pound, and Sanguineti himself. The live vocal elements predominate throughout, Berio's technique of fragmentation and collage acting to develop relationships between phonetics and musical structure as the basis for this piece of music theatre.

As noted in an earlier chapter, the Cologne studio began to change direction under the increasing influence of Stockhausen during the late 1950s and early 1960s, culminating in his appointment to the directorship in 1963. The degree of polarization which followed became so intense that to all intents and purposes the studio became a personal laboratory for the composition of both his live and recorded electronic works. By the date of Stockhausen's succession to the directorship most of his early associates had either left for pastures new or ceased to compose electronic music altogether.

After a series of live electronic pieces, Stockhausen completed one further major tape work at Cologne: *Hymnen* (1967). In the previous year, however, during a visit to Japan, he had completed another work in the same genre, *Telemusik*, at the studio of NHK Radio, Tokyo, to which attention must first be turned.

Japan might seem an unlikely country to have made a significant contribution to the development of electronic music by the mid 1960s. The initiative came from the establishment of an avant-garde in Japanese composition soon after the Second World War, inspired at least in part by the rapid development of communications with the Western world. Two composers, Toshiro Mayuzumi and Makoto Moroi, were instrumental in introducing the new medium to a totally unsuspecting public long before many Western nations had even begun to consider its potential.

During the autumn of 1954 a group of technicians and producers at NHK Radio began some elementary experiments in electronic sound generation using an array of laboratory oscillators and tape recorders. Early in 1955 this group of pioneers received details of facilities installed at Cologne, and using these as a basis began work on constructing a system of their own. Moroi visited the Cologne studio in the autumn of the same year, and on his return commenced work with Mayuzumi on the production of the first pieces of Japanese electronic music in the newly completed NHK studio.

Mathematics, inspired by their encounter with serialism, provided a primary structural basis for their compositions. In *Variations on the Numerical Principle of 7* (1956) the influence of the Cologne school is especially evident, for the piece was based on a tuning scale of $49\sqrt{7}$, recalling the proportional approach to pitch specifications employed by Stockhausen in his *Studie II*.

By this time other Japanese composers were becoming attracted to the medium. One group, known as *Jikken Kobo* (Experimental Laboratory) were granted access to the recording facilities owned by the Sony corporation and began to produce a series of simple *concret* pieces under the leadership of Toru Takemitzu. In 1960 they transferred their activities to a new studio at the nearby Sogetsu Art Centre, which continued in operation until 1966.

An interesting precedent for Stockhausen's *Telemusik* was realized by Mayuzumi at the NHK studio in 1957. This work, entitled *Aoi-no-Ue*, is a partially electronic realization of an eighteenth-century Noh play, oscillators being substituted for the flutes, and noise and pulse generators for the percussion.

Stockhausen's visit to the NHK studio in 1966 undoubtedly influenced the subsequent course of Japanese electronic music, for many of the works which followed showed a more subtle approach to the medium, particularly as regards the handling of timbre. Moroi's *Shosange* (1968) is based on modulations of traditional temple instruments including the triton, shakuhachi, and shamusen. Mayuzumi's *Mandala* (1969) is a reflection on the cosmic philosophy of the Buddhist religion, pure electronic sounds being complemented by manipulations of human voice sounds.

The musical contrast between *Telemusik* and *Kontakte* is very strong, for over the intervening six years a marked change in Stockhausen's compositional outlook had taken place, not least from an acquaintance with the music of Varèse. The universality of *Poème électronique* inspired a growing interest in other cultures, hence the motivation to travel to Japan to investigate at least one of these national traditions at first hand.

The sound sources for the work consist of electronic sine- and triangle-wave generators, function (impulse) generators, temple instruments, and a kaleidoscope of folk and religious music recordings from Bali, Japan, Vietnam, Hungary, Spain, Russia, the Amazon, the Sahara, and Brazil. The processes of amplitude and ring modulation are widely employed, resulting in transformations of the national sources which are so extreme that the original characteristics are only occasionally discernible, such instances providing powerful vistas of the familiar in a sound world which is predominantly synthetic.

The work is divided into thirty-two sections, each introduced by the recorded sound of a Japanese temple instrument. These signals mark the passage of time, heralding a change in material, and a new set of modulatory processes. In some instances they stand out in isolation, in others they become extended and treated as an integral part of the section itself. The choice of temple instrument on each occasion has a direct bearing both on the length of the section it introduces, and also on the temporal ordering of the work as a whole. Strokes on the *keisu* at the start of sections 11 and 22 divide the work into three primary parts, approximately in the durational ratios 5 : 7 : 9. The use of this metal plate chime reflects its traditional role as a means of signifying a change of ritual during the Buddhist ceremony of worship.

Each part is subdivided by the higher-pitched *rin* bell, announcing the start of sections 8, 16, and 24. The majority of the remaining sections are signalled by strokes on one of a family of three wood-blocks. The deep-sounding *mokugio* introduces every sixth section, starting with section 3. Within this overall framework the middle-sounding *bokusho* introduces a total of eight sections starting with the first, and the high-sounding *taku* a total of twelve sections, starting with the second.

Section 31 stands out as a major exception to this arrangement. Following a fusion of transposed and modified *bokusho*, *mokugio*, *rin*, and *keisu* elements in section 29, this penultimate section is heralded and dominated by a gentle chorus of four large temple bells.

A marked degree of mathematical organization is evident, not only in the proportions used for the sectional durations, clearly derived from a Fibonacci series, but in the meticulous specifications used for the modulaton and filtering procedures which recall the tightly ordered organization of *Studie II* and *Kontakte*. The choice of material, and the refinement of its handling, result in a piece which flows with an apparent timelessness which surpasses even *Gesang der Jünglinge*. The piece is thus not a collage of disparate events but a delicately coloured perspective which owes much to the Japanese Noh drama.

*Hymnen* is a *tour de force* which lasts for almost two hours. The choice of material, the national anthems of countries drawn from all over the world, and electronic sounds both from studio generators and also from the ether, shows a clear affinity with the sources used for *Telemusik*. The methods of organization and transformation, however, result in a work which is significantly different.

The use of short-wave receivers to capture many of the anthems not only emphasizes the characteristics of radio communication as a means of linking nations, but it also introduces a recognizable process of initial transformation in terms of filtering and atmospheric interference, the severity of which depends on the distance of the transmission and the general reception conditions. This international flavour strongly echoes the concepts which lay behind Varèse's ill-fated *Espace*.

The work is divided into four regions, each dedicated to a particular composer. Within each region there are a number of centres which usually consist of a pointed reference to a particular anthem or group of anthems. Between these centres the processes of development and metamorphosis act to build linking bridges in an architecture which aims to unify all the constituent elements as parts of an ordered universe.

The first region, dedicated to Boulez, has two such centres: the Internationale and the Marseillaise. The piece starts with a mêlée of short-wave radio sounds, obtained by rapidly tuning from station to station. This chaotic assault on the ear, augmented by hissings, roars, and distorted glissandi, moves erratically towards a semblance of order, provided by the two centres mentioned above. *En route* the listener is made aware of other electronic elements and anthems (notably that of the German Federal Republic) and also shadows of an underlying harmonic structure derived from the anthems themselves.

Further elements appear, with a disruptive effect on the main progression of events. Four times the flow is completely broken by the ghostly calls of a casino croupier. Another digression is created by a two-minute polyphonic recitation on the various shades of red available in Windsor and Newton's artists' water-colours.

The disintegration of the first region leads to an extended bridge passage of flood-like sounds which rush up the audio spectrum to become the chatter of birds before descending once more into the depths, heralding the second region, which is dedicated to Pousseur. This has four centres, the first, the anthem of 'the German Federal Republic, which has already been alluded to, proving the most significant. After a cavernous, almost unrecognizable echo of the Marseillaise, achieved by playing the recording at an eighth of the correct speed, the great hymn by Haydn boldly bursts forth, only to be immediately dislocated by a barrage of interruptions which include the juxtaposition of hymn fragments, sporadic gating of the sound, freezing of motion in the form of an extended chord which subsequently slides outwards pitchwise in both directions, and finally the superimpositions of different strands to create a polyphony.

Under such an assault the anthem suddenly vanishes, fleeting reappearances becoming submerged in the bridge to the second centre, a compilation of African national anthems. These in turn become amalgamated with a synthesized version of the opening of the Soviet anthem to create a third centre. The flow is then dramatically interrupted by a studio recording of a conversation between Stockhausen and his assistant during the preparation of the piece. Stockhausen refers to this as his own personal centre where time—future, past, and present—becomes reduced to a single dimension.

The African anthems then resume their dialogue with the Soviet anthem as before, only to dissolve away as the music moves towards the third region. This section, dedicated to Cage, continues with a meditation on the Soviet anthem, which steadily develops into a full centre. The use of synthetic rather than natural sounds gives an unearthly feel to this exposition, the harmonic flow becoming increasingly disrupted as the processes of amplitude and frequency modulation become dominant features, culminating in another 'frozen' chord. The centre then gently dissolves by means of a slow downwards transposition of the chord, in semitone steps, fading away into a background of morse signals. These sounds from the ether form the bridge to the second centre, based on the American national anthem.

The latter enters brightly, only to fall victim to extensive fragmentation, created by the interpolation of extracts drawn both from other anthems and from popular songs. The British anthem makes a few brief appearances here. Although never accorded a centre in its own right, this anthem is heard fleetingly on a number of occasions during the piece, including, a little perversely, the bridge to the African centre.

The dissolution of this centre advances on several levels. The background of radio interference increases in intensity as if to suggest a worsening of reception conditions. Concurrently the pitched material becomes fragmented, only to polarize as yet another 'frozen' chord is in turn subjected to spatial modulation as if encapsulating the sound universe. The chord, and the rest of the fragments, then abruptly disappear, leaving the background mush of static to form a bridge to the next centre.

With the sudden intrusion of another studio conversation, this time remarking on the need to jump from America to Spain in a few seconds, the music plunges into the third centre, a wild fresco reflecting the colourful nature of the Spanish nation. Successive multitracks of the Spanish anthem spiral upwards to become high-pitched streams of sounds which finally fade into the distance. After a short pause these return to descend into deep resonances, marking the start of the fourth region.

This last region, dedicated to Berio, is the most economical in terms of material. It is also the most monumental, marking the fusion of elements into coherent pillars as the last steps on the path to unity. The first centre, the Swiss national anthem, sung, not played, has been ghosted in short fragments as far back as the end of the Spanish centre in the previous region. These interjections become stronger and more recognizable before themselves becoming caught up in the process of transformation towards mobile streams of sound.

The second and final centre is an amalgam of three elements: a slow pedal of deep rumblings, the reverberated cries of voices, and a rich downward spiral of electronic tones. The first of a further three interjections by the croupier leads to the development of a massive downward-moving timbre cadence, an idea foreshadowed in Křenek's *Pfingstoratorium—Spiritus Intelligentiae, Sanctus*, where frequencies which slide off the bottom of the spectrum are replaced by new elements entering at the top. A slow duet for electronic tones over a continuing pedal leads, after the second and third croupier interjections, to a brief recapitulation of ideas from earlier regions. During this process the sounds of a single man breathing in his sleep become apparent, providing the final bridge into silence. The slow recitation of the word 'pluramon' as a final element of this centre identifies it as the Utopian realm of *Hymunion in Harmondie under Pluramon*, the name being a play on *hymn union, harmonia mundi*, and *pluralism monism*.

Two other versions of *Hymnen* exist: *Hymnen mit Solisten* (1966–7) and *Hymnen mit Orchester* (1969). The former involves the whole of the electronic tape with an added part for a small group of soloists. The latter uses only part of the tape, from the third centre in region two to the end of region three. In both cases the instrumental scores are notated in terms of written instructions and simple signs. Unlike *Kontakte* these instrumental augmentations were added as options subsequent to the production of the main tape, and in no way detract from the conception of the original version as a complete work in its own right.

The reasons for describing *Hymnen* in such detail are threefold. Firstly, the work is arguably the most important tape piece to emerge from the 1960s, achieving a stature which remained unrivalled throughout the 70s. Secondly, its large-scale integration of synthetic and natural sound material provides an excellent example of the marrying of ideas and techniques gestated in the schools of *elektronische Musik* and *musique concrète*, in a manner anticipated by Varèse in his *Poème électronique*. Stockhausen's mature and perceptive handling of the *objet trouvé* provided all the necessary ingredients for a music drama worthy of Wagner, a comparison which he himself has acknowledged. Thirdly, the work owes almost nothing to the voltage-control revolution which was gaining momentum at the time of its production. *Hymnen* was painstakingly constructed using procedures which were for the most part manually controlled, refining techniques which had been developed during the 1950s. The piece, nevertheless, was in no sense dated by the manner of its construction. The musical ideas and the quality of their expression looked forward to the next decade, pointing to the earlier-mentioned dichotomy which arose between increasing sophistication in voltage-control technology and the artistic shortcomings of electronically controlled processes.

With the expansion of interest in electronic music during the 1960s other studies began to grow in importance. Henry, it will be recalled, had left Schaeffer's studio in 1958 to found his own private studio, Apsome. His output continued to be prolific, well over fifty works being produced during the first ten years of this studio's existence. In addition to concert works he has composed tapes for film, theatre, and dance. His ballet *Le Voyage* (1961–2), choreographed by his close friend Maurice Béjart, describes the journey from death into reincarnation, as told in the *Tibetan Book of the Dead*.

*La Reine verte* (1963), again choreographed by Béjart, utilizes both electronic and natural sources, the latter consisting of a piano, percussion, and textless vocalization from a group of singers. Great pains were taken to establish a strong continuum of timbre between these elements, shaped by the natural formants of the vocal sounds.

*Variations pour une porte et un soupir* (1963) is his most overtly *concret* piece of the period. Three basic sources were employed: the sigh of breathing, both inhaling and exhaling, pitched sighs obtained by playing a musical saw in a variety of ways, for example bowing or rubbing, and the squeaks and groans of unoiled door hinges. The degree of transformation applied is for the most part kept to a bare minimum. It is the character of the sources, and the skilful juxtaposition of the resultant recordings, which structure the work.

Henry's Catholicism led him to compose several works with a

religious setting. In 1964–5, for example, he composed four electronic interludes based on the Gospels according to Matthew, Mark, Luke, and John. These were followed by *Messe de Liverpool* (1967) and *Messe pour le temps présent* (1970).

Pousseur worked at the APELAC studio in Brussels during the 1960s before moving on to take up the directorship of the University studio at Gent. Two of his works stand out as being of particular significance: *Trois visages de Liège* (1961) and *Jeu de miroirs de Votre Faust* (1966). The former is a more refined work than his earlier *Scambi*, completed at Milan. The style, however, is strongly derivative of Cologne works from the middle and late 1950s. It employs a text, a group of short poems by Jean Séaux, reflecting the industrial and social life of this Belgian city. The other source material is predominantly electronic, filtered noise bands and both ring- and amplitude-modulated tones providing rich sonorities, frequently the subject of glissandi. The voice transformations are relatively mild, simple collage and reverberation adding a mobility to the recitation of text without destroying its intelligibility. *Jeu de miroirs de Votre Faust* is an electronic commentary on his full-scale opera *Votre Faust*, a work which took him almost six years to complete (1961–7). Once again vocal elements, both spoken and sung, predominate, with only minor transformations being applied to their content.

Yet another protégé of Cologne, Bengt Hambraeus, returned home to work primarily in the Swedish Radio studio at Stockholm. After composing a series of short background pieces for radio and television during the late 1950s, he produced a major concert work, *Tetragon*, in 1965. The style is strongly reminiscent of the more mature electronic works of Luening and Ussachevsky. A variety of instrumental sounds are subjected to simple tape-manipulation techniques such as multi-layering, variable-speed processing, and head echo from channel to channel to produce a powerful reworking of conventionally scored material.

The Munich studio proved an active centre during the 1960s, despite major changes in its administration, culminating in a complete removal of the system to the Hochschule für Gestaltung, Ulm, in 1966. Much of the original equipment was built and paid for by the successful electronics firm Siemens. This resulted in a studio of some sophistication, differing markedly from its European counterparts in the use of a punched tape control system. Whilst strongly reminiscent of the RCA synthesizers, this programming facility proved altogether more flexible, mainly as a result of the enhanced range of controllable synthesis and treatment devices.

Despite the advanced state of design, the studio was originally intended first and foremost as a facility for producing background sound-tracks for radio and television, thus restricting the scope for the production of concert works. In 1964 Mauricio Kagel produced a realization of Cage's *Imaginary Landscape No. 3* for electronic tape and percussion, a testament to a composer who proved a major inspiration for his own compositional style. Herbert Brün also spent some time at Munich before moving to the University of Illinois in 1963, completing a short piece, *Klänge unterwegs*, in 1961. Yet another expatriate of Cologne, Ernst Křenek, visited the studio during 1966–7 to produce a tape for a short television opera, *Der Zauberspiegel*.

The university studio at Berlin achieved some importance, mainly as a result of the activities of Boris Blacher. Blacher, very much the elder statesman (b. 1903), had established a considerable reputation with the German public over many years, particularly in the field of opera. His excursions into the electronic medium occurred at a very late stage in his career, and were restricted for the most part to the preparation of taped interpolations for inclusion in large-scale choral and orchestral works. These included a full-scale opera, *Zwischenfälle bei einer Notlandung* (1964–5), scored for voices, orchestra, and tape, to a libretto by Heinz von Cramer.

The Warsaw studio made a significant contribution to the flowering of contemporary Polish music after the 1956 uprising, sustaining a level of activity second to none. These achievements, unfortunately, have passed almost unnoticed outside Poland itself, for few of these electronic works have ever been heard in Western Europe or America. Krzysztof Penderecki took an active interest in the studio, exploring its capabilities as a tool for generating and manipulating new tone colours in works such as *Psalmus* (1961) and *Brygada śmierci* (1963). Instrumental writing, nevertheless, has remained his main means of expression, frequently employing performance techniques closely allied in their effect to the characteristics of electronic composition. By the middle of the decade the studio was attracting composers from other countries. One of the first, François-Bernard Mâche, an affiliate of the RTF studio in Paris since 1958, visited Warsaw in 1966 to complete a short *concret*-inspired piece, *Nuit blanche*, to a text by Artaud.

The use of solo instruments with pre-recorded tape features prominently in the works of Andrzej Dobrowolski, a native composer whose works have received increasing attention in recent years. His *Music for Magnetic Tape and Oboe Solo* (1965), *Music for Magnetic Tape and Piano Solo* (1972), and *Music for Magnetic Tape and Double Bass Solo* (1977) all display a deep preoccupation with the interplay of rich electronic textures with an extended palette of live instrumental sounds.

Studios were also established in Denmark (Copenhagen, 1956) and Norway (Oslo, 1961) by the state broadcasting corporations. Although the output from these studios was relatively modest during these early years the contributions of Per Nøgård and Arne Nordheim should not be overlooked. Nøgård has gained a considerable reputation within Denmark as a strongly avant-garde composer, pursuing post-Webern techniques of serialism, and his work at Copenhagen stimulated considerable interest in the potential of the electronic medium. His pieces include *Dommen* (1961–2), an extensive work for tape, soloist, and orchestra, and *Labyrinten* (1966–7), a short opera. Nordheim's work at Oslo resulted in a number of works, the first, *Katharsis* (1962), taking the form of a ballet for orchestra and tape. His style is less formalized than that of Nøgård, displaying a more developed sensitivity towards nuances of timbre. The manipulation of naturally produced music material on tape as a restrained enhancement to live performance proved a particular attraction. His *Epitaffio* (1963) for orchestra and tape, for example, uses the latter part only sparingly, mainly to introduce montages of choral singing to which the instruments respond.

The 'closed door' policy of the BBC Radiophonic Workshop, and the continuing lack of support from other institutions, severely retarded developments in Britain during the 1960s. Roberto Gerhard was the only major composer to be granted prolonged access to the Workshop facilities during this period. This permitted him to produce a number of pieces, primarily for radio, working both at the BBC and at his own private studio in Cambridge. His *The Anger of Achilles* (1963), for orchestra and tape, won the Italia prize for composition in 1965.

Tristram Cary continued to work in his own private studio, first in London, and then from 1963 until his departure for Australia in the early 1970s at Diss, Norfolk. The majority of his compositions have been written for radio, television, and film rather than concert-performance. *The Little Island* (1958), for example, is a charming cartoon with an electronic sound-track which is integral to, and not merely background for, the visual action.

Daphne Oram continued to develop her Oramics system at Fairseat, producing, like Cary, a succession of film scores. Music for theatre works also figured prominently, including *Rockets in Ursa Major* (1962), *Hamlet* (1963), and *Purple Dust* (1964). Another private studio was founded in London during the late 1950s by Ernest Berk to provide electronic music for the Modern Ballet Group, a venture which ran for well over a decade.

The general lack of facilities in Britain led several composers to improvise in a manner strongly reminiscent of the early struggles of Luening and Ussachevsky in America more than a decade previously. One result was the establishment of a rudimentary studio by Brian Dennis in an attempt to integrate electronic elements into music for schoolchildren.

Perhaps the most significant development in this sphere was the formation of a collective between the composers Hugh Davies, Don Banks, Anthony Gilbert, David Lumsdaine, and the flautist Douglas Whittaker during the mid 1960s. This pressure-group stimulated considerable interest in the medium amongst the younger British composers via seminars given for the Society for the Promotion of New Music. These activities drew the electronic engineer and composer Peter Zinovieff into their midst. Zinovieff, who was in the process of establishing his own studio at Putney, London, sensed the potential for developing commercial voltage-controlled equipment to satisfy a growing demand, and thus it was that EMS Ltd., London, was born.

By the end of the decade institutions in Britain, principally universities, were beginning to respond. After one abortive attempt at Manchester University, permanent studios were established at Cardiff, Durham, Goldsmiths' College, London, and York, soon to be followed by a host of others. Electronic music had at last become a permanent, if rather new, part of the British compositional scene.

Utrecht, the last of the second-generation European studios to be considered here, proved to be especially important to the development of the medium. As an Institute of Sonology within the University of Utrecht, this centre was able to make advances on several fronts, both in scientific research and development and also in the theory and practice of composition. The early acquisition of a computer led to whole new spheres of investigations, complementing and augmenting the sophisticated custom-built voltage-controlled system evolved during the late 1960s and early 70s.

Although this studio officially dates from 1961, some preliminary work was carried out at Eindhoven during the late 1950s by composers such as Henk Badings, Dick Raaijmakers, and Tom Dissevelt, using items of equipment supplied by Philips, the entire operation being subsequently transferred to Utrecht. It was the appointment of Gottfried Michael Koenig as artistic director in 1964, however, which heralded the start of a full-scale research and development programme. The introduction of a comprehensive course in sonology attracted, and has continued to attract, students from all over the world, providing a powerful theoretical base for the production of works by both established and up-and-coming composers.

The voltage-controlled equipment was constructed to an exacting specification, thus ensuring that the control networks functioned reliably and predictably. Until the introduction of direct computer-control facilities in the mid 1970s sequencers provided the primary means for programming events. Despite this new technology the studio retained its older 'classical' equipment for those who wished to work in a more traditional manner.

Electronic synthesis governed by strict syntactical considerations became a major feature of the studio's output of works, aided in due course by the calculative capabilities of a digital computer to produce constructional data from sets of algorithms. This trend diverged sharply from the freer, more intuitive compositional directions pursued by Stockhausen at Cologne during the 1960s, allying itself more closely to the mathematical approaches of Xenakis, whilst sustaining a strong regard for the post-Webern tradition of serialism.

Koenig's *Terminus II* (1966–7) is characterized by a continuous variation of timbre, all the sounds being derived from an initial complex of sliding oscillator tones. Continuity is achieved by presenting the sounds in the order in which they were derived, tending to a generative process of transformation. The use of mathematically determined procedures becomes more apparent in his next series of compositions entitled *Funktion Grün* (1967), *Funktion Orange* (1968), *Funktion Gelb* (1968), and *Funktion Rot* (1968), leading in turn to *Funktionen Blau, Indigo, Violett,* and *Grau* (1969). These were all derived from a series of composing programmes entitled PROJECT 1, first conceived at the Mathematical Institute of Bonn University during a visit in 1963–4. In the absence of direct computer control of studio equipment at this stage analogue control tapes were used in place of the sequencer, voltages being encoded as frequency functions via a pair of modulators and demodulators.

*Chants de Maldoror* (1965–6, revised 1968–9) by Rainer Riehn makes a virtue of the normally unwanted electronic distortions which can inadvertently occur when operating a studio, for example hiss, mains hum, and over-energized feedback. These sources are subjected to elaborate juxtaposition and montage to create a piece of rich, fast-moving sonorities.

In America, work at the Columbia/Princeton Center continued apace during the 1960s The RCA synthesizer Mark 2 proved highly attractive to the East Coast schools of composition, who for the most part shared a common interest in transferring 'note/event' styles of writing to the electronic medium. There were some, however, who shared the European bias towards less restricted concepts of sound structure and transformation, and the limitations of the synthesizer in this respect led in due course to the introduction of additional synthesis and treatment facilities, including voltage-controlled modules.

Babbitt continued to work extensively with the RCA synthesizer during the early part of the decade. *Vision and Prayer* (1961) combines a live part for a soprano, based on a text by Dylan Thomas, with an all-electronic tape. The techniques employed contrast sharply with those of a work such as Berio's *Visage*. The voice part remains distinctively normal in its presentation throughout, the synthesized material, highly instrumental in nature, being restricted to particular sections of the work. With no attempt being made to relate these elements in terms of any continuum of timbre the dialogue is distinctly uneasy, highlighting the artificial nature of the electronics.

*Philomel* (1963–4), based on a setting of a poem by Hollander on the *Metamorphoses* of Ovid, is a more integrated piece, again for soprano and tape, the latter combining electronic sounds with manipulations of the voice part. The text is a scenario describing the metamorphosis of the tongueless Philomel into a nightingale. Such an effect demanded a conscious interplay between the natural and electronic elements, the latter being employed to produce a rich polyphonic textures suggesting the atmosphere of the forest in which the event takes place. His *Ensembles for Synthesizer* (1963), a wholly electronic piece, is more complexly ordered than its earlier counterpart, *Composition for Synthesizer*. Babbitt here was particularly concerned to explore further the manipulation of complex textures, unobtainable in live instrumental performance.

Mario Davidovsky's association with the studio proved to be long and productive. After some preliminary experimentation with all-electronic sounds he turned his attention to the use of electronic sounds in combination with live instruments, composing a group of pieces, *Synchronisms 1* to *6*. In *Synchronisms No. 1* (1963) for flute and tape, *Synchronisms No. 2* (1964) for flute, clarinet, violin, cello, and tape, and *Synchronisms No. 3* (1964–5) for cello and tape, the source material is worked in a highly sectionalized manner. The constant changes in format from instrumental sounds alone, to instrumental sounds plus tape, or to tape alone highlight the wide variety of natural and artificial timbres obtainable from these resources through the processes of juxtaposition. In *Synchronisms No. 4* (1966–7) for boys' voices or mixed chorus and tape, *Synchronisms No. 5* (1969) for percussion and tape, and *Synchronisms No. 6* (1970) for piano and tape Davidovsky adopts a more flexible approach to compositional procedures, integrating rather than contrasting the live and electronic resources.

İlhan Mimaroğlu also made extensive use of the Columbia/ Princeton facilities, displaying like Davidovsky a keen interest in the integration of electronic and instrumental sounds. His style of composition, however, despite the sophistication of the facilities at his disposal, is highly reminiscent of the traditional 'cut and stick' approaches of the 1950s. Such meticulous attention to detail greatly enhances the essentially dramatic nature of much of his writing, which is rich in timbral and dynamic contrasts. Rather than integrate live and recorded material in performance he has preferred to create works for tape alone, manipulating natural sound sources in a manner highly reminiscent of *musique concrète*.

*Bowery Bum* (1964), for example, is based entirely on the sounds of a plucked rubber band, subjected to simple filtering and tape manipulation. The visual arts, in particular painting, have provided a major stimulus for his compositions—*Bowery Bum* was influenced by Dubuffet. *Le Tombeau d'Edgar Poe* (1964), based on the text of the same name by Mallarmé, is reminiscent of Davidovsky's early *Synchronisms* in its use of juxtaposition. The treatment of the text is strongly derivative of Berio's *Thema*, involving filtering, montage, fragmentation, and reverberation.

The influence of Berio may also be detected in *Prelude XII*, the last of a set of *Preludes* composed during 1966–7. Here a setting of a poem in Turkish by Orhan Veli Kanık is clearly influenced by phonetic considerations, the speech formants influencing the electronic background in a manner which recalls the synthetic speech components of Berio's *Visage*. This penchant for vocal transformation reveals itself again in the last movement of a more recent work: *Music for Jean Dubuffet's 'Coucou Bazar'* (1973).

The work of Mimaroğlu contrasts sharply with the more esoteric styles of composition practised by Babbitt and his followers. Such diversity from a single studio, however, is a compliment to its administration for adopting such an open attitude towards intending composers, and a reflection of the more universal approach to electronic music composition generally fostered during the 1960s and 1970s.

Jacob Druckman's association with the studio commenced in 1966. His style of composition, although clearly identifiable with the East Coast avant-garde, shows a particular regard for the larger-scale manipulation of timbre and texture. *Animus I* (1966) for trombone and tape, is characterized by a strong sense of association between the electronic and instrumental sounds, the links being strengthened by the inclusion of trombone material and transformations thereof in the tape part. In *Animus II* (1967–8), for mezzo-soprano, percussion, and tape, the voice provides a bridge to the electronic material, the latter including a collage of speech fragments, complementing the textless vocalization of the mezzo in a manner owing much to the influence of Berio.

In *Animus III* (1969), for clarinet and tape, the instrumental part is particularly demanding, requiring the production of an extended range of timbres. The tape part includes both clarinet and vocal elements, the latter being matched by the live shaping of formants achieved by varying the mouth excitation of the reed. A further performance element is added by the incorporation of a feedback loop to produce delayed repetitions of the clarinet part, almost qualifying the piece for inclusion under the heading of live electronic music. The animation of the electronic material evokes a powerful dialogue with the clarinet, creating an impression that all the electronic sounds are somehow a live reaction to the antics of the performer.

A later work, *Synapse → Valentine* (1969–70), for double bass and tape, finds Druckman yet again attempting to throw a new perspective on the integration of live and electronic elements. In sharp contrast to his earlier works, this two-movement work treats the two components as entirely separate forces, exploring the qualities of contrast and opposition rather than unity. This dualism is extensively developed, the bass player being required to execute virtuosic feats of rapid pizzicatos, double stops, trills, and tapping of the instrument, combined with a vocal contribution of speech fragments, both sung and spoken.

Perhaps the most significant piece to emerge from Columbia/Princeton during the 1960s was *Time's Encomium*, composed in 1969 by Charles Wuorinen. Wuorinen, a former pupil of both Luening and Ussachevsky, had been a student at Columbia before joining the staff of the music faculty in 1964. *Time's Encomium* was a commission from Nonesuch Records, who had recognized the talent of this promising young composer from his wide-ranging output of traditionally scored music. The piece received instant and widespread acclaim, leading to the award of the 1970 Pulitzer prize for music. The source material was generated entirely from the RCA synthesizer, further treatment in the form of reverberation, filtering, and ring modulation being applied in one of the Center's analogue studios.

The opening sequence of contrasted chords shows a keen awareness of the textual refinements which are possible from electronic sources, the progression into motivic fragments and thence to a slowly evolving complex of sustained and individually enveloped pitches providing a framework ripe for development. The influence of his teachers is unmistakable: one of the recurring motivic fragments, a 'galloping' sequence of pitches, for example, directly recalls the opening of Luening's *Gargoyles*. Wuorinen's deep regard for considerations of larger-scale shaping and organic growth, however, ensure that such clearly identifiable fragments do not become reduced to mere patterns.

Developments in the Experimental Studio at Illinois proceeded on an altogether broader front. Luening and Ussachevsky, it will be recalled, had discovered Lejaren Hiller and Leonard Isaacson employing the computer as a means of generating compositional data during their 1955 international tour of studios, and it was but a small step to the substitution of electronic devices in place of conventional instruments, to create a hybrid system. The direct use of the computer for the digital synthesis of sound was another application which rapidly gained importance during the 1960s, providing a tempting alternative to the new voltage-control technology. Many composers, nevertheless, continued to prefer analogue methods of synthesis, sustaining a significant level of output for this category.

Hiller composed a number of electronic works before turning more specifically to computer sound synthesis. These included *Machine Music* (1964) for piano, percussion, and tape, and *Suite* (1966) for two pianos and tape. *Machine Music* reflects the style of Bartók both in its use of incisive rhythms and in the adoption of an arch-like structure. The work is divided into eleven sections each using one or a specific combination of the three primary forces in a symmetrical structure of densities, pivoting around the sixth movement. The tape part employs a wide variety of sound sources both live and electronic, subjected to extensive treatment in terms of filtering and all three primary methods of modulation. Ring modulation in particular features prominently, the resultant spectra complementing the inharmonic resonances obtained naturally from the tuned percussion.

The *Suite* is part of a much larger multi-media piece, *A Triptych for Hieronymus* (1964–6), requiring a performance area for dancers and actors, encircled by groups of instrumentalists and loudspeakers. A focal point for the action is provided by the projection of film slides on to a screen. The tape part for this three-movement extract is derived from a colourful mixture of natural and electronic sources, this aural kaleidoscope being combined with the live instrumental material to create a spatial perspective which is closely integrated with the visual action.

The electronic works of Salvatore Martirano delve even further than those of Lejaren Hiller into the possibilities of sound theatre.

His works are imbued with a strong sense of vitality and drive, creating contrasts of colour and style which skilfully conceal his highly organized methods of composition. Jazz has proved a major influence in his output. *Underworld* (1964–5), scored for tenor saxophone, two double basses, four percussionists, and tape, indeed, is almost entirely based on a jazz idiom, elevating the pre-recorded electronics to a role which appears as alive in its synthesis as the instrumental performance.

*L's GA* (1967–8) is a full-scale electronic dramatization of Lincoln's Gettysburg Address, the political nature of the text providing the motivation for an almost grotesque excursion into the world of the surreal. The work starts with deep organ-like sounds, created by pumping low-frequency sine tones from loudspeakers down large tubes of cardboard, normally intended for storing carpets, the results being recorded by microphones. The reading of the Address is similarly subjected to a live process of transformation by the inhalation of helium gas, causing the voice of the reader to rise uncontrollably in pitch to a child-like gabble. The accompanying collage of electronic and instrumental sound elements rises to a crescendo, the tension being released by the banal outpourings of an electronic organ with full vibrato, caricaturing the style of American electioneering.

Herbert Brün's move to Illinois provided a useful European influence on the studio's output. His earlier work at Cologne had inspired a particular interest in linguistics, leading him to explore parallels between musical and verbal communication. *Futility* (1964) consists of an alternation between wholly electronic passages and recorded fragments of a self-composed poem, a sense of continuity being created by shaping the synthetic material to match the natural inflections of the spoken part. Later works such as *Soniferous Loops* (1965) and *Non Sequitur VI* (1966) translate these processes of formant shaping into the sphere of live instrumental writing, used in combination with electronic tape.

The works of Kenneth Gaburo are amongst the most significant to emerge from Illinois during the 1960s. Like Brün, he took a keen interest in phonetics, exploring vocal transformations in a manner yet again owing much to the influence of Berio. *Antiphony III* for chorus and tape (1962) and *Antiphony IV* for voice, piccolo, bass trombone, double bass, and tape (1967) both involve elaborate treatment of phonemes. The former involves a lively interplay between the live vocalists, uttering speech elements rich in sibilants and plosives such as 'k', 's', and 't', and the tape part which consists of similar material subjected to extensive juxta-position, transposition, and reverberation. *Antiphony IV* calls upon a wider range of resources, the instrumental elements, used in both live and tape parts, extending and characterizing further the pitched inflections of the vocal material.

Jazz elements, too, figure prominently in some of his works, for example *Lemon Drops* (1965), *Exit Music II: Fat Millie's Lament* (1965), and *For Harry* (1966). *Lemon Drops* is a short all-tape work derived entirely from an electronic tone generator, the incisive rhythms and clearly articulated keyboard-like sounds developing in a manner appropriate to a jazz improvisation. *Exit Music II* commences with two gentle and repeating rhythmic patterns which slowly change in content. The quiet entry of an untreated excerpt from a big-band piece seems to evolve naturally from the opening texture, growing in volume to become the dominant feature before fading again into the background. *For Harry*, Gaburo's last piece at Illinois before he moved to take up an appointment at the University of California at San Diego, is a tribute to the composer Harry Partch. The latter's rejection of the conventional in terms of musical instruments and tuning systems had led him to pursue in isolation the cause of new acoustic instruments and associated timbres, in his own way developing concepts not unconnected with the expanded sound world of electronic music. Gaburo's tribute delicately explores the world of microtones and subtle rhythmic combinations, creating a captiv-ating aura of timbres.

The San Francisco Tape Music Center existed in its original form until 1966, when it was resited at the Tape Music Center at Mills College, Oakland. This move was not accompanied by the studio's two founders, Ramon Sender and Morton Subotnick. Sender chose to continue his activities at Donald Buchla's private studio at Berkeley, California, concentrating increasingly on improvisatory techniques.

Subotnick moved to New York University to develop another studio, based on a Buchla system, for the Intermedia Program at the School of Art. His output at SFTMC, although prolific, has similarly received little recognition, being eclipsed by his later work at New York. One clear reason for this is the preponderance of incidental music for plays in these early works. His later work at New York resulted in a number of large-scale pieces realized via the Buchla synthesizer. *Prelude No. 4* (1966) for piano and tape reveals a highly instrumental approach to electronic writing. *Silver Apples of the Moon* (1967), a commission from Nonesuch Records, demonstrates even more clearly his adherence to 'note/event' methods of organization. A wide variety of timbres and intricate durational structures are employed, the latter assisted to no small extent by the use of a sequencer.

*The Wild Bull* (1968), also a commission from Nonesuch, is characterized by more elaborate applications of sequencer control, resulting in intricate and imaginative shapings of the sole sound source, a sawtooth oscillator. The rapid interplay between different dynamics and timbres generates a strong rhythmic drive which at times creates the feel of a free jazz improvisation. *Laminations* (1969–70) for orchestra and tape utilizes large instrumental forces. With such a powerful reserve of live sounds, heavy demands were placed on the synthetic material, for the directly communicative quality of the various instruments made them naturally dominant.

Gordon Mumma and Robert Ashley's private venture at Ann Arbor, Michigan, the Cooperative Studio for Electronic Music, proved highly influential in establishing a major movement in the sphere of live electronics, a development to be discussed in the next chapter. Their studio work during the early part of the 1960s involved the production of pieces not only for tape alone and tape plus instruments, but also what might be described as an intermediate category, tape plus instruments plus live electronics.

Their styles of composition show a considerable indebtedness to the techniques of jazz, albeit of a progressive nature. The very names of their work suggest a less than academic attitude towards electronic composition, borne out by the colourful, freely structured nature of their content—for example, *A Slice of Life* (1961) and *Eimert Plays Basie* (1961) by Ashley, and *Commodious Means* (1962) by Mumma.

The years 1964–6 marked the peak of their work in the Ann Arbor Studio. Ashley's *The Wolfman* (1964) exists in two versions, one for jazz trio and tape, the other for amplified voice and tape. The former version, prepared for the Bob James Trio, involves a performance of a blues song in conjunction with a tape of heavily modulated speech components, the latter at times completely swamping the live instruments. In the second version the voice replaces the instruments with a mimic of the tape, taking the form of a succession of sustained vocal sounds which are subjected to rich distortions by the application of live acoustic feedback between the performer's microphone and his loudspeaker. *Untitled Mixes* (1965) was also written for the same jazz trio, the instrumentalists being required to imitate the tape material with a variety of plucking, sliding, and exotic percussion effects.

Mumma's *Peasant Boy* (1965) is a very similar piece to *Untitled Mixes*, scored for the same jazz trio and tape, again with the intention that the instrumentalists should imitate the tape sounds. Neither piece, however, is totally successful in achieving an integration of live and electronic elements. The solutions to these problems of relating instrumental and electronic material for Mumma and Ashley lay in eliminating the need for a pre-recorded tape part, thus cultivating a more interactive environment for the realization of their compositions.

Steve Reich founded his own private studio in San Francisco towards the end of 1963, moving it to New York in 1966. His two major tape works, *Its Gonna Rain* (1965) and *Come Out* (1966), both use short verbal phrases as the starting-point for progressive transformations. The basic processes involved were essentially very simple. In *Come Out*, the fragment 'Come out and show them' is intially presented as an untreated repeating loop for almost thirty seconds. This in itself creates a developing musical experience, for the ear becomes increasingly aware of the inner acoustical detail of the fragment in terms of pitch, inflection, and rhythm. Transformation then proceeds by using two identical loops of this source simultaneously, starting in perfect unison and then slowly slipping out of synchronization. This phasing effect gradually introduces echo effects for the shorter elements such as 'c' and 't', whilst the longer ones become extended. As the slippage progresses, juxtaposition and overlay ensue, creating new formant structures. Subsequent multiplications of the loop channels to produce four, eight, or even more loops ensure that the original sense is completely lost in an ever-extending montage of rhythmic and timbral elements. Such a process was readily translatable to live performance; hence his subsequent interest in applying this technique to ensembles of instruments, both acoustical and electronic.

Several other American composers developed a preference for electronic musical instruments on the concert platform, notably Terry Riley and Philip Glass, and these activities will be considered under the heading of live electronic music. Riley, however, like Reich, worked on studio pieces whilst developing his own style of instrumental composition. During 1961 he spent a short while at the San Francisco Tape Music Center, producing a number of sketches, including an electronic version of his *In C*, normally performed live with any combination of instruments which might be available. His tapes *Poppy Nogood and the Phantom Band* (1968) and *A Rainbow in Curved Air* (1969), based on electronic keyboards, with addition of a soprano saxophone in the former instance, could not have been performed live in view of the use of elaborate multitracking and tape feedback. To ears conditioned by modern pop-music techniques, the effects merely suggest recordings of particularly versatile performances, from some viewpoints a considerable virtue.

Electronic composition in Canada remained strangely isolated from allied developments in America and Europe, attracting few performances outside the country and very little attention from the mainstream of musical criticism. Paradoxically some of the most interesting works in the field of computer sound synthesis in the 1970s have emerged from Canadian studios, and this unjust state of neglect is at last beginning to change.

The oldest studio, run by the National Research Council in Ottawa, continued in operation under the direction of Hugh Le Caine. István Anhalt completed a series of pieces, *Electronic Composition Nos. 1 to 4*, between 1959 and 1961 which were accorded performances in America alongside works from the better-known composers Wuorinen, Luening, and Ussachevsky. The fourth piece, indeed, was completed at the Columbia/Princeton Center. Anhalt's style contrasts significantly with many of the East Coast American composers, showing a greater affinity with the subtleties associated with European schools of composition, such as Milan. His treatment of timbre and pitch organization is most sensitive, displaying a coherence which arises naturally out of the sound shapes themselves, rather than some predetermined formalistic structure.

The main impetus to developments in Canada, however, stemmed from the founding of a studio at the University of Toronto in 1959, initially under the directorship of Arnold Walter. Walter collaborated with Myron Schaeffer and Harvey Olnick in a number of ventures, including two electronic tapes for television films, *Summer Idyll* (1960) and *Project TV* (1962), and one for a ballet *Electronic Dance* (1963). Pauline Oliveros visited the studio in 1966, producing a wealth of compositions, including *I of IV*, *II of IV*, *III of IV*, *IV of IV*, and *NO MO*. Many of these works were the products of simple generative and treatment processes, resulting in a performance style of electronic composition which could be transferred to the live concert platform.

The Toronto studio was initially equipped with a number of custom-built devices. These included a Hamograph, a special form of reverberation unit constructed from a spiral of steel mesh, an adapted keyboard controlling a bank of tuneable oscillators and band-pass filters, and a multi-head tape recorder fitted with individual drive controls for tape loops. The Hamograph was a device capable of controlling the amplitude of up to twelve different channels of sound, each driven via a tape control loop and an associated on/off gate activated via a Schmitt trigger and an associated level detector. Tape-recorded signals thus provided a primary means of process control until the advent of voltage- and digital-control technology in the mid to late 1960s.

During the decade other universities in Canada established studios: McGill (Montreal) and Vancouver in 1964, Simon Fraser in 1967, and Laval a year later. The work of Murray Schafer first at Montreal and then at Simon Fraser is notable for its emphasis on electronic music for schools and colleges. Like Brian Dennis in England, he concentrated on the presentation of the medium as a creative tool accessible to all without recourse to complex technological procedures. Such a desire to achieve a directness of contact with the tools of synthesis has only to be taken one stage further to enter the sphere of live electronics.

# 8 Live Electronic Music

Live electronic music or, to be more specific, compositions wholly or largely based on live synthesis became a major sphere of activity during the 1960s. Antecedents are numerous, stretching back to Cahill's Dynamophone and the subsequent proliferation of electronic musical instruments during the inter-war period. A more positive antecedent, however, lies in the compositions of John Cage during the 1940s and 50s which introduced a far less stylized approach to live electronic sounds. Instrumental imitation forms but one aspect of the developments to be discussed under this heading, for the latter were primarily motivated by a desire to transfer studio procedures to the concert platform in a manner which was not limited by traditional performance practice. Schaeffer's ill-fated attempt to generate the final stages of his works live at the first public concert of *musique concrète* is perhaps the most interesting early excursion into this type of composition.

Cage's growing interest in live electronics provided the catalyst for the birth of a number of live electronic ensembles in America who, with some justification, considered themselves the pioneers of a new art form which embraced aspects of progressive jazz and even rock. It is to Europe, however, that attention is first turned, for it was here that the most coherent transition from established studio techniques to live synthesis occurred.

Kagel's *Transición II* (1959) for piano, percussion, and two tape recorders has been claimed as the first example of the use of a tape recorder as a live performance aid. The percussionist plays on the sound-board, strings, and rim of the piano whilst the pianist plays the keys. One tape recorder reproduces material recorded prior to the performance whilst the other is used to record extracts of the performance itself to be cut into loops and reproduced as an echo of events past. Stockhausen's interest in live electronics stems from 1964. For the next two years he worked intensively in the Cologne studio, composing three pieces for the genre: *Mikrophonie I* (1964), *Mixtur* (1964), and *Mikrophonie II* (1965).

*Mikrophonie I* is a work which uses a large tam-tam as the sole sound source. Two microphones are held on either side of the instrument, each connected to an amplifier and loudspeaker via an adjustable band-pass filter. Six performers are required, two activating the tam-tam, two varying the positioning of the microphones, and two controlling the settings of the filters and associated amplifiers. The score specifies the production of a wide variety of sounds from the tam-tam. These include vocal-like resonances, generated by rubbing the surface with cardboard tubes, deeply reverberant sounds from soft mallet-strokes, sharp percussive effects from striking the surface with hard rods of wood, metal, or plastic, and effects like atmospheric noise, achieved by scraping or brushing. The microphones and filters act to highlight and modify timbral features which can only be detected very close to the surface of the instrument.

*Mixtur* is an altogether more complicated work technically, requiring five orchestral groups, four ring modulators, and associated sine-wave generators. The original version required large groups of woodwind, brass, pizzicato strings and harp, bowed strings and percussion. A later version (1967) was scaled down to a more modest ensemble of instruments. Only the percussion group remains unmodulated, the sounds of the tam-tam being highlighted via a contact microphone and amplification system. The sounds from each of the other four groups are captured via microphones and fed to one side of a ring modulator, a sine tone being fed to the other to provide a modulating frequency.

The electronic processes in this work differ from those used for *Mikrophonie I* in one important respect. Whereas the latter work is based on subtractive synthesis, using filters to isolate and highlight components in an already complex sound, *Mixtur* features additive synthesis, using modulating frequencies to generate additional partials in the form of sum and difference tones. The frequency settings of the oscillators at times drop into the sub-audio range, unbalancing the ring modulators to the point where the wave function acts as an amplitude modulator for the instrumental material. Once again a sectionalized structure is employed, resulting in twenty 'moments', each incorporating a simplified notation to specify textural effects rather than exact scoring.

*Mikrophonie II* is perhaps the most significant of this trilogy of pieces, scored for Hammond organ, choir, four ring modulators, and tape. The tape consists of short extracts from three former works, two instrumental—*Carré* (1959–60) and *Momente* (1961–4) —and one electronic—*Gesang der Jünglinge*. Despite the inclusion of these recorded passages, the work is based predominantly on live electronic techniques. The quotations from *Gesang* and the use of a text drawn from *Einfache grammatische Meditationen* by Helmut Heissenbüttel highlight Stockhausen's continuing interest in the study of phonetics in relation to electronic music. The choir comprises twelve singers: two groups of three sopranos and two groups of three basses. The sounds from each group are fed to one side of a ring modulator via microphones, the Hammond organ replacing hand-tuned sine-wave oscillators as the modulatory source for the complementary inputs. Modulation thus occurs only when a choral group and the organ sound together. At all other times these sources are perceived naturally, the organ adopting a very low profile relative to the vocal parts. This increased flexibility of ring modulation results in elaborate transformations, foreshadowing the complex timbres incorporated in both *Telemusik* and *Hymnen*.

Stockhausen's next live electronic work, *Solo* (1966), was prepared during his visit to the NHK Studio in Tokyo. *Solo*, as the title suggests, is a work for any single melody instrument, originally either a flute or a trombone, and a complex tape feedback system regulated by four assistants. A single tape loop is stretched between a stereo tape recorder, set in record mode, and a tension pulley several feet away. As the loop passes from recorder to pulley it is monitored by six playback-head assemblies, mounted on stands which are adjustable in a horizontal plane. The positioning of the heads is critical, for precise delays are specified between sounds being fed to the record head and their reproduction at each of the playback heads. Microphones are employed to pick up source information from the instrument. The outputs from the playback heads are fed to a mixing desk where the assistants regulate both their live distribution between four loudspeakers and also the level of direct feedback to the record lines. The cumulative effect of this looping process is a permuting series of patterns which merge eventually into a stream of continuous sound. The latter is then punctuated by cutting off the feedback gain completely for short intervals, creating new blocks of sound which similarly permute. A heavy onus is placed on the partnership skills of the instrumentalist and his assistant. The score offers a choice of six formal schemes, each demanding very precise actions on the part of the performers.

After *Hymnen* Stockhausen returned to live electronics with an increasing interest in improvisatory techniques for ensembles, working from minimally notated scores. Improvisation, however, is in many respects a misnomer, for the very minimalism of the material demands the most disciplined of interactions between the players if the composer's intentions are to be satisfactorily fulfilled. It became clear to Stockhausen that such performance demands could only be fulfilled by forming his own ensemble of players who could learn over a considerable period of time how best to work as a cohesive group. This ensemble drew together a group of distinguished composers and performers, including Alfred Alings, Harald Bojé, Johannes Fritsch, Rolf Gelhaar, and Alfons and Aloys Kontarsky.

His next composition for the genre, *Prozession* (1967), is an intricately programmed series of processes based on a scheme of + (more), − (less), and = (same) signs which control the change in state of features such as pitch and amplitude, and also larger aspects of form such as the number of repetitions or the number of sections. The content is derived from fragments of earlier works assigned to particular instruments: *Mikrophonie I* for the tam-tam, adaptations of *Gesang der Jünglinge*, *Kontakte*, and *Momente* for the viola, *Telemusik* and *Solo* for the electronium (an electronic keyboard instrument), and *Piano Pieces I–XI* (1952–6) and *Kontakte* for the piano. The electronic element, apart from the electronium, is provided by two microphones, two filters, and amplitude regulators controlled by an additional performer.

*Kurzwellen* (1968) for piano, electronium, tam-tam, viola, and four short-wave radios is more readily identifiable as a descendant of *Hymnen*. Once again, two microphones and filters provide an active means for modifying the sounds electronically, an extra dimension being added by the use of a contact microphone to amplify the viola. Each instrumental player uses his own short-wave radio to select source material out of the ether, these elements providing the basis for instrumental enhancement and electronic modification. This greater freedom of choice is countered by a stricter degree of control over the processes of development and interaction, still using the same system of +, −, and = signs.

*Aus den sieben Tagen* (1968), although not specifically a

composition requiring electronics, has frequently been performed with their use. Scored for an unspecified ensemble, the work consists of fifteen texts which have to be interpreted in a collective composition. Despite this apparent move into the sphere of free improvisation, the work, through its texts, demands the expression of ideas in a manner which requires the highest qualities of discipline and rationality from the individual.

Stockhausen, in his own performances, has preferred to restrict the electronic element to the same treatments employed in the works just described: microphones and filters. This emerging characteristic highlights the restraint he has chosen to adopt in incorporating live electronics into his music. His contributions to the sphere of live electronic music have thus proved more coherent artistically than many of the products of the electronic improvisation groups shortly to be studied. On the debit side, however, it may be argued that Stockhausen has yet to develop the full potential of the live medium, known procedures being preferred to more experimental ones.

In *Spiral* (1968) for a soloist with short-wave receiver, the electronic processes are reduced merely to the level of selection from a ready-made source of material, with no further application of processing. *Mantra* (1970), however, exhibits a return to a more involved use of electronics which has inspired a number of imitators. The work is scored for two pianists, a short-wave radio or a tape of short-wave sounds, two ring modulators, two oscillators, wood-blocks, antique cymbals, and sound projection, the latter aspect being controlled by an assistant. This return to the individual performer and a closely notated score results in a piece which is strongly reminiscent of a much earlier style of composition.

The suggested scoring for *Ylem* (1972) signalled the adoption of a slightly freer attitude towards live electronic devices. No fewer than four of the nineteen elements making up the ensemble are wholly or partially electronic. At the first performance these consisted of an electronium, an amplified cello fitted with a foot-operated filter, a keyboard synthesizer, and a VCS 3 synthesizer manufactured by EMS, used to process the amplified sounds of a saxophone/bassoon. The variety of facilities offered by the synthesizers presented considerable scope for live synthesis as well as treatments. The score instructions, however, restrict their role primarily to the production of a web of timbres around a selected group of sounds, providing links for the other players.

Stockhausen's ensemble at Cologne Radio was not the only live electronic group to flourish in Germany. After a difference of opinion in 1970 both Fritsch and Gelhaar left his group to form an independent ensemble, Feedback, in association with David Johnson, John McGuire, and Michael von Biel, among others. With no overriding allegiance to Stockhausen they became free to develop other aspects of live electronic music using ideas generated by the group.

The live electronic ensembles which emerged elsewhere in Europe during the 1960s concentrated for the most part on group improvisation. One of the first, Gruppo di Improvvisazione Nuova Consonanza, was established by Franco Evangelisti in Rome in 1964, attracting a wealth of composer participants over the years. These included Mario Bertoncini, Aldo Clementi, Roland Kayn, and Ivan Vandor from Europe, and Larry Austin and John Eaton from America. Their works were essentially group efforts, based predominantly on traditional instruments and voice. Their primary objective lay in the development of performance techniques which would produce sounds of an electronic nature from these natural sources—for example, high squeaks from wind and brass instruments and bowed percussion. Electronic sources nevertheless were used from time to time, principally an electronic organ and a group of oscillators. Filters and ring modulators provided the primary means for sound processing. Towards the end of the decade their improvisations began to include passages for pre-recorded tape, introducing a more formal element into the shaping of their compositions.

A rival ensemble, Musica Elettronica Viva, was founded in Rome during 1966 by a group consisting for the most part of expatriate American composers. These included Allan Bryant, Alvin Curran, Jon Phetteplace, Frederic Rzewski, and Richard Teitelbaum. MEV established a well-equipped studio of their own to assist in the development of their resources for live synthesis, and this led, as a by-product, to the production of one or two pieces for voices or instruments and pre-recorded tape. The bulk of their activities, nevertheless, were directed towards live performance and their compositions steadily developed in the opposite direction, from pieces with a well-defined format to increasingly freer styles of improvisation.

The specifications for their earlier works give an indication of the variety of resources they employed: for example, *Variations IV* (1966) for instruments, voice, transistor radios, Volkswagen bus, garden hose, pebbles thrown on auditorium roof, wooden chairs, stone floor scraped with various materials, and magnetic pick-ups used with loudspeakers to create feedback. This piece was an adaptation of Cage's *Variations IV* (1964), performed simultaneously with *Solo for Cello*.

Later works displayed an increasing use of electronic equipment, including tape-delay systems, contact microphones, Moog synthesizer modules, neurological amplifiers and associated electrodes to decode alpha waves generated by the brains of selected performers, and photocell mixers. The latter, developed by Rzewski, were operated by light-pens, providing a powerful aid to sound projection via multi-channel amplification systems.

The concerts given by groups such as MEV caused a considerable stir in musical circles, not least for the highly theatrical nature of their presentation. Whereas Stockhausen's semi-improvisatory works imposed the discipline of a score or set of instructions on the players, the works of MEV concentrated more specifically on the individual motivations of the players as the basis for a structure, responding to, rather than interpreting, ideas for an overall plan. Pieces such as *Spacecraft* (1967–8), *Free Soup* (1968), and *Sound Pool* (1969), largely conceived by Rzewski, extended the participatory element to the audience themselves, the latter being encouraged to react to and influence the evolution of the works. In *Spacecraft* the primary objective was the liberation of the performer from his environment, starting with his own musical tastes, and proceeding through the processes of interaction with others towards a communal art of music making. This development of a social art led in *Sound Pool* to an integration of both teaching and performance skills, the more able musicians being directed to organize and assist weaker players in their endeavours to contribute ideas to the general flow.

Similarities exist between MEV and the British Group AMM, founded in 1965 by Lou Gare, Keith Rowe and Eddie Prevost in association with Cornelius Cardew and Christopher Hobbs. This combination of jazz and avant-garde musicians led to an interesting fusion of musical ideas. In the early years the group concentrated upon the search for new sounds and performance techniques, using contact microphones and a variety of electro-mechanical aids. Their musical outlook, however, became first narrowed and then confused by increasingly extreme political ideas, leading to the formation of a breakaway group known as the Scratch Orchestra in 1969 under the leadership of Cardew, Michael Parsons, and Howard Skempton. Gare and Prevost continued to run AMM for several years, directing it towards a more conventional type of jazz ensemble with a decreasing emphasis on electronics.

A growing interest in live electronic music in Britain towards the end of the 1960s led to the formation of other ensembles, notably Gentle Fire and Naked Software. Both groups benefited considerably from the skills of Hugh Davies. His gifts for designing unusual transducers out of materials such as scraps of metal and wood, rubber bands, and coils of wire attached to suitable electrical pick-ups such as contact microphones, provided them with a wealth of cheap and versatile performance aids.

Two Cambridge research fellows, Roger Smalley and Tim Souster, formed a group called Intermodulation in 1969, which specialized in the performance of works for instruments and live electronics. Smalley's first piece to involve live electronic modulation, *Transformation I*, scored for piano, two microphones, ring modulator, and filter, was completed early in the same year. The similarities in scoring with Stockhausen's *Mantra* become all the more striking when it is appreciated that Smalley's piece appeared a year earlier. The parts for both the pianist and the electronics operator are precisely notated, though the score allows some flexibility in the synchronization of its various layers.

With Smalley's departure for Australia in 1976, Souster restyled the group under the new name of 0 dB, concentrating on works which incorporated strongly rhythmic features drawn from both the music of Africa and Western rock, for example his own *Afghan Amplitudes* (1976) and *Arcane Artefact* (1976). Rock and jazz influences, albeit of a progressive type, also figure prominently in the works of David Bedford and Barry Guy. In the late 1970s contemporary jazz entered into a period of revolution, following paths very similar to those pursued by the more 'traditional' avant-garde some ten years previously. Live electronics became an integral part of this quest for new styles not only in Britain but also elsewhere in Europe and America. The uncertainty presently associated with this progressive genre, however, prevents any authoritative assessment of its likely destination.

John Eaton's own venture promoting the Synket as a concert instrument led him to compose a number of pieces for live performance. The presentation of his *Songs for RPB* for soprano, piano and Synket at the American Academy in Rome in 1965 is the first recorded occasion upon which a portable synthesizer was used on stage. Eaton was particularly interested in the use of quarter-tones, and these feature in many of his works. His *Concert Piece for Synket and Symphony Orchestra* (1967) matches the Synket against two orchestral groups tuned a quarter tone apart. The ability to vary the tunings of the synthesizer accorded it a powerful role as an intermediary, generating rich timbres to complement the variety of textures obtainable from combinations of instruments. *Blind Man's Cry* (1968) for soprano, Synkets, and Moog synthesizer initiated a trend towards works for ensembles of synthesizers, the increased resources permitting a more versatile approach towards scores for live electronics. His *Mass* (1970) for soprano, speaker, clarinet, three Synkets plus one derivative—a Synmill—Moog synthesizer, and tape-delay system shows an even greater preoccupation with the development of connections between live and electronic sounds, the high shrieks of the soprano and clarinet blending into clusters of sine tones whilst the Synkets imitate percussion and string instruments.

In Japan Takehisa Kosugi entered the field of live electronic music as early as 1961 with *Micro I*, a piece for solo microphone. His association with the Sogetsu Art Centre led to the formation of a collective, Group Ongaku, which devoted itself to live improvisation.

Toshi Ichiyanagi, having completed a number of studio compositions at the NHK Studio from 1962 onwards, turned his attention towards live electronics, like Kosugi associating himself with the Sogetsu Art Centre. The use of sound in association with sculpture provided a particular fascination for him. In 1964 he constructed a system for an art gallery in Takamatsu city where an exhibition of sculpture was accompanied by a soundscape of photocell-controlled oscillators, operated by the movement of passers-by. In 1966 he constructed a similar system for a department store in Tokyo, this time for an exhibition of kinetic sculptures. Environmental music, controlled or at least influenced by the audience, was not unique to Japan, however. Tristram

Cary, for example, constructed a six-oscillator system for an escalator at the 1967 EXPO exhibition, controlled by the movement of passengers.

The development of live electronic music in America during the 1960s was dominated by performance ensembles, in some instances of a collective type, concerned with the development of group projects, in others firmly led by a specific individual. Cage's group at Stony Point, New York State, clearly belonged to the latter category, although the subsequent migration of several members of his ensemble to live electronic music groups based all over the world suggests a strong fermentation of the former approach. His performers included David Tudor, who remained a close associate for many years, Michael von Biel, David Behrman, Toshi Ichiyanagi, Alvin Lucier, Gordon Mumma, Pauline Oliveros, and Christian Wolff.

Cage's *Music for Amplified Toy Pianos* and *Cartridge Music*, both composed in 1960, marked an auspicious start to the decade. In the former piece a single performer plays any number of toy pianos to which contact microphones have been fitted. In the latter, gramophone cartridges, into which all manner of objects have been inserted, and contact microphones attached to any responsive surface, provide a rich, if somewhat unusual, source of material. To the casual observer the results are an instant, if at times unpleasant, type of *musique concrète*. Since the sounds are entirely the products of performance actions, however, any comparison with the output of the Paris studio is, to say the least, misleading. Cage had moved away from such predetermined orderings of material manipulation towards an electronic art which was truly live.

In 1961 he produced an electronic version of *Winter Music*, a work which was originally written for one to twenty pianos in 1957. This may be performed simultaneously with his next piece, *Atlas Eclipticalis* (1961–2), for chamber or orchestral ensemble, with contact microphones, amplifiers, and loudspeakers operated by an assistant. The instrumental format is variable, up to eighty-six parts, and the work may be played complete, or in any part thereof. The score is distinctive for its notational detail. Most of Cage's compositions from this period are laid out graphically, leaving much to the interpretative skills of the performers. The material for *Atlas Eclipticalis*, however, is largely the product of indeterminate selection, resulting in a colourful if perplexing constellation of sounds.

Indeterminacy and variable instrumental formats are primary characteristics of a series of pieces entitled *Variations I–VIII*, composed between 1958 and 1968. *Variations II* (1963) for any number of players using any sound-producing means calls upon contact microphones or any other suitable transducer to amplify the vibrational characteristics of the selected sources. David Tudor gained a reputation for his performances of the work using a piano fitted with contact microphones to the frame and sound-board, and gramophone cartridges to the strings. Later *Variations* employed more bizarre resources. *Variations V* (1965), for example, calls for film, slides, pre-recorded tapes, and dancers, the latter triggering the audio-visual elements by breaking light beams focused on photoelectric cells. Robert Moog designed special distance-sensitive antennae as additional controlling devices. This work was specially written for the Merce Cunningham Dance Company, a troupe which enjoyed a long and fruitful association with Cage and his associates.

Cage's boundless enthusiasm for pastures new led him into the field of computer sound synthesis in 1969 with *HPSCHD*, a joint project with Hiller which will be returned to in a subsequent chapter. A discussion limited to his electronic pieces gives a very narrow vista of this pluralistic composer. It is this very quality which recognizes no boundaries to means of artistic expression that has influenced so many composers and elicited a grudging respect even from those who find his work perplexing, frustrating, or annoying in the extreme.

Although Tudor became recognized primarily as a performer of other composers' works of live electronic music, he also contributed several pieces of his own to the genre. *Fluorescent Sound* (1964), written for Stockholm's Museum of Modern Art, utilized the resonances of fluorescent light tubes, amplified and distributed via loudspeakers. *Rainforest* (1968) incorporates a system of specially designed loudspeakers, consisting of electromagnetic coils with their moving parts attached to a variety of resonators instead of the normal paper cones. These transducers added rich harmonics, distorting the electrical signals passed to them for acoustic output, in this instance generated from a bank of oscillators manipulated by two performers.

Behrman, after a short spell working in the studio at Brandeis University, Waltham, set up his own experimental studio in New York during 1966. His piece *Wave Train* (1966) relies significantly on controlled acoustic feedback between guitar pick-ups attached to the strings of the piano and the monitor loudspeakers to which these signals are fed. Considerable skill is required in setting the gains of these pick-ups: too high a level results in a permanent and unpleasant 'howl-around' whilst too little merely amplifies the damped, basic characteristics of the strings. A median setting produces the desired rich resonances as the excitement of the strings becomes self-perpetuating.

Behrman was a member of the Sonic Arts Union, an influential group of live electronic music composers and performers, formed in 1966. The other members were Robert Ashley, Alvin Lucier, and Gordon Mumma. Ashley and Mumma, it will be recalled, had established the Cooperative Studio for Electronic Music at Ann Arbor, composing several tape compositions before turning almost exclusively to the live medium. Lucier's contact with studio electronics started in 1965 subsequent to his appointment to the staff at Brandeis University. Tape compositions, however, were very few, the facilities being used primarily for developing his performance ideas.

Mumma's first major work of live electronic music, *Medium Size Mograph*, was completed in 1963. This piece for piano, four hands, and 'cybersonic' equipment utilized custom-built, portable electronics both to modify the piano sounds and also to translate the latter into control functions for the electronic generators. In *Mesa* (1966) for cybersonic metal reeds, a member of the accordion family is wired up to an arrangement of transducers, modulators, and filters, acting to transform simple melodic phrases into complex successions of sounds, rich in non-harmonic partials. The controls for the electronics, as in all these pieces, are contained in a box slung around the performer's neck. Alterations to device settings may thus be made whilst performing the instrument. In later works such as *Cybersonic Cantilevers* (1973) the audience became a source of control information for the work, recalling the participation pieces of Musica Elettronica Viva.

Ashley developed a particular interest in the use of live electronics in music theatre. In 1965 he composed *Lecture Series*, a piece for speaker, public address system, electronic processing equipment, and related 'events'. This interest in speech, which stems back to his tape piece *The Wolfman*, was developed further in *Purposeful Lady Slow Afternoon*, the first part of a larger work entitled *The Wolfman Motor City Revue* (1968). This piece is built around an amplified reading of a woman's first sexual experience and the aftermath. A discreetly associative visual element is supplied by two sequences of film slides projected simultaneously on different screens.

Lucier was the most adventurous member of the group. *Music for Solo Performer* (1965) is the first live electronic piece to have used amplified alpha brain waves, here combined with resonating percussion instruments, gating devices, and pre-recorded tapes of electronically processed waves. *North American Time Capsule* (1967) was written in response to an invitation from Sylvania Electronic Systems to compose a work using a prototype for a new design of vocoder which employed digital sampling techniques. The score consists merely of a set of instructions, thus leaving much to the imagination of the performers. Eight vocoders are required, processing the sounds of a chorus who are free to describe aspects of their civilization through speaking or singing, in any language, to the future discoverers of the time capsule deep in space. Additional sonic aspects of contemporary life may also be incorporated, for example the sounds of vacuum cleaners, electric shavers, motor cars, or aircraft, along with the sounds of musical instruments.

Later works are even more theatrical in their staging. *Vespers* (1968) requires several performers to walk about a darkened stage carrying electronic location detectors which respond to the presence of a number of solid objects positioned strategically within the performance area by clicking at different rates, the nearer the object, the faster the clicking.

In *I am Sitting in a Room* (1970) Lucier returned to a simpler technology, using a chain of microphones, tape recorders, and loudspeakers on stage to generate cumulative reiterations of a source text reading. The use of acoustic linking from recording to recording adds an extra dimension to the progressive transformations, for the resonances of the room enhance the sound as it radiates from loudspeaker to microphone.

Reich's live electronic music shows a marked preference for keyboards, used in a conventional performing role alongside more traditional instruments. Pattern-generating procedures continued to form the basis of his works, for example *Phase Patterns* and

*Four Organs*, both written in 1970. Terry Riley followed a similar path as regards choice of instruments, but with a greater emphasis on improvisation. *Persian Surgery Dervishes* (1971), for example, has received remarkably different performances in view of the freedom accorded to the players.

La Monte Young and more recently Philip Glass developed ensembles much in the same vein as those of Reich and Riley. Glass has proved successful in cultivating a more popular image, concentrating, with works such as *Contrary Motion* and *Music in Fifths* (1969), on slowly-changing timbres and harmonies produced from electronic musical instruments.

The percussionist Max Neuhaus produced notable realizations of Brown's *Four Systems* (1964), Sylvano Bussotti's *Cœur pour batteur* (1965), and Cage's *Fontana Mix-Feed* (1965) before concentrating more specifically on his own compositions. The scores for these three works gave ample scope for instrumental interpretation. *Four Systems*, for example, consists merely of a series of horizontal lines differentiated in thickness and length. Amplification and controlled feedback from loudspeaker to microphone provided the primary means of electronic enhancement, inducing resonating instruments such as cymbals and gongs to vibrate with rich timbres.

The general growth of interest during the decade led to the First Festival of Live Electronic Music at the University of California in 1967, followed five years later by a spectacular international collaboration, ICES 1972, held in London. The latter festival, which included as a special event the chartering of a train for performers and audience which ran between London and Edinburgh, brought together composers and performers on a scale which is never likely to be equalled again, for the subsequent proliferation of activities, especially in the field of rock and pop, makes it impracticable to assemble such a comprehensively representative collection of musicians. ICES included several rock concerts, a strong portent of the gathering strength of commercial electronic music, to which attention must now be turned.

# 9 Rock and Pop Electronic Music

Electronic jingles invade the lives of millions every day via the media of radio and television. These ephemera, while familiarizing the general public with the nature of synthesized sounds, have debased electronic music to the level of an advertising aid. Such a widely recognized application, however, is only one step higher in the public consciousness than rock and pop music which uses electronically generated material as a matter of course. Today the commercial digital synthesizer is ubiquitous, serving in many instances both the serious and the popular music sectors with equal success. As a result the primary distinctions have become those of application rather than of technology. This situation contrasts sharply with the circumstances surrounding the pioneering phase of synthesized rock and pop music. Here experimentation by a number of leading artists with new methods of sound production inspired a range of technical developments which were to prove highly influential on the evolution of the electronic medium as a whole, and it is this fascinating albeit relatively brief era of exploration which provides the focus for this chapter.

During the late 1960s rising expenditure on basic electronic mixing and amplification equipment by the commercial sector led to the acquisition of studio and stage facilities which eclipsed those offered by all but the most prestigious of the institutions hitherto discussed. An increasing curiosity with devices for the synthesis and processing of sound led a number of leading rock and pop groups to acquire facilities of considerable sophistication, offering creative opportunities which far exceeded those available to most serious electronic composers.

Popular music has made some use of electronic devices since the 1920s, for it was not unknown for dance bands of the period to use simple amplification on occasions, and by the end of the next decade the Hammond organ was in regular use. It was the growth in popularity of the electric guitar during the 1950s, however, which heralded the start of major developments in this sphere. Initially this instrument was equipped with a pick-up at or near the bridge, an amplifier, and a loudspeaker, the system producing a bright but essentially faithful reproduction of the strings' vibrational characteristics. Over the years a number of electronic sound-processing devices have been added in an effort to improve the versatility of the instrument. Some of these are adaptations of equipment commonly to be found in an electronic music studio. Others have been more specifically engineered as enhancements for the guitar.

Facilities for tonal modifications were originally limited to simple bass and treble controls integral to the amplifier. In due course more flexible filtering facilities were added, providing additional control over the important middle-frequency areas. Reverberation and echo quickly proved popular means of enhancement, such effects being generated usually via a spring delay unit, or a device known as a Copycat. The former facility, as has already been noted, suffers from an unevenness of response, resulting from resonances which occur at a number of frequencies. Since reverberation plates are both expensive and far from portable, considerable pressure was exerted on manufacturers to produce better-quality spring units, sometimes incorporating three or more coils in an attempt to even out individual resonances.

The Copycat, a direct descendant of Schaeffer's Morphophone, is a compact tape-loop delay system providing, normally, between three and five playback heads, suitably spaced to provide an irregular pattern of delays. Careful regulation of the playback levels, and the degree of feedback supplied to the record head in addition to the source signals, allows an acceptably smooth prolongation of all but the most percussive guitar sounds.

Tremolo was another treatment which found early favour. This characteristic, derived from the Hammond organ, is produced by a special amplitude regulator which modulates the gain of applied signals by a few decibels at a repetition speed of about 7–11 Hz. Pitch vibrato could not be generated electronically except with extreme difficulty until the introduction of digital signal-processing devices during the 1970s, and the presence of frets on the fingerboard restricted the performer's ability to produce such an effect himself. The Hawaiian guitar provided the only practical alternative, its hand-operated lever acting to adjust the tension, and hence the tuning, of the strings.

More marked manipulations became possible with the introduction of the wah-wah and the fuzz-tone effects. The wah-wah consists of a tuneable low-pass filter coupled to an amplitude regulator, the device normally being controlled via a foot pedal. The effect of linking an increase in amplitude with a rising frequency of cut-off is very similar onomatopoeically to a 'wah-wah'-like sound, the brightness of timbre rising and falling with the gain. The fuzz-tone generator is a special type of frequency multiplier, like a ring modulator, which transforms the guitar into a harsh and aggressive sounding instrument by adding rich and complex partials to each note.

Special limiters were introduced as sustaining devices, artificially prolonging the duration of individual notes or chords by automatically compensating for the loss in gain which occurs during the decay portion of each envelope. If the limiter also rounds the initial attack transients the result is a smooth organ-like sound which permits an extremely legato style of playing.

The terms 'phasing' and 'flanging' have variously been applied to a number of processing techniques which introduce very small time delays into applied signals. When these are mixed with their sources a complex interaction occurs, resulting in an augmentation of certain frequencies and a cancellation of others. The effects become particularly marked if the time delay is varied dynamically, for this leads to a modulation of the interactions, perceived as a complex 'squeezing' of the sound, as if moulded by an unseen hand reaching through the timbral spectrum. If the source and processed signals are fed to separate speakers, the characteristics of frequency cancellation and augmentation are set up as a result of acoustic interations, creating strange illusions of spatial movement.

A variety of methods may be employed for the generation of such delays. One of the simplest requires two tape recorders operating at the same speed and set in record mode, both receiving a common feed from the source signal. Providing the distance between the record and playback heads is identical both recorders will reproduce the source simultaneously. If a pencil is inserted between the heads on one of the machines and pushed against the tape, the deflection of the latter increases the effective distance the tape has to travel by a fractional amount, delaying its arrival at the replay head, relative to the other machine. An alternative approach, resulting in a slightly different characteristic subjectively, is to modulate the speed of one machine very gently. Both techniques, however, are very difficult to regulate, and have generally been discarded in favour of analogue and, more recently, digital delay lines which achieve the desired effects electronically. The latter are frequently used in live performance to considerable effect. The timbral subtleties of these devices, however, can only be explored properly in the more disciplined environment of a studio.

The electric guitar was not the only instrument to benefit from electronic improvements over the years. Electronic keyboard instruments were subject to similar modifications, in some instances being developed into comprehensive synthesizers in their own right, offering a number of performance facilities. This trend has led to a considerable blurring of the boundary between what would normally be considered an instrument and a fully equipped studio system. Several manufacturers, such as the successful firm of Roland, having concentrated initially on products in the former category, are now producing equipment which is as relevant to the electronic composer as to the rock or pop musician.

One or two instruments have, nevertheless, retained their identity against the tide of technological change. The electronic piano, for example, has remained popular with many bands and groups, its artificial sound gaining a status of its own. By far the most unusual design to survive is the Mellotron or Chamberlin, a keyboard instrument which reproduces sounds previously recorded on an array of tape loops, each of the latter being assigned to a specific key.

The steady integration of electronic devices with more traditional instruments in rock and pop music has established a technical link to the main genres of electronic music. Artistic links, however, have been far more tenuous, for the philosophical and stylistic differences have not proved easy to bridge. Furthermore, excursions into new sound worlds by rock and pop musicians have often lacked any sustained development. Many a group, in search of an individuality which will assure success, has experimented with electronics in the early stages of its career, only to return to more traditional resources as the years have advanced.

One widely known style of electronic music which has established a bridge across this divide was launched by Walter Carlos in 1968 with his album *Switched on Bach*. This, and its sequel,

*The Well Tempered Synthesizer*, issued the following year, consists entirely of electronic realizations of selected works by Bach, created via a Moog synthesizer. The response of the popular market was without precedent, resulting in sales of these records which quickly surpassed the entire world-wide production of conventional recordings of the works of Bach.

This evident interest in electronic popularizations of the classics encouraged others to follow suit. The Japanese composer Isao Tomita has achieved particular success with his electronic arrangements, starting with his album *Snowflakes are Dancing* (1974), based on the piano works of Debussy. These realizations are concerned less with the overt sensationalism of Carlos and more with a considered exploration of the subtleties of texture obtainable from electronic orchestrations.

Extracts from classical works either synthesized or performed conventionally in association with electronic elements, have appeared in a number of rock pieces, although not always to good effect. The inclusion of the Hallelujah Chorus from Handel's *Messiah* in *The Six Wives of Henry VIII* by the group Yes (*Yes Songs*, 1973), for example, serves to confuse rather than consolidate an already convoluted collage of musical fragments.

Emerson, Lake, and Palmer adopted a more considered approach to the integration of classical material into a popular idiom, carefully preserving the spirit of the sources in their own recordings. Their *Pictures at an Exhibition* (1971) provides a striking example of their skills, unaltered quotations from the original Mussorgsky and elaborate synthesized manipulations providing the outer extremes of a carefully constructed framework of rock and classical styles.

Electronically processed material has appeared in several rock compositions since the mid 1960s. Isolated examples may be traced back to the previous decade, for example the use of speeded-up recordings of voices to create high-pitched and childlike twitterings by the Chipmunks in both *The Witchdoctor* (1957) and *The Chipmunk Song* (1958). It was the Beach Boys, however, who provided the main stimulus for electronic rock music with their use of vocal tape transformations and the sounds of a Thérémin in *Good Vibrations* (1966) and *She's Goin Bald* (1967). The Tempophon is employed extensively in these pieces, providing progressive transpositions of pitch without alteration to the tempo.

The Beatles, after preliminary experimentation with simple tape loops and reversed playback of recordings in *I'm only Sleeping* and *Tomorrow Never Knows* from their album *Revolver* (1967), incorporated a number of more elaborate tape transformations in their next record, *Sgt. Pepper's Lonely Hearts Club Band* (1967). The song *A Day in the Life*, for example, incorporates multi-tracking techniques which could never have been realized live, and was indicative of an important trend in rock towards the greater flexibility of studio-engineered music, rather than straight reproductions of concert pieces. Live performance, however, remained the *raison d'être* for most rock groups, leading in turn to an increasing demand for more sophisticated performance facilities.

Pre-recorded tapes provided one solution to the problems of stage presentations. In their album *Anthem of the Sun* (1967–8), the group Grateful Dead introduced a tape interlude between two songs which incorporated elaborate transformations of vocal, percussion, piano, and electronic sounds in the form of a montage. In *Aoxomoxoa* (1969) electronic treatments feature extensively in the songs themselves, particular use being made of phasing, modulation, filtering, and multitracking via a tape-delay system. Several of these effects were nevertheless generated live, in an effort to reduce the dependence on pre-recorded material.

One motivation for the use of electronic techniques in rock pieces of the late 1960s and early 70s was undoubtedly a desire to evoke the twisted and blurred imagery associated with the act of drug-taking. *Their Satanic Majesties Request* (1967) by the Rolling Stones, for example, is permeated with electronic distortions of the instrumental material which verge on the bizarre.

Frank Zappa and the Mothers of Invention have used electronics in several of their albums, moving from studio-produced treatments in *Uncle Meat* (1967–8) to synthesizers in live performances for release such as *Roxy and Elsewhere* (1974). Considerable skills were demanded of their keyboard player, George Duke, in performing both on conventional instruments and also on synthesizers during the piece. The challenge of this new performance art was pursued by several other rock musicians, including Rick Wakeman of Yes, Brian Eno of the Matching Moles and Roxy Music, amongst other ensembles, and Keith Emerson, of Emerson, Lake, and Palmer.

Yes paid particular attention to the use of extended electronic interludes in their songs, creating works of symphonic proportions. In *Close to the Edge* (1972) Wakeman exhibits a considerable feat of dexterity, manipulating synthesizer, organ, Mellotron, and piano for long periods in this four-movement work. Similar displays of virtuosity are exhibited by Eno in albums such as *Little Red Record* and *Roxy Music* (1972). Eno, perhaps more than any other instrumentalist of his time, attempted to forge close links between rock and avant-garde styles of composition. His solo work *Discreet Music* (1975) might equally well have been included in the earlier discussion of studio electronic works, for the procedures employed show a close affinity to the tape works of Steve Reich. Two melodic lines provide the sole sources of material, subjected to tape echo, tape delay, and simple filtering. The structure of the piece is that of a continuous process of transformation, based on a series of repeating and permuting patterns which slowly change in complexity and texture.

Emerson's skills have already been alluded to in considering *Pictures at an Exhibition*. Similar feats of performance are evident in *Toccata* from the album *Brain Salad Surgery* (1973), a piece based on the fourth movement of Ginastera's first piano concerto. Here the Mellotron is dispensed with completely, the synthesizer being used primarily as an instrumental imitator. Despite the more adventurous experimentation of performers such as Eno, rock music has tended to restrict the use of live electronics to the latter role. Noise effects and repeating sequencer-controlled patterns have featured in some works, but the nature of most rock styles and the relative ease of keyboard control have favoured more conventional approaches to synthesis. Far more varied uses of synthesizers in live performance have been demonstrated by several of the electronic ensembles discussed in the preceding chapter.

Soft Machine is an example of a British group, originally specializing in avant-garde jazz, who developed a rock image through the use of electronics Their earliest works, *Soft Machine* (1968) and *Soft Machine II* (1969), display an imaginative use of 'wah-wah' effects on both guitar and vocal material. Their later albums, involving the use of synthesizers, are less distinctive, mainly as a result of their elementary use of these devices as keyboard substitutes.

Whilst the medium of rock retained a strong preference for tonal harmony, texture provided the primary key to a more versatile use of electronics. The German group Tangerine Dream, formed by Edgar Froese in the mid 1970s, has proved one of the most adventurous in exploring the use of synthesizers. Froese had become aware of the advantages of studio multitracking in preparing his own solo album *Aqua* (1973–4) and *ngc 891* (1974) and the characteristics of carefully ordered montage are evident in releases such as *Rubycon* (1975) and *Cyclone* (1978). The group's concern with the manipulation of timbre is emphasized by their unusual instrumentation, drums, percussion, and guitar figuring far less prominently than is usual in most rock music. Synthesizers, electric piano, and Mellotron provide the primary sources, augmented at times by the use of solo woodwind instruments such as flute, cor anglais, and clarinet.

A very close sense of integration between these sources is achieved in many of their pieces. Towards the end of 'Madrigal Meridian', from *Cyclone*, the perceptual boundary between the natural and synthetic sound worlds is completely confused by the use of a string-tone synthesizer which creates an astonishingly realistic impression of the natural instruments.

More novel applications of electronic techniques are to be found in the recordings of groups such as Pink Floyd and, to a lesser extent, Velvet Underground and Jimi Hendrix. Pink Floyd have made extensive use of synthesizers and pre-recorded tape in their works, frequently exploring more exotic effects of sound transformation applied to a variety of *concret* sources. Albums such as *Atom Heart Mother* (1970), *Meddle* (1971), and *The Dark Side of the Moon* (1972–3) exhibit strong socio-cultural characteristics in their integration of instrumental material with many environmental sounds such as the mooing of cows, footsteps, frying eggs and bacon, football crowds, clock chimes, and the mechanical clatter of cash registers. These pieces differ, nevertheless, from works drawing upon similar material in the mainstream of electronic composition, for the instrumental parts display a strong adherence to traditional rock orchestration and principles of tonal organization.

'Echoes', which occupies the entire second side of *Meddle*, is especially notable for its sensitive and coherence use of electronic material. This is most evident in an extended central section which effects a subtle transformation from the regular pulsing of a percussion backing pattern, left exposed at the end of a vocal section, to a ghostly timeless world of distant cries and undulating moans, only to return to the security and immediacy of simple diatonic harmony and metre with a reappearance of the vocal material. A debt to Stockhausen is evident, especially in the closing section, which incorporates an upwards-moving timbre continuum of successive vocal glissandi.

The music of Velvet Underground shows some affinity with the words of La Monte Young and Riley, for their violist, John Cale, had migrated to rock after playing for both musicians. Although their use of cyclic variation anticipates similar techniques employed by Eno, the style is wilder and altogether more adventurous. The group was originally formed by Andy Warhol for a multi-media show entitled 'Exploding Plastic Inevitable', staged in a New York night-club during 1965. Music from this production formed the basis of their principal album *Andy Warhol's Velvet Underground Featuring Nico* (1967–9). Their use of electronics contrasts sharply with that of Pink Floyd, with an emphasis on heavy modulation or even sheer distortion. This aggressive rock style was also pursued by guitarist Jimi Hendrix, who displayed a particular predilection for the fuzz-tone generator in albums such as *The Jimi Hendrix Experience* (1967–8).

By the late 1970s the pioneering phase of electronic rock and pop music had run its course. Individuality had been largely replaced by a significant degree of uniformity in both technical and musical terms as commercial manufacturers flooded the market with low cost analogue synthesizers offering broadly similar characteristics. The ramifications of these developments were soon to affect the medium as a whole, forcing fundamental changes in the relationship between the creative artist and his tools, not least as the result of an increased dependence by composers both popular and serious on the characteristics of highly engineered systems, for the most part designed to be of general rather than specialized appeal. The course of these developments was to be affected by a fundamental and far-reaching change in the technology itself from an analogue to a digital domain, and it is to the evolution of the latter that attention must now be turned.

# The Digital Revolution

# 10 The Birth of Computer Music

The term 'computer music' embraces a wide variety of compositional and performance activities, ranging from the generation of conventionally notated scores based on data calculated via the computer to the direct synthesis of sound in a digital form within the computer itself. With just one or two important exceptions, in particular Bell Telephone Laboratories, most of the pioneering work during the 1950s and 60s was carried out at universities and other non-profit-making institutions dependent on public funds. Although the 1970s saw the development of a growing number of mass-produced all-digital products the main revolution in the manufacturing sector dates from the early 1980s and the birth of the MIDI synthesizer.

During the early years of computer music research the only tools available were mainframe computers, large and expensive items of equipment designed in the first instance as a general purpose tool for scientific and commercial data processing. Such resources were initially few and far between and had to be shared with many other users. Towards the end of the 1960s more compact and less expensive models became available, and as a result some studios were able to acquire their own dedicated facilities, starting a trend towards self-sufficiency which was to gather momentum during the 1970s. These machines proved particularly suitable for hybrid synthesis, a technique which involves the use of a computer as a control facility for an analogue system of generators and processors, but their scaled down processing capabilities initially proved a major drawback for more demanding applications such as the direct synthesis and processing of sound material in a digital form.

This situation was to change dramatically as the years advanced, for the continuing development of digital technology during the decade led to a succession of new minicomputers which were soon to rival the power and speed of much larger machines for a mere fraction of their cost. By 1980 the microcomputer revolution was gathering pace, and this not only brought computing resources for music to the desktop of the individual but also facilitated the construction of purpose-built systems for audio synthesis.

Before these developments are studied in detail, it is helpful to outline the basic characteristics of a traditional computer since they provide important clues to the ways in which digital processors have been used for music applications. The distinctions between the various classes of computer, from the largest mainframe to the smallest desktop micro, are essentially a matter of degree. A basic system will usually incorporate the following items of equipment, known generally as hardware:

1. A bank of digital storage locations, known as the memory.
2. An operational control system, known as the central processing unit or CPU.
3. An input device such as keyboard, used to pass externally prepared information to the system.
4. An output device such as a visual display unit (VDU) or a printer, used to recover information from the system in a readable form.
5. Auxiliary storage devices such as a magnetic disk or tape drive, used to store bulk information in a digitally coded form.

Fig. 61 illustrates the configuration of a traditional mainframe system.

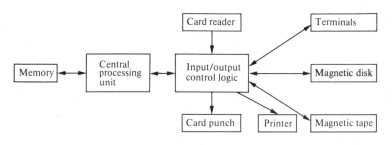

**Figure 61**

Prior to the 1960s most computer users had no option but to prepare their programs on punched cards or paper tape using special mechanically driven data preparation machines. Tasks would then be submitted to the machine and processed one by one, with no opportunity for any direct interaction between the programmer and the computer. In due course the emphasis shifted towards more direct communication facilities for individual users, leading to the introduction of terminals which combined a conventional typewriter keyboard with a simple daisy wheel or dot matrix printer, the latter producing hardcopy output at a modest speed. As a result larger installations were able to accommodate several users working simultaneously, the computer multiplexing between the various tasks so rapidly as to appear committed to each terminal. Today typewriter terminals have largely been replaced by VDUs, and punched cards or paper tape have almost universally been discarded in favour of the magnetic floppy disk which provides an altogether more powerful and convenient means for the storage of individual programs and data.

The memory of a computer is organized in a manner similar to that of the digital memory sequencer, described in Chapter 6. Each memory location is assigned a unique address by which it may be referenced, the number of digital storage bits depending on the individual architecture. Older computers frequently assigned a fixed number of bits to each basic storage unit. Known as words, these ranged in capacity from eight to twelve, sixteen, eighteen, or even twenty-four bits per location. Over the years there has been a general trend towards a slightly different method of organization which restricts each location to eight bits but allows the addressing system to combine locations, for example as pairs to create sixteen-bit words, or as groups of four to create thirty-two-bit words. This principle is known as byte addressing, the term byte referring to each unit of eight bits. In all cases control over memory addressing and the storage and recovery of information from each location is exercised by the CPU. Unlike the memory sequencer, access to locations need not necessarily be sequential, for the CPU is able to move its address pointer directly from one location to any other. This freedom gives rise to the term random access.

The size of the memory imposes an important constraint on the computer's operational characteristics. Until the advent of the microchip, memory was a major item of expense, in the early 1960s costing as much as £1 a byte. By 1980 equivalent memory had become available for less than a hundredth of this amount and this rapid decline in price continued apace. Just a decade later desktop computers with memory capacities of between 0.5 megabytes (500 000 bytes) and upwards of 16 megabytes (16 000 000 bytes) had become commonplace both in the office and also increasingly in the home. The early pioneers of computer music worked with mainframe computers offering perhaps 1 or 2 megabytes of memory at the most, and even this resource would have seemed generous to those who worked with the first generation of minicomputers, which were often restricted to no more than 64 kilobytes (64 000 bytes) and sometimes as little as 4 kilobytes (4000 bytes) of memory.

The CPU itself acts as the administrative and operational heart of a computer. In addition to controlling the memory and the peripherals it includes an arithmetic logic unit (ALU) which executes arithmetic operations such as add, subtract, multiply, and divide, and also logic operations such as AND, OR, NAND, and NOR. To facilitate the rapid processing of digital information the CPU normally includes a number of registers or binary counters. The memory is treated as a general work area for digital information passing to and from the CPU. This information may consist either of instructions, such as 'move the contents of location $x$ to the CPU', or of data, for example the contents of location $x$.

The sequences of instructions which operate the computer are organized into a program, loaded for execution into a contiguous block of memory locations. The instructions themselves enter the system in the first instance via one of the input devices, frequently used programs being stored on magnetic disk for rapid loading into memory as and when required. Since these programs are non-permanent and easily altered, they are known collectively as software.

A distinction can be made between two specific types of program. The first type, usually described as applications software, consists of programs written by a programmer to carry out specified tasks, ranging from word processing to the calculation of a payroll or a set of mathematical procedures. The second, known as the operating system, is a special program or set of sub-programs which has to be loaded into memory as soon as the computer is switched on. Its purpose is to control the various functions of the computer, such as loading and supervising the use of applications programs, and managing the storage of data and program files on disk. Since key parts of the operating system have to remain loaded at all times the amount of free memory available for user programs is invariably less than the quoted memory size, a factor which can sometimes pose problems with smaller computers.

Early types of memory were known as core, since they operated on a magnetic principle of storage which allowed automatic retention of information during periods when the computer was switched off. In such instances it was not always necessary to reload the system every time the computer was switched on again. Most modern memory is volatile, which means that unless some form of battery back-up facility is available all information disappears whenever the power is disconnected. In such cases a complete reinitialization is always required.

With the birth of the microcomputer the initial booting of such systems was simplified by adding a special memory chip known as a BIOS (Basic Input/Output System) which holds a permanent record of key components of the operating system, automatically accessed as soon as the machine is switched on. Such memory is generally known as ROM (Read Only Memory) to distinguish it from RAM (Random Access Memory), a term used to describe conventional memory or core, which can be overwritten with new information at any time.

Direct specification of instructions for a computer is known as machine-level programming. In its most primitive form this involves entering each command as a number which translates directly into its binary coded equivalent, and such a code is both difficult to prepare and also very hard to check. A more practicable method, known as assembly programming, involves entering the instructions in the form of simple mnemonics, which are easier to assimilate externally. These are then translated internally into equivalent machine instructions by a special interpreter program supplied by the computer manufacturer.

Programming in assembler code allows the selection of the most efficient sequence of instructions to achieve a particular objective, and this facility can be of the utmost importance in applications where speed is of the essence. From a programmer's point of view, however, there are a number of drawbacks. In particular, such direct control of a computer's processor is extremely complex and time-consuming to prepare, even the simplest mathematical operations requiring a considerable number of assembler statements. A more serious, longer-term disadvantage is the dependence of such programs on the computer for which they were originally written. Different models use different instruction sets, demanding laborious reprogramming before such software may be ported from one machine to another.

To overcome such difficulties a number of universal high-level programming languages have been developed. These employ simpler directives which are semantically more powerful, a single command replacing an entire sequence of low level machine instructions. Such a facility is provided via special compilers which act to translate instructions written in the syntax of the language into the machine code appropriate for the particular computer. Programs prepared in this manner are machine-independent, for with a few minor alterations they may be readily transferred from one make of computer to another.

ALGOL (ALGOrithmic Language), BASIC, C, COBOL, FORTRAN (FORmula TRANslation), LISP, and PASCAL are among the most common high-level languages in use today. Although these greatly simplify the task of programming, the machine code they generate is rarely as efficient as that obtainable by programming directly in assembler. In a modern high-speed computer using a well written compiler the resulting loss in performance may be small enough to be of no material consequence. During the pioneering era of computer music, however, the combination of much slower processors and older, less efficient compilers made this trade-off between speed and ease of programming far more significant.

The first attempts at harnessing the computer as a tool for synthesizing sound date from the mid 1950s. During this period the research division of Bell Telephone Laboratories, New Jersey, became interested in the possibilities of transmitting telephone conversations in a digitized form by converting the analogue information into equivalent patterns of numerical samples at one end of the line and performing the reverse process at the other. The complexities encountered in multiplexing several conversations together down a single line, and then separating them again at the other end, led to the use of the computer as a development aid.

The telephone system only requires an acceptable fidelity over a relatively small frequency bandwidth, concentrated towards the lower end of the audio spectrum. The research team quickly realized that, despite some major technical obstacles, there was a distant possibility that full audio bandwidth transmission systems could be developed, capable of handling broadcast-quality music information.

It was in such a climate of investigation that one of the Bell engineers, Max Mathews, began exploring the use of the computer itself as a means of calculating and generating sound samples. His first attempts consisted of two experimental programs: MUSIC I which appeared in 1957, quickly replaced by MUSIC II early in 1958. Both of these produced very simple sounds, MUSIC I being restricted to one and MUSIC II to four triangle-wave functions.

The computer employed, an IBM 704, was by modern standards, very slow and extremely limited in its capabilities, even when programmed directly in assembler code. The first commercial computer had been marketed by Remington Rand in 1951, but it was not until IBM entered the field with their 701 model in 1953 that the industry began to make any significant progress in marketing. The 704, its immediate successor, was thus still a relatively primitive machine relying almost entirely on valve technology.

The introduction of transistor-based circuits in the late 1950s radically altered the outlook for computer technology, and by the end of the decade faster and less cumbersome machines were appearing on the market. Bell Telephone Laboratories took delivery of one of these second-generation computers, an IBM 7094, in 1959, and it was for this machine that Mathews produced his first comprehensive direct synthesis program, MUSIC III, completed early in 1960.

By now several composers and engineers were showing an interest in the project. James Tenney became directly involved with developments at Bell, soon to be followed by Hubert Howe, Godfrey Winham, and Jim Randall at the University of Princeton, New Jersey. The next, improved, version of Mathews' program, MUSIC IV, produced in 1962 in association with Joan Miller, provided the basic model for a whole family of derivatives, subsequently to be implemented in a number of centres all over the world.

The earlier mentioned differences between high- and low-level programming techniques become of importance in tracing the evolution of these versions. MUSIC IV, like its predecessors, was written almost entirely in assembler code, in this instance for the IBM 7094. Princeton, conveniently, had purchased just such a machine shortly after Bell, enabling a copy of this program to be implemented with a minimum of difficulty. Several improvements were introduced at this second centre, the new version being renamed MUSIC IV B. Particular attention was paid to the intelligibility of the program to prospective composers, an aspect which previously had not commanded sufficient attention.

Developments in computer technology were nevertheless sealing the fate of these two versions before work had been completed. With the advent of integrated circuits, providing a means of incorporating several miniaturized transistors within a single moulding, a third generation of computers emerged, launched by IBM in 1965 with their series of System 360 models. The increased capabilities of these machines were accompanied by radical alterations to the internal machine functions, and thus the methods of assembler programming.

In an attempt to avoid short-term obsolescence and to make MUSIC programs more generally available to centres not equipped with IBM machines it was considered prudent to prepare versions which were written in FORTRAN, one of the oldest and most widely available high-level languages. The first of these, MUSIC IV F, was written by Arthur Roberts in 1965, soon to be eclipsed by a more comprehensive version. MUSIC IV BF, written by Howe at Princeton during 1966–7 and subsequently improved by Winham. These programs, inevitably, were less efficient in their execution than those written directly in assembler code, making them particularly unpopular with computing centres hard pressed with conflicting demands on their resources.

Mathews, meanwhile, continued to develop his own versions at Bell Telephone Laboratories, completing an all-FORTRAN MUSIC V in 1968. This program was moderately successful in overcoming the inefficiencies of the language by means of a major reorganization of several of the internal synthesis functions, bearing in mind the particular characteristics of FORTRAN compilers. The result was a simpler program, more readily understood by composers with little or no prior experience of computer operation, but lacking a number of refinements. A number of large centres, however, chose this version as the starting-point for their own programs, in some instances developed almost out of all recognition from their ancestor.

The advantages of low-level programming were not neglected. Barry Vercoe, whilst working at Princeton, developed during 1968 a very fast version of MUSIC IV B, entitled MUSIC 360, for the corresponding IBM range of machines. After moving to Massachusetts Institute of Technology in the early 1970s he developed a compact version, MUSIC 11, in 1973, written in assembler for the PDP 11 range of computers manufactured by the Digital Equipment Corporation. This program is of particular significance, for as a result of major improvements in efficiency as regards processing demands and use of memory space, the MUSIC approach to direct synthesis became accessible to a family of much smaller computers, sufficiently modest in cost to be considered viable purchases for many studios. Further, in the version retained at MIT, major advances were made in the input facilities for composers, including such aids as an interactive computer graphics system and conventional music keyboards, to be used in association with the more usual teletypewriter or VDU.

Another version, MUSIC 10, written for the larger PDP 10 range of machines, was produced by John Chowning and James Moorer at the University of Stanford, California, in 1975, further improvements being implemented both at Stanford and at the newly established Institut de Recherche et Coordination Acoustique/Musique (IRCAM) in Paris. Recognition of the increasing importance of the programming language C led Richard Moore to develop CMUSIC, a much expanded version of MUSIC V, at the University of California, San Diego in 1985. In a similar move Barry Vercoe translated MUSIC 11 into a C version known as CSOUND at MIT in 1986.

In general terms these programs are similar in their construction. The differences occur primarily in their relative efficiency and versatility, and the formats of the sound-specification procedures offered to the composer. The basic principles of digital sound production have already been outlined in considering the characteristics of sequencers. If a sound is to be synthesized digitally the computer must be programmed to calculate the corresponding pressure-wave characteristics in terms of discrete numerical samples, the latter being passed for translation into equivalent voltage steps via a digital-to-analogue converter. The fidelity of the result, it will be recalled, is dependent both on the rate at which these samples are produced and on the numerical accuracy of their values.

The wave-generation process itself is based on the principles of additive synthesis, building up composite sample patterns from sinusoidal components. To avoid excessive computation, blocks of memory, typically 512 words long, are set aside for the storage of wave forms in the form of numerical tables. A sine-wave oscillator may thus be simulated by storing a numerical representation of a single cycle as 512 discrete steps in one of these blocks and repeatedly scanning through the values to generate a continuous function. Such a technique shows a strong similarity to that employed for generating audio or control waves from a sequencer.

The frequency of waves produced by this technique depends both on the speed at which the samples are finally output to the converter and on the number of samples used to represent each fundamental cycle. Applying a sampling rate of 10 000 samples per second in the above instance would result in a sine wave of 10 000/512 = 19.5 Hz, approximately. Doubling this rate to 20 000 samples per second would increase the frequency in proportion to about 39 Hz. In the case of a sequencer programmed to generate a single wave function, it is possible to control the output frequency by manipulating the rate of sampling. Such a technique was impracticable in the case of the MUSIC programs in view of the need to synchronize the processes of component addition to a fixed rate of sampling.

A different method of extracting wave-form samples from the memory blocks had thus to be evolved, where the frequency of repetition would be determined by modifying the number of samples used to represent each cycle, whilst keeping the sampling rate constant. To return to the example above, at a sampling rate of 10 000 the output frequency could be doubled from 19.5 Hz to 39 Hz merely by reading every second sample in the memory block. The entire wave would then be scanned after 256 steps instead of 512. Reading every fourth sample will quadruple the frequency, and so forth. Since the memory block is read as a continuous loop, location 1 following location 512, no problems are encountered in extracting sample values at intervals which do not repeat an exact number of times within the table length, for example every third or every fifth sample.

Whilst this technique permits the generation of multiples of 19.5 Hz, or subdivisions from repeated readings of each sample in turn, it does not allow the production of any other frequency. This difficulty is overcome by the application of a simple interpolation routine to calculate function values which lie between adjacent elements in the wave table as and when required. Generation of a 100 Hz wave at a sampling rate of 10000 samples per second, for example, demands the extraction of values every 5.12 elements.

The primary disadvantage of this approach to digital synthesis lies in the steady reduction in the number of samples available for each cycle as progressively higher frequencies are generated. Fortunately the ear is reasonably tolerant of the consequential increase in distortion towards the upper regions of the audio spectrum, providing sufficient samples are available for lower components. A critical situation is reached, however, when the wave representation has become reduced to two samples per cycle. This occurs at a frequency corresponding to half the sampling rate, referred to as the Nyquist frequency. Any attempt to generate frequencies above this value leads to the generation of a beat frequency which folds back into lower-frequency regions. Generation of a 7000 Hz wave at 10000 samples per second, for example, will introduce an additional component at 10000 − 7000 = 3000 Hz.

The Nyquist frequency thus marks the upper limit of the usable synthesis spectrum, a sharp low-pass filter being inserted in the output of the D-to-A converter to suppress any spurious components which may be generated above this point. A sampling rate of 10000, allowing a bandwidth of 5 kHz, may be adequate for speech but is far too slow for high-quality music synthesis, which demands a bandwidth of at least 16 kHz (32000 samples per second) and preferably 20 kHz or more to ensure accurate reproduction of the entire audio spectrum. Another factor influencing the quality of digitally generated sound is the numerical accuracy of the samples themselves. Since the precision of successive whole-number approximations to a continuous function depends on the range of values which may be used for this quantization process, the key factor is thus the number of bits available for each sample, typically sixteen for a modern high-performance system. The pioneers of computer music were often restricted to converters which offered much lower sampling rates and bit resolutions, with often serious consequences for the quality of the material thus generated. These issues will be examined more closely in subsequent chapters.

The quest for high fidelity in a digital synthesis system leads to other problems. If the computer is to calculate and output the samples in 'real' (or more correctly 'actual') time, then increasing the sampling rate will reduce the time available between samples for their computation. The steady improvements in digital processing power over the years have proved crucial in this respect and this factor perhaps above all others has influenced and constrained the development of more efficient and versatile tools for computer music.

In the case of the MUSIC family of direct synthesis programs the precision of the internal calculation processes and the levels of complexity which are demanded by composers quickly lead to processing requirements which are beyond the real-time capability of the host computer. In such situations the only practicable way of overcoming this hurdle is to allow the computer to calculate the information over whatever period of time proves necessary, accumulating the samples in the first instance on an auxiliary storage device such as a magnetic disk or tape. As a subsequent process the resulting audio data is then recovered sequentially and passed to a D-to-A converter at the required sampling rate. Stereo output doubles both the processing and storage requirements since each channel requires its own set of samples. In practice samples are usually interleaved, leaving the control system for the associated pair of converters to decode the information correctly.

In the past the delays which composers have encountered in working with such systems have often been quite considerable. On a typical mainframe computer of the 1960s or 70s upwards of ten or twenty minutes of processing time could be required for each minute of sound. If the computer happened to be especially slow or the synthesis instructions particularly complex it was not unknown for this ratio to increase to 100 or even 200 to 1. In view of these heavy demands composers would often wait several hours before their tasks were completed. Such environmental conditions contrasted sharply with the immediacy of response encountered in the analogue studio. The compensations lay in the range and flexibility of the synthesis facilities which are provided for the composer, in particular the ability to specify refined and precisely ordered sounds via a musically orientated syntax. In due course, with the implementation of these programs or their derivatives on increasingly powerful personal workstations, the true value of such an open environment for composing computer music became more generally appreciated.

A central concept of the MUSIC family of programs is the division of synthesis tasks into two components, the orchestra and the score. The 'orchestra' is constructed from statements which define a network of unit generators and processors, generally representing recognizable studio devices such as oscillators, filters, envelope-shapers, and reverberation units. In due course a number of more specialist unit generators were added to programs such as CSOUND as a direct result of research into new algorithms for the synthesis of sound. Since these devices are software simulations the only limit on the number of unit generator definitions is the maximum workspace available in memory. The 'score', as its title suggests, provides performance data for the orchestra. Suitable sequences of control information must be provided for each unit generator, including details of starting times and durations for each set of values, as well as the values themselves. Oscillator wave-shapes are specified via function-generating routines which accept simple variables such as the relative strengths of the selected harmonic components and then produce the corresponding wavetables.

In many versions of the MUSIC programs function-generating routines may be employed to replace the normal exponential attack and decay characteristics of envelope-shapers with customized curves. Such a facility allows a powerful measure of control over the evolution of timbre since it is possible to build up sound complexes from sinusoidal components, individually regulated in terms of pitch and also amplitude. The accuracy and attention to detail afforded by this additive synthesis method allows for very fine crafting of the resulting sound material. The quantity of information which has to be provided for this method of synthesis is nevertheless considerable, and in many situations it is more convenient to use other synthesis methods which require less-detailed information. Particular consideration has been given to the characteristics of amplitude and frequency modulation in this context in view of the limited number of parameters involved. Since the control of one unit generator oscillator by another merely requires the insertion of suitable link commands in the orchestra specification, such techniques are relatively easy to implement and leave ample scope for experimentation.

The work of John Chowning at Stanford has proved particularly significant in this context. During the late 1960s he began detailed investigations into the characteristics of frequency-modulated sounds using the computer as a synthesis source. He discovered that the application of frequencies of deviation greater than the carrier frequency itself led to the production of unusual acoustic phenomena. Such modulatory conditions, when studied mathematically, suggest an oscillation which deviates into a negative frequency region for part of its cycle. A wave of 150 Hz subject to a deviation of 200 Hz would thus be modulated between 350 Hz and –50 Hz. The ear, however, does not recognize negative frequency components as a downwards extension of the normal audio spectrum. Instead they are perceived as positive frequencies, but with an inverted wave-form or phase. The modulation characteristic will thus appear as follows:

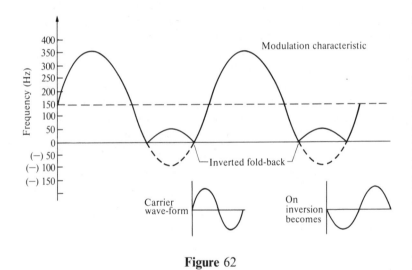

**Figure** 62

Identical effects occur to the side bands generated by the process of modulation itself, those bands which lie below 0 Hz being folded back into the audio spectrum with an inverted phase. It will be recalled that under normal conditions frequency modulation results in a symmetrical distribution of side bands either side of the carrier frequency, the spacing and number of side bands generated from a particular carrier being regulated by the frequency of modulation, and the deviation.

If negative side bands are generated, however, the distribution ceases to be symmetrical. Consider, for example, the result of modulating a carrier of 200 Hz with a frequency of 70 Hz, the latter producing a peak deviation of 250 Hz. Theory predicts the generation of side bands of varying amplitudes at 270, 340, 410, 480, and 550 Hz above the carrier, and 130, 60, –10, –80, and –150 Hz beneath, the three negative values being folded back with an inversion of phase.

The aural effects become especially meaningful if such characteristics are varied dynamically. If the modulating wave is changed from 70 Hz to 73 Hz in the above instance, the spacings of the upper side bands increase proportionately to 273, 346, 419, 492, and 565 Hz. The lower side bands, however, will change in frequency to 127, 54, –19, –92, and –165 Hz. The negative components, upon fold-back, thus gain in frequency, moving in the opposite direction from their positively generated neighbours.

The effects of crossing side bands radically alter the perceived characteristics of the modulated sound. In particular they exhibit a remarkably 'alive' quality as they permute, due to the complex phasing which occurs between the components. Within the precise domain of digital synthesis, control over these characteristics may be accurately exercised via the three basic variables of the carrier frequency, $c$, the modulating frequency, $m$, and the deviation, $d$.

During the 1970s, with assistance from James Moorer, Chowning continued his research into FM techniques, paying particular attention to the possibility of synthesizing instrumental timbres by suitable combinations of $c$, $m$, and $d$ values. Bell and brass sounds proved particularly productive avenues of exploration, sometimes necessitating the use of double or triple modulators with multiple carriers.

Only very minor modifications to the internal sample-generation routines of MUSIC-type synthesis programs were necessary to accommodate the specification of negative frequency components, and Chowning's models soon became widely used and extremely popular with computer music composers. His own works *Sabelithe* and *Turenas* (an anagram of 'natures'), written in 1972, convincingly demonstrate the richness and variety of timbres which may be produced by such a technique. Unfortunately, FM sounds, like the products of so many other specific synthesis techniques encountered in the medium, have proved vulnerable to over-indulgent and sometimes insensitive usage. The composer is presented with a particularly difficult task in employing modulation synthesis, even when working from one of Chowning's models, for the variables available for manipulation can seem very remote from the acoustic phenomena they produce. Chowning himself was subsequently to tackle this particular drawback to FM with considerable success in partnership with Yamaha, who implemented an expanded set of his algorithms as the basis for their range of all-digital MIDI synthesizers, launched in 1983.

The inclusion of filter units in MUSIC orchestras results in complex and time-consuming calculations during the sample-generation process. Max Mathews omitted filters altogether in his original version of MUSIC V, forcing composers to create such timbral modifications by manipulating the wave-generation functions directly, This restriction seriously impeded the creative use of the program, and as already noted many centres have subsequently modified the software to provide such a facility. Well-developed programs such as MUSIC 360 and MUSIC 11 provide a comprehensive range of filter types covering all the standard modes, for example low-pass, high-pass, band-pass, and band-reject.

Digital reverberation units offer a technique of sound enhancement unparalleled in the analogue domain. Computing techniques allow the generation of multiple delayed images without any of the inherent mechanical distortions produced by spring or plate units. Such facilities are thus particularly valuable in direct synthesis for they supply a versatile means of adding warmth and perspective to sounds which would otherwise tend to sound dry and clinical. Like filters, however, reverberation units make heavy demands on the computer, and thus must be used sparingly.

The pioneering work carried out at Bell Telephone Laboratories, MIT, Princeton, and Stanford encouraged other centres throughout the world to establish computer music facilities. By the end of the 1970s MUSIC programs had been installed in centres as far apart as Melbourne in Australia, Ontario and Waterloo in Canada, Marseilles and IRCAM in France, Durham, Glasgow, and London in Great Britain, and

Padua in Italy. In America itself many other universities had installed facilities, including Columbia, Illinois, Indiana, Michigan, New York at Buffalo, and Queens College, New York.

From an artistic viewpoint the creative potential of these direct-synthesis facilities had yet to be fully explored. The reasons for this latency are numerous, not least the fundamental difficulties experienced by many composers in working creatively with a system which demands the specification of ideas via a coding system of alphanumeric characters and offers little opportunity for interactive experimentation. One notable improvement to the data-coding system was developed at Stanford by Leland Smith. Using MUSIC V he produced a more accessible musical syntax for specifying details of pitch and rhythm via a special sub-program entitled SCORE (1972). In addition, routines were included for applying processes of transposition and transformation, creating in effect a simple composing facility. The degree of flexibility attained, however, was necessarily limited by MUSIC V itself.

Mathews had briefly turned his attention to auxiliary input methods during the mid 1960s, developing a graphical facility for the entry of simple score details to MUSIC IV in association with L. Rossler. This project, however, terminated with the removal of the IBM 7094 computer from Bell Telephone Laboratories. Apart from Vercoe's own graphical input system for MUSIC 11 at MIT, allowing data to be entered and displayed using conventional notation, no other sustained attempt had yet been made to develop a visual input system specifically for this family of programs. During the early years advance was hindered by a poor standard of audio fidelity, largely due to substandard conversion facilities. A predominance of experimental pieces by scientists rather than accomplished composers also contributed to a general air of scepticism in musical circles.

The experimental nature of the early works realized at Bell Telephone Laboratories is reflected in their titles: for example, *Variations in Timbre and Attack* (1961) and *Five Against Seven— Random Cannon* (1961) by John Pierce, or *Noise Study* (1961) and *Five Stochastics Studies* (1961) by James Tenney. *Bicycle Built for Two* (1962) by Max Mathews achieved some notoriety as an early example of digital speech synthesis, inspiring a research interest in this major aspect of communication theory.

Bell Laboratories provided the proving ground for another

influential pioneer of direct-synthesis techniques, Jean Claude Risset. After completing an impressive piece, *Little Boy* (1968), Risset returned to his native France to further developments both at Marseilles and at IRCAM. During the 1970s he produced a number of pieces, including *Dialogues* (1975) for flute, clarinet, piano, percussion, and computer-generated sounds, and *Songes* (1978), an essay in transformations from violin and flute sounds to the complex timbres of frequency-modulated tones. Special modifications to MUSIC V and MUSIC 10, both implemented at IRCAM allowed the input of short extracts of externally generated source material via an analogue-to-digital converter. This information was then analysed digitally, providing the data necessary for modification and re-synthesis, in combination with internally generated sounds.

Digital signal processing has become an important technique for composers of computer music, for it facilitates an integration of natural and synthetic sound worlds with a degree of refinement unattainable in an analogue studio. By the early 1980s many studios had installed A-to-D converters to digitize and process externally generated sound material and the commercial sector soon grasped the potential of sampling as an alternative to wave-form synthesis for the synthesizer market.

It will be recalled that the analogue studio offers a number of processing techniques for natural sources, such as filtering, modulation, reverberative enhancement, and tape manipulation. The scope of transformations which may be effected, however, is subject to a number of limitations, for it is not possible to perform a complete analysis of the sonological components. The characteristics of pitch and duration, for example, cannot satisfactorily be isolated one from another. Variable-speed processing results in proportional changes to both components, and the 'snapshot' sampling mechanisms of the Tempophon provide a very poor quality of reproduction. In the digital domain, where each second of sound may be quantified in terms of many thousands of discrete numerical samples, the constituent components of frequency, amplitude, and time may be accurately isolated by means of mathematics.

Work on the programming routines necessary for such complex operations began at Bell Telephone Laboratories during the 1960s. The most significant advances, however, were pioneered at Stanford by James Moorer, who succeeded in transforming a computational nightmare into a musically understandable set of procedures. During the 1970s he produced a number of miniatures to illustrate the use of such techniques, including *Perfect Days* (1975) and *Gentlemen Start Your Engines* (1977). Both incorporate speech sources and make extensive use of pitch and durational manipulations. *Perfect Days* also employs an interesting technique known as cross-synthesis, where one sound is used to control the articulation of another.

The basis for such a technique is to be found in the functional characteristics of the analogue vocoder. This device, it will be recalled, provides a dynamic analysis of the frequency spectrum of an applied sound via a bank of band-pass filters. If the amplitude functions thus derived are used to control the operation of another identically tuned bank of filters, these characteristics may be superimposed on any sound applied to the input of this second bank. The computed application of such a technique to digitized signals permits not only a more accurate superimposition of characteristics but also the introduction of subtle variations. In *Perfect Days* speech elements are used to articulate the sounds of a solo flute, resulting in a degree of animation which touches on the surreal.

Speech generation and manipulation feature in the works of Charles Dodge, a composer closely involved with the development of direct-synthesis facilities at both Columbia and Princeton Universities. His strong commitment to serial principles of musical organization results in a style of composition which contrasts sharply with the freer methods of expression adopted by West Coast composers. In *Speech Songs* (1973) the phonemes of his text are subject to strictly ordered permutations within a strongly sectionalized formal scheme.

Such indebtedness to the teachings of Babbitt are evident in his other computer-generated works, such as *Changes* (1969), *Earth's Magnetic Field* (1970), *Extensions for Trumpet and Tape* (1973), and *In Celebration* (1975). His choices of textures are predominantly instrumental in nature, the precision of the computer being exploited to provide a refined measure of control over the processes of synthesis. *Changes* evolves as a textural interplay between three contrasting elements: percussion-like sounds, pitch sequences, and chords. Some instrumental sounds are clearly identifiable, for example, the insistent tapping of a side-drum towards the beginning of the work, and brass notes reminiscent of a horn or trombone. A consistent mobility of timbre, however, prevents such associations from acquiring any sense of permanence. The entire piece is given a strong sense of propulsion by its jazz-orientated organization of rhythm. *In Celebration*, like *Speech Songs*, incorporates vocal syntheses, cross-synthesis leading to a convincing parody of vocal part-singing.

A number of composers have worked with MUSIC programs at Princeton, including Benjamin Boretz, Jim Randall, Barry Vercoe, and Jonathan Harvey. The principles of serialism feature strongly in many works. *Group Variation II*, realized by Boretz in 1973, for example, is a taut, pointillistic composition built upon a strictly organized scheme of 'note/events'.

Randall's works were amongst the first to be realized at Princeton. His *Quartets in Pairs* (1964) is a very brief contrapunctual study in 'note/event' organization, employing three simple timbres: an approximation to a violin, an approximation to a clarinet, and a sine wave. Once again the computer is treated as a virtuoso performer, executing melodic leaps with a dexterity unattainable from natural instruments and providing with ease intricate rhythmic patterns such as seven against six and five against nine.

Randall's *Mudgett: Monologues by a Mass Murderer* (1965) is an altogether more substantial work which shows a careful regard for the subtleties of timbre and articulation offered by digital synthesis. Only two of the projected four or five movements were completed, entitled 'Electronic Prelude' and 'Toronto'. The text purports to describe the events leading up to the execution of Herman Webster Mudgett, alias Dr H. M. Holmes, in Philadelphia's Moyamensing Prison in 1886. The first movement uses wholly synthetic sounds, rich textures being built up from overlapping sequences of sustained pitches, some displaying a gentle vibrato which varies in speed. An abrupt ending heralds the second movement which combined synthesized material with a pre-recorded tape of a soprano, the latter source, apart from simple editing and ' sections of double-tracking, being left untreated. The style is strikingly reminiscent of Schoenberg's expressionist period, in particular his *Pierrot Lunaire*, the connection being reinforced by a liberal use of *Sprechstimme*.

*Synthesism* (1969–70) by Barry Vercoe displays more than a passing affinity with the sounds and methods of organization employed by Stockhausen at Cologne during the 1950s. Streams of filtered noise are blended with sounds built up out of distinct tones, using a tuning principle which divides the octave into sixteen equal parts. The latter ratios, as a geometric series, are also used to control the organization of durations and attack rates. A specifically American influence on this expatriate New Zealand composer may be detected in the emphasis given to rapidly articulated sequences of pitches which display an angular contour through the use of random-number biasing in their selection.

*Synapse* (1976) for computer tape and viola, a later work realized at MIT, displays a sensitive regard for the performance characteristics of the live instrument. The synthetic material is carefully articulated to complement the wide-ranging affectations of the viola part whilst still retaining an independent identity.

Jonathan Harvey, one of the foremost members of the British avant-garde, realized a piece entitled *Time Points* during a year's period of study at Princeton, 1969–70. This study was conceived as a manipulation of a series of fixed timbres, articulated in terms of their pitch, duration, dynamics, and vibrato. Such an economy of means resulted in a clear and well-defined aural perspective which highlights the integrity of the chosen types of sound. A more recent work, *Mortuos Plango, Vivos Voco*, realized at IRCAM in 1980, is an important addition to the repertoire of works which employ digital signal-processing. The piece is based on the sounds of the great tenor bell at Winchester Cathedral, and the voice of Harvey's own son, Dominic, who was a chorister there from 1975 to 1980. Its title is taken from the inscription around the bell, the full text providing the source material for the boy. The pitch and time structure of the work is based entirely on the rich irregular harmonic spectrum of the bell. The eight sections are each based on one of the principal eight lowest partials. Chords are constructed from the repertoire of thirty-three partials, and modulations from one area of the spectrum to another are achieved by means of glissandi. Constant transformations between the sounds of the boy's voice and that of the bell act to unify the contrasting sources of material.

Developments in direct synthesis at Illinois have been influenced by the long-standing interest in computer-assisted composition inspired by the work of Lejaren Hiller. MUSIC-type programs have thus been treated as part of a much larger programme of research and development in musical composition.

Two composers, John Melby and Herbert Brün, have made particular use of computer-generated sounds. Melby's works display a clear affinity with the East Coast school of serialism. *Of Quiet Desperation* (1975) is characterized by rich textures and at times a strikingly lyrical treatment of melodic elements. *Concerto for Violin and Computer Tape* (1979) is an altogether more taut and dramatic work, paying due regard, as in the case of Vercoe's *Synapse*, to the expressive capabilities of the solo instrument.

Herbert Brün's compositions are somewhat enigmatic, for his highly individual ideas lie closer to those of John Cage than his earlier associates in Cologne and Munich. He has composed a number of works employing computer synthesis wholly or in part, including *Soniferous Loops* (1965), *Infrandibles* (1968), and a trilogy, *Dust, More Dust, and Dustiny* (1976–7). The last-mentioned group of works was composed and realized acoustically via a special synthesis program entitled SAWDUST, which permitted Brün to work with the smallest parts of wave forms, linking, mingling, or merging such components to create composite shapes. The latter were then treated either as periodic waves by means of cyclic repetition, or as passing moments of orientation in a predetermined process of gradual transformation.

Brün's decision to write his own synthesis routines rather than use a MUSIC program was indicative of a growing trend towards alternative approaches to digital sound-production, both in software and in hardware. The systems which resulted are generally more economical in their use of resources and in many instances interactive in operation. Their evolution has been influenced to some extent by the hybrid approaches which reached their zenith of development during the early 1970s. The principal antecedents of the latter have already been discussed, namely the RCA synthesizers and the digital sequencers added to voltage-controlled systems. The desire to explore more versatile methods of analogue device control naturally directed attention towards the possibilities of using the computer.

One of the earliest investigations into hybrid synthesis was initiated by James Gabura and Gustav Ciamaga at the University of Toronto during 1965–6, resulting in a real-time control system for two Moog voltage-controlled oscillators and two custom-built amplitude regulators, using an IBM 1620 computer. In 1967 Lejaren Hiller and James Beauchamp attempted to obtain sufficient funds from the National Science Foundation for the construction of an elaborate hybrid system at Illinois. Sadly, the application was turned down both on this occasion and again in 1969, when it was resubmitted by Hiller in a revised form subsequent to his move from Illinois to the State University of New York at Buffalo.

Interestingly it was Max Mathews himself who pioneered the first fully developed hybrid system in America at Bell Telephone Laboratories, unveiled in a paper delivered to a conference on 'Music and Technology' organized by UNESCO in Stockholm in 1970. This system, known as GROOVE (Generated Real-time Output Operations on Voltage-controlled Equipment), utilized a Honeywell DDP-224 computer which, for its time, was both fast and efficient. To this was attached a large auxiliary disk storage unit, a tape drive, and an interface for the analogue devices, incorporating twelve eight-bit and two twelve-bit digital-to-analogue converters, and sixteen relays for switching functions. An additional pair of converters provided the horizontal and vertical coordinates for a cathode ray display unit.

The latter facility provided the composer with a visual representation of his control instructions, as interpreted by the computer. The software generated a linear time-scale along the horizontal axis, the sensitivity of which could be varied by the composer. This span, typically ten seconds, acted as a basic timing-block or page, the screen automatically clearing at the end of each page to display the next. Up to ten different functions could be displayed without undue overcrowding.

The inclusion of a graphical monitoring system is of particular interest, for such a comprehensive visual representation of the device control functions, linked to a real-time generation system, brought the composer into intimate contact with the processes of synthesis. Device commands were entered via a conventional typewriter terminal, using a mnemonic code, the computer translating them into sequential control values for transmission to the analogue device interfaces. Several ancillary input devices were provided specifically for the purpose of varying selected device functions during the performance of a computed score of control data. These consisted of a twenty-four-note keyboard, four rotary knobs, and a three-dimensional joystick, the voltage outputs from the knobs and joystick being multiplexed to a single analogue-to-digital converter for registration by the computer. The keyboard was connected directly to a twenty-four-bit register, each key controlling the state of a uniquely assigned bit.

The output of control data to the studio interfaces was regulated via a variable-rate clock pulse generator. Since the computer acts as a control device in a hybrid system and not as a source of audio signals, adjustments to the clock rate vary the rate of change of events, not the nature of the events themselves. A useful parallel may be drawn with the shift-pulse control system of a simple digital sequencer.

The performance of a composition could be halted at any point by depressing a special key. The control functions were then examinable in detail via the graphical display, alterations could be made, and the instruction sequence run forwards or backwards for a short distance to assess the effects of such changes.

The analogue section of the system was notable for its modularity. In addition to a basic configuration of twelve voltage-controlled oscillators, seven voltage-controlled amplifiers, and two voltage-controlled filters, a wide variety of signal-processing functions could be selected from an array of seventy-two operational amplifiers mounted on plug-in cards. Fifty fine-resolution potentiometers were provided for the manual specification of constants associated with these amplifiers. Interconnections for the entire audio system were routed via a 500-element central patch-field.

Clearly, in a hybrid system, where the synthesis of sound is entirely dependent on analogue devices, little scope exists for developing input methods which are not specifically tied to the functional characteristics of the devices themselves. Nevertheless the ability to interact directly with the processes of sound generation, calling upon the enhanced control capabilities of a digital computer, creates a highly attractive environment for developing and evaluating compositional ideas.

The degree of interaction permitted varies considerably from one system design to another. In GROOVE, Mathews clearly intended the composer to work with traditional programming techniques in the first instance, any interactive modifications to be applied at a later stage. As the following extract from his paper delivered at Stockholm demonstrates, he viewed his system as an instrument which, once configured, could be freely influenced in its performance in the manner described above:

The composer does not personally play every note in a score, instead he influences (hopefully controls) the way in which the instrumentalists play the notes. The computer performer should not attempt to define the entire sound in real time. Instead the computer should contain a score and the performer should influence the way in which the score is played . . . The mode of conducting consists of turning knobs and pressing keys rather than waving a stick, but this is a minor mechanical detail . . . The program is basically a system for creating, storing, retrieving and editing functions of time. It allows the composition of time functions by turning knobs and pressing keys in real time; it stores time functions on the disk file; it retrieves the stored functions (the score), combines them with input functions (the conductor functions) in order to generate the control functions which drive the analogue synthesizer and it provides for facile editing of time functions via control of 'programme' time.

GROOVE remained operational for almost a decade, its fate being sealed by the withdrawal of the Honeywell computer towards the end of the 1970s. An emphasis on research rather than production has left a modest repertoire of works for posterity, the majority being composed by Joseph Olive and Emanuel Ghent. Perhaps the best-known piece to be realized via GROOVE is Ghent's *Phosphons*. This is essentially two pieces, a tape work which may be performed alone, and a light composition, stored as control instructions for a dimmer unit on perforated paper tape. In a full performance these two parts are synchronized with each other and with the movements of dancers, choreographed by Mimi Garrard.

Whilst Mathews was developing GROOVE at Bell Telephone Laboratories, another major hybrid system, MUSYS III, was under construction in London under the direction of Peter Zinovieff. For its time this system was perhaps the most attractive computer music facility available anywhere, whilst certainly being one of the cheapest in terms of capital costs. The venture was all the more remarkable for being a private one, well established before any useful financial contributions could be made from the profits of his commercial company, EMS.

Zinovieff started the construction of his studio in 1962, basing it initially on traditional, manually controlled sound-generation and processing devices. By the time this system had become operational in 1963, he was already carrying out preliminary investigations into the possibilities of voltage control, and over the next few years the studio was gradually expanded to accommodate new devices based on this design principle. This in turn generated a need for a more sophisticated system of operation, answered in the first instance by the construction of an elaborate sequencer during the period 1966–8. The project, however, was to prove a major disappointment, for the resultant device incorporated over 700 different controls, presenting the composer with formidable practical difficulties.

It was a suggestion by an associate, Mark Dowson, that the computer might provide a more viable method of sequential control which led to the purchase of first one, and then a second PDP 8 minicomputer, and the commencement of work on a hybrid synthesis system. By the end of 1969 most of the hardware interfaces had been designed and assembled by David Cockerell and Zinovieff, and within a few months MUSYS III was operational, using software specially written by Peter Grogono.

The decision to use two small computers instead of one larger machine allowed the control program to be divided into two sections, one concerned with the translation of higher-level arithmetic and logic instructions into time-ordered sequences of device commands, the other with the transference of these commands to the associated interfaces. A small disk unit provided an immediate data-storage facility, accessible by both computers.

The analogue system consisted of three types of devices, classified as follows: (i) devices equipped with integral digital-to-analogue converters; (ii) voltage-controlled devices which could be connected to the computing system via a set of general-purpose converters; and (iii) devices restricted to manual operation only.

In the first category the primary sound source consisted of a bank of 252 oscillators, divided into three groups of eighty four. Each group provided a seven-octave range of tempered pitches with the choice of sine or square wave forms, or a combination of both. Problems with frequency drift were overcome by a special tuning program which checked and adjusted the oscillator outputs relative to a reference crystal-clock frequency.

In addition to the oscillator bank, four digitally controlled sine/square oscillators were provided. Each of these could be manually switched between two frequency ranges, one covering the audio spectrum, the other providing control waves down to 0.01 Hz. A further oscillator provided an especially stable audio source, tuneable by the computer in three ranges, with a choice of a sine, square, or triangle wave form. Two digitally controlled noise sources were also included. The first consisted of a white-noise generator connected to a tuneable filter, the computer controlling the degree of coloration in terms of the centre frequency and bandwidth selected for the latter device. The second noise source was a percussion unit offering a varied palette of effects, generated by feeding pulses or bursts of noise into a network of resonating filters.

Powerful filtering facilities were provided in the form of a bank of sixty-four band-pass units tuned a semitone apart. Both the $Q$ and the through gain of each unit could be directly manipulated by the computers. The bank functioned in a number of modes. As a general timbral shaping facility it could be used to process audio signals either generated within the system, or supplied from an external device. In addition the bank could be transformed into an audio source in its own right by selecting the sharpest $Q$ settings and operating a special switch which supplied 'pink' noise to the inputs. Under these conditions the filters resonated to produce sine tones at their centre frequencies. Less acute $Q$ settings led to the generation of narrow noise bands. The bank could also be used as an analyser by monitoring the high $Q$ responses of each unit to applied signals and storing the information digitally on the disk. The line spectra thus extracted could then be studied either as a numerical print-out or as an oscilloscope display. Reversing the process permitted the use of vocoder techniques or, with skilful data-processing, a restricted form of cross-synthesis between sources. Additional filtering facilities were supplied in the form of a secondary bank of twelve filters spanning a six-octave range and two tuneable filter units, each offering a band-pass or band-reject mode response and a variable $Q$. Nine digitally controlled amplifiers providing up to 56 dB of attenuation were available for the general regulation of signal levels within the system. Envelope-shaping facilities were provided in the form of three simple attack/decay modulators and one special master envelope unit, the latter providing a more refined method of shaping. The attack/decay modulators provided exponential response characteristics, the timing of each segment being adjustable between an almost instantaneous 1/1000 sec and 1 sec in eight steps. The master envelope unit consisted of an integrator, used to control the gain of an associated amplifier. An ability to regulate the rate of integration in attack (positive) and decay (negative) modes via the computers allowed the generation of a wide variety of envelope characteristics.

Three other digitally controlled integrators, each generating a voltage function, and four digital-to-analogue converters provided the means for linking the computers with devices in the second category. These consisted of a small voltage-controlled synthesizer, known as the VCS 4, and four separate high-quality voltage-controlled oscillators, offering a choice of sawtooth or triangle wave forms. The synthesizer comprised six voltage-controlled oscillators, two envelope-shapers, two ring modulators, two tuneable filters, two spring reverberation units, four output amplifiers, and a pair of four-octave keyboards. A simple patching system allowed the connection of the computer interfaces listed above to the control break-points of selected device functions. In due course the VCS 4 was replaced by the much larger Synthi 100 synthesizer, a commercial product of EMS.

The third category of devices provided a variety of independent manually operated facilities, including ring modulators, filters, line amplifiers, limiters, reverberation units, and auxiliary coloured-noise sources. In addition both two- and four-track recording facilities were provided.

From the composer's point of view such a range of device characteristics afforded considerable flexibility. At one end of the scale the computer could be used to control every aspect of a synthesis task, using a comprehensive program of operational instructions entered via a teletypewriter. At the other, an entirely 'classical' approach was possible, operating devices by hand.

In designing MUSYS particular attention was paid to the problems of interaction with the computers themselves. In hybrid synthesis, it will be recalled, the primary task of the control system is to transfer information to and from the device interface registers at clock-controlled intervals. At the lowest, and most detailed, level of specification the composer has to supply the computer with a complete set of register values for each clock pulse. In MUSYS such information could be entered using either a conventional teletypewriter or a specially constructed console. The latter provided quick access to each of the device registers via a panel of push-buttons, the contents of the selected register being displayed as a binary pattern of lights. New values could then be transmitted direct to the register by depressing buttons to change the light states, the effects on the associated device function being immediately perceived.

Sequences of register values could be passed for storage or

retrieved via a spinwheel which increased or decreased the timing pulse counter setting according to the direction of rotation, the counter acting directly upon the internal data array pointers. Although this technique facilitated a step-by-step assembly of entire control programs, its primary value was as an interactive aid to composition at higher levels of device specification, involving the use of macro-programming statements entered via the teletypewriter. The device data generated from these statements could then be performed under computer control, and modified where necessary by stopping the program at appropriate points and switching to console mode. Once new values had been entered and the effects verified by running the program a short distance via the spinwheel, control could be restored to the computer.

During 1970 a number of composers attended a short inaugural studio course funded by the British Arts Council. These included Don Banks, Edward Cowie, Anthony Gilbert, Jonathan Harvey, David Lumsdaine, and Keith Winter. The commercial nature of this studio and a lack of institutional support, however, severely restricted access to others in subsequent years, and the hybrid system was dismantled in 1979. Nevertheless, a number of works were produced during the early part of the decade. In 1971 Harrison Birtwistle composed *Chronometer*, an extensive work based almost entirely on elaborate manipulation of clock sounds. The sophistication of the MUSYS system permitted Birtwistle to employ subtle processes of timbral shaping and transformation, focusing attention on the inherent variety of characteristics which may be derived from such sources. Hans Werner Henze used the studio on a number of occasions, completing one all-electronic work, *Glass Music*, and tape parts for two orchestral works, *Violin Concerto No. 2* (1971) and *Tristan* (1973). In the *Concerto* the tape part is restricted to a recitation which undergoes a number of transformations in a manner reminiscent of Berio. In *Tristan* a similar treatment of a reading of part of the Tristan story is combined with large blocks of electronic sound, the latter being used to heighten the tension of the orchestral climaxes.

A third major hybrid system was completed at the Elektronmusikstudion (EMS), Stockholm, in 1972. Work had been initiated as early as 1964 under the direction of Karl-Birger Blomdahl, the newly appointed head of music for the corporation. His premature death in 1968 forced Swedish Radio to reconsider their commitment, and after negotiations with the Government the project continued in association with the Ministry of Education.

The original brief was most exacting, demanding (1) an instantaneous response from the computing system, (2) that the control system should be so simple that virtually no composer should encounter difficulties using it, and (3) that the quality of synthesis should meet the highest specifications. No expense was spared in designing devices to meet the last requirement. The stability and accuracy of the oscillator bank, for example, is second to none.

All the necessary interfaces for the application of digital control were build into the devices themselves. External control facilities such as sliders and knobs were completely dispensed with, a special numerical 'dialling' system being substituted for manual operation of the studio. Each device function is associated with a set of split metal contacts consisting of pairs of flat metal plates inlaid with a number, for example:

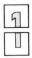

**Figure** 63

By means of a metal brush a numerical value may be selected and transmitted to the associated interface by shorting the contacts of suitable combinations of digits. The system provides a visual verification of the selection by illuminating the values from underneath. The numbers may be changed by using the brush to activate new digits column by column, the old values being automatically cancelled.

Connections and disconnections between devices are made via a similar system of shorting studs, repeated brush strokes switching the selections on and off alternately. The connection states are indicated by a series of repeater visual display banks mounted over each of the device groups, individual lights being allocated for each possible connection which may be made to and from the units concerned.

It is thus possible to play the studio in real time by manually selecting the states of device-control functions and interconnections, and experimenting with static sound building blocks in a manner not unlike that achievable via the button panel in MUSYS.

The range of facilities provided is extensive, comprising twenty-four oscillators with a choice of seven different wave forms, a noise generator offering both 'pink' and 'white' characteristics, two third-octave filer units of twenty-eight channels each, three ring modulators, two amplitude modulators, four reverberation units, two general-purpose amplifiers, and four output-channel amplifiers.

The studio first became operational in 1966 using an elementary digital recording system which allowed step by step sequences of device settings to be assembled on magnetic tape. Such a facility was both cumbersome and prone to errors which were difficult to correct. The first steps towards the provision of computer control were taken in 1968 when land-lines were installed to connect the studio to an external machine in the University of Stockholm.

This situation was far from ideal, for the operating facilities were as remote as those commonly endured by early users of MUSIC direct-synthesis programs. A journey across the city was necessary to punch out specifications on cards, for execution at the convenience of the computing centre. The administrative changes which occurred during the same year, however, led to the injection of new funds, and the placing of an order for a PDP 15 computer from the Digital Equipment Corporation. This package was installed late in 1970, and the first software package, EMS 1, became available for use in the spring of 1972.

EMS 1 provided the composer with a powerful and easy-to-use specification language. In its original version, however, it suffered from one major limitation, for no provision was made for entering or modifying data direct from the studio console. Entire sections of a piece had thus to be entered in the form of a complete series of programming statements with no opportunity for interaction except by using the teletypewriter or VDU, any alterations requiring a complete recompilation before the effects could be monitored aurally. Later EMS programs are more flexible in this respect.

The remoteness of Stockholm from the rest of Europe has tended to restrict the production of works to Scandinavian composers. Works by Lars-Gunner Bodin, Knut Wiggen, and Tamas Ungvary are amongst the most significant to emerge from this studio. Wiggen's works, such as *Resa* and *Sommarmorgan*, are notable for their rich and sensitively shaped textures. As the director of the computer-controlled studio, he was instrumental in stimulating the development of composing programs such as his MUSIC BOX which accept musical ideas in the form of mathematical procedures or rules and generate corresponding control data for the devices.

Ungvary developed this aspect further, producing his own composing program COTEST in the mid 1970s. His *Axonel II* for flutes and computer-generated sounds (1978) is based on two primary ideas: progression from the extreme polarities of electronic and instrumental music towards a homogeneous musical unity, and development of the flute's inner tension, which gives rise to stuttering and crying, towards a more lyrical and ornamental mode of expression. A more recent program, IMPAC, written by Michael Hinton, has proved especially suitable for interactive working, building up ideas from simple components to create sound complexes which may be easily modified and juxtaposed.

The use of the computer as a tool for generating data structures from higher orders of compositional specifications may be traced back to the pioneering work of Lejaren Hiller and Iannis Xenakis in the late 1950s. Both composers were concerned primarily with the production of printed material for translation by hand into conventionally notated scores, ready for instrumental performance. Their interests in electronic music, however, provided a natural link with the sphere of digital sound synthesis, and led to a fostering of techniques which combined both aspects of computer composition.

Hiller gained some notoriety for his collaboration with John Cage over the production of material for *HPSCHD* (1967–9). Many of the composing sub-routines and processes used by Hiller in this work were derivatives of those used first in the *Illiac Suite* (1956) and subsequently in the *Computer Cantata* (1963). In the *Illiac Suite*, Hiller, assisted by Leonard Isaacson, experimented with a number of stylistic models. The first movement is concerned with the production of tonal melody and harmony in two- and four-part counterpoint. The second movement restricts the latter element entirely to note-against-note principles of organization, highlighting the diatonic nature of the interweaving melodic lines. In the third movement a more progressive style is suggested by using the computer to manipulate note rows. Finally, in the fourth movement a more radical idiom is created by allowing probability theory, rather than structural rules of tonal and rhythmic organization, to determine the evolution of the material. The *Cantata*, composed in association with Robert Baker, was his first piece to employ computer-generated sounds, used in association with more traditional electronic and natural sound sources, including the voice. The specifications of pitches, durations, amplitudes, and timbres were all determined via random-probability programs, operating on the distribution of pitches contained in a short extract from *Three Places in New England* by Charles Ives.

In *HPSCHD* similar techniques were applied to extracts from piano works by Mozart, Beethoven, Chopin, Schumann, Gottschalk, Busoni, Schoenberg, Cage, and Hiller. Cage had become preoccupied with the use of chance elements in musical composition, in particular those which could be derived from principles described in the ancient Chinese book of *I Ching*. Further material was derived by running a program to perform twenty realizations of Mozart's *Musical Dice Game*.

The work is of indeterminate length, from one to seven harpsichords and one to fifty-one tapes of computer-generated sounds. The score consists of the tapes, and seven solo parts for the players, each of these elements lasting twenty minutes. In performance *HPSCHD* lasts a minimum of twenty minutes, with no upper limit on its maximum duration, for the performers are at liberty to start any solo or any tape at any time. In its recorded version computer-generated instructions are provided for control of the settings of a conventional hi-fi stereo set, involving the listener in the act of performance.

A special synthesis program was constructed using routines adapted from Mathews' MUSIC IV B. Each note specification consisted of a simple timbre selected from a choice of sine-, sawtooth-, or square-wave characteristics, an attack time, a decay time, an overall duration, and a maximum amplitude, all these details being supplied by the composing program. Hiller used the same basic system for the production of computer sounds for another piece, *Algorithms I* (1968), scored for flute, clarinet, bassoon, trumpet, harp, violin, cello, bass, percussion, and tape.

The achievements of Xenakis in the field of computer music

are perhaps better known, at least in Europe. His use of digital sound-generation techniques is a relatively recent development, interest in more active uses of the computer being hitherto directed towards the manipulation of visual effects, including laser beams.

His critical attitude towards the electronic medium as a whole is revealed in an essay entitled *New Proposals in Microsound Structure*, first published in 1968 and subsequently added to his extensive treatise, *Formalized Music*.

Since the war all 'electronic' music has [also] failed, in spite of the big hopes of the fifties, to pull electro-acoustic music out of its cradle of the so-called electronic pure sounds produced by frequency generation. . . . Only when the 'pure' electronic sounds were framed by other 'concrete' sounds which were much richer and much more interesting (thanks to Edgard Varèse, Pierre Schaeffer and Pierre Henry), could electronic music become really powerful. The most recent attempts to use the flower of modern technology, computers coupled to converters, have shown that in spite of some relative successes, the sonorous results are even less interesting than those made ten years ago in the classic electro-acoustic studios by means of frequency generators, filters, modulators, and reverberation units.

Xenakis first began experimenting with the computer as a compositional aid in 1956, using an IBM 7090. The first fruits of its labours, *ST/10-1, 080262*, a work for instrumental ensemble, received its first performance on 24 May 1962 at the headquarters of IBM France. The program used to prepare this work, written in FORTRAN, embodied a mechanical version of theories first explored in an earlier work, *Achorripsis*, for twenty-one instruments (1956–7). These were based on the use of a minimal structure to control the generation of data according to the laws of probability. Factors such as the time of occurrence, the type of timbre, the choice of instrument, the gradient of glissando, the duration, and the dynamic of each component sounds are thus governed by large-scale determinants, which bias the probability weightings used in the data-generation process.

Several compositions were produced using modifications of the ST/10 program, including *ST/48-1, 240162* for large orchestra, *Atrées* for ten soloists, and *Morsima-Amorsima* for piano, violin, cello, and double bass, all three pieces being completed in 1962. During the 1970s Xenakis worked primarily at the Centre d'Études de Mathématique et Automatique Musicales

(C.E.M.A.Mu.), Paris, producing such multi-media works as *Polytope de Cluny* (1972–4) and *Diatope* (1977), each composed and controlled in performance via the computer, using two special programs prepared in collaboration with Cornelia Colyer. *Polytope de Cluny* is an automated light/sound composition employing 600 electronic flashes, three 2-watt lasers, and seven-track electronic tape, first staged in the Cluny Museum, Paris. *Diatope* similarly employs 1600 electronic flashes, four lasers, and twelve-track tape, originally commissioned by the Georges Pompidou Centre, Paris, of which IRCAM is part. Sound localization and the flash and laser events in both pieces are controlled by associated digital tapes.

Towards the end of the decade Xenakis turned more specifically to computer-generated sounds preparing a series of programs under the generic title of UPIC with Guy Medique at C.E.M.A.Mu. This developed into a long-term project which has undergone a number of revisions in terms of both hardware and software as the years have advanced. The initial phase resulted in a suite of three programs hosted on the Centre's own Solar 16-65 minicomputer. The first of these, UPIC-A, provided a basic pedagogical tool for the synthesis and study of sounds. UPIC-B allowed externally generated material to be input to the system for analysis, using an A-to-D converter. Auxiliary tape and disk storage facilities were used to assemble a comprehensive library of digitized sound sources, each carefully catalogued according to its acoustical components. The addition of a graphics unit permitted the composer to display these functions and alter their content interactively. The latter facility was taken a stage further with UPIC-C, which incorporated an advanced facility for kinetic picture manipulation. In common with other software synthesis systems of the period none of these versions could operate in real time. The solution lay in the development of custom-designed hardware, which was introduced in stages as the necessary technology became available. By the end of the 1980s UPIC had been transformed into a portable and completely interactive system of considerable versatility, and the functional characteristics of this more recent version will be returned to in due course.

Gottfried Michael Koenig began investigating aspects of computer-aided composition at Utrecht during the early 1960s, producing two programs which generate printed data: PROJECT 1 (1964) and PROJECT 2 (1970). The purchase of a PDP 15 computer by the Institute of Sonology permitted him to transfer his work from the main university installation to more congenial surroundings, and made it possible for others to participate in a broader-based programme of research into computer music.

PROJECT 1 was closely modelled on the traditional principles of serial composition and offered only a limited measure of control over the processes of data generation. Like the ST programs of Xenakis it was conceived solely as a personal composing system. PROJECT 2, in contrast, was specifically intended for general use, offering a far more flexible range of facilities. This program incorporates a set of probability functions which may be utilized to control the selection of numerical values from a table of possibilities via a random-number generator. Various types of weighting are offered. A function called ALEA, for example, will make entirely random selections from a table of values, each element once chosen remaining eligible for reselection. Another, called SERIES, will remove values from the table after selection to prevent repetitions occurring. When all the available elements have been used up the function may be programmed with a fresh copy of the table. A different type of selection procedure is provided by a function called TENDENCY. This allows the composer to apply 'masks' to the random-number generator, dynamically adjusting the range of values from which it may make choices.

The selection and control of functions and their associated data tables and the production of musical score characteristics from their output is carried out via three sub-programs concerned respectively with the three basic parameters of pitch, time, and dynamics.

Koenig used PROJECT 1 to generate two instrumental works: *Project 1—Version 1* (1966) and *Project 1—Version 3* (1967), both for instrumental ensemble. Having launched PROJECT 2 with a piece entitled *Uebung fuer Klavier* (1970), he commenced work on a number of improvements to the software, extending the range of options available and adding facilities for interactive specification. At the same time he encouraged other researchers at Utrecht, who were working more specifically upon techniques of digital synthesis, to adapt their systems to accept input specifications directly from his programs. In due course a link was established with VOSIM, a hardware system developed by Stan Tempelaars between 1975 and 1978 from a software model formulated by Werner Kaegi during 1973–4. This latter system is significant not only for its use of mixed digital technology, but also for its unique principles of operation.

Kaegi, as a specialist in phonetics, was especially interested in the production of quasi-speech sounds. His researches showed that a considerable number of these could be generated by the skilful manipulation of a pair of oscillators, programmed to generate pulsed trains of single waves. Although the control specifications for these trains are necessarily complex, the basic principles of operation are straightforward to understand. The wave characteristic itself consists of a sine-squared function, the primary variables being the duration of each cycle and the delay before its repetition.

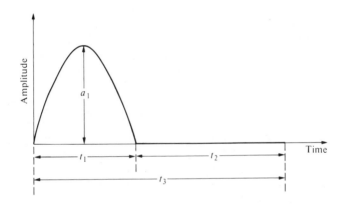

**Figure 64**

The fundamental pitch of the output is determined by $t_3$, this being the sum of the period of the wave pulse itself, $t_1$, and the delay before its repetition, $t_2$. In addition a strong formant is generated at the frequencies $1/t_2$. The nature of the sounds thus generated becomes of particular interest when the time constants are dynamically varied. Random variation of $t_2$ will introduce significant noise elements, variation of $t_1$ whilst $t_3$ is kept constant produces diphthongs, and progressive changes to $t_3$ will result in glissandi. Control over the amplitude of the sounds merely requires adjustments to $a_1$.

Other digital synthesis systems developed at Utrecht during the 1970s include PILE (Paul Berg, 1975–6), POD (Barry Truax,

1972–5), and FMS (W. Matthews, 1976). The latter system is of a mixed digital type, using the PDP 15 to control a bank of FM generators. PILE and POD are both software packages generating sounds entirely within the computer for conversion by external D-to-A converters.

Berg has been particularly interested in the realization of generalized composing rules rather than the exercise of direct control over acoustical characteristics such as frequency, intensity, and duration, and this is reflected in the process-orientated nature of the input language for PILE. The POD system, in contrast, whilst providing for the application of compositional rules, deliberately directs the composer towards the manipulation of acoustic parameters. Debts to both Xenakis and Koenig are evident in Truax's use of stochastic procedures and tendency masks to generate and control the production of data, the more detailed the specifications the more predictable the final result. The latter characteristic encourages what is known as a 'top down' approach to composition, where the large-scale determinants are established first and the inner details supplied at a later stage.

The POD system (the title is an acronym for POisson Distribution) consists of a number of separate programs specifically designed for the smaller computer. These were developed over a number of years, first at Utrecht, and then at Simon Fraser University, Vancouver, and at Stockholm. After a preliminary program, POD 4, three main versions, POD 5, POD 6, and POD 7, were created, each offering the composer a different range of synthesis facilities.

Both POD 5 and POD 6 operate as interactive, real-time synthesis programs. In POD 5 sounds are generated additively by scanning pre-stored wave tables. In POD 6 synthesis is achieved entirely via frequency modulation following the principles established by John Chowning. Apart from the wave-form tables the control data values in both cases are not explicitly supplied by the composer except in the rarest of circumstances. These are generated by the random-probability routines in response to higher-level compositional specifications.

In contrast, POD 7 sacrifices the benefits of real-time synthesis for the advantage of more refined sonological specifications made possible by calculating all the sample values first and then passing them to the converters. The availability of all three programs as subsets of a complete system allows the composer to choose freely between them according to the nature of his work.

The limitations of software synthesis for real-time operation were partly overcome by the development of a version of the POD system for the Stockholm Studio in 1978 which transfers the processes of sound generation to the analogue devices, leaving the computer with the less demanding task of calculating control data.

*Nautilus*, for solo percussion and four computer-synthesized soundtracks, composed by Truax in 1976, provides an impressive example of the versatility of the POD system. The use of tendency masks to control the frequency and density of FM components leads to subtle shadings of texture and a strong sense of organic development within the sounds themselves. Spatial location receives particular attention, the elements being subjected to rotation in both directions. The careful addition of reverberation leads to an illusion of nearness when movement is rapid and distance when the images become almost stationary.

The live part shows some affinity with the principles employed in Stockhausen's *Zyklus*, for solo percussion. The performer stands in the centre of four families of percussion instruments (drums, woods, hard metals, soft metals) and is free to choose between eight available score parts, the only constraint being a requirement to alternate the direction each part follows around two sides of the instrumental layout. The synchronization between tape and live parts is thus intuitively controlled by the performer.

A more recent work by Truax, *Aerial*, for French horn and tape (1980), achieves a particularly strong sense of integration between the live and recorded material. A sense of association with the imagery of natural landscapes is achieved by means of sound clusters which suggest the shapes and colours of mountains, clouds, and lakes.

A similar feeling of identification with nature through sound is evoked in the works of Jean Piché. *Heliograms* (1978) realized via POD, is a representation of four solar photographs taken outside the earth's atmosphere. An analogue mix-down of thirty-two syntheses incorporating both additive and FM techniques results in a work of powerful proportions, all the more remarkable when the modesty of the computing resources is taken into account.

By the beginning of the 1970s digital technology was at last advancing to the point where the construction of hardware digital oscillators and signal processors became a practical proposition. Max Mathews, in describing his GROOVE system at the 1970 UNESCO conference in Stockholm, accurately predicted the coming of such devices although he could scarcely have envisaged the scale and speed of the developments which were to follow. In the same way that the exclusiveness of the 'classical' analogue studios was largely to disappear as a result of the development of the mass-produced voltage-controlled synthesizer, so the world of computer music was soon to leave the enclosed environment of the academic institution and become accessible to all via a second and far more substantial flowering of the commercial sector, this time in the digital domain.

As a result of this ever growing accessibility the identity of key works of lasting importance has become obscured by the wealth of output (good, bad, and indifferent) which now pours forth from systems ranging from the most modest home synthesizer to the largest university studio. The sheer pace of technical development has presented major problems for many composers, for the quantity of new information which has to be absorbed every time a new system or device becomes available can prove a major impediment to the creative process. As will be seen in due course the need for better man/machine communications on a level which encourages rather than hinders the creative process was to become a major issue during the 1980s and early 90s, and important progress is now being made in this area. Tracking the evolution of the technology itself over the intervening period is both fascinating and rewarding, not least in preparing the ground for any future appraisal of its artistic significance. Despite the rapid pace and diversity of developments distinct trends can be identified and followed through their various stages of evolution, and it is to these that attention is now turned.

# 11 New Horizons in Digital Technology

In the preceding chapter it was shown how the evolution of the commercial computer from the early 1950s to the late 60s can be divided into three important phases: (1) first-generation computers based on valve technology, (2) second-generation computers based on transistor technology, and (3) third-generation computers based on integrated circuits.

As part of the underlying trend towards increased power and reduced component size the design of faster and more compact memory banks assumed particular importance in this context. Second-generation computers still required separate components for each memory location, and although the initial savings in space and cost brought about by the move from valves to transistors were clearly impressive it was still necessary to use several thousand individual parts to assemble even a relatively small memory bank. The subsequent introduction of technology which could integrate a number of circuits within a wafer of silicon led to the fabrication of first tens, then hundreds, and eventually thousands of logic gates as part of a single moulding, occupying no more than a square centimetre or so on a printed circuit board. Within less than twenty years the capacity of a single memory chip was to expand from just a few hundred to more than a million bytes.

Integrated circuits were soon to revolutionize many other aspects of computer design, ranging from the interfaces required to control the flow of instructions and data to and from peripheral devices to the operational heart of the system itself, the central processing unit. Here the fabrication of suitable chips proved to be a much greater challenge, for unlike the ordered arrays of gates required for a memory bank a CPU involves highly complex arrangements of logic circuits and cross-connections which cannot easily be reproduced within the physical constraints of a single wafer of silicon. For this reason the CPUs of many early third generation computers were only partially integrated, based on a network of chips each concerned with a particular subset of the processor architecture.

By the end of the 1960s a number of chip manufacturers were turning their attention to the development of a complete computer, or at least its operational core, within a single silicon chip. The functional characteristics required for such a device to qualify as a true microprocessor became a matter of heated debate but some measure of agreement was reached over the following minimum criteria: It should be able to (1) process both text and numbers in conventional digital code, (2) directly address a memory bank of sufficient capacity to hold both a program and its data, (3) provide programmers with a set of instructions sufficient in scope to carry out a significant number of the standard logical and arithmetic operations associated with a conventional computer, and (4) be capable of communicating with a variety of input and output devices.

A microprocessor, thus, has to be able to function as a general purpose computer when linked in a straightforward manner to a conventional memory bank and standard peripherals such as a disk drive, an alphanumeric keyboard, and a visual display unit or printer. In practice many microprocessors have been widely used for applications of a far more restricted nature in functional terms, for example the dedicated control of a specific manufacturing process or such routine aspects of everyday life as the management of traffic signals, car engines, or washing machines. In such situations the software to control the microprocessor is highly specific, and is often stored permanently in an associated read-only memory chip or ROM. A number of applications, including audio processing, have justified the fabrication of microprocessors with very special characteristics, and some of these will be looked at more closely in due course.

The first true microprocessor, known as the 4004, was manufactured by Intel in 1972. By today's standards this device is extremely slow and hard to program, difficulties in the latter context being compounded by the fact that only four bits of data or programming code can be handled at a time. The 4004 was quickly followed by the 8008, which was not only much faster but also able to address eight-bit data blocks directly. By adding power supplies, memory boards, and simple input/output interfaces, pioneers were thus able to assemble the first experimental self-contained microcomputers. These developments received a major boost in 1974 when Intel brought out a new microprocessor known as the 8080, which was notable for both a marked improvement in processing speed and also a more powerful instruction set. The expanding market for microprocessors encouraged some entrepreneurs to start retailing do-it-yourself microcomputer kits, thus stimulating interest from the public at large in the potential of digital technology and thereby establishing a new pastime as a home computer hobbyist. Software support was almost non-existent at this stage, and as a result prospective users were generally left with little more than a tabulation of the basic instruction set and their ingenuity. The formation of self-help groups and the establishment of the first magazines for computer hobbyists, however, soon stimulated a demand for both system and applications software.

By 1975 most of the major digital component manufacturers were adding microprocessors to their product ranges. Motorola, for example, introduced the 6800 processor, Zilog introduced the Z-80, a much improved derivative of the 8080, and MOS Technology introduced the 6501, forerunner of its highly successful derivative, the 6502. Some firms, such as Texas Instruments, concentrated on producing their own versions of popular processors such as the 8080, with the result that a market which was already becoming competitive became fiercely so, driving prices steadily downwards. Intersil set an interesting precedent by producing a microprocessor which emulated the traditionally fabricated central processing unit used in Digital Equipment Corporation's first minicomputer, the PDP 8, thus starting a new line of attack on the more traditional sectors of the computer market.

The full impact of this new technology was quickly felt as in quick succession three companies marketed the first fully packaged off-the-shelf commercial microcomputers, complete with operating system, applications software, and at least one language compiler. These were the Commodore PET, based on a 6502 processor, the Radio Shack TRS-80, based on a Z-80 microprocessor, and the Apple II, based on a 6502. This last machine was destined to become one of the most important computers for music applications, and was still in general use long after both the TRS-80 and the PET had faded into obscurity. Other companies soon entered the market, notably Atari with their 400 and 800 series, once again based on the 6502 microprocessor. The latter machines emulated many of the functional characteristics of the Apple II and marked the start of a protracted and intense rivalry which was to prove of particular significance to the music industry.

Eight-bit microprocessors dominated the microcomputer industry until the early 1980s when the first sixteen-bit versions became commercially available. The processes of transition to these new architectures were to span a number of years, for in many circumstances the limitations of the older technology in terms of speed of operation and the management of instructions and data were outweighed by considerations such as low cost and the availability of tried and tested software. None the less, for applications demanding more processor power such as mathematically intensive data processing, high definition graphics, or music quality audio, it quickly became apparent that the new generation of microprocessors unquestionably held the key to the future.

The first sixteen-bit microprocessor to be manufactured in significant quantities was the LSI 11, which appeared in 1978, mannufactured by Western Digital. This product, like the eight-bit Intersil chip described earlier, emulates the central processing unit of a DEC minicomputer, in this case the highly successful PDP 11. In 1979 Intel introduced the 8086, a sixteen-bit version of their 8080, and within a matter of months Zilog followed suit with a sixteen-bit Z-8000, matched in turn by Motorola with a sixteen-bit 68000.

By 1980 desktop microcomputers were being manufactured in significant quantities for a market still to a large extent dominated by educational and research institutions but now starting to expand rapidly in the domestic sector as the result of a growing number of home users world-wide. The industrial and commercial sectors, however, had yet to be tempted away from the products of traditional computer manufacturers, who were naturally keen to preserve the considerable profit margins associated with the sale of large multi-user mainframe systems. This polarization of objectives between the old established companies and their new rivals was upset dramatically in 1981 when the computing giant IBM entered the microcomputer market with its first personal computer known as the IBM PC, based on a specially modified version of the 8086 known as the 8088. Despite a number of operational shortcomings the PC gradually secured an increasing share of the microcomputer market, its association with the name of IBM providing the necessary pedigree to attract potential purchasers from all quarters.

The steady development of the IBM PC during the 1980s was to have a significant impact on other microcomputer manufacturers. Many smaller companies were forced either to cease production altogether or turn instead to the manufacture of cheap clones of the PC itself, a development which IBM chose largely to ignore, confident in the appeal of its own products. Notable exceptions to this trend were companies such as Apple, Atari, and Commodore, who managed to retain and develop their own share of this market with new ranges of microcomputers offering highly distinctive features. One sphere which showed particular resilience to the growing influence of the IBM PC was the games and general entertainment sector, where budget-priced machines such as the Sinclair Spectrum (based on a Z-80) and the Commodore 64 and 128 series (based on the 6502) maintained their position as market leaders, providing the initial training ground for countless computer enthusiasts, including a significant number who took a specific interest in music applications. IBM attempted to penetrate this lucrative sector with a version of the PC known as the PC Junior, but this product was not a marketing success and was soon discontinued.

A unique collaboration between the British Broadcasting Corporation and the microcomputer manufacturer Acorn resulting in the BBC Micro is of some interest in this context. This machine, based on the 6502 microprocessor, dominated the UK educational market during the early 1980s, its exposure via the medium of television serving to stimulate widespread interest in computing amongst the public at large. Outside the UK, however, this machine remained almost unknown. Perhaps the most striking example of the differences which can occur between a national as opposed to an international market in this context is the situation which developed in Japan, where the market became dominated by indigenous electronics and computer conglomerates such as NEC, with only limited penetration from foreign manufacturers such as Apple or IBM.

While the microcomputer industry was coming of age parallel developments were taking place in the field of computer music technology. One of the first designs for a mixed digital system, VOCOM, was produced by David Cockerell and Peter Eastty for

Peter Zinovieff at his EMS studio in England in 1972. This consisted of a bank of digital oscillators controlled by the same PDP 8 minicomputers used to run MUSYS. As early prototype devices these oscillators had to be built using discrete components. The advent of the microprocessor, however, soon led to a more streamlined approach to the design of such hardware.

In 1975 John Appleton, Sydney Alonso, and Cameron Jones, working at Dartmouth College, New Hampshire, produced the prototype for an all-digital synthesizer based entirely on a network of integrated circuits and an integral microprocessor. In 1976 the New England Digital Corporation was established to manufacture the system, known as the Synclavier, a venture which was to prove a lasting commercial success with the release of a series of upgrades and new versions over the years, leading to many improvements in terms of both its functional characteristics and also the quality of sound production.

The main synthesis engine of the original Synclavier consists of a bank of timbre generators, each providing a choice of twenty-four sinusoidal harmonics for each voice. The number of voices available depends on the version, the smallest providing eight and the largest upwards of thirty-two. The user can configure these generators directly using a push-button console, thus requiring no detailed knowledge of the programming code used internally by the synthesizer. Although the designers originally intended the Synclavier to be primarily a performance instrument interest in the use of proprietary software for voice editing and programmed control led quickly to the addition of a VDU and an associated alphanumeric keyboard. Disk storage facilities for programs and data were initially restricted to a single floppy disk unit, but these were subsequently expanded to include a hard disk drive offering a much larger capacity.

The control system is based around a specially designed sixteen-bit microprocessor known as ABLE and an associated memory bank, the latter being used primarily as a multi-channel sequencer for the storage of performance data. The primary input device for registering and performing sound events consists of a five-octave keyboard which may be split functionally into two sections, each controlling a separate voice or group of voices. Envelope characteristics for each key selection are entered via push-buttons with a facility to program both the overall envelope and also the envelope of individual harmonics for each note.

Fine tunings of pitches, time constants, and amplitudes are sp̃-
fied via a continuously adjustable knob, coupled to a group ̣
function buttons and a digital display which gives a numericar
reading of the current settings. One or a pair of foot-pedals may
optionally be connected as auxiliary performance aids, one regulating volume, the other any other selected variable, for example
the overall envelope duration. A touch-ribbon controller permitting continuous pitch variations is also available as an alternative
to the music keyboard, copying a principle first explored in the
Ondes Martenot. As an alternative to additive synthesis the
Synclavier offers frequency-modulation facilities for each voice. A
very distinctive FM timbral characteristic is generated by a special option which allows four voices to track each other, slightly
mistuned.

The design of the Synclavier from the first to the most recent
versions has been heavily influenced by the requirements of the
commercial music sector, a trend encouraged by a marketing
decision taken at an early stage to secure its status as an expensive up-market product, geared specifically to the needs of the
most ambitious and affluent rock and pop musicians. Back in the
1970s, however, as the first commercial synthesizer of its type, it
was to prove a major focus of attention for the computer music
community as a whole, not least for those working with software
synthesis systems in institutions, who quickly recognized the significance of an all-digital product which permitted the generation
of a large repertory of music material instantly, rather than waiting minutes or even hours for the results of software synthesis
programs. More recent versions of the Synclavier include
improved facilities for the display and manipulation of synthesis
data such as wave-shapes and envelope characteristics, and a signal processing facility for externally generated sound material,
input using an A-to-D converter.

Although much of the underlying software is hidden from the
normal user, access to some of the basic programming facilities
allowed the composer Joel Chadabe to develop a special interactive performance program known as PLAY in association with
Roger Meyers in 1978. This permits a performer to superimpose
continuous variations on a pre-programmed sequence of events,
fed to the synthesizer as control information from a specially prepared disk file. For his own purposes Chadabe added two capacitive field detectors, modern equivalents of the Thérémin sensors,

control devices, the distance of his hands from the detectors regulating the course of the performance program. In 1986 New England Digital started manufacturing a direct-to-disk multi-track recorder, which when combined with a Synclavier creates a sophisticated digital recording and sound synthesis system.

The Synclavier was soon to have a major rival. Two Australians, Peter Vogel and Kim Ryrie, having established a company for manufacturing special effects boxes for film studios in the mid-1970s, quickly turned their attention to the construction of a prototype audio processor known as the QASAR M8, completed in 1978, leading in turn to a fully developed digital synthesizer known as the Fairlight Computer Music Instrument or CMI, available from 1979 onwards.

In the Fairlight, synthesis from first principles using mathematically generated wave data is replaced by sampling technology, where externally generated sounds are digitized and their patterns stored in memory for processing and re-synthesis. The patterns can either be loaded from a library of sources consisting of a series of voice module cards supplied by the manufacturers, or sampled directly from an external sound source via an A-to-D converter. The early versions of this synthesizer are controlled by a pair of standard eight-bit 6800 microprocessors, but more recent versions have been substantially re-engineered to take advantage of the more powerful sixteen-bit 68000 family of microprocessors. Two six-octave keyboards, an interactive graphics unit, and an alphanumeric keyboard are provided as standard features, with the option of adding up to three foot-pedals as auxiliary performance aids. Sound specifications such as the control of dynamics or timbre may either be entered in a mnemonic code using the alphanumeric keyboard, or edited interactively on screen in graphical form using the light pen. It is also possible to use the latter facility to draw wave-shapes directly, which then may be freely combined and shaped dynamically to generate more complex timbres.

As is the case with the Synclavier the user is heavily insulated from the processor functions by a hidden layer of proprietary software. At first sight this design approach, which was to become a common characteristic of many commercial synthesizers, has distinct advantages since it forces manufacturers to provide the user with a comprehensive set of well documented tools. However, this lack of direct access to the synthesis engine itself, particularly in the case of sophisticated and expensive up-market systems such as the Synclavier and the Fairlight, has often proved a source of some frustration especially for those users who have come to expect a similar degree of programming flexibility to that afforded by traditional software synthesis systems. These drawbacks apart, both the Synclavier and the Fairlight were to prove of the utmost significance in shaping the development of the synthesizer industry during the 1980s, the techniques of additive and FM synthesis in the former and sampling in the latter providing the basis for three of the most important synthesis methods in use to the present day.

Four other commercial synthesizers dating back to the late 1970s merit consideration in the current context: the PPG Wave 2.2 from Germany, and the Crumar General Development System (GDS), the Con Brio ADS 200, and the Synergy from the USA. The PPG Wave 2.2 is a digital synthesizer with a particularly extensive array of control facilities for direct programming by the user. The data for the oscillator wavetables is selected from a library of almost 2000 wave-forms stored in a special ROM. Once loaded these wave-forms can be manipulated using a bank of control knobs which allow the specification of amplitude envelopes and frequency and filtering modifications in a manner which closely corresponds to the procedures used to operate a conventional voltage-controlled synthesizer. Direct control of the digital functions such as voice selection and loading of data into memory is accomplished via a simple keypad, and a five octave music keyboard serves as the primary performing interface. In due course the PPG Wave 2.2 was superseded by the PPG Waveterm, a much improved version which like the Fairlight allows the direct sampling of externally generated sounds via an A-to-D converter as an alternative to the factory supplied wavetable bank. The computer interface is also upgraded with the inclusion of a graphics screen which can be used to edit and display sound parameters.

The Con Brio provides a pair of five octave keyboards, a video display monitor, and a panel of push-buttons and rotary knobs for the entry of timbral and dynamic specifications. A typewriter terminal or VDU may be added as an optional extra, allowing operational details to be programmed in the form of a mnemonic code. The ability to migrate freely between gestural and strictly notated control over device functions is a particularly distinctive feature, recalling the flexibility of a system such as MUSYS.

The GDS and the Synergy started out as research projects, based on a prototype design for a bank of digital oscillators first suggested by Hal Alles of Bell Telephone Laboratories in 1979. The GDS was originally intended as an intermediate test bed for the Synergy, but such was the interest stimulated by its special characteristics that it was manufactured as a product in its own right before the design for the Synergy had been completed. The commercial version is equipped with a single five-octave keyboard, a video display monitor, an alphanumeric keyboard, and a number of rotary knobs, sliders, and joysticks. This synthesizer differs from most of its contemporaries in allowing the composer to program its functions using a standard high level language such as FORTRAN. In view of the amount of work in computer-assisted composition carried out using such languages during the 1960s and 70s this decision to marry composing and synthesis facilities in a commercial product is of some significance.

The Synergy, which finally appeared on the market in 1981, is quite different from the GDS in many respects, being intended specifically as a performance instrument with a single six-octave keyboard. The design is altogether more compact with a special control panel of knobs and push-buttons instead of a VDU and an associated alphanumeric keyboard. Nevertheless, particular care has been taken to ensure that this simplified interface can provide a significant degree of operational versatility when the synthesizer is used live on stage, anticipating a design principle which was to be adopted by most keyboard synthesizers during the 1980s and 90s.

Although systems such as the above were designed increasingly to service the requirements of the rock and pop music industries one product dating from 1979 stood out against this trend. This was the DMX-1000 from the USA, manufactured by Digital Music Systems. It consists of a very fast purpose-built digital signal generation and processing system, assembled from special integrated circuit building blocks known as bit slices and designed to be attached to any suitable control computer. When the DMX-1000 was first released most general-purpose microcomputers still lacked sufficient processing resources to operate the system properly, and for this reason users had to turn to a minicomputer such as the PDP 11. Although the system was clearly intended for institutional users in the first instance, often able to negotiate access to a suitable host machine without too much difficulty, the needs of those less fortunate were answered by a special version known as the DMX-1010, which includes a small LSI-based PDP 11 as well as the signal .processor itself. The software synthesis program MUSIC 11 served as the model for the main control language, MUSIC 1000, but the freedom to program the system directly using its special instruction set soon led others to develop a number of alternative software packages, for example Barry Truax, who released a version of his POD programs for the DMX in 1983. Digital signal processing of externally generated material is also possible using the DMX-1000, its superior processing speed allowing continuous passages of sound to be manipulated with some degree of flexibility in real time.

With hindsight the historical significance of the DMX-1000 is far greater than many commentators have hitherto chosen to accord it. In functional terms the system anticipated the chip-based digital signal processor or DSP, and as will be seen in due course this particular family of microprocessors has led to the development of a new set of high performance tools for real-time computer music systems which have assumed considerable importance in the 1990s.

Outside the commercial sector a number of other all-digital systems were developed during the late 1970s. In 1976 James Beauchamp, K. Pohlmann, and L. Chapman constructed a prototype digital synthesizer at Illinois University, controlled by a small TI 980 computer with just 8K of memory. In 1978 Mike Manthey, using a slightly larger TI 960 computer, developed a mixed digital system known as the EGG synthesizer at the University of Aarhus, Denmark. Another project dating from this period was directed by Giuseppi di Giugno at IRCAM between 1976 and 1978, resulting in four systems known as the 4A, the 4B, the 4C, and the 4X, the last-mentioned being subsequently released as a commercial product. The 4A consisted of 256 digital oscillators and envelope-generators, providing additive synthesis facilities under the control of a PDP 11 computer with up to four different wave-shapes in use at any one time. The 4B and the 4C both provided FM synthesis facilities from a smaller bank of sixty-four oscillators and thirty-two envelope-generators, the latter model being controlled by a PDP 11, the former by its newer microprocessor version, the LSI 11. Parallels may be drawn between these systems and Truax's POD 5 and POD 6 programs, the former being based on hardware synthesis techniques, the latter on conventional software methods.

The command language for these first three di Giugno synthesizers was originally written in assembler code, placing heavy demands on the programming skills of the composer. By 1980 Curtis Abbott had developed a higher-level control language for the 4C version, known as 4CED, which permitted the use of more musically orientated procedures without any serious loss of flexibility or computational efficiency. As with most of the all-digital hardware systems so far discussed real-time performance was a primary design objective, and particular attention was paid to the operational characteristics of the man/machine interface. Much of the compositional work carried out at IRCAM using the di Giugno synthesizers has tended to favour a foreground/ background approach where the composer or performer interacts with a basic program of operations, pre-programmed into the system before the performance starts. In such an environment it is possible to use an alphanumeric computer keyboard as the primary means of control, provided that the associated VDU provides constantly updated information as to what the computer is actually doing. Today the mouse-driven graphics facilities provided as a standard feature of most modern desktop computers offer alternative and particularly powerful tools for such interactive working. In the case of the 4C text mode operation was favoured, requiring the performer to keep track of programming structures rather than rely on graphic displays or arrays of icons. To assist the input of information an array of sixteen potentiometers was provided, freely assignable as control devices for individual performance parameters.

The 4X model differs significantly from its predecessors since it provides extensive facilities for digital signal processing, allowing up to sixteen different channels of externally generated material to be processed simultaneously in real time. This version offers a number of features broadly similar to the DMX-1000, in particular an advanced programming language which allows the composer to assemble chains of devices from modular components and then manipulate these composite instruments in a manner similar to that used by the MUSIC family of programs. Notable compositions realized using the early di Giugno synthesizers include *Anthony* (1977) by David Wessel, using the 4A, and *Light*

(1979) by Tod Machover, using both the 4A and the 4C systems. In 1980 Machover combined the facilities of the 4A and 4C with those offered by MUSIC 10 running on the PDP 10 mainframe computer at IRCAM to produce *Soft Morning, City!* for tape, soprano, and double bass. Use here was made of Moorer's digital signal-processing techniques to incorporate material provided by the soprano Jane Manning in the tape part of the work. Perhaps the most significant work yet to have been produced using the 4X live on stage is *Répons* by Pierre Boulez, first composed in 1981–2 and then subsequently revised a number of times, in which six percussion soloists are subjected to live treatment in a dialogue with an ensemble of twenty-four players.

Although the 4X is possibly the most powerful and versatile real-time synthesis system to date from the late 1970s, with hindsight equal if not greater significance can be attached to the development of the SSSP synthesizer, the product of the Structured Sound Synthesis Project initiated at the University of Toronto, Ontario, in 1977, but unfortunately terminated prematurely in 1983 when funding ceased. The scale of this venture and the care taken to evaluate the artistic and technical deficiencies of existing facilities before embarking on its design resulted in the construction of a system which was to provide one of the most important models for others to aspire to during the 1980s, both in the commercial and the non-commercial sectors.

The project, co-ordinated by William Buxton, culminated in the construction of a versatile digital synthesizer, controlled by a PDP 11 computer. At the heart of the hardware lay a bank of sixteen digital oscillators which generated up to eight different wave forms, stored in special memory banks. Four different synthesis modes were available: Independent Voice Mode, Bank Mode, Frequency Modulation Mode, and VOSIM mode. In Independent Voice Mode each oscillator was treated as an individual voice, using a fixed timbre selected from one of the eight source wave forms. In Bank Mode any number of oscillators up to a maximum of sixteen could be used in parallel to create a single voice. If sinusoidal functions were selected, additive synthesis techniques could be employed with up to sixteen independently controlled partials. In Frequency Modulation Mode, pairs of oscillators could be coupled to produce complex spectra in accordance with Chowning's principles. VOSIM mode was a direct implementation of Kaegi's methods to create vowel-like sounds.

Up to four output channels were available which, when coupled to a special digitally controlled channel-distribution network, could be projected between a maximum of sixteen different loudspeakers. An additional mixing system, inserted between the synthesizer and the channel-distribution network, allowed the addition of up to sixteen different external sources to the output. .

Perhaps the most interesting feature of the system concerns the facilities it provided for man/machine communication. At the basic level of operation commands could be entered using a conventional alphanumeric keyboard. The primary design objective, however, was to provide musically attractive methods of contact with the synthesizer. In place of traditional input aids such as knobs, sliders, and joysticks, all of which suffer from the limitations of a fixed mechanical travel, a series of continuously rotatable plastic bands was provided for the entry of data by means of physical hand movements. These allowed existing internal function values to be incremented or decremented, depending on the direction in which the bands were rotated, and were normally used in conjunction with the main input device, a special interactive graphics unit.

The facilities offered by the SSSP synthesizer established a standard for communications which was second to none. The composer was free to enter and display control data in a number of ways. For example, if the intention was to produce a 'note/event' type of piece using tempered pitches, the associated software allowed the use of traditional musical notation, the screen displaying a window of the score on a pair of staves in its upper part and a list of permissible operations such as 'append', 'change', and 'delete' in the lower. Scrolling of the score in both directions was controlled by one of the band regulators, a simple but very effective improvement on conventional cursor control methods. Access to display characteristics was achieved via a tracking cross which could be moved to any position by using a mouse. The latter device consisted of a simple tracker ball in a small moulding, which when moved about on a flat surface produces corresponding movements of a tracking cross or pointer on-screen, a forerunner of the standard mouse used with a modern microcomputer. Manipulation commenced with the selection of a mode of operation. This was achieved by moving the cross until it was positioned over the corresponding entry in the list, and then clicking a button on the mouse itself to register the choice. The cross could then be moved to the score area and used to modify the displayed data in the manner selected. In the case of 'append', where the purpose was to add notes, the cross was positioned over the desired point of entry and the mouse button clicked again. This caused the cross to disappear, to be replaced by a small marker and a linear display of note types from a demi-semiquaver to a semibreve, the latter in the interests of clarity being displaced towards the right of the screen. The cursor was then used to manipulate the note-type display, the desired neume being positioned over the marker. Depressing another control button on the mouse caused the neume to be entered into the score, the unwanted elements disappearing to be replaced once again by the tracking cross.

This level of flexibility extended to the other modes of data entry and display. These permitted the specification of acoustical data such as frequency, timbre, and envelope via similar processes of visual manipulation. To assist the composer the graphics software offered a variety of display methods, depending on the intended action. Sound envelopes, for example, could be drawn in on a supplied grid, the software assisting in the rectification of obvious mistakes such as envelopes which do not progress continuously in a left-to-right direction when measured along the time axis.

Other actions, such as the entry of data for an FM sound, led to a portioning of the screen into segments, each concerned with a specific variable, for example the wave-form of each oscillator, the duration of the sound, the frequency of the carrier, or the modulation index. This mixture of numerical and graphical data was easily manipulated via the mouse, especially when used in combination with the band regulators. If so desired numerical data could be displayed in the form of slider settings, shown as crossbars on vertical lines which moved up and down in response to the physical movement of the regulators. Yet another display mode offered a perceptual model of the sound, of particular use in evaluating elements such as vowel formants, generated by means of the VOSIM option.

The design revolution of the 1980s in digital engineering was to lead to a succession of low-cost synthesizers which emulate many of the features pioneered by the SSSP. These products were associated with the continuing growth of the microcomputer industry and an increasing awareness of the potential of hardware tools which have been specially engineered or adapted for audio synthesis and processing. One of the most distinctive characteristics associated with development of microcomputers has been their use of visual display facilities as the primary means of communication with the outside world. Prior to this computer manufacturers had paid surprisingly little attention to improving the performance of input/output facilities for the individual user, assuming, as it turned out incorrectly, that the alphanumeric code provided by devices such as the traditional teletypewriter was perfectly adequate for the majority of applications. Even the early VDUs, which first appeared in significant quantities during the mid-1970s, were for the most part restricted to simple character displays, providing little more than a visual alternative to the printed output produced by a typewriter terminal. Software facilities for entering and editing text were generally very basic, with little support for users other than those primarily engaged in writing programs or word-processing. High-resolution graphics facilities such as those used for the development of the SSSP were for the most part bulky, and exceedingly expensive, the laser printer was still in its infancy, and the only practical means of reproducing such information accurately in hardcopy was the slow and often cumbersome graph plotter.

In their search for a cheap and convenient means of visual communication a number of microcomputer manufacturers turned their attention to the domestic television, developing special modulators which translate computer data into broadcast picture signals, input to the set via a standard aerial socket. Whereas the resulting picture quality is invariably inferior to that obtainable from a modern high-definition graphics monitor these devices had a considerable impact on the computing industry as a whole since they offer a cheap and easily programmable means of displaying both text and graphics simultaneously, with the added dimension of colour.

Desktop publishing, including such diverse applications as the preparation of flowcharts for business and commerce and the drawing of engineering diagrams, was thus but a small step away, and microcomputer manufacturers, realizing the importance of these new and as yet untapped markets, began to invest heavily in the design of high-quality visual display facilities. Thus the general purpose WIMP (Windows, Icons, Mouse, Pointer) environment was born. In the field of music the development of such resources was to acquire a particular significance as the technology improved, for it became possible to use such systems to display and manipulate music scores in common music notation, acoustic diagrams, or indeed any functional aspect of sound generation and processing which could be usefully represented in a graphical form.

The emphasis on developing visual interfaces for general computer applications overshadowed a more restrained but growing interest in the possibilities of computer-generated sound. The starting-point in this context was the simple loudspeaker provided by most microcomputers to alert the user to certain important operational conditions, for example that the machine has switched on and booted successfully, or that a serious system or user error has occurred. The most basic method of sound production for this purpose involves the application of on/off voltage pulses of fixed amplitude from a simple one-bit generator directly to the speaker coil. No D-to-A converters are required for this direct coupling and sound production is limited to pulse patterns of a fixed amplitude. Despite the severe limitations of such a resource a number of early enthusiasts were sufficiently motivated by the availability of a programmable audio generator, however basic, to start developing programs which played tunes or even simple chords, achieved by clever programming of the pulse generator to produce patterns which fool the loudspeaker voice coil into movements which reproduce a range of wave-form functions. Ingenuity sometimes knows no bounds and some programmers have managed to synthesize short extracts of recognizable speech using this method, leading to the production of some elementary 'speak and spell' programs. Such material is clearly of limited value for any serious compositional purposes but when it is combined with visual aids it can prove a viable resource for a number of educational applications such as aural training or teaching the basic rules of harmony and counterpoint.

Some microcomputers such as the original Apple II and the IBM PC provide no other means of sound generation. Others, even of a relatively early vintage, offer more versatile facilities but progress in this respect has been slow and inconsistent. In the case of the Atari 400 and 800 additional hardware provides four independent sound channels, each controllable in terms of pitch and also amplitude. The repertory of sounds is still limited to pulse patterns but there is some scope for shaping the timbre via a pair of dynamically programmable high-pass filters. Commodore introduced altogether more elaborate synthesis facilities for their 64 and 128 models based on a hybrid arrangement of three digitally controlled analogue oscillators which offer a choice of three basic wave-forms and the facility to program the pitch, duration, amplitude, and overall envelope of each note/event.

Given its lack of any such hardware enhancements the rise in popularity of the Apple II to become the most popular model for music applications during the late 1970s and early 80s might appear a little strange. The primary attraction lay in the general versatility of this highly successful microcomputer, not least for its graphics capabilities, which were well in advance of its competitors. Additionally, Apple had been far-sighted enough to provide spare slots within the machine for the insertion of extra hardware. This encouraged other manufacturers to market a range of specialist products, including a number designed specifically for sound synthesis. One of the first of these, known as Music System from Mountain Computer, appeared in 1980 and consists of two plug-in cards which provide sixteen individually programmable hardware oscillators and a pair of eight-bit D-to-A converters for stereo output. Other manufacturers, notably ALF with its nine-voice MC1 card and Sweet Micro Systems with its six-voice Mockingbird card, were soon competing for a share of this growing market for computer-generated sound, although the resources they provided proved to be rather limited in scope. The ALF system, for example, just generates square waves, albeit subjected to some ingenious processing to allow the production of a range of distinctive timbres.

Although good graphics facilities were clearly important for a number of music applications attention naturally gravitated towards more conventional performance aids such as the music keyboard. In 1981 a system known as the alphaSyntauri appeared on the market comprising a four octave keyboard, a pair of foot-pedals and a plug-in interface card, packaged together with a matching set of Mountain Computer boards for an Apple II. The accompanying software includes an editor for the synthesizer voices accessed using alphanumeric keyboard and graphic display facilities of the host computer and also a sequencing package which stores performance data on floppy disk. Various functions can be controlled using either the foot-pedals or the games paddles normally provided with the computer. A rival system, also based on the Mountain Computer cards and an Apple II, soon followed from Passport Designs. Known as the Soundchaser it too offered a music keyboard and accessories, supported by sound editing and sequencing software.

The early 1980s marked a watershed in the development of commercial systems for electronic and computer music as the underlying technology progressively shifted from the analogue to the digital domain. One factor, however, was to prove an unfortunate impediment to this process of change, and this concerns the very variable audio fidelity of many of the all-digital products produced during this transitional period of development. Although quality is undoubtedly a factor related to cost, even systems such as the Fairlight and the Synclavier were initially not without some shortcomings in this respect.

It has been shown that two factors ultimately constrain the fidelity of digital sound; the rate at which the acoustic wave is sampled and the numerical accuracy of the samples themselves. The significance of a particular speed of sampling can readily be appreciated given the basic rule that the upper Nyquist limit of the audio frequency spectrum is equal to half the sampling rate. In practice this upper bandwidth limit has to be reduced as a consequence of the requirement to insert a sharp analogue low-pass filter in the final output stage to attenuate any frequency components which exceed the Nyquist frequency.

In discussing the characteristics of filters for analogue synthesizers it was noted that even the sharpest filters cannot cut off signals exactly at a specified frequency. This attenuation takes effect over a spread of frequencies at a rate which may range from perhaps just 3 dB per octave for a gentle roll-off to 80 or 90 dB per octave for the best 'brick wall' filters. For this reason filters for converters are usually designed to start their attenuation at no more than about 85 to 90 per cent of the Nyquist frequency. The significance of this factor can best be illustrated by reference to the international standards for digital audio which have been developed for recording and broadcasting. Digital links for broadcasting have been used in many countries since the early 1970s, and this has led to the early standard of 32 kHz as the sampling rate for FM quality radio transmissions. At first glance this may seem a little low since the Nyquist frequency is only 16 kHz, well below the upper limit of hearing, which is generally taken to be between about 18 and 20 kHz. If the associated low-pass filter is set 10 per cent below this the effective bandwidth reduces to 14.5 kHz. The latter, however, matches the frequency restriction imposed on FM radio broadcasts in most countries, and listeners are unlikely to detect any significant defects as a result of sampling errors providing the filter circuits are adequate.

Non-broadcast audio systems, however, are not subject to such restrictions. LP records, for example, are perfectly capable of reproducing the entire audio spectrum from about 20 Hz to 20 kHz, and this was an important benchmark in determining the sampling rate for the first digital medium for the domestic market, the compact disc. For this a standard of 44.1 kHz was decided upon, resulting in a Nyquist frequency of 22.05 kHz, which leaves sufficient headroom for a low-pass filter with a cut-off frequency of about 20 kHz. In due course the recording industry introduced another standard which uses the still higher rate of 48 kHz, and this has been adopted for more recent digital recording systems such as digital audio tape (DAT).

The significance of the second factor determining audio quality, the accuracy of the sample values themselves, requires a more detailed explanation. It will be recalled that the binary system follows a simple power-of-two progression when calculating the maximum number of different values which can be represented by a specific number of bits, for example eight-bit samples can represent 256 different values, twelve-bit samples 4096 values, and sixteen-bit samples 65 536 values. This quantizing factor determines the maximum dynamic range or signal-to-noise ratio which can be achieved using conventional sample coding in a digital audio system. Measured logarithmically the dynamics encountered in the concert hall will typically embrace a range of about 70 to 80 decibels between the softest and the loudest sounds. Analogue tape recorders, even those fitted with noise reduction facilities, require the compression of such information to a range of about 65 to 70 dB at the most, and in the case of LP records or stereo FM radio it has to be reduced still further to about 50 dB.

In the case of a digital audio system it can be shown that each extra bit employed for coding sound samples increases the dynamic range by about 6 dB, thus an eight-bit system has a range of 48 dB, a twelve-bit system a range of 72 dB, and a sixteen-bit system a range of 96 dB. It would thus appear, for example, that if a system generates eight-bit sound samples at 32 kHz, it will match the specifications of FM radio in terms of dynamic range as well as bandwidth. Unfortunately this does not prove to be the case, for the nature of the digital medium conspires to produce a type of distortion at low amplitudes which is far more objectionable subjectively than simple electrical measurements might otherwise suggest.

In analogue systems dynamic range is usually measured in terms of the signal-to-noise ratio, defined as the difference in amplitude between the residual noise level of a system, and the level at which the electronic circuits begin to overload and distort the wave-form of the signal. Since most residual noise manifests itself as a low-level hiss in these circumstances the ear is often able to ignore it providing the amplitude of the reproduced signal itself is at least 10 dB or so louder. Most importantly, even if the listener is aware of some hiss in quiet passages of music, the signal itself will usually retain its underlying clarity.

The same is not true in the case of digital audio systems. Here there is no such quantity as residual noise, since reducing a digital signal to zero amplitude produces a null string of samples and thus no output. Instead, noise manifests itself in terms of the numerical errors which are generated when approximating sample values, a factor which increases proportionally as the amplitude of the signal decreases. In an eight-bit system the samples for a signal at maximum amplitude will be quantized to the nearest value on an integer scale which accommodates 256 steps from peak to peak. If, however, the signal is reduced in amplitude by just 30 dB the number of steps available to quantize the signal will reduce to just eight, resulting in significant quantizing errors. These are perceived as a direct and particularly unpleasant distortion of the signal itself. Although some ingenious coding techniques exist for reducing the effects of such errors electronically it is now well recognized that the dynamic range of a digital system has to be significantly better than that of an equivalent analogue system if the ear is to make a favourable comparison. For FM radio quality, thus, sampling accuracies of at least twelve or thirteen bits are generally required, giving a dynamic range of 72 to 78 dB.

This factor is of particular significance when considering the performance of byte-orientated synthesis systems. Given that the processing engine of a digital synthesizer has to generate samples in real time, any decision to use more than one byte for each sample may result in a significant increase in the time taken to compute the values. This certainly proved to be the case with eight-bit microprocessors which can only handle one byte of data at a time. As a result many of the early commercial digital synthesizers, from the original version of the Fairlight to the much smaller systems based on the Mountain Computer boards, were limited to eight-bit samples even though low cost D-to-A and A-to-D converter chips of a much better resolution were available from component manufacturers. The general updating of commercial synthesizers from an eight- to twelve-bit sample standard during the first half of the 1980s led to noticeable improvements in their quality, and as technology improved still further, spurred on to no small extent by the development of the compact disc player and related products, so sixteen-bit systems finally became the rule rather than the exception.

At the start of the 1980s the commercial market divided into three distinct sectors. Products such as the Fairlight and the Synclavier were opening up important markets for digital technology at one end of the spectrum, counterbalanced by a diverse collection of built-in or add-on synthesis systems for the microcomputer market at the other. In the middle lay by far the largest sector, still dominated by analogue voltage-controlled synthesizers both large and small, but poised for what was to prove a design revolution of the utmost significance.

The key to this development lay in the forging of a historic agreement signed by all the leading manufacturers of synthesizers world-wide concerning a common protocol for connecting different items of equipment together at the control level. One of the most serious deficiencies of existing systems was the lack of any consistency between the control voltage functions used by one manufacturer and those of any other. Attaching a Buchla keyboard to a Moog synthesizer, for example, would result in some quite bizarre results as a result of their different voltage-to-pitch laws. This less than satisfactory situation still prevailed when a number of manufacturers began to design some experimental digital interfaces for their products at the start of the 1980s. Although connecting unmatched voltage-controlled devices together will usually produce some form of response, any mismatch in a digital system will usually produce no response at all. Thus prototype systems such as the Key Code System of Yamaha and the SCI Digital Interface of Sequential Circuits were quite unable to communicate with each other. Given the success of a general drive amongst computer manufacturers to establish common communications standards throughout the industry such a situation became rapidly untenable.

The idea of establishing an industry-standard digital protocol for connecting synthesizers and associated peripherals together at the control level was first put forward informally at a meeting of the National Association of Music Merchants (NAMM) in the early summer of 1981. This American organization had become an important international forum for the music industry, and attracted representatives from companies world-wide, including most of those specifically involved in the design and manufacture of electronic musical instruments and synthesizers. The initiative for a universal communications system came from Dave Smith, the president of Sequential Circuits, who persuaded Roland and Oberheim to nominate representatives to participate in a joint feasibility study with Chet Wood, one of his chief design engineers. Progress was swift, and within a matter of months Smith was in a position to call a meeting with a larger group of manufacturers, which now included Kawai, Korg, and Yamaha. The outcome of discussions was positive and encouraging, and at an Audio and Engineering Society convention held just a few weeks later Smith and Wood formally presented their proposal for a USI (Universal Synthesizer Interface). Although this constituted little more than an outline description of a protocol to transmit note/event information between synthesizers it laid the foundations for what was to become a highly significant communications system.

With the AES presentation the debate finally entered the public arena, and a more detailed proposal was presented to a meeting of NAMM in January 1982, attended by representatives from CBS/Rhodes, Emu, Kawai, Music Technology Inc. (Crumar), Oberheim, Octave Plateau, Passport Designs, Roland, Sequential Circuits, Syntauri, Unichord (Korg), and Yamaha. Despite some improvements which had been made to the engineering specification the suggested communications protocol was still at this stage restricted to the transmission of basic 'on/off' note/event information. A number of companies objected to this limitation on the grounds that any universal protocol should be capable of carrying a far more comprehensive range of data, including any information necessary to configure the synthesis devices themselves. Arguments also developed over the hardware specification for the interface itself and as a result agreement was only reached in principle, pending further discussions.

During the summer of 1982 the initiative passed largely to the Japanese, leaving just Sequential Circuits to represent American interests. The collective enthusiasm of this new grouping of companies quickly paid dividends, and by September the draft of a considerably expanded specification was complete, as was the final choice of an acronym, the Musical Instrument Digital Interface, or MIDI. This development was finally announced to the world by Robert Moog in an article which appeared in the October edition of the magazine *Keyboard*. This personal seal of approval from such a respected pioneer of the synthesizer industry had a significant impact on the more traditional and generally sceptical sectors of the music industry. By the end of the year both Sequential Circuits and Roland were manufacturing synthesizers with MIDI-compatible interfaces, and their demonstration at the January 1983 meeting of NAMM finally persuaded the industry as a whole that this was a development which had to be taken seriously. The final, definitive MIDI specification, Version 1.0, was published in the spring of 1983 by the newly formed MIDI Association, and by the end of the year most synthesizer manufacturers had started to incorporate MIDI as a standard design feature of their products.

Although an exhaustive description of MIDI is beyond the scope of this book a number of its basic features need to be considered since they provide important clues to the significance of the protocol for the many systems which rely on its control. The expansion of the acronym itself is very misleading and has been the cause of much misunderstanding through its use of the word 'interface'. In computing terms an interface is usually defined as a hardware device which translates one form of data representation into another. By this definition D-to-A and A-to-D converters are clearly interfaces, as are the various ports fitted to microcomputers to allow communication with external disk drives, printers, or other computers. MIDI does indeed require special hardware interfaces to translate information from one format into another but the MIDI specification itself is principally a detailed description of a communications protocol for the transmission and reception of music data. Aside from one or two basic electrical features the physical design of a MIDI interface and how the information is represented and interpreted internally are matters for the individual manufacturer to resolve. In the case of a digital synthesizer this interface is simply required to convert data from one digital format into another. An analogue synthesizer requires a completely different type of interface incorporating a D-to-A and an A-to-D converter to translate suitable MIDI information into control voltages and vice versa. These so called 'retrofit kits' have proved very popular with owners of traditional synthesizers from manufacturers such as Moog, Buchla, and ARP, since they neatly circumvent the problems of compatibility discussed earlier.

MIDI is a serial communications protocol, whereby all commands and data are transmitted as a single sequential stream of bits down a single cable. A parallel communications system was considered, but this option was rejected on the grounds that the multi-core cabling required to transmit information in this manner would have been bulky, relatively expensive, vulnerable to accidental damage, and also particularly susceptible to electrical interference if more than a metre or so long. Artists were quick to point out the practical problems of performing on stage, not least the common requirement to locate synthesizers and keyboards some distance apart, and the presence of all kinds of cabling for amplifiers and loudspeakers which are vulnerable to many forms of electrical interference. In such situations a fully screened serial communications system is the only reliable medium for the transfer of digital information.

There are some important electrical differences between a MIDI system and a standard serial communications system for a microcomputer. Essentially the former senses interruptions in current flow while the latter senses voltage pulses. Conversion from one mode of operation to the other is nevertheless relatively straightforward in hardware terms, and this has proved helpful in designing MIDI interfaces for a number of microcomputers. The MIDI specification makes one important stipulation in this context, that opto-isolators must be used on the data lines of all MIDI ports to protect equipment. An opto-isolator is a combination of a light-emitting diode which can be switched on and off to represent equivalent binary data states, and a corresponding photoelectric cell which detects these changes. By using light as a buffering mechanism all kinds of electronic problems can be avoided, for example the creation of ground loops between equipment which can upset digital data, or the accidental transmission of large voltage spikes which can damage other equipment.

There are three types of MIDI port: MIDI IN, MIDI OUT, and MIDI THRU. In each case the electronic circuitry terminates in a conventional 5-pin DIN socket, allowing the use of screened connecting cables with a DIN plug at either end. Just two pins are required for MIDI transmissions, any radiation being suppressed via a third pin which is used to connect the cable sheathing to earth. Since MIDI signals are transmitted in one direction only the purpose of MIDI IN and MIDI OUT ports is for the most part self-explanatory. MIDI synthesizers can be expected to provide both of these ports and full bidirectional communications between any two of these can be achieved using just a pair of MIDI cables.

More complex configurations require careful planning. At first sight it might appear that all that is necessary to link three or more synthesizers together is a simple chain of connections from one MIDI OUT port to the next MIDI IN port, the output port on the last synthesizer being looped back to the input port on the first to complete a circular communications chain. Unfortunately this arrangement will rarely work, for there is no requirement in the MIDI specification for signals received at the MIDI IN port of a device to be echoed automatically at the corresponding MIDI OUT port, and many synthesizers cannot support this special mode of operation. The onwards transmission of such material is the sole purpose of the MIDI THRU port, but potential cabling difficulties do not stop here since a number of cheaper synthesizers omit this port altogether on the grounds that it is only classified as optional in the original specification.

In the case of simple MIDI interfaces for microcomputers the lack of a THRU port is fortunately less of a problem since most MIDI software is designed to use the MIDI OUT port in a suitably intelligent manner, combining any incoming signals for onwards transmission with new information generated by the computer itself to form a composite stream of data. Specialist books on MIDI offer countless suggestions on how best to connect a number of devices together, but in many situations there is no one ideal solution. This situation has eased significantly in recent years by the introduction of special electronically driven MIDI MERGE and MIDI THRU boxes which provide what are in effect programmable digital telephone exchanges for the routing of complex interconnections.

The quantity and nature of the data transmitted by MIDI

varies significantly according to the context. At the heart of the various categories of MIDI commands lie the codes used to control the performance of a synthesizer, known collectively as channel voice messages. These are used to transmit data for individual note/events, for example the activation of a voice in a synthesizer in response to the depression of a key on a music keyboard. The 'note on' (sometimes referred to as 'key on') message consists of three bytes, containing three separate items of information. The first byte, known as the status byte or instruction code, signals the start of a new MIDI message, and also identifies its purpose. The second byte identifies the pitch of the note as a simple numerical value which must lie in the range 0 to 127 since MIDI only allows the use of seven bits per byte for the storage of data. In normal use each of these numbers is identified with a specific key on an equal-tempered keyboard, for example middle C corresponds to a value of 60, and concert A, nine semitones above, corresponds to a value of 69. Some synthesizers allow this data to be modified internally to produce other temperaments, or to be transposed up or down a specified number of semitones. While the former facility has some value for playing ancient music and the latter can be a bonus for a keyboard player suddenly faced with a request to play a piece in a different key, this fundamental rationalization of frequency information in terms of fixed pitch specifications has implications for the serious composer. In particular it is not very practicable to use standard MIDI messages for the dynamic control of frequency spectra except in some very limited ways which will be discussed shortly.

The third byte in a 'note on' message is reserved for keyboard velocity information. This is used to denote the volume level, based on the proposition that the faster a key is struck on a conventional keyboard instrument the louder it will sound, the data once again being quantized as a value in the range 0 to 127. Not all MIDI keyboards can sense this performance characteristic, in which case a default value of 64 is automatically transmitted instead. While this method of dynamic control relates well to traditional keyboard skills associated with instruments such as the piano the correlation is less obvious when controlling sounds which require continuous control over nuances of both pitch and dynamics, for example strings or woodwind. In these circumstances merely sensing initial key velocity will provide insufficient gestural information, necessitating the use of supplementary channel voice messages which are provided specifically for the registration of additional performance characteristics.

Glissandi or some degree of variable pitch tuning can be achieved by using a three-byte channel voice message known as 'pitch bend', which modifies the basic pitch setting in discrete steps. In this case the second and third bytes are read together as a single item of data, allowing very fine gradations of control with a maximum permitted resolution of fourteen bits (16 384 discrete steps). MIDI does not specify what range of pitch detuning this range of numbers should correspond to, and the usefulness of this feature thus depends very much on the functional characteristics of the synthesizer concerned. Since the usual device for controlling pitch bend is a hand-operated bidirectional wheel, designed to return to its median position as soon as it is released, accurate regulation of pitch in this manner can become a highly speculative operation.

Two other channel voice messages, one a more sophisticated version of the other, are provided to allow further modification of the primary 'note on' data. Referred to as 'key pressure' or 'aftertouch' messages these codes allow subsequent changes in key pressure to be transmitted as a sequence of values which may be used to alter pitch or volume settings dynamically. Although this information is clearly useful for adding performance nuances cheaper MIDI keyboards are often unable to provide it. Similarly, many synthesizers will only respond to the simpler of the two messages and several entry-level models cannot respond to either. The basic 'key pressure' message is a single parameter which reflects an average value for all the keys currently depressed. Only two bytes are required, the status byte and a second byte which contains the overall pressure value on a scale from 0 (no pressure) to 127 (maximum pressure). The more elaborate polyphonic message monitors the depression of keys individually. Three bytes are required for this command, a status byte, a second byte containing the note number, and a third byte containing its pressure, once again measured on a scale from 0 to 127.

Commands such as 'pitch bend and 'key pressure' considerably increase the amount of MIDI data which has to be transmitted since they actively sense any change in the device settings and immediately generate an updated message. This situation contrasts sharply with the single three-byte message sent just once whenever a new 'note on' action is sensed, and has some important implications for the general management of MIDI information.

Since the duration of a note is not transmitted (in a live performance this would require knowledge of the future) an equivalent 'key off' message has to be sent when the key is released. MIDI allows two means of achieving this. The first and more usual method uses a matching three-byte message but with a different status byte which tags it as a 'key off' command. The second byte, as before, identifies which note is to be switched off, and the third byte the release velocity. In many systems the latter information is entirely redundant, although a few synthesizers can use this information to modify the decay of the note's envelope. The second method, less common initially but now growing in popularity, simply sends another 'key on' message for the note with a velocity of zero.

Two further channel voice messages are provided, 'program change' and 'control change', concerned respectively with directing the flow of information and the configuration of the hardware. 'Program change' is designed to signal to the synthesizer that a different voice is to be selected. Only two bytes are required for this command, a status byte, and a data byte which represents a program (= voice) number in the range 0 to 127. To add an element of confusion some synthesizer manufacturers automatically add one when interpreting the binary code which is transmitted so that it corresponds to voice numbers in the range 1 to 128. Furthermore, the interpretation of the program number depends entirely on the configuration of the voices within the synthesizer itself at the time of transmission. Accidental loading of the wrong bank can result in unexpected and quite grotesque results, a situation all too familiar to composers who regularly use sequencing programs to store their works for later performance and then forget to log the precise specifications for the associated voice bank.

The versatility suggested by this facility to choose from up to 128 voice selections is tempered slightly by some practical considerations. In particular most synthesizers are only able to store a maximum of 64 different voices in a voice bank at any one time and some only permit 32, or as few as 16. An overriding restraint is the fact that MIDI can only handle a maximum of 16 different channels of voice data at any one time, but this is usually a rather less pressing issue. Flexibility to change voices during a performance is often a more important consideration than the capacity to indulge in orchestral textures more extensive than those associated with a late-nineteenth-century symphony or a grand opera.

As noted earlier, MIDI is a serial communications protocol, requiring all information to be directed down a single data line. Voice messages intended for two or more separate channels have to be multiplexed together and then extracted correctly as the flow of MIDI information is passed down the chain to the various hardware devices. The key to differentiating between signals for different channels lies in the status byte which introduces each channel voice message. The first four bits in the status byte identify the type of command, and the second four bits identify the channel number. Thus if a pair of synthesizers in a MIDI chain is set to receive information just on channels 1 and 2 respectively and an attempt is made to play the system using a keyboard set to transmit on channel 1, only the first synthesizer will respond. If a second keyboard is added to the chain and set to transmit on channel 2, then two totally independent lines of communication will have been established. If so desired, channel information can be ignored altogether by receiving (but not transmitting) devices by disabling the internal number filter, in which case all channel voice messages will be treated as relevant regardless of their number.

This particular feature forms one of a group of channel mode messages which are embedded as a special set of codes in the 'control change' command, which is otherwise used to modify the status of key hardware components in a MIDI system. It requires three bytes; the usual status byte, a second byte to identify the control device to be altered, and a third byte to specify its new setting. The original MIDI specification designated the assignment of just two control device numbers, 0 and 1, leaving individual manufacturers to determine the designation (if any) of the others. 0 is the control number for a pitch bend regulator, but this code has become redundant with the introduction of the special 'pitch bend' channel voice message described earlier. 1 is the control number for a modulation wheel, a device included in many synthesizers to regulate the amount of vibrato for a voice if its synthesis algorithm requires this parameter. As to the other control device numbers, many manufacturers have chosen to follow the allocations used by Yamaha, for example 2 for a breath controller, 4 for an adjustable foot-pedal control, 6 for a data entry knob or slider, and 64 for a sustain pedal. The original MIDI specification reserved numbers 0 to 63 for continuous controllers and numbers 64 to 95 for switches, but these designations have been subject to some change over the years. Numbers 92 to 95, for example, are now used for variable data such as depth of tremolo (92) and chorus effects (93).

Turning to the data itself, in the case of a switching device such as a sustain pedal only two states need to be recognized, and as a result values in the range 0 to 63 are simply interpreted as 'off', and values in the range 64 to 127 as 'on'. In the case of continuously variable controllers, however, there is an altogether more serious issue to be addressed. The limitation to just one data byte for a device control code severely restricts the attainable quantization of the associated function. Whereas 128 steps might be considered adequate for the regulation of volume this is clearly an inadequate number for a smooth glissando. With hindsight the simplest solution might have been provision of an additional data byte for these values in the message, allowing functions to be represented as 16 384 discrete steps, as is the case with the 'pitch bend' channel voice message. Instead the convention has been to divide up device codes 0 to 63 into pairs, 0 with 32, 1 with 33, and so on. By restricting the logical device numbers for variable controllers to the range 0 to 31, two messages can thus be sent for each control change, the data value in the first element of the pair representing the most significant byte and the data value in the second element the least significant byte of a composite fourteen-bit MIDI data value. The requirement to send six bytes for each change of value rather than four is nevertheless an undesirable overhead in terms of data density, especially if a number of controllers are active at any one time.

Channel numbers 121 to 127 are the ones specially set aside for the channel mode messages. In ascending order their designations are as follows: 'reset all controls', 'local control', 'all notes off', 'omni mode off', 'omni mode on', 'mono mode on', and 'poly mode on'. As in the case of channel voice messages the same three-byte format is used, although only 'local control' and 'mono mode on' require use of the third byte to convey associated data values. The mode commands 'reset all controls' and 'all notes off' are self-explanatory. 'Local control' affects the relationship between a keyboard and the associated voice banks in a synthesizer where both components are integral to the design. As in the case of the device control codes for switches, if the second byte contains a value of between 64 and 127 local control is switched on, in which case the keyboard will drive both the internal voices and also any external devices which have been connected by MIDI on an appropriate channel. If instead the second byte contains a value between 0 and 63 local control is switched off, in which case MIDI information is still transmitted to external devices but the connection from the keyboard to the internal voices is disabled.

'Omni on' and 'omni off' are the channel mode commands which determine whether a synthesizer voice will respond to all voice messages regardless of the channel number, or on just one designated channel. The 'mono mode on' and 'poly mode on' commands determine whether a voice is to be monophonic or polyphonic, up to the maximum number of notes the hardware will allow to be generated simultaneously (typically 8 or 16). If two or more notes are activated simultaneously in the former mode only one will actually sound, usually the highest. If the third byte of the 'mono mode on' command is set to zero then alternate transmission of the two 'mono' and 'poly' messages will simply switch all the voices on all channels between the two modes. If the third byte of the 'mono mode command' is non-zero, however, its numerical value will signal how many channels, numbered in ascending order from channel 1, will be set to mono, the prevailing status of the other channels remaining unaltered.

All the possible combinations of the above commands are rationalized as four standard operating modes, which are defined as follows: MODE 1, 'omni on/poly'; MODE 2, 'omni on/mono'; MODE 3, 'omni off/poly'; and MODE 4, 'omni off/mono'. MODE 1 is the default mode which every item of MIDI hardware should support. MODE 2 is particularly applicable to voltage-controlled synthesizers which have been retrofitted with MIDI since they are generally only capable of generating monophonic sounds and lack the additional hardware necessary to decode information for different channels. MODE 3 is potentially the most powerful since it allows polyphonic operation of up to sixteen different voices, each controlled on a different channel. MODE 4 is essentially a monophonic version of MODE 3 for use with solo voices on individual channels.

It will now be clear from even this cursory examination of the MIDI protocol that the amount of information which may be transmitted in some circumstances can be quite considerable. It has been shown that the performance of a single note requires a minimum of six bytes of information, three to switch it on and three to switch it off. Although the basic sequence of 'note on' and 'note off' messages required to generate a slow monophonic melody will be very modest, the density of traffic will increase substantially if any active sensing channel commands such as key pressure are used to refine the pitch or amplitude characteristics. Playing notes faster will increase the data flow, as will the transmission of polyphonic, as opposed to monophonic, data. Under extreme conditions the density of traffic can indeed increase to the point where MIDI itself reaches its operational limit. What then happens is a situation similar to a traffic jam, with delays in transmission as channel commands are forced to queue. Once these delays begin to exceed about 50 to 100 milliseconds the ear may well become aware of a lack of precision when an attempt is made to activate large clusters of notes on several channels simultaneously. To understand the nature and extent of this problem it is necessary to look more closely at the electronic specification of MIDI.

During the early 1980s the standard operating speeds for serial transmission between computers and peripheral devices such as printers and VDUs were still relatively slow. The origins of this communications method go back to the early 1950s when manufacturers began to tackle the problems of connecting keyboard terminals to computers in a manner which would accommodate the use of significant lengths of cabling. The earliest operating speeds were extremely slow, typically 110 bits of digital information per second (110 baud), sufficient to drive standard mechanical teletypewriters at about 11 characters per second. With the advent of more modern terminals the need arose for higher speeds of transmission: 300 baud soon replaced the old 110 baud standard, and in due course this was upgraded first to 1200 baud and then to higher multiples thereof. By the time a standard for MIDI was first being discussed 9600 baud had become the normal maximum baud rate for serial communications, with a few computers already able to support the next multiple of 19 200 baud.

Although synthesizer manufacturers could only guess what

densities of control information might be demanded in future systems they deduced, correctly, that even a transmission rate of 19 200 baud was likely to prove too slow for the flow of control data in some circumstances. The next multiple, 38 400 baud, would have satisfied their criteria but the MIDI committee settled instead for the slightly lower speed of 31 250 baud, which happens to be an exact division (1/32) of 1 megahertz, the basic clock speed used by many first-generation microprocessors. Proposals to double or even quadruple the speed of MIDI have been put forward on a number of occasions, but the investment in equipment for the existing specification has been so substantial that the current baud rate is likely to remain the industry standard for some considerable time.

Each byte of MIDI information consists of eight bits, the first bit being used as a flag to indicate whether or not the byte is a status byte (set to 1), or a data byte (set to 0). This explains why only seven bits can be used for data in a single byte, and fourteen bits for data in a double byte, representing a total of 128 and 16 384 integers respectively. In transmission terms, however, each MIDI byte requires ten bits, since both a start bit and a stop bit are added to allow for error checking. At a rate of 31 250 baud, therefore, a maximum of 3125 bytes of MIDI information can be transmitted per second, or, viewed another way, a typical three-byte channel voice message takes about 1 millisecond to complete. Since all MIDI data has to be multiplexed as a single data stream it can now be seen how the margin between detectable and non-detectable delays in response is of some significance, this boundary lying theoretically somewhere between 50 and 100 supposedly simultaneous messages. When the continuous flow of data from active sensing devices is taken into account it becomes clear that saturation of the transmission line is more than just a possibility. In practice the actual delays which occur are further influenced by electrical considerations and the physical routing of the MIDI cables, but the introduction of MIDI signal merging and splitting devices has helped to minimize the effects of latency in large networks.

In addition to the basic channel messages described above MIDI provides an additional set of commands known as system messages which are used to send global information to the system as a whole. One in particular, known as 'system exclusive', holds the key to what has proved to be one of MIDI's most powerful features, an ability to switch with just a single status command to a special mode of operation which allows the transfer information of any type from one device to another, the only requirement being strict adherence to the MIDI data format which as already noted prohibits any use of the highest order bit in each byte for any data. The primary purpose of this mode is to provide individual synthesizer manufacturers with a facility for transmitting their own special system set-up messages between devices via MIDI, for example the detailed specifications of voice algorithms.

Each participating manufacturer is allocated a special version of the two-byte command, the first byte containing the standard 'system exclusive' status byte and the second byte a unique identifying number. The latter ensures that the information which follows is not erroneously intercepted by other devices. Once this command has been issued the manufacturer is entirely responsible for determining the use of the data bytes which follow with no restriction as to their number, this mode remaining in force until the status byte of any other MIDI command is transmitted, at which point normal MIDI operation is resumed. Voice editing is an important aspect of any serious use of MIDI synthesis facilities and this is an area where computer graphics support has proved particularly useful.

Perhaps the most unexpected use of 'system exclusive' mode has been as a communications channel for transferring audio samples between synthesis devices. It is particularly unfortunate in this respect that MIDI limits data to seven bits per byte, for as a result eight-bit sound samples require two bytes instead of one and sixteen-bit samples three bytes instead of two, introducing a significant element of redundancy into the transmission process. Today much faster interfaces are available for the transfer of digital audio data from one item of equipment to another, but for many years this special use of MIDI has provided a cheap and easy solution to what otherwise can prove a difficult communications problem. The transfer of audio samples provides one of the few examples of an application which has led to a major addition to the original MIDI specification. As sampling techniques gained in popularity it was quickly recognized that without any established guide-lines audio information would be transmitted in a variety of incompatible formats. To overcome this the Sample Dump Standard or SDS was introduced, imposing a strict set of rules for the coding and transmission of audio data files.

A number of other system messages are available, principally concerned with the transmission and synchronization of timing information. In live performance such information is not generally required since each new event is manually activated by an action such as depressing a new key. If, however, the sequence of commands thus generated is to be recorded for subsequent replay then timing information has also to be registered. In the case of a MIDI system serviced by a single sequencer, all timing information can be generated internally by the latter device and it is not necessary to access the MIDI clock. When two or more sequencers are to be used together synchronization is only possible using a common clock counter, in which case the simplest solution is to use MIDI timing messages which have been specially developed for this purpose.

Timing information is also important whenever MIDI devices are used with other equipment which uses different synchronization facilities. The most likely code to be encountered is SMPTE, an abbreviation for the Society of Motion PicTure Engineers, developed in 1967 for the synchronization of video and audio information, and now widely used in the recording industry. Here time is measured in terms of 'frames' per second, necessitating a conversion facility if standard MIDI time codes are to be translated into SMPTE and vice versa. To assist in this process MIDI has more recently adopted a timing protocol known as MTC with a new set of messages which recognize the use of frames per second as a unit of time.

MIDI is best suited to the synthesis of very specific genres of music information which although extensive in scope are by no means all-embracing. However, given the success of MIDI as the universal standard for the medium, even designers of more specialist systems at the frontiers of technical and musical research have come to realize the importance of providing suitable interfaces for this universal means of communication. Having thus traced the early development of the microcomputer and the evolution of digital synthesis techniques up to the birth of MIDI the stage is now set for a study of the hardware products which followed.

# 12 The MIDI Synthesizer

At the start of the 1980s the voltage-controlled synthesizer dominated the electronic music industry. The previous decade had seen steadily increasing sales not only from long-established manufacturers such as Moog, Buchla, ARP, and EMS but also newer competitors such as Casiotone, Korg, Roland, Sequential Circuits, and Yamaha. As a result the market for such products not only embraced the music education sector as a whole but also the rock and pop music sectors, both professional and amateur. By contrast digital applications were still largely confined to specialist groups of users, at one extreme serviced by large and expensive synthesizers such as the Fairlight and the Synclavier, and at the other by relatively basic facilities for microcomputers. Digital products had yet to make a significant impact and it thus appeared that the analogue synthesizer had an assured future.

In 1981 Casio launched a miniature all-digital synthesizer known as the VL-1, costing less than a hundred dollars. This consists of a tiny keyboard of just over two octaves, a bank of five voices controlled by a set of push-buttons, a 100 note sequencer, and a rhythm unit offering a choice of ten different patterns. The synthesis facilities are fairly rudimentary and of only moderate fidelity but this pioneering product marked an important turning point in the development of products for the music industry. Although several commentators initially dismissed the VL-1 as merely a toy others quickly realized the underlying significance of a system which embodied the essential elements of a programmable digital music synthesizer for little more than the price of an up-market scientific calculator. It is interesting to note in this context that by far the greatest proportion of the manufacturing costs of the VL-1 was associated with ancillary items such as the case, the keyboard, and the push-buttons. All the synthesis processes are carried out by a specially fabricated VLSI chip costing a fraction of any alternative architecture based instead on discrete analogue components.

The VL-1 provided a major stimulus to two other manufacturing sectors which are closely linked with that of the music synthesizer. The first of these concentrates on the most basic types of electronic keyboard, products which use an electronic means of sound production but are specifically engineered to function as a simple instrument with a fixed repertory of voices. The second concerns sound systems for the video games market, characterized by products which range from cheap self-contained systems complete with control paddles which plug directly into the aerial socket of a domestic television to sophisticated arcade machines designed for the purposes of gambling. All three sectors shared a common aim at this time in seeking the development of low-cost high-performance sound chips which could offer a range of functional characteristics from sound effects to a useful repertory of musical timbres.

Casio soon built up a range of digital synthesizers which despite being designed largely for the lower end of the market began seriously to challenge traditional analogue products from firms such as Moog and EMS. The CT-701, for example, which appeared only a matter of months after the VL-1, provides a five-octave keyboard, twenty preset voices, a rhythm box, and a sequencer. Moreover, it is polyphonic, allowing up to eight notes to be sounded simultaneously, and in addition incorporates a light-pen facility for reading in music information from scores which have previously been transcribed into a bar code format using strips similar to those used for registering goods at a supermarket check-out. Although this input method can only be used with specially pre-coded scores, a number of which are provided with the synthesizer, it clearly demonstrates the potential of a music data input technique which depends on digital rather than analogue technology.

The year 1981 saw Yamaha's first steps into the digital arena with the launch of their GS1 and GS2 synthesizers. These were by no means cheap products (the GS1 cost as much as a small Synclavier) but they served as important prototypes for their highly successful and influential DX series of all-digital synthesizers which were introduced within two years. Strictly speaking the GS synthesizers are of a hybrid construction since analogue circuits are used extensively for the last stages of synthesis to modify the tone by means of filtering and tremolo or chorus effects. The heart of the voice generation system none the less is entirely digital, and it is the design of this section which is of particular interest here.

The complex arrays of chips and wiring interconnections to be found inside the GS1 and GS2 give a clue to the experimental nature of these products. They were built to look outwardly like small grand pianos, the hammers, strings, and sound board section being replaced by a network of electronic circuits. Their primary repertory of digital voices also reflects this intention. The quantity of individual components used in these synthesizers and the generous layout of the circuit boards themselves indicates clearly that Yamaha's own development of VLSI chip technology was still at a relatively early stage, but the more pressing need was to obtain feedback from customers as to the strengths and weaknesses of this new approach to synthesizer design.

As regards the digital circuits themselves, a significant feature is the use of frequency modulation techniques to generate timbres instead of conventional additive methods. Yamaha had the foresight to patent a series of hardware algorithms for FM synthesis, thus effectively preventing any other manufacturer from developing rival FM systems. As noted in an earlier chapter these were developed in partnership with John Chowning at Stanford University, building upon his pioneering work in this area during the late 1960s and early 70s, which made extensive use of the MUSIC family of software synthesis programs. This linking of advanced institutional research and commercial expertise for the mass-production of new musical products was to reap rich rewards. The implementation of FM techniques in the GS1 and GS2 was far simpler than that subsequently adopted for the DX series but these keyboard synthesizers clearly demonstrated the power and versatility of such algorithms as a method for generating musical sounds, the instantaneous response of the specially designed hardware contrasting sharply with the non-real-time environment of traditional software-based computer music systems. As products of a pre-MIDI era, however, with no facilities for directly accessing synthesis algorithms or performance data, the scope for experimentation beyond the factory-supplied preset voices was very limited.

Most of these restrictions were removed in the DX series of synthesizers, launched in 1983. In contrast to the GS models these are compact, portable, and most importantly based on MIDI. The initial range was entirely keyboard-based, with versions ranging from the flagship DX7 to the more modest DX21, differences of scale being reflected in the number and sophistication of the FM algorithms provided. The latter may be programmed either directly in the manner described below or indirectly using a MIDI-based voice editing program hosted on an associated microcomputer. Within two years the range had been expanded to include voice-only systems such as the TX816 and TX802, designed for remote operation via MIDI either from a master keyboard such as the Yamaha KX88 or another keyboard synthesizer such as a DX7. Whereas the functional characteristics of a TX802 correspond closely to those offered by a single DX7 the TX816 is an altogether more powerful device, consisting of eight DX7 voice modules mounted in a single rack.

The sound generation system for each voice in a DX7 consists of six oscillators which can be arranged in different configurations by selecting from a table of thirty-two basic algorithms. One algorithm specially configures all the generators as a parallel bank of six individually programmable audio oscillators, the outputs being directly mixed to produce a simple blend of timbres without any frequency modulation. The other algorithms comprise a mixture of parallel and serial connections, in some instances creating a sequence of three or even four oscillators in a single FM chain. These carefully researched extensions of the basic two-oscillator FM principle greatly expand the variety of timbres which can be generated by this means. A further enhancement consists of a feedback facility for one of the oscillators which can be used to introduce a degree of resonance to the sound.

Considerable thought has been given to the facilities for controlling the frequency and amplitude settings for each oscillator. Since a fundamental characteristic of most synthesizer voices is a distinctive timbre which will transpose consistently up or down in pitch, the basic frequency settings for each oscillator are normally specified in the form of ratios of the chosen key selection which can either be limited to simple multiples or sub-multiples to create harmonically related spectra or include fractional ratios to create more complex sounds. Alternatively the oscillators can be individually assigned a specific fixed frequency value which is retained regardless of the key selection. Suitable combinations of fixed and frequency mode oscillators for the various algorithms can then be used to introduce a variety of effects, for example timbres which vary according to the key selection or which include a range of noise-like components.

The provision of separate envelope generators for each oscillator allows for considerable flexibility in determining the evolution of both timbre and volume. Additional function generators permit other characteristics to be superimposed on the resulting sound such as frequency and/or amplitude vibrato, and variations in the fundamental pitch. The specifications for up to thirty-two different sounds can stored in the internal voice bank of the synthesizer (expanded to sixty-four in later versions), this information being loaded either from a special plug-in cartridge or input from an external source using MIDI in 'system exclusive' mode. The internal bank provides the primary working area for voice development and performance, a battery back-up ensuring that the information is not lost whenever the synthesizer is switched off. A library of 128 factory-produced voices can be accessed via a special ROM cartridge, and erasable RAM cartridges may be used for the storage of user-defined voices.

The general performance characteristics of the DX7 are further extended by the availability of keyboard sensing circuitry which takes advantage of several of the special options offered by MIDI. These include the ability to measure the velocity with which individual keys are depressed and then use this information to modify the maximum amplitude settings of selected oscillators to varying degrees, thus providing a powerful tool for controlling both the amplitude and the timbre of FM sounds as performance features. In addition the pressure exerted on individual keys after the initial stroke can be actively sensed and utilized to modify a selection of control settings. This facility is very useful for applications such as generating the subtle pitch variations which are associated with striking the keys of an acoustic instrument such as the clavichord, or for introducing a variable pitch or amplitude vibrato. Another enhancement consists of a comprehensive range of microtuning facilities to create different scaling systems as locally applied modifications to the standard equal temperament scaling of the standard MIDI pitch codes.

In the case of the early DX synthesizers only one voice can be active at a time. Later versions, such as the DX7 Mark II launched in 1985, allow two voices to be active, thus expanding the timbral possibilities of the system. In this model the user has the option of either mixing the two output signals together to create a multi-timbral blend or splitting the voices so that one voice responds to notes below a selected breakpoint on the keyboard and the other to notes above. Other enhancements include facilities for panning the voices stereophonically across two output channels and independent control of locally applied modifications such as the transposition of pitch data up or down by a specified number of semitone steps. Yamaha also produced an enhanced version of this synthesizer, which incorporates a floppy disk unit for the storage of data, a useful alternative to the plug-in RAM cartridge.

Direct voice editing is carried out using the alphanumeric display screen, a data entry slider and a series of push-buttons, many of which have a dual function as voice selection buttons when the synthesizer is used in performance mode. Here the problems faced by manufacturers in devising compact but usable editing facilities for digital synthesizers are clearly illustrated. On the original DX7 the display is so small that only one control parameter can be viewed at a time. Although the control panel is well organized and straightforward to operate, with the effects of any alterations instantly audible, the inability to cross-reference other parameter settings at the same time or to view envelope functions graphically is a major drawback. The enlarged display facilities provided for the DX7 Mark II are an improvement since they allow a number of related parameters to be viewed at a time, but still only in an alphanumeric form.

Attention has already been drawn to the acoustical deficiencies which can result from inadequate sampling rates, too few bits to represent each sample, and shortcomings in the synthesis process itself. Measured against all-digital products of the period, from the Mark II Fairlight to systems based on the Mountain Computer boards, the perceived quality of the DX7 is as impressive as the versatility of its performance. Although its full technical specification has never been officially disclosed external measurements by a number of independent reviewers have invariably confirmed the generally favourable verdict of such subjective assessments. It appears, for example, that the original DX7 achieves noise and distortion figures comparable to those associated with a twelve-bit sampling standard, a frequency response in the order of 18 kHz, and a purity of wave-form generation which matches that of a good interpolating wavetable oscillator. While tests on more basic members of the DX synthesizers reveal some design economies later versions such as the DX7 Mark II approach the quality of an audio compact disc.

The launch of such a high-quality all-digital product in 1983 was thus an important landmark, not only for its inclusion of MIDI but also in that it established the credibility of digital rather than analogue methods of synthesizer design. The Yamaha FM patents, however, proved remarkably effective in restraining direct commercial competition, and as already noted other manufacturers were forced to turn to alternative synthesis technologies for the development of competitive products.

A fundamental disadvantage of most conventional synthesis methods, including frequency modulation, is the lack of any direct connection with the natural sound world and the processes of sound generation which are associated with it. In due course reference will be made to digital synthesis techniques which are modelled directly on acoustic principles, but these for the most part are more recent developments and have yet to be exploited to any great extent by the commercial sector. Back in the 1980s the most obvious solution for many manufacturers lay in the design of systems which capture and manipulate the characteristics of the natural sound world itself, and thus it was that attention turned towards the possibilities of digital sampling. The potential of this synthesis method had been convincingly demonstrated by the Fairlight back in 1979, but the development of the MIDI sampler proved to be a rather protracted process. Once this design revolution had gathered momentum, however, its impact on the synthesizer market as a whole was to prove substantial.

A major cause of this extended developmental phase was the relatively high costs of the associated technology during its early years, in terms of both memory requirements and processing power. A major breakthrough occurred in 1981 with the launch of a self-contained sampling keyboard synthesizer known as the Emulator I, manufactured by E-mu for about a quarter of the price of a Fairlight. Although the editing facilities are much more rudimentary it clearly demonstrated the potential of sampling methods as an alternative to wave-form synthesis for the design of keyboard synthesizers. A closer study of this pioneering model provides a useful framework for a discussion of the characteristics of samplers in general.

The operational heart of the Emulator I consists of a Z-80 microprocessor, operating software permanently stored in ROM, and 120 kilobytes of memory for the storage of sound samples, accessed by a series of voice modules which permit the re-synthesis of material via the keyboard in up to eight parts. Although the A-to-D and D-to-A converters are only eight-bit, special companding circuitry is incorporated to compress the dynamic range of sound material on the input side, and expand it again on the output. Such a non-linear method of sampling and internal data compression introduces the possibility of audible companding errors with some types of signal, but from a commercial point of view this drawback was considered less important than the considerable savings in costs which resulted from a reduced memory requirement and the benefits of a dynamic range approaching that of a conventional twelve-bit sampling system.

The sampling rate is fixed at 30 kHz, only slightly below the 32 kHz maximum used by the original Fairlight, but the low-pass filters in the Emulator restrict the bandwidth to 10 kHz, which is well below the Nyquist frequency (15 kHz). Of the memory 8 kilobytes are reserved for system operations, leaving 120 kilobytes for sound samples. This allocation is usually split to allow two sounds to be resident at a time, each occupying a maximum of 60 kilobytes with one allocated to the upper two octaves and the other to the lower two octaves of the four-octave keyboard. At a sampling rate of 30 kHz this restricts the maximum length of each sound to only two seconds, illustrating how critical the factor of memory size becomes when determining the functional characteristics of a particular sampler. The original Fairlight suffered badly in this respect, only permitting sounds with a maximum duration of 1.2 seconds to be sampled at maximum fidelity. The solution here, as with many other early sampler designs, is a facility to sample at a slower rate whenever the duration of the sound is of overriding importance. Unfortunately lowering the sampling rate also reduces the maximum attainable bandwidth in direct proportion, with potentially devastating consequences for the audio fidelity, especially if the source happens to be a sound which is of a rich timbre.

The initial sampling rate is only the starting-point for determining the performance of the system. How this information is then reproduced at different pitches is equally critical. A common practice is to vary the rate at which the voice modules reproduce the sample pattern: double the rate for one octave higher, half the rate for one octave lower, and suitable divisions and multiplications thereof to produce the equal-tempered scalings required for a conventional music keyboard. Since the basic bit pattern of the sound is preserved in this process no additional degradation in quality will normally occur when the material is re-synthesized. The principle disadvantage is the need for individual D-to-A converters for each sounding note if the output is to be polyphonic, adding to the overall manufacturing costs. An alternative is to use a resampling algorithm to produce an equivalent pattern of samples but at a constant sampling rate, in which case all the constituent sounds can be mixed digitally before conversion.

Although the specific technical details of such internal design features are usually of little direct interest to the user the subjective effects of transposition can prove highly significant since they involve processes which are essentially no different from those associated with speeding up or slowing down a conventional tape recording. Changes in pitch also result in proportional changes in prominent characteristics such as the attack and decay times, and other time-varying features such as vibrato will similarly be affected. In the case of the Emulator I the effects of excessive transposition can be minimized by using an optional multi-sampling facility which allows the memory to be partitioned into eight segments instead of the normal two, each assigned to a specific half-octave of keys. If the sound source is an instrument such as a piano a reasonable consistency of timbre can thus be achieved by sampling at eight different pitches, suitably spaced half an octave apart. Unfortunately a price has to be paid in memory terms with the consequential restriction of sampled sounds to an average of no more than half a second each. An alternative use of this partitioning facility involves sampling a different sound for each group of keys to create multi-voice textures or a set of individual instruments such as the components of a small percussion kit.

Recording sounds at one pitch and reproducing them at different pitches is basic to all samplers, and as just illustrated one measure of their overall versatility is the number of different voices and samples that can be handled at any one time. Another is their capacity to process sampled sounds before re-synthesis. Modern samplers with large memories are capable of a variety of sophisticated editing procedures such as the reordering of user-defined sound segments in memory or the dynamically controlled blending of two different sounds to create a new composite sound which can then sometimes be resampled for further processing. Older samplers such as the Emulator I are usually restricted to features such as a simple looping facility to allow a single sound to be artificially sustained and some means of regulating the overall envelope.

Designing a good looping system is no easy task since some sounds are not amenable to such treatment. The basic process starts with the selection of suitable start- and end-points for a loop within the chosen sound. The sampler is then programmed to read through the sound until the end-point is encountered, at which point it is directed back to the start-point for the loop to re-read the intervening samples, this cyclical process continuing until either the activating key is released or a specified number of loops has been completed, whereupon sample extraction proceeds normally to the end of the sound. More sophisticated samplers allow more than one loop segment to be established with the option of selecting one segment as the primary keyboard-controlled sustain loop and specifying a certain number of repeats for the others.

The greatest problem encountered in setting up loops concerns the breakpoint in the loop itself. Any discontinuity in the waveform will result in an audible click and it is thus very important to be able to move either the start- or the end-point of the loop segment sample by sample until the smoothest possible transition is achieved. Unfortunately some samplers will not allow such fine adjustments to be made directly, offering instead an automatic detection process whereby the sampler itself seeks a suitable loop point. While this facility can sometimes be very convenient it cannot always be relied upon to achieve the best possible results. There is a further factor to be taken into account, for even the smoothest join will not remove the subjective effects of any significant differences in the nature of the sound material either side of the loop. The smallest change in overall amplitude of the sound between the start- and end-points can readily result in an audible pulsing, and any variation in pitch even more so. Such problems are well known to those familiar with tape looping procedures where a satisfactory solution can sometimes be effected by joining the ends of the loop together with a long diagonal splice, thus creating a physically engineered transition rather than a direct cut. Many modern samplers offer an electronic means of cross-fading in this manner, but no such method can overcome any significant discontinuities across the breakpoint.

Facilities to superimpose basic attack and decay characteristics and other modulation characteristics on recorded sounds to create new envelopes are very desirable since they allow sound sources to be dynamically shaped in a consistent manner, regardless of their transposition. To this end the Emulator I provides an adjustable three-stage attack/sustain/decay envelope-shaper, along with a number of performance aids such as a pair of modulation wheels to bend the pitch and introduce varying degrees of vibrato, a variable low-pass filter, and a foot-pedal switch which allows notes played in the lower half of the keyboard to be automatically doubled by corresponding notes in the upper half.

Auxiliary facilities for storing and retrieving sampled sounds are essential requirements since samplers invariably use volatile RAM memory. For this reason even the most basic sampler incorporates a floppy disk drive and it is now quite usual for larger models to offer high-capacity hard disk facilities as well either as a standard feature or as an optional extra. Unfortunately manufacturers have attached little importance to standardizing disk formats for sampled sounds and although developments such as the MIDI sample dump standard have provided a general protocol for transferring files of sampled sounds from one sampler to another or from a sampler to a computer it is very rare that the audio data recorded on to a floppy disk by one sampler can be read directly by another. This is all the more irritating since most samplers use industry-standard disk drives which will accept normal 5.25- or 3.5-inch blank disks, widely available from computer suppliers at low cost. These have to be specially formatted using a utility program provided as part of the sampler's own operating system, and it is the lack of agreement over a common protocol for this process which is the primary cause of incompatibility. One or two manufacturers, notably Roland, have used a non-standard drive which requires special 2.8-inch disks, but this initiative to develop a universal storage media specially for samplers has attracted little support from other manufacturers.

The storage capacity of floppy disks is critical when considering their use for storing sampled audio data. In the case of the Emulator I each two-second sound sample requires 60 kilobytes of storage space at maximum fidelity. In the case of a more modern sampler sampling at the compact disc standard of 44 100 sixteen-bit samples per second in stereo rather than mono, the same two seconds of sampled sound will require 176.4 kilobytes. Early

5.25-inch drives, including the type used in the Emulator I, record at a low density and only access one side of the disk. The maximum capacity of each disk is thus restricted to no more than about 180 kilobytes. As the technology improved double-sided drives and higher recording densities were introduced, increasing typical capacities first to 360 kilobytes and then to 1200 kilobytes (1.2 megabytes). From the outset recording densities for the smaller 3.5-inch disk drives have been of a much higher order. As a result even the earliest single-sided versions could usually store up to 360 kilobytes, with double-sided drives offering first 720 kilobytes, and then 1440 kilobytes (1.44 megabytes). Floppy disk drives offering even higher recording densities were introduced during the early 1990s but the medium is likely to remain of limited value for the storage of audio data. Even a 1.44-megabyte disk, for example, can only store about eight seconds of CD-quality sound unless some form of electronic data compression is used. A much better solution is offered by a new generation of hard disk drives which use removable disk packs in the form of a small cartridge with typical capacities of 40 or 80 megabytes, but these particular designs have yet to be widely adopted by sampler manufacturers.

As a product dating from 1981 the Emulator I belongs to the pre-MIDI era. The original model made no provision for controlling the performance of events internally or externally but by 1982 a special 900-note sequencer section had been introduced as an upgrade, creating a versatile and entirely self-contained resource for both composition and performance.

In 1983 developments began to gather pace with the demonstration of the prototype for a sampling keyboard which finally went into production early in 1984 as the Kurzweil 250. The manufacturer was primarily concerned with producing a performance instrument rather than a general purpose sampler and released it in a playback-only version in the first instance. Although additional features such as a sound digitizer and a voice editing program were announced as forthcoming upgrades users had to wait almost two years before the full range of options were made available, these delays being largely attributable to the innovative nature of its technology.

Internally the most important difference between the Kurzweil and its contemporaries concerns the use of floating point numbers rather than integers to represent samples. In essence this involves recoding each sample value in the form of two components, the first being the basic number pattern expressed as a fraction, the other the exponent or multiplier required to rescale this fraction to its true value. Computers have supported both types of data format from a very early stage in their development, and direct synthesis programs such as CMUSIC and CSOUND generally use floating rather than fixed point data formats for their internal computations. In the context of sampler development, however, this implementation broke new ground.

Wave-form components are frequently subjected to a number of arithmetic operations during the processes of digital synthesis and processing. If the samples are stored as simple integers, binary arithmetic dictates that each bit pattern will be shifted one position to the left within the word boundary every time the value is doubled, and one position to the right every time it is halved. If attempts are made to multiply sample values beyond the maximum range permitted by the available bits the highest-order bits will be successively shifted out and lost, resulting in a severe distortion of the sound. Conversely, whenever a sample value is shifted to the right as the result of a division the lowest-order bit will be discarded. In the latter case the effect of this loss of information is rather different since the arithmetic change is essentially a proportional scaling-down of the overall numeric range representing the wave-form, perceived as a general reduction in volume. However, as explained in the preceding chapter, reducing the number of bits used to represent a wave-form affects the underlying numerical accuracy of the samples themselves. Any subsequent multiplication of these values to restore the overall amplitude will therefore also magnify the level of audio distortion thus introduced. To take an extreme case, if a sine wave is digitized as eight-bit bytes at maximum amplitude, attenuated 42 dB by shifting all the sample values to the right a total of seven steps and finally restored to its original amplitude by shifting these values left again a total of seven steps, only the information previously stored in the most significant bit will be recovered, resulting in a sequence of square wave pulses which bears little relation to the original signal. In a more typical case such as a 12 dB attenuation of a full-range signal followed by a matching amplification, two bits of low-order information will have been lost, reducing the effective resolution of the restored signal to just six bits. Although a significant proportion of the original detail will be preserved in this instance the loss in resolution will still be perceived as a marked increase in signal noise, the dynamic range having in effect been reduced from 48 dB to 36 dB.

If the same operations are carried out on samples coded in floating-point format, the potential loss of information through attenuation and amplification can largely be absorbed by changes to the exponent value rather than the fractional data itself. There are nevertheless some important practical issues to be taken into account when considering the use of floating-point rather than integer formats for audio samples. The maximum resolution of a floating point number is determined by the number of bits available to record the fractional component itself, and the absolute range of values which may thus be coded depends on the number of bits available to record the exponent values. In a traditional minicomputer such as the PDP 11 standard integer numbers occupy two bytes (sixteen bits) and standard floating point numbers occupy four bytes (thirty-two bits). Converting an array of integers into equivalent floating point numbers thus doubles the amount of memory space required, twenty-four bits being assigned to the fractional component and eight bits to the exponent value. The extra bits thus provided for basic numerical precision taken together with an associated exponent range of some 256 orders of magnitude are clearly more than adequate to ensure that the accuracy of sixteen-bit integer samples can be preserved intact regardless of any changes in amplitude as a result of complex audio processing operations.

In the case of the Kurzweil 250 a reduced floating-point format is used, based on an eighteen-bit word length. This saves considerably on memory requirements but imposes some limitations on accuracy. Just ten bits are assigned to the fractional value of each sample, leaving eight bits for the exponent. The former constraint limits the maximum signal-to-noise ratio to just 60 dB at full amplitude, but the overall performance is significantly better than that obtained from a conventional ten-bit integer system, especially at lower amplitudes, since the signal-to-noise ratio will remain constant throughout the exponent range. In practice, therefore, the system delivers a perceived quality considerably better than the format might at first suggest.

The entire Kurzweil is controlled by a single sixteen-bit 68000 microprocessor which supervises all processing and communications operations. The operating system and control software are stored in a special read-only memory, additional ROMs providing an extensive library of factory-supplied voices. Instead of storing a representative selection of perhaps six or eight sampled sounds up to fifty separate recordings are digitized for each voice, thus ensuring that no sample has to be used more than twice in servicing the eighty-eight notes on the full-length keyboard. This intensive multi-sampling overcomes most of the problems of transposition discussed earlier and is matched by a facility to perform up to twelve voices at a time. Conventional storage of such information would have required a prohibitive amount of memory space so an analysis of the functional characteristics of each sound is stored rather than the sound itself, reducing the basic sound library to little more than two megabytes.

The digitizing facility is not capable of reducing sampled sounds into such components and handles the data in a more conventional manner, converting the samples directly into a floating-point format before loading them into memory; 512 kilowords (one per sample) are available for this purpose and the sampling rate may be adjusted in ten steps from 50 kHz down to 5 kHz, the maximum sampling times increasing proportionally from 10 seconds at the highest rate to 100 seconds at the lowest. For reasons which have already been outlined, however, the lowest sampling rates are of limited practical value since the associated fidelity is very poor. The absence of any disk storage facilities for the basic Kurzweil is a major drawback when using the digitizer and this necessitates the services of a microcomputer.

Kurzweil encountered significant difficulties in selecting a suitable host machine for this purpose since none of the machines generally available in 1983 proved sufficiently fast and powerful for their needs. The launch of the Apple Macintosh in 1984 provided an attractive solution and a high-speed interface known as the MacAttach was quickly developed for the instrument. The main control panel of push-buttons and sliders provides all the general editing facilities and also controls access to the internal sequencer, which has a capacity of about 7900 notes. Any detailed manipulation of sampled wave-forms or sequences or the scoring of events in common music notation requires the MacAttach facility and appropriate software. MIDI is supported via built-in ports, and many users have found this facility useful for accessing a wider range of sequencing and notation programs.

The marketing of such a powerful sampling keyboard in 1983 provided a major stimulus to other manufacturers. None, however, chose to invest in the floating-point technology of the Kurzweil, concentrating instead on improving the performance of systems based on an integer architecture. In 1984 E-mu replaced the Emulator I with the Emulator II. This added facilities for MIDI, expanded the memory to 512 kilobytes, and increased the disk capacity to a full megabyte. In quantizing terms this sampler achieves a performance equivalent to that of a conventional fourteen-bit linear system by using an alternative method of coding known as delta modulation, where the changes in value from sample to sample are recorded instead of the absolute numerical value of each sample. This dramatically reduces the data storage requirements for sampled sounds to just eight bits per sample, but once again there are drawbacks in terms of both the lack of compatibility with other more conventional sampling formats and also the increased risk of introducing other types of signal distortion under certain conditions, in particular rapid changes in signal levels as a result of sharp attack transients or percussive sounds.

The improvements to the Emulator II were accompanied by a significant increase in price when compared with the previous model, reflecting a similar marketing strategy to that adopted by both Synclavier and Fairlight on the release of their own Mark II systems. Any notion that the sampler industry was destined to become the exclusive preserve of those willing to pay ever higher prices for the privilege was dealt a mortal blow in the same year with the release of the Ensoniq Mirage, a sampler offering an attractive range of facilities and performance specifications for a fraction of the price of an Emulator II. These include 128 kilobytes of memory, an integral floppy disk drive, a 31.25 kHz sampling rate and a non-linear, eight-bit conversion system similar in operation to that of the Emulator I. The low-cost MIDI sampler had come of age.

Akai's first MIDI sampler, the S612, appeared in 1985, the first of a range of models from this manufacturer and distinguished by the lack of an integral keyboard. Despite its rather basic facilities for editing and a memory restricted to just 43 kilowords (one word = 1.5 bytes in this context) the S612 set new standards with its use of twelve-bit sampling with linear converters, associated with a maximum sampling rate of 32 kHz. Sequential

Circuits responded with the Prophet 2000, a keyboard sampler offering twelve-bit resolution, a basic 256-kiloword memory split into two banks, and a maximum sampling rate of 42 kHz, sufficient for full audio bandwidth recording. Each of its memory banks may be partitioned into eight blocks for multi-sampling, and the editing facilities allow two separate loops to be set up within each sound. Later in the same year Korg introduced the DSS-1, a keyboard sampler which is similar to the Prophet 2000 in its use of twelve-bit sampling and a 256-kiloword memory, but differs in its provision of a better range of sampling rates including both the 32 and the 48 kHz industry standards. In addition the DSS-1 incorporates wave-form synthesis facilities more usually associated with a traditional synthesizer, heralding a mixed sampling/synthesis design technology which was to become popular in the late 1980s with products such as the Yamaha SY77, to be described later. In the case of the Korg the user can either draw in wave-shapes directly or specify a timbre in terms of the relative strengths of up to 128 individual harmonics.

In common with FM or additive synthesizers, samplers require adequate display facilities to assist editing. Given the complex nature of audio waves some form of graphical monitoring is highly desirable, especially when selecting segments of sound for looping or splicing. Unfortunately most MIDI samplers just provide a small liquid crystal display and many of the early models are restricted to alphanumeric character information only. The Akai S612, Prophet 2000, and Korg DSS-1 are all deficient in this respect and the same holds true for both the S-10 and the S-50 sampling keyboards from Roland, which followed in 1986. In the case of the S-50, however, a solution is provided in the form of a special link adaptor which permits a computer monitor to be attached for the display of functions graphically. Both offer twelve-bit resolution but with a maximum sampling rate of just 30 kHz. The smaller S-10 provides 128 kilowords of memory, sufficient for just four seconds of sound at maximum fidelity. In contrast the S-50 provides 512 kilowords of memory, sufficient for a number of multi-sampling applications. One notable feature of both samplers is their ability to re-synthesize from memory with up to sixteen notes sounding simultaneously, compared with eight in the case of the Prophet 2000 and Korg DSS-1, and just six in the case of the Akai S612.

Akai's answer to these more sophisticated samplers was the

S900, a substantially re-engineered version of the S612, offering 512 kilowords of memory, eight voices, and a maximum sampling rate of 40 kHz. It was Ensoniq, however, which signalled a new phase in sampler development with the EPS, which appeared towards the end of 1986. This offers a wide selection of sampling rates up to a maximum of 52.1 kHz, twelve voices (extending to twenty at lower sampling rates), a 512-kilobyte (256-kiloword) memory which is expandable to 1024 kilobytes (512 kilowords), and, most significantly, a sampling resolution of thirteen bits. This improvement in quantization accuracy is further enhanced with the use of sixteen-bit (two-byte) words for the storage of samples, the three extra bits allowing an extended integer scaling of dynamic levels internally without loss of accuracy.

At the top end of the market Fairlight finally caught up with Synclavier in terms of basic fidelity with the Mark III version of the system, which offers full sixteen-bit sampling. A further incentive for improvements in fidelity came from the main audio industry with the release of a number of 'tapeless' studio recording systems which use digital sampling and high-capacity hard disk storage systems as a direct substitute for the conventional tape recorder. Two systems dating from this period are worth noting in the current context. The HDU system from PPG is a sixteen-bit system which samples in mono or stereo at 44.1 kHz. In addition to a suite of basic editing facilities a number of useful signal processing functions are offered such as time compression and expansion, a form of vocoding which allows a variety of manipulations such as the transposition of pitch without altering the speed. The 85-megabyte disk provided with the early versions of the system allows just twelve minutes of mono recording and only three minutes in full four-track mode. As a machine for preparing pop jingles it initially had few rivals.

The AudioFile from AMS is an altogether more substantial system allowing up to eight tracks of tapeless digital recording with sixteen-bit mono or stereo sampling at a selection of rates which include the 44.1 and 48 kHz industry standards. The disk facilities are expandable, allowing the system to be upgraded to take advantage of the range of high-capacity disk drives which have become available since the end of the 1980s. These have developed rapidly from an initial capacity of about 300 megabytes to about 1200 megabytes (1.2 gigabytes) by the early 1990s, and such facilities are clearly now more than adequate for most recording applications. A 600-megabyte disk, for example, will allow the AudioFile system to record up to about 50 minutes of stereo material at its highest sampling rate.

As regards MIDI samplers the move to sixteen-bit sampling was heralded by Greengate towards the end of 1986 with the DS:4, quickly followed by Casio with their FZ-1 keyboard sampler, released early in 1987. The FZ-1 aroused particular interest in view of its extremely competitive price and the fact that such a high-quality product should come from a manufacturer which hitherto had built its reputation principally on entry-level systems more likely to be used for entertainment rather than serious composition or performance. The only major limitations of the FZ-1 concern the maximum sampling rate, which is just 36 kHz, and a restriction to just eight voices. These apart, other notable features include memory facilities with a basic capacity of one megabyte (512 kilowords), expandable to two megabytes (1024 kilowords), and a good range of editing facilities which include a graphics window which is especially useful for locating suitable start- and end-points for loops.

The FZ-1 was soon to have a rival, the Prophet 3000 from Sequential Circuits, offering two megabytes of memory and sixteen-bit resolution at the three industry-standard sampling rates of 32, 44.1, and 48 kHz. Initially, like most samplers from this period, it suffered from the limitations of a floppy disk drive as the only facility for storing samples. Within a matter of months, however, a hard disk option was released which uses the Small Computers System Interface (SCSI), a fast communications link developed by the computer industry especially for use with high speed peripherals such as disks. Following this lead other manufacturers such as Akai, E-mu, Ensoniq, Korg, and Roland introduced SCSI-based hard disk systems as options for their new ranges of samplers. These facilities transformed the working environment for the serious composer or performer, offering typically 20 or 40 megabytes of data storage in the first instance, but with the possibility of further expansion at a later stage if needs demand. This choice of an industry-standard interface was to prove significant in another respect since it provided a high-speed gateway not merely from a sampler to its own hard disk, but from sampler to sampler or sampler to microcomputer, thus providing a very attractive alternative to MIDI for the high-speed transfer of audio data between devices.

Whereas the launch of the first twelve-bit MIDI samplers encouraged most manufacturers quickly to follow suit, the general upgrade to a sixteen-bit standard proved to be a far more protracted affair. Roland, for example, retained a twelve-bit format for the S220, an improved version of the S-10 released in 1987, and also for the S550, a development of the S-50 released in 1988, in both cases still limited by a maximum sampling rate of 30 kHz. Indeed their first sixteen-bit sampler, the S330 released later the same year, only achieves this specification at the output stage by means of special hardware which interpolates twelve-bit samples from the main processor. In a similar vein E-mu retained their special non-standard data compression technology for new versions of the Emulator II, the Emax and the Emax SE, released in 1988, the primary technical improvements being a SCSI hard disk option, an increase in the maximum sampling rate to 42 kHz, and an expanded library of factory-supplied sounds. E-mu took an important initiative over the vexed question of different sampling rates and data standards with these models, providing software utilities which will convert audio data files obtained from other sources via the MIDI sample dump facility or SCSI to conform to their own special specifications.

The year 1988 saw the release of the highly successful E-mu Emulator III, which delivers true sixteen-bit quality in stereo or mono at a number of sampling rates including 44.1 kHz. Four megabytes of memory are provided as standard, expandable to eight or sixteen megabytes, further facilities including an integral hard disk with support for SCSI and a comprehensive suite of editing facilities, supported by a liquid crystal display panel with graphics capabilities. In addition to SCSI and MIDI yet another communications facility is provided in the form of a conventional serial computer port. Akai responded with the S1000, released in 1989 offering very similar operational characteristics, for example sixteen-bit sampling in mono or stereo at 44.1 kHz, one to eight megabytes of memory, a hard disk option, SCSI communications, and a comparable suite of editing facilities with graphics support.

By the end of the 1980s the basic problems of fidelity in MIDI samplers had finally been surmounted, leaving the flexibility of the hardware and its operating software as the primary features distinguishing one sampler from another. Since editing facilities are largely a matter of software several manufacturers have been able to improve the performance of their products in the field through the release of upgrade programs which can be installed in a matter of seconds from a floppy disk. Other features are intrinsic to the hardware architecture, for example the number of voices available or the duration of samples which can be loaded into memory. Characteristics such as these require additional or replacement hardware, and beyond basic facilities such as expansion slots ready to receive extra memory cards the scope for improvements here to existing models has remained rather limited.

Despite the relentless advance of digital engineering a number of manufacturers continued to make extensive use of analogue circuits until the late 1980s. In many cases their conversion to the new practices was progressive, leading to a number of interesting products *en route* which combine elements of both technologies. The design principles involved here were by no means new, for they had already been successfully developed for systems such as EMS in Stockholm and MUSYS in London during the late 1960s and early 70s. The principal advantage lay in the ability to control the functional characteristics of analogue devices accurately in a digital domain without incurring the processing overheads associated with real-time digital synthesis.

Antecedents of this new generation of hybrid synthesizers include the eight-voice Trident from Korg, the OBX series from Oberheim, the sixteen-voice Rhodes Chroma, the Jupiter series from Roland, and the Prophet series from Sequential Circuits. One noticeable difference between these machines and their more traditional voltage-controlled ancestors is the replacement of patch chords or shorting-pin connectors with electronic routing facilities, making it possible to store settings in a small memory bank for instant recall at the press of a button. With the introduction of MIDI some synthesizer manufacturers saw the advantage of taking this process a stage further and replaced voltage-controlled oscillators with digitally controlled equivalents. Similar engineering changes were also applied in some instances to associated signal processing devices such as filters and envelope-shapers, but this was by no means a universal practice. Other manufacturers introduced all-digital oscillators with integral D-to-A converters for systems which otherwise remained entirely analogue.

Such details are not always clear to the casual observer and commercial considerations often conspire to obscure the true nature of the underlying technology. In the case of a manufacturer such as Roland, however, the hybrid nature of their MIDI synthesizer designs is well documented. Their favoured principle has been a combination of digitally controlled analogue oscillators with a selection of voltage-controlled processors such as filters, amplifiers, modulators, and envelope generators, and this configuration forms the basis of their early Juno series of MIDI synthesizers, for example the fully programmable six-voice Juno 106. A similar arrangement is used in their subsequent JX series of synthesizers, for example the six-voice JX8P, or the twelve-voice JX10. The latter model, introduced in 1986, is essentially two JX8Ps combined as a single instrument, with additional support from a built-in digital sequencer which uses a plug-in cartridge to store performance data. Each voice uses a pair of oscillators offering a choice of four basic wave-forms; sawtooth, square, pulse, and noise. A separate attack/decay/sustain/release (ADSR) envelope-shaper is provided for each oscillator and the resulting signals can either be mixed directly or cross-modulated. Modulation of pitch is also possible either via a low-frequency oscillator or by using function patterns generated by an envelope-shaper, and further timbral modifications can be made using a voltage-controlled filter or a voltage-controlled amplifier. Keyboard velocity can also be sensed and applied as a control variable, and up to 100 preset voices can be stored in the internal memory. With their full support for MIDI control these JX and Juno synthesizers integrate readily into any performance configuration. Functionally, however, they are representative of a very different design philosophy from that associated with an all-digital synthesizer such as the DX7.

The achievements of Casio merit special attention at this point, not least for their production of a versatile range of all-digital synthesizers at very low cost during the mid-1980s. This CZ series, like the FZ-1 sixteen-bit sampler, took some commentators by surprise. From the original CZ-101 to more sophisticated but far from expensive versions such as the CZ-3000 and CZ-5000 the key to success here lay in the use of a synthesis technique which is potentially no less powerful than that of FM. As in the latter case the secret lies not so much in the individuality of the technique itself, known as phase distortion synthesis, but in the method of its implementation.

The principles of phase distortion synthesis as implemented by

Casio are essentially very simple. The basic technique of digital wavetable synthesis has already been described in connection with the MUSIC family of direct synthesis programs. In this context it has been shown how calculating a single cycle of a selected wave-form as a table of values and then scanning it cyclically to extract a continuous function is computationally far more efficient than repetitively calculating each value in turn from first principles. Different frequencies at a chosen sample rate can be generated by varying the incremental value and, for the highest quality of output, interpolating samples which lie at points between the values stored in the table rather than rounding to the nearest stored value. Providing the incremental value is constant, at least on a cycle-by-cycle basis, the resulting function will accurately reflect the stored wave-form.

In the case of phase distortion synthesis, instead of extracting samples at a constant increment per cycle, the incremental step is varied during the course of each cycle. As a result the extrapolated function is distorted in a controllable manner. In some respects this technique has much in common with the analogue pulse width modulation techniques described in connection with the early Cologne studio, but the use of ramp, triangle, or sinusoidal functions rather than just square waves greatly expands the degree of timbral flexibility. Superficially this would also appear to satisfy the underlying principle of FM modulation, where the frequency input to one oscillator is modulated by the output from a second oscillator. In functional terms, however, there are important differences in the ways in which control can be exercised over the generation and variation of timbres.

The basic control facilities for voicing the Casio CZ synthesizers consist of a series of digital envelope generators which vary the degree of phase distortion dynamically during the evolution of a sound. Eight basic wave-forms are provided for the phase distortion process itself; sawtooth, square, pulse, a double sine consisting of two asymmetric cycles, a hybrid between a sawtooth and a pulse, and three resonated versions of sawtooth, triangle, and trapezoid wave-forms. More complex wave-forms can be produced by pairing any two of these component functions.

Casio was not alone in seeking out new and distinctive synthesis methods. Sequential Circuits developed a technique known as vector synthesis for their Prophet VS which provides powerful and yet easily programmable facilities for generating complex wave-forms where up to four basic wave-forms can be selected and instantly mixed via a joystick to create a new composite wave-form. The intuitive nature of this technique contrasts sharply with the complexities of FM algorithms, and although there are inevitably some practical limitations its ease of use proved very popular, especially among those users who normally would venture no further than the basic bank of preset voices provided by the manufacturer. Further refinements include separate envelope-shaping and filtering facilities for each wave-form generator.

An important new trend in synthesizer technology was signalled in 1986 by Kawai with the release of their K3 digital wave memory synthesizer, a product which undoubtedly influenced Yamaha in the design of their successor to the DX7, the SY77. Prior to the K3 the synthesizer market could be seen to be developing broadly on two fronts, one concerned with the development of digital oscillators in conjunction with either digital or analogue signal processing facilities, the other concerned with the re-synthesis of sampled sounds. Kawai realized that combining the two approaches could greatly expand the versatility of a system, providing the implementations were suitably compatible. In electronic terms there is no material distinction to be made between generating sound material from a function table by cyclic extraction and reading through a stored file of sound samples, either straight through or with some intermediate looping process. Roland were preparing the ground here with synthesizers such as the D-50 and D-110, which complement their S-10 and S-50 samplers in using sampled wave-forms which have been specially pre-processed for use as synthesizer voices, with complete 'single shot' recordings for percussion effects and looped extracts for more sustained sounds such as strings, woodwind, or brass. The latter technique, known as linear arithmetic, provides a natural complement to synthetic methods of synthesis and it was thus a small but significant step to the design of systems which combine both aspects.

The K3 includes a bank of thirty-two preset wave-forms covering a variety of timbres of both natural and synthetic origin. Wave-forms can also be generated by means of additive synthesis either internally or by importing suitable data from an external source. Both factory-supplied and user-defined wave-forms can be directly accessed via two individually programmable digital oscillators, allowing the construction of a wide variety of composite wave-forms. Subsequent processing is largely analogue in this instance, the facilities including voltage-controlled filters and envelope-shapers and a stereo chorus effects unit. This additive/sampled synthesis approach was extended further in the K5, released in 1987, several of the voltage-controlled modules in the signal processing section having been replaced with digitally controlled equivalents. With the K1, released in 1988, the facilities are expanded still further with a resident library of 256 sounds of both natural and sampled origin, any four of which can be blended together to create new voices which may be refined further using an extended range of signal processing facilities.

Although Yamaha's patents on its hardware implementation of FM synthesis indeed proved a major deterrent to other manufacturers wishing to emulate this particular synthesis principle this embargo was to be broken in 1987 by Korg with the release of their DS-8 digital FM synthesizer. This offers a much simpler user interface to the algorithms, which are in turn restricted to two-oscillator pairings rather than the four- or six-oscillator groupings used in the Yamaha DX series. Timbral richness is achieved by offering a choice of basic oscillator wave-shapes which are already rich in harmonic content, for example sawtooth, square, bright sawtooth, and bright square, the degree of modulation being regulated via an envelope-shaper which directly manipulates the modulation index. Korg's reputation for innovative technology had already been established with products such as the DSS-1 sampler or the still earlier DW series of synthesizers, which in the context of MIDI were among the first to employ all-digital wavetable synthesis techniques. The M1 music workstation which followed in 1988 not only offers a combination of sampling and additive synthesis techniques, augmented by an aperiodic wave-form generator for the production of percussive sounds, but also includes an eight-track sequencer, allowing a complete performance to be built up layer by layer without any external assistance.

With the notable exception of Casio's flagship CZ-5000 synthesizer which offers basic eight-track sequencing facilities as a built-in facility, such an integration of synthesis and sequencing technologies within a MIDI synthesizer had hitherto been most unusual, but this was soon to change as other manufacturers launched rival systems. Ensoniq, for example, include a eight-track sequencer as part of their SQ80 synthesizer, released in 1988 as a partner for the EPS sampler. The sound library for the SQ80 consists of seventy-five sources, ranging from basic sawtooth and square waves via a variety of additively produced wave-forms, to a collection of sampled instruments such as bass, piano, and voices, augmented with a representative selection of percussion sounds.

One year later two other important synthesizers were launched, the Ensoniq VFX, and the long-awaited replacement for the Yamaha DX7, the SY77. These models offer a powerful range of synthesis facilities, in both cases divided into two distinct sections for programming purposes, the first being concerned with all the primary stages of synthesis, the second with an optional range of digital signal processing effects. A closer look at their architectures reveals just how dramatic has been the scale of developments in this sector of the synthesizer industry since the early years of MIDI.

The Ensoniq VFX offers twenty-one independently programmable digital oscillators, drawing on a bank of 109 basic waveforms which can be modified to generate a total resource of 1800 variants. These comprise strings, brass, breath, bass, tuned and untuned percussion sounds, both sampled and synthesized, as well as an extensive array of more basic electronic sounds which include many single-cycle wave-forms of varying complexity. Each oscillator provides a basic voice, and up to six of these components can be combined to generate a composite keyboard sound. Voice modification facilities include three six-stage envelope-shapers, two independent dynamic digital filters, and a variety of modulation sources including a low-frequency modulator which offers seven different wave-shapes and a programmable delay. The effects section provides fifteen different configurations including several types of reverberation as well as echo, delay, and chorus effects.

One important characteristic of a synthesizer is its capacity to generate polyphonic textures. By the early 1980s most synthesizers were capable of generating at least eight notes simultaneously. While this was a major advance on older voltage-controlled systems, which are often only capable of monophonic sound production, even this capacity soon proved inadequate for the developing world of MIDI. If longer-sounding notes are not to be cut off prematurely in complex passages twelve- or even sixteen-note capability is highly desirable, and in the case of the VFX no less than twenty-one different notes can be active at any one time. Multi-timbral facilities extend the textural possibilities of polyphonic note generation still further by allowing two or more different voices to sound together, either as a simple blend or as independently controlled components. Early multi-timbral MIDI synthesizers often limited the latter mode of operation to a basic division of the keyboard into two or more keygroups with a separate voice for each section. With the VFX true independent voicing is possible with the facility to use up to twelve different voices at any one time mapped across the entire keyboard range, each voice controllable by a separate MIDI channel. No internal sequencer is provided with this system, necessitating the use of an external control facility if full advantage is to be taken of the synthesizer's capabilities.

The Yamaha SY77 offers a comparable range of facilities with the added advantage of an integral sequencer. With this synthesizer all sixteen MIDI channels can be used simultaneously, extending the orchestral capabilities to the maximum permitted by the protocol. To support this two autonomous synthesis technologies are provided, each allowing the simultaneous generation of up to sixteen different voices. Careful programming of the synthesizer can thus allow the production of textures made up of thirty-two different elements. The two technologies are known respectively as advanced frequency modulation (AFM) and advanced wave modulation (AWM). AFM is an extension of the FM system used in the DX7, still relying upon groupings of six oscillators but with a choice of forty-five rather than thirty-two algorithms. Although voices developed using a DX7 can be converted to run on the SY77, the true potential of the new system can only be realized by exploring its extended range of FM facilities, notably a choice of sixteen different wave-forms rather than just a simple sine wave and the ability to tap three oscillators rather than one to generate feedback signals for timbral enrichment by means of resonance. The AWM facility is a full sixteen-bit 48 kHz sampling system drawing upon an extensive bank of factory supplied sounds. From these two sources a number of different synthesis chains can be constructed. Both modulation facilities can be used independently, with their voices routed directly to the stereo output amplifiers either separately or as a simple audio mix. Alternatively AWM waves can be used as control signals for selected operators of an AFM generator, thus producing a variety of complex and dynamically varying modulations.

Further timbral modifications can be achieved by routing AFM or AWM waves through a digital filtering section. This forms the first stage of an all-digital effects unit, which like the equivalent section in the Ensoniq VFX facilitates a variety of signal processing functions. The options available include panning facilities, eight types of reverberation, and a variety of echo, delay, and modulation effects. As in the case of the DX7, Yamaha achieve a level of functional flexibility which is second to none and at the same time manage to offer the less adventurous user a generous and suitably diverse selection of factory-generated sounds. Two banks of presets are permanently stored in read-only memory, each offering a repertory of sixty-four voices. Two of these voices are sampled percussion kits with individual instruments assigned to specific keys. A further sixty-four user-defined voices can be created in a programmable memory bank, supported by a floppy disk facility which can also be used to save data from the sequencer. Additional factory-produced voices may be imported via a plug-in cartridge facility. The biggest drawback here is the lack of any facility to import sampled sounds from any other source. This deficiency has been rectified in the SY99, an upgraded version of the SY77 released in 1990 which supports use of the MIDI sample dump protocol for this purpose.

The combination of wave-form and sampling synthesis facilities with both a digital processing section and also a sequencer results in a remarkably self-sufficient system for the composition and performance of music. This integration of so many hardware items which hitherto had generally been developed as separate products is particularly interesting since for many users it conveniently circumvents the need to understand the intricacies of MIDI communications. There are, however, several categories of MIDI device which cannot be so conveniently subsumed into a single system without a significant loss of functionality. In this context the introduction of keyboard-based percussion facilities such as the above has not been without its critics. On the one hand they allow access to an important repertory of sounds as a simple extension of the keyboard. On the other they completely destroy any practical link to the art of percussion playing.

Similar controversy initially surrounded the development of keyboard-based string synthesizers during the 1970s, which proved especially popular with German rock and pop groups such as Tangerine Dream. In the case of drum machines a continuing interest in the traditional performance art has encouraged the manufacture of a number of specialist synthesizers which are designed specifically for use with electronic sensing pads activated by stick or finger strokes, but even these products have been overshadowed by a growing number of automatic percussion generators which can be programmed to produce a variety of patterns using no more than a simple array of buttons. The popularity of such techniques as a convenient means of dispensing with the services of a trained percussionist provides an important clue as to why so much popular music in recent years has been characterized by backing material which displays remarkably similar characteristics from one album to another.

Electronic drum machines and sensors were in existence long before 1983 but the lack of a unified communication system to link the various components created major problems of compatibility. MIDI provided an extremely effective solution to such problems and these pioneering designs were soon discarded in favour of MIDI-based alternatives. Most of the major synthesizer manufacturers have developed drum machines of some description over the years but these have faced fierce competition from specialist manufacturers such as Simmons, who produced the first complete electronic drum kit, and Linn, generally recognized as being the inventor of the digital drum.

Simmons has enjoyed a lasting success for many years in this market sector, their initial all-analogue SD55 system leading directly to the popular SDS series, which ranges from early models such as the SDS7 and SDS8 to more recent versions such as the all-digital SDS800. Their concern for the performer is particularly evident in the well-crafted design of their drum pads which are well liked by many professional percussionists. Linn established their reputation with the 9000 series, which combines a versatile sequencer with a sophisticated high-quality drum synthesizer. In 1987 a collaboration between Akai and Linn led to the manufacture of a system known as the ADR15, which combines a sampling system for the direct capture of new sounds with a sequencer which can be driven by either pressure- or velocity-sensitive buttons or by external drum pads, thus creating a powerful facility for live and/or sequence-assisted performance. The use of twelve-bit samples at up to 40 kHz compares favourably with the general sampling standards of the time, but even here sixteen-bit sampling was already making its presence felt with products such as the Alesis HR16 drum machine. The latter offers no fewer than forty-eight sixteen-bit velocity-sensitive pads which can be programmed using an extensive library of both acoustically sampled and electronically generated sound sources.

Roland's DDR30 and its associated set of six drum pads, introduced in 1985, is representative of a first-generation MIDI drum kit from a mainstream synthesizer manufacturer. The sounds are configured by modifying four basic sources in terms of their pitch, timbre, and envelope. Up to eight variations can be specified for each drum pad and a working repertory is assembled and stored in memory as a complete kit. Up to thirty-two of these kits can be resident in memory at any time, allowing access to an extensive library of material at the push of a button. The DDR30 was designed specifically as a performance tool for a live percussionist, and thus lacks any facility for generating or recording patterns. Roland initially saw rhythm generation as a quite separate application, regarding it as a by-product of the basic accompaniment presets which had become a standard feature of keyboards designed specifically for the home entertainment market. Such facilities are provided by the TR505 rhythm box, which appeared in the same year, offering a basic repertory of percussion sounds and programmable patterns which are accessed via a simple push-button panel. This device was replaced by the TR626 in 1987, which offers an expanded range of thirty digital voices, eight individual audio outputs, forty-eight preset, and forty-eight programmable patterns.

By 1988 firms such as Yamaha and Korg had added drum machines to their product ranges. Yamaha's RX7 offers a basic library of 100 sampled sounds using sixteen-bit resolution, foreshadowing the AWM facility incorporated in the SY77. These sounds range from electric bass, marimba, and orchestral sounds to a comprehensive collection of drum and cymbal sounds which include nine different bass drum samples, ten different snare samples, two rim shots, seventeen tom-toms, four cymbals, and four hi-hats. Although the machine can be operated using external drum pads it is better suited to pre-programmed modes of operation which use its internal sequencer. The facilities for direct performance, for example, consist of a standard set of twenty-four press keys which are neither pressure- or velocity-sensitive. The system is capable of sixteen-note polyphony, and the sequencer, memory permitting, allows up to 100 patterns to be stored of between one and ninety-nine bars in length. Simple programming procedures allow any one of the 100 factory voices to be assigned to any key or any combination of keys thereof. In addition each sound can be edited in terms of its basic pitch, overall amplitude, decay, and stereo pan position.

In common with so many of Yamaha's products the RX series of drum machines are not so much components to form part of a system, but complete performance tools in their own right. A rather different philosophy is encountered with Korg's DRM-1 digital rhythm module, which also dates from this period. Here the emphasis is clearly biased towards the performer with the inclusion of a built-in pad-to-MIDI converter. The sequencer section is also rationalized to allow efficient interaction under performance conditions, the emphasis being on the direct recording of backing patterns for a complete song rather than the overlay of basic patterns to be pre-programmed into the system. The voice section consists of a small bank of internal sounds and four ROM cartridge slots on the front panel which will also accept sound cards from Korg's earlier DDD-1 and DDD-5 drum machines. When fully populated the system library can hold up to fifty-five different sounds, accessed by sixteen drum kit programs, each of which can contain up to sixteen variants.

The basic differences between the characteristics of a drum machine and those of a rhythm generator can be further illustrated by comparing the Korg DRM-1 with products such as the Roland R-8 Human Rhythm Composer, which appeared in 1989. The latter is specifically designed for the generation of automated rhythm tracks, combining an internal library of sixty-eight percussion sounds with a sophisticated multi-track sequencing facility which is operated via a push-button editing panel. Drum pads or other performance aids are clearly of no relevance here, and the R-5 is best suited for compositional applications which specifically require the construction of elaborate rhythmic patterns.

Although drum pads represent the most important family of performance tools other than keyboards for MIDI a number of other instrumental transducers have been developed since the mid-1980s. Perhaps the most conspicuous instrument to have been targeted in this respect is the electric guitar, leading to products such as the Yamaha G10 MIDI guitar system and the Casio PG380 MIDI Synth guitar. The G10, which appeared in 1988, was one of the first products of this type successfully to overcome the technical problems encountered in converting guitar pitches into equivalent MIDI codes. Although the fingerboard and frets very closely resemble the equivalent parts of a conventional guitar the similarities end here, since there is no guitar-like body, the latter being replaced by a small box underneath the playing area which contains the electronics. The device is simply a controller, producing basic electronic signals which are converted into MIDI data by an associated device known as the G10C guitar-to-MIDI converter, which in turn has to be connected to an associated synthesizer before any sounds can be produced. In contrast the Casio PG380 combines a MIDI-based pick-up system with an integral synthesizer module which offers sixty-four preset sounds, supported by plug-in ROM cards which expand the repertory to over 1000 sounds. In all other respects this product looks and plays like a conventional instrument, the natural profile of the guitar sound box providing ample storage space for all the electronics.

In terms of new areas of development it has been wind and brass instruments which have so far attracted particular attention, not least for the fact that emulation of their functional characteristics has proved relatively straightforward in engineering terms. In 1987 Akai introduced two special MIDI controllers, the EVI (Electronic Valve Instrument) and the EWI (Electronic Wind Instrument). Both are designed for use with an EV2000 voicing unit, which contains special synthesis modules for these instrumental families, but the controllers can also be connected directly via MIDI to any suitable synthesizer.

The EVI is closely modelled on the acoustic trumpet, consisting of a rectangular tube with three valve-like press switches, a mouthpiece, and what appears to be a small bell. In reality the latter disguises a fourth valve and a set of roller sensors which control octave switching across a range of seven octaves. Two other sensors are provided on the opposite side of the tube to the main valves, one controlling pitch bend, the other affecting the subtleties of pitch which occur when a trumpeter alters the lip pressure on an acoustic instrument. The EWI has no bell and offers a simplified wind fingering system using press keypads in association with a roller-based octave switching system on the underside for the left thumb, matched with pitch bend sensors for the right thumb. Although key and octave selections determine the basic MIDI pitch information to be generated, overall dynamic and expressive control information is obtained by detecting wind and lip pressure respectively.

Yahama also introduced a wind controller, the WX7, in the same year. As with the EVI and EWI, MIDI performance data is generated by a combination of key selections and wind and lip pressure. A standard woodwind fingering is used to produce a basic chromatic scale, transposition over a six-octave range being controlled by thumb-operated buttons. Particular care has been taken with this controller to provide facilities for customizing its response to the requirements of the individual user. To this end the plastic mouthpiece can be set to emulate the response of a recorder, or alternatively a saxophone or clarinet. In addition the instrument's sensitivity to changes in wind pressure can be adjusted, as well as the point at which it will start to 'speak'.

Commercial products such as the WX7 or the EWI and EVI have important links with a number of performance transducers which have been developed by the institutional research sector, and these will be studied in the next chapter. A similar linking of interests can be identified in connection with the development of devices for digital signal processing. It has already been noted how with synthesizers such as the Ensoniq VFX and the Yamaha SY77 the facilities for shaping voice material are complete processing sections in their own right. Such digital signal processors, however, were by no means new to the world of MIDI since a number of self-contained effects units had been on the market for some time. Yamaha, for example, released a sixteen-bit reverberation unit, the REV1, in 1984, followed early in 1985 by a cheaper but in many respects no less versatile version known as the REV7, the main difference being a reduced sampling rate of 31.25 kHz rather the 44.1 kHz used by the REV1. Over thirty different factory preset programs are offered by the REV7, ranging from room and hall types of reverberation to simple chorus and flanging effects. A rival product from the same period offering very similar facilities is the Lexicon 224X.

By far the most popular Yamaha effects unit, however, has

been the SPX90, which was to follow in 1986, updated first as the SPX900 and subsequently as the SPX1000. The SPX90 significantly extends the facilities of the REV7 into a true multi-effects processor which includes other features such as pitch shifting and multiple delay echo. The versatility of the SPX processors, not least the freedom to choose and program the individual effects, inspired other manufacturers to follow suit, leading to products such as the Alesis Quadraverb, the Eventide H3000 Ultra-harmonizer, and the Korg A3 signal processor. A notable design feature of the A3 is the use of rotary knobs to adjust parameter settings rather than the usual array of buttons. These greatly speed up the process of adjusting parameter values, an important consideration when working in a performance environment. Forty-one different effects are available on the A3, the number in use at any one time (up to a maximum of six) and the order of chaining being determined by a preset connection patch which is selected from a bank of twenty different configurations. The Eventide H3000 Ultra-harmonizer is a more specialist effects processor, a development of earlier models such as the H910 and H949 and primarily intended for applications such as multiple pitch shifting, enhanced by associated effects such as delay, flanging, and reverberation.

The significance of MIDI as regards the dynamic operation of these effects units varies considerably from one product to another. In the case of a machine such as the Eventide H3000 Ultra-harmonizer special care has been taken to integrate the various processing control parameters with the performance characteristics of a MIDI keyboard such as note range and key pressure, velocity, and/or release. It is thus possible to use the H3000 as if it were a conventional MIDI-controlled synthesizer. Most systems of this type, however, restrict the use of MIDI to program change commands and no more than one or two performance parameters. It is thus quite normal to use such facilities without any reference to MIDI whatsoever, and there are a number of high-quality signal processors in regular use in both synthesis and recording studios which do not support MIDI at all.

The subject of sequencers provides a natural link back to the earlier discussion of the microcomputer and its contribution to the development of the medium. Synthesizer manufacturers have naturally always been anxious to cultivate and retain their own particular share of a highly competitive market, and as will be seen shortly the microcomputer as a third-party product offering facilities which can freely be exploited by any researcher or entrepreneur posed a major threat to such an objective. The development of sequencing facilities either as free-standing devices or, as just illustrated, as an integral part of a modern synthesis workstation is thus of particular significance in this context.

Early entry-level products such as the Casio SZ-1, Roland MSQ-100, and the Yamaha QX7 offer a relatively basic range of characteristics in terms of total note capacity, number of simultaneous tracks, and facilities for storing sequences from one session to another. All three rely primarily on simple cassette storage facilities which are extremely slow and unreliable. In addition the editing facilities are limited and cumbersome to use. These drawbacks were soon addressed with products such as the Yamaha QX1, which is altogether more sophisticated, offering a total capacity of 80 000 notes (as against just 1800 notes in the case of the Casio SZ-1), eight-track recording, a disk-based storage system for sequencing programs, and a well-thought-out pushbutton editing facility.

Even the QX1, however, was soon to face stiff competition from computer-based alternatives, for despite the evident ingenuity of manufacturers such as Yamaha all such systems still suffered from one major drawback, the restrictions of a small LED display panel for editing voice and sequencing data, and the lack of choice as to the editing facility itself. Synthesizer manufacturers have gone to great lengths to try and overcome such difficulties, and sequencers which date from the latter part of the 1980s such as the Akai/Linn ASQ10, the Yamaha QX3, and the Alesis MMT8 have won many friends for their ease and simplicity of operation. In performance situations considerations such as these are often of paramount importance. In the studio, however, greater significance will often be attached to factors such as the refinement of control afforded and the capacity to carry out editing tasks which may at times prove quite complex, and in these circumstances the WIMPS environment has many advantages. To understand the true significance of the latter not only for sequencing but also for many other applications it is necessary to return to the development of the microcomputer and its associated technology from the birth of MIDI onwards.

# 13 From Microcomputer to Music Supercomputer

At the start of the 1980s the microcomputer was still regarded by many as little more than an experimental tool which catered for a range of minority interests. Large and expensive mainframe computers dominated the computing industry and like the analogue synthesizer their long-term prosperity seemed assured. Few could have anticipated that by the end of the decade the centre of gravity would have changed so dramatically in favour of powerful desktop workstations, providing processing facilities which for many applications have proved equal or even superior to those offered by traditional computers.

A significant feature of the first phase of microcomputer development was the rapid proliferation of different machine architectures, each offering a unique set of functional characteristics and in many instances enjoying only a relatively short production life. By the dawn of MIDI a general rationalization had begun, encouraging microcomputer manufacturers to adopt a more generic approach to the design of new models. This new climate of stability provided an important stimulus to the embryonic music software industry, able at last to develop products with a reasonable life expectancy.

Although the introduction of the IBM PC established the status of the microcomputer in the eyes of the industry as a whole it was the launch of the Apple Macintosh in 1984 which established the more interesting technical agenda for the rest of the decade. One of the most distinctive features of this machine is its mouse-driven graphics interface, which provides not only a sophisticated environment for interactive programming but also a simple and yet powerful means of controlling the operation of the entire system from the moment it is switched on. The value of a WIMPS environment for music applications had been demonstrated by the SSSP project back in 1977 but this was the first time that such a comprehensive set of graphical resources had become available as a standard facility for a general purpose microcomputer. The versatility of the Macintosh is further enhanced by a particularly efficient machine architecture, based upon a sixteen-bit 68000 microprocessor. Later versions of the Macintosh from the II series introduced in 1986 onwards use much faster versions of this microprocessor, starting with the 68020 and progressing in due course to the 68030. As a result later machines such as the IIfx and the IIci offer particularly powerful processing capabilities with the added enhancement of advanced colour graphics.

Although the WIMPS environment is now ubiquitous the PC family was one of the last to adopt it, progress here having been retarded by some shortcomings in the original design. The first series of XT machines were fashioned very much in the mould of the traditional VDU terminal, the user interface amounting to little more than a basic alphanumeric keyboard and an associated video monitor, intended primarily for the display of alphanumeric character information. This only requires a relatively modest resolution in terms of screen dots or pixels and the picture quality of the earliest PCs is inadequate for any serious graphics applications. The video hardware of the XT was upgraded in due course, but this exposed other shortcomings in the original design such as the lack of adequate memory and processing capabilities to support a comprehensive WIMPS environment.

The turning-point in the fortunes of the PC came with the introduction of the more advanced AT series in the mid-1980s, based initially on the 80286 microprocessor, an upgraded version of the original 8088. A succession of new graphics cards and associated monitors with increasing resolution and also support for colour soon followed, supported in turn by more powerful AT PCs with larger memories, better peripherals, and an improved operating system. The introduction of the 80386 microprocessor towards the end of the decade, quickly followed by the even faster 80486, led to the manufacture of AT PCs which could rival the best machines in the Macintosh II series. Steadily increasing production levels and a matching fall in the price of components led to a progressive reduction in prices, helped to no small extent by the growing number of clone manufacturers who freely copied the PC's architecture. The final ingredient, a versatile WIMPS software environment known as Windows 3, was released by Microsoft in 1990 and proved an instant success.

This enduring battle between the Macintosh and the PC has tended to overshadow the development of other microcomputers which have proved of particular significance in a musical context. In the field of scientific research, for example, the Macintosh has faced intense competition from the Sun, a powerful if relatively expensive graphics-driven workstation which has been used for a number of important computer music projects since its introduction in the mid-1980s, especially in Europe at institutions such as IRCAM. A more recent challenge to be discussed later dates from 1988 with the release of a revolutionary microcomputer from NeXT, which set new standards for the sector in terms of audio-visual facilities, basic processing power, and suitable environments for software development.

At the other end of the scale, Apple's long-standing rivals Atari and Commodore soon responded to the Macintosh with a series of new models. 1985 saw the launch of three machines from Atari, the 130 ST, the 520 ST, and the 1040 ST, all based on the 68000 microprocessor and offering a high-resolution interactive graphics environment very similar to that provided by the Macintosh. Subsequent upgrades have included the Mega ST, which offers memory expansion facilities and a detachable rather than an integral keyboard, and the STE, which provides further enhancements such as extra ports for data input and output and an improved sound system with direct memory access. The launch of the TT in 1990 based on the 68030 microprocessor signalled a major upgrade in terms of processing power. To achieve this performance, however, Atari had no option but to make radical changes to the internal hardware architecture and this has necessitated modifications to much of the music software originally written for the ST range.

Commodore responded with the Amiga family of computers in late 1985, starting with the 1000 model, which is based on the 68000 microprocessor and a graphics-driven operating system. Subsequent versions include the smaller 500, which has proved especially popular with the home entertainment market, and the larger 2000, designed to increase sales to the scientific, business, and commercial market sectors. As in the case of Atari increasing competition from upgraded versions of the Macintosh led in due course to the introduction of a powerful 3000 series based on the 68030 microprocessor. Other important architectures emerged in national rather than international contexts, for example the Archimedes from the UK company Acorn, which uses a special microprocessor known as ARM. This was redesigned as the

A3000 in the late 1980s and has been particularly attractive to schools as a powerful successor to the BBC Micro.

Notwithstanding the success of the Macintosh, Apple continued to market the Apple II, introducing a substantially upgraded version known as the Apple IIGS in 1986. This uses a special sixteen-bit processor, the 65C816, which not only emulates all the functions of the original 6502 to ensure full compatibility with earlier Apple II models but also provides a high resolution WIMPS environment very similar to that offered by the Macintosh.

All of the microcomputers discussed above incorporate improved facilities for sound synthesis with the notable exception of the PC series, which has retained the rudimentary one-bit system used in the original XT even for the more recent versions based on the very fast 80486. Models in the Atari range incorporate a basic three-voice synthesizer chip manufactured by Yamaha, capable of generating elementary tone sequences and sound effects. Up to four independently regulated sounds can be generated simultaneously, but with the original ST series only 64 kilobytes of RAM can be allocated for the direct output of audio with a maximum sampling rate of 16 kHz, which after internal filtering restricts the bandwidth to about 7.5 kHz. As just noted, with the STE machines Atari upgraded the sound system to allow the output of sampled sounds in stereo with eight-bit resolution direct from the main memory, and this improvement brought their audio facilities more into line with those of machines such as the Commodore Amiga. One of the most distinctive features of the latter is the inclusion of a special synthesis chip which can be used to generate recognizable speech whenever complete words are typed into the microcomputer. For music or sound effects a four-voice, eight-bit system with stereo outputs is provided with a usable bandwidth of about 7.5 kHz. Once again both wavetable synthesis and synthesis from sampled sounds held in memory are available. The Archimedes offers very similar facilities to those of the Amiga with stereo outputs of eight-bit resolution and direct access to synthesized or sampled sounds from memory, but with eight rather than four voices and an optional special plug-in card with an integral A-to-D converter which allows sounds to be sampled directly.

The sound systems for the Apple Macintosh and the Apple IIGS are of particular interest since they set new standards of versatility and general fidelity for the microcomputer industry during the mid-1980s. In the case of the IIGS an eight-bit digital oscillator chip (DOC) is used, designed by Ensoniq originally as the main audio processor for their Mirage synthesizer. Although many of its intrinsic functions are implemented in the IIGS, for example wavetable synthesis with up to thirty-two oscillators or the multiple sampling of sounds direct from memory, the A-to-D facility and the second output channel for stereo operation are not supported. The sound hardware in the Macintosh is quite different from that of the IIGS, consisting of an Apple design built from discrete components in the early versions, much of this circuitry being replaced by custom chips from Sony in the Macintosh II series. The sampling rate is 22.05 kHz, which happens to be half the 44.1 kHz industry standard used for compact discs, but the bandwidth is sharply reduced to just 7.5 kHz by the internal filters. Three basic forms of synthesis are provided, simple square wave generation for simple 'alert' signals, sampling direct from memory, and wavetable synthesis with up to four voices.

Although facilities such as the above marked a major step forward in the provision of sound resources for microcomputers they still did not match the performance of a well-engineered synthesizer. Where these machines have really come into their own is with applications which bypass the internal sound circuitry altogether, either to service external synthesis devices via MIDI or to host fast audio co-processors, attached to high-quality A-to-D and D-to-A converters.

It will be recalled that there are important differences between a MIDI interface and a conventional serial port, in terms of both the nature of the electrical signals transmitted and also the data transmission speed itself which does not conform to any of the standard baud rates adopted by the computer industry. These problems of compatibility can be overcome in two ways, the choice depending to a large extent on the functional characteristics of the microcomputer concerned. The first solution requires an external MIDI-to-serial data converter inserted between the MIDI system and a spare serial port on the microcomputer. Although the electrical conversion of the associated signals requires relatively simple hardware, arbitrating between the MIDI data rate and the speed of the serial port is not always so straightforward. If the latter is restricted to a maximum speed of

19 200 baud, or worse still 9600 baud, then some form of buffering has to be provided.

An early design such as the module manufactured by Sound Composition Systems (SCS) contains an eight-kilobyte memory buffer precisely for this purpose, but products of this type will only work properly if the density of MIDI traffic is sufficiently light or intermittent for the buffer to absorb any possible overrun. If continuous MIDI information such as pitch bend messages is transmitted to the microcomputer the buffer will quickly overflow, resulting in loss or corruption of the data. To reduce the chances of this occurring the SCS unit contains special circuits to filter out active sensing information, but this inevitably degrades the usefulness of such an interface. Fortunately computers such as the Apple Macintosh and the Commodore Amiga incorporate a more sophisticated type of serial port which allows the baud rate to be programmed internally to the 31 250 baud rate required by MIDI. In these cases no buffering is required in the interface itself and the risks of data corruption during transmission are effectively eliminated.

The second solution requires a special MIDI interface card which is fitted directly to the main control bus of the microcomputer itself. The electronics are necessarily more complex in this case since the card has to communicate directly with the CPU. Although inherently more expensive, this method neatly circumvents the compatibility problems described above in connection with add-on modules for serial ports. Roland pioneered this type of interface for the PC with their MPU-401 card, and most MIDI software for this family of microcomputers requires the use of either this card or one which is functionally compatible.

One or two manufacturers, notably Atari and Yamaha, have produced microcomputers with integral MIDI interfaces. In the case of Atari all models from the ST series onwards include a pair of MIDI IN and MIDI OUT ports as a standard feature, making these microcomputers particularly attractive for music applications. The first Yamaha music microcomputer, the CX5M, was an addition to their DX range of MIDI equipment, designed in the first instance as a self-contained workstation which combines facilities for FM synthesis with the programmable features of a control computer. When the system first appeared in 1985 products such as the DX7 synthesizer and the QX7 sequencer already provided the primary tools for a programmable MIDI system, but Yamaha were aware of the growing attraction of graphics-driven facilities for advanced editing and sequencing applications. Unfortunately they based their system on an architecture which was to have a limited life-span despite early support from a number of major Japanese electronics manufacturers, and as a result the technology of the CX5M was soon rendered obsolete by developments elsewhere and the system was withdrawn in 1988. This architecture, known as MSX, was devised by Microsoft specifically for the eight-bit Z-80 microprocessor with the object of producing a compact microcomputer complete with operating system, a BASIC language interpreter stored in a small ROM of only 32 kilobytes, an equivalent amount of RAM for general programming, and support for peripherals such as a keyboard and printer.

Although the MSX specification permits the addition of a disk-based operating system the CX5M does not support this facility, using instead a set of ROM cartridges to provide the basic software and RAM cartridges of rather limited capacity for the storage of user data from one session to another. Three further components complete the basic system, a VDU display to match the integral alphanumeric keyboard, a MIDI music keyboard, and a special plug-in module which is a complete FM synthesizer designed to interface directly to the MSX system. Known as the SFG01 this is basically a scaled-down version of a DX9 with just four operators and eight algorithms, the associated software consisting of a voice editor, a sequencer, and a special program which allows the user to compose and synthesize scores using conventional music notation.

Yamaha's second microcomputer system, released in 1989 as the C1, has proved much more successful since it uses a standard 80286 PC AT architecture. The MIDI facilities are comprehensive, consisting of two MIDI IN, one MIDI THRU, and eight MIDI OUT ports, all separately programmable. Unfortunately these ports are not MPU-401-compatible, and although some software manufacturers have produced Yamaha-compatible versions of their programs specially for the C1 others have yet to follow suit.

Whereas the market for MIDI synthesizers world-wide has shown some consistency as regards the relative popularity of particular makes from one country to another the same cannot be said for microcomputers and their associated MIDI software.

Here rather different trends have emerged, particularly noticeable when comparing developments in the USA with those in Europe, and largely due to the effects of different marketing strategies and pricing policies adopted by manufacturers from one country to another over the years. During the initial period of MIDI development Apple's computers were aggressively marketed in the USA at highly competitive prices, and as a result sales of both the Apple IIGS and the Macintosh to music users not only outstripped those of the IBM PC but also those of Commodore and Atari. In Europe Apple demanded much higher prices for their microcomputers and peripherals and this led the price-conscious music industry to turn to other machines, notably the Atari ST, which became the most popular choice for MIDI applications in countries such as the UK and Germany.

By 1990 the most pronounced effects of these variations in hardware prices from country to country were beginning to disappear, helped by the introduction of a much cheaper range of Macintosh microcomputers for European as well as American markets and also the growth of interest on both sides of the Atlantic in its now primary competitor the rapidly improving PC. As a result, with the development of MIDI software for other microcomputers such as the Amiga and the Archimedes the prospective purchaser faces a wide-ranging and at times very confusing choice of facilities.

The repertory of MIDI software can be divided into a number of categories. These include composition and performance, music notation, sequencing, voice editing, and various educational applications such as aural training and music theory. The use of the computer as an aid to composition has already been cited in connection with the work of Hiller and Xenakis during the 1950s and 60s and Chadabe during the 1970s. The continuing work of Chadabe and his associates led to three innovative MIDI programs from Intelligent Music for the Macintosh: Upbeat, Jam Factory, and M. Upbeat is a rhythmic programming system which allows patterns to be generated and edited using a graphics interface. What distinguishes this from a conventional sequencing program is the availability of extended editing facilities which allow data such as key velocities, durations, or the density of events to be modified using computer-generated probability functions. In addition it is possible to change performance data dynamically, allowing alterations to be made intuitively using the mouse.

The notion of 'jamming' as in a jazz session lies at the heart of Jam Factory, an improvisation program where the performer first defines basic ideas in terms of fields of pitch data, selects an initial set of computer-driven performance algorithms, and then proceeds to modify their operation interactively using the mouse as a master controller. At the heart of the process lie four instruments, each of which has to be initialized with a basic note pattern, usually input via a MIDI keyboard. This data is then analysed to produce a set of probability tables which record how often a particular note follows (1) a single note, (2) a two-note sequence, and (3) three-note sequences, in a manner reminiscent of the Olson and Belar composing machine. Re-synthesis proceeds by random or pseudo-random selection of pitch and duration values, suitably weighted according to these tables. The ability to alter the course of events using the mouse results in a very flexible performing tool which permits the generation and shaping of a variety of textures of varying complexity and density in a 'top down' manner similar to that of the POD programs of Barry Truax and the PROJECT programs of Gottfried Michael Koenig, where control over the course of events is exercised on a macro rather than a micro level.

In some respects M has much in common with both Jam Factory in terms of the interactive processes of its operation and also Upbeat in terms of the number of different tracks which can be manipulated simultaneously, but the arrangement of the screen icons reveals a much stronger emphasis on compositional processes which have to be worked out in advance rather than interactively during the course of a performance. These require the user to input a basic set of note patterns via MIDI and then provide control data for an associated set of re-synthesis algorithms which allow regulation of parameters such as event density, duration, and repetition. A number of layers can be specified in this manner, allowing the composer to build up rich textures using a selection of different voices.

Music notation programs vary considerably in terms of both sophistication and emphasis. At one extreme there are a number of advanced typesetting packages which are capable of producing scores of the highest quality, suitable for publication. One of the first of these programs, SCORE, dates back to the 1972 program of the same name, produced by Leland Smith for use with MUSIC V. This provided the starting-point for the development of MS, which was designed more specifically as a general-purpose score writing program, and it was this that led to the commercial version of SCORE, released for the IBM PC just over a decade later. As already noted the PC initially lacked good interactive graphics facilities and as a result users of the early versions of this program could only enter score details in terms of alphanumeric character strings, a process which some found rather cumbersome especially when proof-reading and correcting the results. Another disadvantage was the lack of support for MIDI, which given the limitations of the sound system of the PC precluded any serious audio proofing. Both drawbacks have been fully addressed in more recent versions of SCORE, distributed by Passport Designs, which allow interactive editing of data on-screen as an alternative to text mode entry and also support the use of MIDI for both audio proofing and data input from any suitable keyboard or sequencer via an associated transcription program known as Escort.

HB Music Engraver, for the Macintosh, differs from SCORE in being designed from the outset as a fully interactive menu-driven graphics system, the user accessing a series of dialogue boxes to change the functions of the mouse and also select the symbols to be used in pasting up the score. Audio proofing is possible using either the internal synthesis facilities of the Macintosh or an external synthesizer, accessed via MIDI. In terms of the range and versatility of facilities both SCORE and HB Music Engraver qualify as typesetting programs of considerable refinement. Issues such as the precise shape and position of neumes or the trajectory of beamings are very important to professional engravers and it is a matter of personal taste which of these programs is the more proficient. There are, nevertheless, a number of other notation packages which come quite close to these professional systems in terms of flexibility and refinement. Representative packages in this latter category include Copyist from Dr T for the Atari ST, Professional Composer from Mark of the Unicorn for the Macintosh, and Finale from Coda, originally developed for the Macintosh but now also available in a Windows 3 version for the PC.

All of these offer a number of features in common, and any one can be considered representative of the genre. Finale, for example, allows data input either from a live performance using a MIDI keyboard, or a multi-channel MIDI sequencer file, or via the mouse, with full support for multi-channel MIDI playback. In addition data can also be edited in its MIDI code format, allowing access to performance details such as the choice of channel or dynamic levels. Instant piano score reductions of orchestral textures can be obtained, clefs changed, and parts transposed and printed out individually. Further refinements include the ability to vary the trajectory and thickness of beaming, the positioning of text, and the scaling of music details.

The boundary between notation and sequencing software is further obscured by a number of compound packages which embrace both aspects with almost equal weighting. Despite its name, Notator from C-Lab for the Atari ST falls into this category, as does Personal Composer from Jim Miller for the PC and Concertware+MIDI from Great Wave Software for the Macintosh. C-Lab and Personal Composer combine powerful score writing facilities (up to thirty-two staves per page in the case of C-Lab) with multi-track sequencing facilities (sixty-four tracks in the case of C-Lab, thirty-two in the case of Personal Composer). The original Concertware program (later updated as Concertware+) is primarily a score writing program with a synthesis option which allows material to be checked aurally using the internal sound system of the Macintosh. Three separate but linkable modules are provided: Music Writer, Music Player, and Instrument Maker. The first allows scores to be constructed on-screen using either the mouse or the alphanumeric keyboard or a combination of the two, the second translates basic score details into a control sequence for the Macintosh sound system using a factory-supplied repertory of synthesized sounds, and the third allows the sounds to be constructed directly using a graphics tool to specify wave-form components. Although the sound capabilities of the Macintosh are necessarily limited in scope Concertware+ provides a sufficient range of resources to qualify as an integrated music writing, synthesis, and performance system. With Concertware+MIDI the addition of a software driver for MIDI makes it possible to use the sequencer as the master control facility for an external synthesizer.

Programs primarily intended for sequencing form by far the largest category of MIDI software. Facilities for the display and editing of data in common music notation as well as MIDI formats are generally included as a matter of course but often lack the sophistication of a more specialist engraving program. Some are designed to complement true music notation programs, for example Performer from Mark of the Unicorn for the Macintosh, which is a companion to Professional Composer. Most are able to accommodate a full set of sixteen MIDI voice tracks and more sophisticated versions offer twenty-four or more, allowing a number of sub-tracks to be used for selected voices.

The distribution of these programs between microcomputers gives a useful indication of their relative popularity for MIDI applications. By the end of the 1980s the leaders in terms of choice of software were the Atari ST and the Macintosh, with a slight numerical advantage in favour of the former. Fewer programs had been developed for the PC by this stage but this imbalance has been substantially corrected in the early 1990s as the popularity of this microcomputer for music applications has steadily grown. In contrast Commodore and Acorn have yet to attract a truly comprehensive repertory of programs, not just for sequencing but also for MIDI applications in general, but here too the availability of software is now much improved.

One reason for this has been a notable trend towards software portability with the release of a number of programs in versions for more than one microcomputer. Steinberg's pioneering Pro-24 sequencing package for the Atari ST, for example, was subsequently produced in a version for the Commodore Amiga, and their more recent program Cubase can be obtained in versions for the Atari ST and the Macintosh. Passport Designs have gone one stage further with their main sequencing program Mastertracks Pro, which has been released in versions for the Apple IIGS, the Commodore 64, 128, and Amiga, the Atari ST, the IBM PC, and the Macintosh. Reference has already been made to the availability of Finale for both the Macintosh and the PC, and even more specialist programs such as M can now be obtained in versions for the Amiga, the Atari ST, and the PC, as well as the original written for the Macintosh.

Voice editing software by its very nature is specific to a single-synthesizer architecture, demanding the purchase of several programs if a number of different synthesizers are thus to be configured. For many users the extra expense is more than outweighed by the ease and refinement of working afforded by a WIMPS-driven environment. These programs often include additional banks of ready-to-use voices to supplement those provided by the synthesizer manufacturer and are produced by a number of software houses such as Dr T (Atari, Macintosh, PC, and Amiga), Sound Quest (Atari, PC, Amiga), Steinberg (Atari), and Opcode (Macintosh).

Educational software covers a variety of musical subjects and enjoys a history which started well before the advent of MIDI. A succession of basic music packages were produced for the original Apple II during the late 1970s and early 80s but the limitations of the one-bit sound system severely restricted their usefulness. The introduction of add-on sound facilities such as the Mountain Computer board was thus especially important for this market sector since they allowed the generation of polyphonic textures, especially useful for aural training or the teaching of harmony and counterpoint. Machines such as the Commodore 64 and the Atari 400 with built-in synthesis capabilities had a distinct advantage over the basic Apple II in this respect and both were well represented in the initial repertory of educational programs. Most of these have long since disappeared from sale or regular use but several of the MIDI-based packages available today owe their origins to these pioneering products. This is an area ripe for further development, not least in terms of software, which is of a less elementary nature than has generally been the case hitherto. Representative aural training packages include the Guido Music Learning System from Delaware University, which is available in versions for the Macintosh and the PC, and Perceive from Coda for the Macintosh. Programs for learning the rules of harmony and counterpoint include MacVoice from Carnegie–Mellon University and Palestrina from Dartmouth College.

The use of microcomputers for sample editing provides an important link between MIDI synthesizers and the earlier-mentioned use of co-processors to create high-performance audio workstations. The best-known software packages include products from Blank Software (Macintosh), Digidesign (Atari and Macintosh), Dr T (Amiga, Atari, and Macintosh), Steinberg (Atari), and Turtle Beach (PC family). In discussing the characteristics of MIDI it was seen how the special 'system exclusive' mode permits the exchange of audio data between devices via a standard MIDI link. The biggest drawback to this method of communication is the significant delays encountered in the transfer of even just a short sound extract. When a microcomputer is linked to a sampler in this manner for the purposes of sound editing this problem becomes all the more significant if the former lacks facilities for direct audio proofing. In this situation sound data has to be transferred back to the sampler via the MIDI link before the results of any alteration can be verified. The introduction of SCSI-based communications as a much faster alternative to MIDI for a number of samplers has eliminated the worst effects of this latency but even so the need to operate two separate items of equipment every time an edit is to be checked can still prove extremely irritating.

Faced with such hurdles many users have found the limited facilities provided by the Macintosh or the Atari STE for the output of sound direct from memory the lesser of two evils. The optimum solution in all these cases is now a high performance D-to-A converter card connected directly to the internal communications bus of the host microcomputer. These have become available for a number of microcomputers in recent years and in many instances are capable of converting audio data at industry-standard sampling rates in mono or stereo with full sixteen-bit resolution.

Memory size is as important a factor in the current context as in the earlier discussion of sampler development. Microcomputers such as the Atari 520 ST, the XT PC, and the Commodore Amiga 500 are limited to a usable free memory capacity of only 0.5 megabytes or thereabouts, and this is before taking into consideration the space required for the editing program itself. At the other end of the scale models such as a 386 or 486 PC clone, a Macintosh IIfx or IIci, or an Amiga 3000 can all accommodate at least eight and in some cases up to sixteen megabytes of memory. If memory is limited it is sometimes possible to use the computer's own hard disk as an intermediate storage facility, the editing program controlling the transfer of sound segments into memory as required. Such disk-to-memory transfers will sometimes involve momentary delays but if this internal shuffling of data is efficiently organized and suitably buffered the process will often be transparent to the user.

When the terms of reference are extended from the editing of sounds for a sampler to the editing of complete digital recordings the boundary between the active generation and processing of digitized sound for creative purposes and more general uses of digital audio in the recording industry for mixing and editing becomes very tenuous. One software package for the Macintosh,

Alchemy from Blank Software, stands out for special consideration in this context in view of its exceptional versatility in both
spheres of application. On the one hand, it is a powerful sixteen-
bit editing and processing program for the Macintosh, suitable
for use with a variety of samplers. On the other, it can be used to
mix and edit complete audio files from hard disk, manipulate
sound information from newer multi-media tools such as CD-
ROM audio, and provide a compatible environment for a number of specialist digital audio processing systems.

The introduction of high-quality co-processing hardware has
added an important new dimension to the use of microcomputers
for audio. Systems such as those developed around the Sound
Accelerator card from Digidesign for the Macintosh and Atari
ST or the Dyaxis sub-system from Studer/Editech for the
Macintosh have facilitated dramatic improvements in performance and versatility. Both systems incorporate stereo sixteen-bit
converters which operate at the 44.1 kHz in the case of the
Sound Accelerator and 32, 44.1, or 48 kHz in the case of Dyaxis.
Digital audio input/output ports are also provided, and these
greatly extend the flexibility of these systems since it is possible to
communicate directly with other digital audio equipment without
any intermediate conversion into an analogue format.

Whereas Dyaxis is designed primarily for the professional
recording studio the Digidesign system embraces not only recording but also a range of synthesis and processing applications of
particular interest to composers. The development of the Sound
Accelerator card was largely inspired by an earlier suite of software programs developed for the Macintosh. The first of these,
Sound Designer, appeared in 1985 as an editing system for the
E-mu Emulator II sampler, subsequently supported by a music
score editor known as Music Designer. Extension of support to
other samplers such as the Sequential Prophet 2000 and the Akai
S612 soon followed, leading to further additions as the range of
commercial samplers steadily expanded. In 1986 a software synthesis package, Softsynth, was introduced, offering a bank of
thirty-two oscillators with a choice of wave-forms, each controllable by a forty-stage envelope-shaper and a fifteen-stage frequency envelope, with a facility for FM operation. In due course
a much more powerful version known as Turbosynth was
released, providing a comprehensive range of synthesis and signal
processing functions which include modulation, filtering, delay,

pitch shifting and looping, as well as a facility to process externally sampled sounds.

It was soon observed that these programs suffered not only from the processing limitations of the host microcomputer but also from the restricted fidelity of its audio system. The Sound Accelerator card, which appeared in 1988, addressed both issues, leading to the introduction of an integrated system known as Sound Tools in versions for the Macintosh in 1989 and subsequently the Atari ST in 1990. The system consists of two basic elements, the Sound Accelerator card, and an updated version of Sound Designer known as Sound Designer II, to which a number of additional hardware and software facilities can be added. The new versions of Sound Designer offer both sample editing and also digital mixing and processing of complete audio files. The main card includes hardware for stereo D-to-A conversion only, matching A-to-D facilities requiring installation of a second card. Alternatively an external bidirectional interface unit can be used to connect the main Sound Accelerator card directly to a DAT recorder via a digital communications port. Digidesign software programs such as Softsynth and Turbosynth can take advantage of the enhanced processing facilities offered by the Sound Accelerator card, and it is also possible to use third-party products such as Alchemy.

Systems such as Sound Tools and Dyaxis are based on a special family of microprocessors known generically as digital signal processors or DSPs. These can be programmed to service a range of applications and are in principle just as accessible to a software developer as any general purpose microprocessor. The hardware architectures, however, are very different, the concept of a single CPU being replaced by one of a set of sub-processors, linked together to create an efficient pipeline for synchronous computing. A useful analogy is that of a factory which builds just one car at a time, the workers taking turns to insert specific parts, as opposed to a continuous assembly line where several workers can work simultaneously and thus much more efficiently on a succession of cars.

In the field of digital audio the DSPs were foreshadowed by a number of systems built at various institutions from discrete components, for example the 4X developed at IRCAM and the digital oscillator bank designed by Hal Alles of Bell Telephone Laboratories. Two further pioneering systems merit particular attention in this context, the System Concepts Digital Synthesizer and the Lucasfilm Digital Audio Processor. The System Concepts Digital Synthesizer was developed for the commercial market by Jim Samson from a prototype known as the Samson Box, the result of a extended project at Stanford University which occupied much of the 1970s. Like the 4X the synthesis hardware is built from arrays of logic gates, optimized for the tasks of audio signal generation and processing. Extensive use is made of pipelining to speed up chains of signal processing steps and the overall performance of the system is both fast and efficient.

The Lucasfilm Digital Audio Processor is of special interest since its digital signal processing section, although built largely from discrete components, uses design principles remarkably similar to those associated with the internal design of a modern, chip-fabricated DSP. This system was the brainchild of James Moorer, who moved to Lucasfilm from Stanford soon after completing his work on MUSIC 10 in the mid-1970s. With assistance from James Snell he began work on the project in early 1980, and by 1983 the system was operational. Although designed specifically for the needs of the film industry, which has not been noted in the past for particularly good standards of audio fidelity, it was engineered to the highest specifications, with a capacity to process up to sixty-four channels of sound information at a 50-kHz sampling rate mapped across a bank of eight processing modules, controlled in turn by a 68000-based microcomputer. Each module offers a wide variety of functions, ranging from filtering and pitch shifting for individual channels to multi-track editing and mixing, accessed via a series of consoles which link sound and vision for film production.

In the same way that Intel is credited with the manufacture of the first microprocessor in 1972 a similar distinction can be advanced for their production of the first general-purpose DSP chip in 1978, the 2920. As a novel and untested architecture attempting to penetrate a well-established market for conventional microprocessors its impact was fairly modest, its disappointing speed serving to mask the true significance of the special technology. In 1980 NEC introduced a much faster and more powerful DSP known as the muPD7720, and this inspired a number of major microprocessor manufacturers to start developing rival products of an even higher specification, a race which was won by Texas Instruments with the release of their TMS 32000 in 1983.

The novel characteristics of these signal processors require some qualification since it follows that any computing architecture which is optimized for specific modes of operation will inevitably prove more efficient for some types of data processing and less so for others, and there are thus important differences between the functional characteristics of one DSP and those of another. The TMS 32000, for example, is most efficient for applications such as computer graphics and the on-line control of industrial processes. Nevertheless, the architecture was sufficiently attractive to persuade several research groups to investigate its use for audio applications, and this led to construction of a number of 32000-based experimental real-time synthesizers in the mid-1980s. Such developments were helped significantly by the introduction in due course of faster versions of this DSP as the 32020 series, notably the 320C25, which eliminates a number of these programming difficulties by means of an enhanced instruction set.

The release of the TMS 32030 at the end of the decade signalled a design change of particular importance for audio applications through its use of a thirty-two-bit floating-point architecture instead of the fixed-point architecture used in all earlier versions of the TMS series. The significance of restricted integer word lengths when processing audio data has already been discussed at some length, in particular the serious loss of quantizing accuracy which occurs when a signal is attenuated significantly as a result of one process, only to be boosted again subsequently. The fixed-point versions of the TMS series, in common with rival products such as the MB87064 from Fujitsu or the WE DSP16A from AT & T, use integer word lengths of sixteen bits, requiring skilful and time-consuming programming if the adverse effects of amplitude scaling are to be minimized. Another fixed-point family of DSPs known as the 56000 series, introduced by Motorola in the mid-1980s, addresses this problem by using twenty-four-bit rather than sixteen-bit word lengths for the internal storage of data. As a result conventional sixteen-bit audio samples can be attenuated internally by up to 64 dB before any detectable loss of quantization accuracy occurs.

Given this advantage it is not surprising that the majority of DSP-based audio systems developed during the late-1980s have been based on one of the 56000 DSPs, notably the general purpose 56001. These include the Digidesign Sound Accelerator discussed earlier and also the audio section of perhaps the most advanced microcomputer to emerge from this period, the NeXT, which integrates both microcomputer and DSP technology as part of its basic architecture. Three microprocessors are employed for this purpose, a fast 68030 main processor, a 68882 co-processor specifically designed to speed up floating-point calculations, and a 56001 DSP for the processing of both sound and vision, the latter supporting sixteen-bit stereo D-to-A converters which operate at 44.1 kHz and also a high-resolution graphics system. With computer music as well as general audio applications in mind a comprehensive software tool-box is provided, allowing easy installation of traditional synthesis programs such as CMUSIC or CSOUND or one of a growing range of new applications which are under development at a number of institutions around the world. Accessories such as a high-resolution laser printer, MIDI interface, A-to-D converters, and a bidirectional DAT interface complete this powerful, and in musical terms very attractive, microcomputer.

The early 1990s has seen the trend towards thirty-two-bit floating-point architectures strengthened by the introduction of DSPs such as the WE DSP32 from AT & T and the 96000 from Motorola, and the next generation of music systems currently under development is already taking advantage of these new computing engines. Nevertheless, even DSPs as fast and powerful as these still suffer from some practical drawbacks. In particular they are generally not designed to cope with the more general processing or housekeeping tasks which are an unavoidable part of any computing process, and these have usually to be delegated to the host microcomputer. This can lead to a serious loss in overall efficiency if communications between the host and the DSP become saturated or the host itself is too slow.

Two related lines of hardware development are providing possible solutions to such problems. One of these concerns the development of alternative co-processor architectures which subsume most if not all the advantages of a DSP approach and at the same time reduce the demands made on the host system to a minimum. The other avoids DSPs altogether and relies instead upon continuing improvements in the performance of the conventional microcomputer itself, which have proved very substantial in recent years as the result of the introduction of faster and more powerful versions of standard microprocessors such the 80486 and the 68040. This particular line of development, although now undoubtedly delivering some impressive results, is still restrained by the fact that such systems retain the traditional concept of a single CPU, which in the end is only capable of processing one operation at a time. Many computational tasks, not least those in a music context, require several processes to be executed in parallel, for example the synthesis of a polyphonic texture from several independent voices, or the filtering of individual channels in a digital mixer. With a single CPU such parallelism has to be simulated by processing small quantities of data for each component in turn in a cyclical fashion, and this explains why the time taken to process a CSOUND score depends not only on the complexity of each instrument but also on how many instruments are active concurrently.

If there is no further scope for increasing the power of a single microprocessor the next logical step involves connecting two or more microprocessors together in parallel and the development of a suitable control system which can dynamically schedule concurrent tasks between them in an efficient manner. Unfortunately if this line of hardware development is taken too far it can prove very hard to achieve even any further increases in performance since in the case of conventional microprocessors or DSPs the proportion of time consumed in managing the system rises rapidly in proportion to the number of active processors in the network. Typically, adding a second processor will only increase the throughput of the system by about 50 per cent, and adding a sixth processor to an existing network of five will often prove highly counter-productive since this can actually reduce the overall speed of the system. Overcoming inter-processor communication bottlenecks for parallel computing systems has demanded a fundamental reappraisal of the ways in which such engines are put together. One solution which has stimulated particular interest in the field of computer music since the late 1980s has been the construction of massively parallel systems from hundreds or even thousands of very simple microprocessors which are sometimes little more than basic logic gates, with the object of developing models which have the capacity to emulate the neural networks which operate within the human brain. Such systems facilitate the development of systems which explore aspects of artificial intelligence, of particular value in the development of more intuitive interfaces for composer–machine communications as well as powerful and versatile computing engines for the synthesis and processing of compositional material. A notable example of such a massively parallel resource which has been used for music applications is the Connection Machine, built at MIT in 1987–8.

Another approach has resulted from a European initiative based upon a very special type of microprocessor known as the transputer, designed by Inmos in the United Kingdom during the mid-1980s. This is essentially a complete microcomputer fabricated as a single chip which incorporates a processor, memory, and a set of high speed input/output communication links which allow two- or even three-dimensional networks of tens or even hundreds of these devices to be assembled and programmed with relative ease. The key to the performance of the transputer lies both in its internal architecture, which allows the programmer to write routines which involve serial or parallel algorithms, and in the communication links themselves, which consist of single wires transmitting or receiving data as a high-speed serial stream in place of the normal parallel bus structure used by conventional microprocessors. A number of European research groups developed prototype systems for computer music during the early 1990s based on networks of transputers, and interest is steadily growing in the possibilities of this rather unusual technology.

The choice and availability of facilities for programming is becoming a major issue as new and more complex hardware architectures become available. The time taken to write a complicated synthesis task in the assembly language or machine code of a processor can prove a formidable prospect even for an experienced programmer, and the results do not always seem to justify the effort. Newer high-speed processors, including the transputer, are often of a RISC (Reduced Instruction Set Computing) type which, as the acronym suggests, involves a streamlined hardware architecture and a considerable reduction in the number and variety of machine instructions available. Such characteristics require the acquisition of new programming skills if efficient algorithms are to be written directly in this manner. This has led to some criticism of the RISC approach on the grounds that ease of programming should be as important if not a greater priority than basic machine efficiency. As a result new architectures are now increasingly expected to be well supported with software tools for writing programs at both low and high levels. This is not the case with most of the DSPs described above, for with few exceptions they cannot directly accept programs written in languages such as C or Pascal.

A good example of a new type of processor which does meet such programming requirements is the i860, introduced by Intel in 1989 and used as the main computing engine for the IRCAM Musical Workstation, completed in 1991. This microprocessor combines the concept of an extended RISC design with the pipelined construction of a DSP to create a very powerful hybrid architecture which combines hardware features specifically designed for high-speed signal processing applications with an efficient system of overall management, with the added advantage of an enhanced instruction set which fully supports both integer and floating-point mathematics and also more powerful programming languages such as C. This functional integration removes an important bottleneck in a traditional host microcomputer/DSP system since much of the burden of control can be shifted from the i860 host to the i860 system itself. Although direct networking of several i860s in parallel is again ultimately constrained by the bandwidth of the communications bus, the introduction of a special module which integrates an i860 with a transputer has opened up the possibility of developing audio supercomputers of unprecedented power.

In designing the IRCAM Musical Workstation a more pressing consideration was the choice of a host microcomputer for a more modest configuration of i860s which could immediately support a wide range of music software with good graphics, high capacity disk storage facilities, sound input and output, and communication interfaces to other devices such as DAT recorders and MIDI equipment. Such requirements were readily met by the NeXT after some modifications to its basic operating software. The i860 system itself is modular, with the option of one, two, or three identical plug-in cards, each containing a pair of i860 microprocessors, a high-speed memory bank with shared access, and associated control and communications hardware.

A sophisticated tool-box has been developed for this system with comprehensive support for both high-level and low-level programming. Considerable attention has been paid to the use of interactive graphics as the primary medium for working where individual processes may be viewed as 'objects', easily interconnected and intercepted for development or modification using MAX or ANIMAL, special programming environments developed at IRCAM. The release of the workstation by Ariel as a commercial product in 1991 has made it possible for the composing community at large to take advantage of the wide range of facilities offered by this advanced system.

High-speed general-purpose microprocessors, newer RISC-based designs such as the i860, thirty-two-bit floating-point DSPs, and the various architectures which are being developed for the construction of parallel computers are opening up possibilities for composers and researchers which could scarcely have been envisaged at the beginning of the 1980s. Exploiting the latest hardware tools to construct ever faster and more versatile computing engines is only of limited value in the longer term if the resulting products are not to be made generally available to prospective users at a realistic cost and supported by an adequate repertory of suitable software. Considerations such as these have ensured sustained interest in traditional direct synthesis programs such as CMUSIC and CSOUND, which continue to be used by a number of institutions and individuals both for composition and also research. The increasing power of general-purpose microcomputers has not only allowed the direct installation of such systems on the personal desktop but also dramatically reduced the waiting time for even the most complex of 'scores' and 'orchestras'. Indeed, some of the very latest standard computing platforms are powerful enough to allow a growing repertory of material to be synthesized at industry-standard sampling rates without any intermediate delay.

Strong evidence of the continuing interest in direct synthesis techniques is provided by the Composers Desktop Project established in York during the mid 1980s, with the object of marketing an affordable music system which could run software synthesis programs such as CMUSIC and CSOUND and also provide an environment for developing other packages of special interest to composers. Cost considerations in the European context led to the choice of the Atari 1040 ST rather than a Macintosh as the host microcomputer, the only additional items of hardware required consisting of a high-capacity hard disk drive for storing sound files and a special interface developed by the CDP itself to allow communications between the Atari and an associated commercial digital tape recorder. The latter facility provides the A-to-D and D-to-A converters for the input and output of sound material and also serves as a general-purpose recording facility for the mastering of complete pieces.

In addition to the development of a number of useful software utilities such as a program for editing and mixing sound files, some newer synthesis algorithms have been specially implemented for the CDP, notably a program for phase vocoding. Simple analogue vocoding, where audio information is analysed by a bank of filters into a set of varying amplitude values for subsequent re-synthesis, has already been described in connection with Meyer-Eppler's preliminary investigations into speech synthesis in Germany just after the Second World War, leading in turn to Moorer's development of more sophisticated algorithms for digital filtering at Stanford during the mid 1970s. The key to a true vocoder capable of accurately re-synthesizing sound spectra from a succession of snapshot filter frames lies in the retention of information concerning the phase of the individual spectral components, hence the name. This additional data also allows the composer to effect a variety of useful transformations during the re-synthesis process such as accurate transposition of the harmonic spectra without altering the temporal evolution of the constituent events, or the stretching of material in time without affecting its pitch. A number of researchers worldwide have contributed to the development of the phase vocoder algorithms, and their greater accessibility through initiatives such as the CDP is to be welcomed.

The 1980s saw the development of a number of other synthesis algorithms, with a particular emphasis on those which imitate natural sounds such as bowed and plucked strings, woodwind and brass, and the human voice. Direct modelling of the acoustic process has proved especially successful in this context, resulting in a realism which is not always practicable using additive synthesis or FM techniques. Such modelling is particularly powerful since the composer is able to exercise direct control over the components of the acoustic model and produce extensive transformations which cannot be matched by any known procedures for manipulating acoustically generated sources.

Two algorithms merit special attention since they both are now widely available for general use, notably as additional unit generators for programs such as CSOUND. The first of these, the Karplus-Strong algorithm, emulates the vibratory behaviour of a plucked string, and the second, FOF (Fonction d'Onde Formantique), that of the human singing voice. The work of Kevin Karplus and Alex Strong in string modelling during the late 1970s, further refined by David Jaffe and Julius Smith at Stanford University, has resulted in a synthesis tool of considerable versatility. The basic acoustic model is simulated in the form of a variable length digital delay line, energized by noise and incorporating a feedback path via an attenuator, coupled to an adjustable low-pass filter which induces resonances akin to those of a vibrating string. Suitable adjustments of these parameters can alter the decay of the string sound from a plucked characteristic to a sustained one, with the possibility of changing pitch not only in discrete steps, but also by means of glissandi, thus introducing powerful facilities for gestural control. Further adjustments allow the percussive characteristics of plucked string sounds to be transformed into a number of drum-like timbres.

The second algorithm, FOF, was originally developed by Xavier Rodet, Yves Potard, and Jean-Baptiste Barrière at IRCAM for CHANT, a software program which allows composers to emulate the characteristics of the singing voice. Modelling of the latter requires the use of four or five FOF generators connected in parallel, one for each of the primary formants generated by the vocal tract. These are simulated by means of sinusoidal impulses which are individually enveloped to create a band-limited response similar to that which can be obtained by applying a pulse train to a conventional band-pass filter. The FOF algorithm, however, produces far more accurate approximations and can easily be modified to generate different sounds such as bells, gongs, filtered noise effects, or wood percussion sounds. One particular feature is the possibility of using FOF to produce granular textures, opening up a rich spectral sound world which has attracted considerable interest as the result of a system such as POD from Barry Truax which is well suited to such processes amongst others.

As computer music systems have acquired the capacity to synthesize and process an increasing repertory of sound material in real time so attention has turned towards the development of more sophisticated control facilities for their operation. MIDI devices from music keyboards to wind controllers have proved particularly attractive in this context, and for this reason many of the systems described above support their use. Standard MIDI interfaces provide a convenient link for any system which is hosted by a conventional microcomputer but the successful capture and application of complex gestural information is another consideration altogether. Commercial MIDI controllers as yet only embrace certain aspects of instrumental performance but future designs will benefit from the fruits of research currently in progress at a number of institutions.

An important key to progress in this area has been the development of more advanced facilities for the capture and application of gestural information from traditional acoustic instruments, allowing for instance the interaction of a live acoustic performance with the processes of synthesis. One application which has aroused considerable interest is that of the automatic accompanying system where a synthesizer, voiced typically as a piano, intelligently tracks a soloist using a pre-programmed score of the work to be performed. Reproducing the skills of a professional accompanist is a formidable challenge given the subtle variations in tempo and other aspects of articulation from one soloist to another and also the unpredictability of rehearsal as mistakes are made and different passages rehearsed, requiring the accompanying system to deduce what the performer is trying to play, and from what part of the score. The most formidable challenge concerns how best to capture those characteristics of the soloist's own performance which are necessary to ensure both accurate synchronization and also a matching interpretation.

The problems encountered in acquiring such data from conventional orchestral instruments are very much more complex than those associated with pseudo-instrumental controllers with built-in sensors. Although it is possible to fit mechanisms to detect key movements or the direct contact of strings with the fingerboard in the case of fretted instruments such as guitars the only comprehensive source of performance information is the acoustic sound itself. The accurate analysis of acoustic data in terms of the frequency and timing of individual note/events has proved a major engineering challenge, especially in live performance. If the solo instrument is itself polyphonic, for example a piano, such problems are made greater by many orders of magnitude. Long-standing research projects directed by researchers such as Barry Vercoe both at IRCAM and MIT and Roger Dannenberg at Carnegie–Mellon have yielded promising results in this area and commercial accompaniment systems of this order of sophistication are now clearly in prospect.

Gestural capture systems for applications such as performing or interactive composition have opened up other possibilities for interpreting human expression and there are two on-going projects dating from the 1970s which merit special attention in this context. The first of these, UPIC, illustrates very well how the transition from a non-real-time to a real-time environment as a result of the long-term development of a particular system can materially alter the way in which the user interacts with it. The early versions of UPIC, despite the introduction of a graphics inter-face, were clearly composing tools in the sense that the user was encouraged first to develop basic materials in terms of wave-shapes and functions such as amplitude envelopes and then by processes of selection and evaluation work towards the construction of a complete composition as a predetermined set of processes. As the graphics interface became more sophisticated and the response times of the associated hardware progressively shorter so UPIC gradually became interactive, thus developing step by step into a performance instrument. A growing concern of Iannis Xenakis has been to bring the world of sound synthesis within the reach of novice composers such as schoolchildren and this has influenced the development of the graphics interface itself, which in all versions produced so far is driven directly by a hand-held wand or light pen rather than the conventional mouse moved about on a flat surface. In fully interactive versions of UPIC the screen is organized as a very special type of score, essentially a map of sound pictures assembled in a manner analogous to the artist and his palette of paints. These pictures, and their associated performance characteristics can be ordered into regions, for example the basic repertory of source timbres and envelopes, the choice of sound patterns, and the direction and speed at which the material is to be accessed and synthesis. Performance of an UPIC score can thus be rehearsed or entirely intuitive, this flexibility allowing the user to establish a very personal working relationship with the system.

There is much in common between the performing interface for UPIC and the range of conducting facilities for synthesis control developed by Max Mathews over a similar period. In 1975, in response to a request from Pierre Boulez, Mathews began work on more advanced software for operating GROOVE, leading to an early version of his Conductor program, which is designed to interpret performance information provided by a suitable gestural sensor and generate a suitable sequence of synthesis instructions. As the name of the program suggests his preferred controller is the hand-held rod which can move in the air like a conductor's baton and also be used to strike a solid transducer such as a drum skin, or its equivalent.

Mathews's first system, the Sequential Drum, consists of a grid of horizontal and vertical wires and an associated beater. When the latter is used to strike the grid a pair of wires is forced into contact, generating co-ordinates which are then analysed by the Conductor program. What distinguishes this sensor from devices such as a graphics mouse or tablet is the use of a contact microphone to record the strength of each hit. Practical difficulties with the wire grid soon led Mathews to develop another type of surface, the Daton. This consists of a solid but partially tactile skin in the form of a square, supported in each corner by a strain gauge. Drum strokes on different parts of the playing surface will thus produce different responses from each of the gauges, the resulting information being decoded to produce the corresponding co-ordinates.

Although the Daton has proved a useful tool it is Mathews's third system, the Radio Drum, which is perhaps the best known. This allows detection of proximity to the drum surface as well as the surface co-ordinates, thus creating a three-dimensional sensor. The surface itself consists of a network of radio antennae which detect the strengths of signals transmitted from a small radio transmitter incorporated into the head of the drum stick. Multiple sticks may be employed, two being an obvious choice for a single performer, the movements of each stick being individually monitored and processed by the Conductor program, which will output data in a MIDI format.

Considerable performance skills have to be acquired if full advantage is to be taken of the Radio Drum's detection features and the same is true in the case of another gestural capture system developed by Michael Waisvisz at STEIM, Amsterdam, in the mid-1980s, known as The Hands. This is a most remarkable system designed very much to a personal specification but embodying technology which has encouraged others to develop systems offering similar characteristics. The Hands consists of two gloves containing special detectors which monitor the movements of individual fingers and also the movements of the hands themselves relative to one another. The tactile skills necessary to operate the system are developed further in a more recent system from Waisvisz, The Web, which consists of a lattice similar to a spider's web which is manipulated by finger movements, sensors detecting the resulting changes in tension within segments.

Optical sensing techniques have also proved a productive line of research in this context. The possibilities of detecting physical movement by means of light beams and optical sensors had been demonstrated during the 1960s by John Cage among others but the true potential of the medium as a means of gestural capture only became apparent with the development of digital transducers.

Such technology forms the basis of the VideoHarp, first developed by Dean Rubine and Paul McAvinney at Carnegie–Mellon in 1988 and subsequently updated and improved. This device is a MIDI controller which optically tracks the movement of individual fingers on a sheet of glass, illuminated at one end by a neon strip light source. The sensor at the other end consists of a bank of memory cells with a transparent cover, making them sensitive to variations in the intensity of light. This bank functions as a sophisticated lens with a 60 degree line of vision across the glass to the illuminated opposite edge, creating a triangular detection area. When a finger touches the glass surface in the detection area the light beam is partially blocked, the memory cell system allowing detection of both the angle and also the apparent thickness of the interruption. Since the thickness of the finger relative to the total width of the light beam it is interrupting increases the closer it is placed to the sensor this information can be used to map the movement of fingers in a two-dimensional playing area. In the improved version two sheets of glass are used, allowing detection of finger movements from both hands, positioned one on each side.

The dramatic growth in facilities for computer music in recent years, fuelled by the escalating power of the underlying technology, has transformed the outlook for the medium in terms of access to advanced resources both for the individual forced to rely on private means and also for those who work in the increasing number of institutions world-wide which actively support composition and research in this medium. Such accessibility has removed much of the mystique which surrounded electronic and computer music until the early 1980s but at the same time made it very difficult to develop any rational perspective with regard to the vast quantity of compositions which undoubtedly now exist on tape in studios and personal archives the world over. Children who otherwise might never master even the basic skills of a traditional musical instrument are now in large numbers discovering the possibilities of synthetic sound production through contact with synthesizers at school, leading in turn to fierce debates over the extent to which the art and practice of music technology should form part of a general music curriculum.

Maintaining a healthy balance between the development of mass-produced commercial systems at prices which ensure maximum accessibility and the development of more specialist or experimental products for those wishing to explore new techniques of synthesis and processing is a vital objective, and it is most encouraging to note that the considerable industry of many individuals in this context with or without institutional support seems set to continue. A promising trend in recent years has been the growing priority being given to the exploitation of successful research projects for the benefit of the wider community via both the commercial sector and also collectives such as the CDP or PAN (Performing Arts Network), a North American-based organization for the interchange of information which embraces very similar aims.

Many of the issues which have yet to be addressed are by no means new, although the sheer pace of technical developments conspires to obscure them. It is sometimes assumed that the processes of evolution, especially in a scientific context, lead inevitably to a new environment which is better than the one it replaces. Measured in terms of general performance both in terms of processing capabilities and also as a factor of cost it is hard to dispute that this has indeed been the general trend over the years. When the terms of reference are expanded to include artistic criteria it is not so clear that all of these developments have necessarily been of particular benefit to the creative process.

More than fifty years have now elapsed since the establishment of Schaeffer's first research laboratory at the RTF in wartime France and Cage's first excursions into live synthesis. Much progress has been made in developing practical tools and an associated repertory for electronic and computer music since this early period of experimentation and discovery, and those responsible for future developments have a rich legacy of knowledge and understanding of the problems which have to be addressed if this meeting of disciplines is to bear the richest fruit. Major pitfalls, however, await those who choose not to heed the lessons of the past, and a review of some of these form the basis of the concluding chapter.

# 14 Conclusion

The outlook for electronic and computer music offers a highly speculative subject for a concluding chapter. Since the 1980s technology has advanced at such a pace that artistic considerations have not always received the attention that they deserve. There are now, however, some encouraging signs that the medium is moving towards an era of consolidation and reappraisal which will allow a more appropriate balance of interests to be struck.

In the past the functional limitations of audio synthesis and processing systems have materially influenced the way in which they are used, whether for composition or for performance. Such constraints have sometimes been helpful at least in the initial stages of exploration since they establish a clear practical framework for the development of musical ideas, but their true significance becomes all too apparent as soon as any attempts are made to go beyond the operational limits of the system. As their functional characteristics have improved so the technical barriers have been steadily pushed back to expose two complementary issues which are of paramount importance: first, what the creative goals of composers and performers in the future are likely to be, and second, what kind of new tools will be needed to achieve them.

This new environment calls for a reappraisal of the basic terminology used to describe the attributes of the medium. At the very highest level, for example, the distinction between 'electronic' and 'computer' music no longer holds any particular relevance. Until the late 1970s these two technologies and their associated musical repertories developed along very different paths both practically and philosophically. During the 1980s these paths started to converge, but with an increasing emphasis on digital rather than analogue technology. This process of fusion in terms of both technical means and also methods of working was recognized well before the birth of MIDI with the emergence of the more generic term 'electroacoustic music'. There is much to commend this definition since it makes no material distinction between sounds of natural or synthetic origin and also draws attention to their perceived characteristics through the processes of audition rather than the technical means by which they are produced. It thus follows that the success or otherwise of a repertory of electroacoustic music depends on the aural result and not the means by which it is achieved, unless it becomes apparent to the listener that the desired objectives have been compromised by shortcomings in the technology itself or its method of application. As a term of French origin, however, it presents very real problems of a semantic nature to an English-speaking public since unlike words such as 'electronic' or 'computer' it has no obvious roots in everyday life. As a result it too readily conjures up the vision of an art form which is both élitist and inaccessible, hardly a description that the younger generation would normally think appropriate for rock and pop music, which relies so heavily on 'electroacoustic' processes.

This review of terminology begs the question why any qualification of the term 'music' should be necessary in the first place. To many people devices such as guitars, synthesizers, and audio processors are the primary agents for making music, and to their way of thinking it is acoustic instruments which belong to the fringes of the medium rather than their electronic counterparts. Although such a contrary outlook may seem heretical to the classical music lover it is one which is evidently supported by many writers of books and articles on MIDI for the popular press. A more considered perspective seeks a reconciliation of these philosophical differences by recognizing the diversity of sound-producing agents which may be used to generate music and the ability of many of these tools to serve both serious and popular applications alike. What arises from this is the importance of achieving a better understanding of the musical and the technical characteristics of the many tools which have been developed over the years for sound synthesis and processing, and to what extent they have succeeded in enhancing the working environment for the composer and performer.

One of the most disappointing characteristics of developments in the past has been the widespread reluctance of pioneers to study, let alone learn from, the experience of their predecessors. In a number of instances their commitment to new techniques of generating and manipulating sound has led to bitter frustration and disillusionment arising directly from a failure to address fundamental musical problems associated with the medium, many of which had been clearly identified by the mid 1950s. A vital key, which is only now being fully recognized, is the need for a greater understanding of the nature of sound and the complexities of its specification and perception in musical, as opposed to technical, terms.

Attention has already been drawn to the constraints which the characteristics of studio equipment can impose on their creative use. Indeed, during the early years of electronic music they virtually dictated the methods of working. Schaeffer's *musique concrète*, for example, evolved in terms of analyses and transformations which could be obtained exclusively by the physical manipulation of source recordings, in the first instance coded on wax disc. The bond with the latter recording medium was so close, it will be recalled, that the subsequent introduction of the tape recorder as a replacement was viewed with considerable misgivings.

At Cologne, too, the initial desire to synthesize material entirely from first principles, using a single sine-wave generator, resulted in its own methodology. The desire to expand the range of techniques employed in these classical studios fermented quite naturally from a growing curiosity with the new medium, searching new horizons in the pursuit of originality. Progress was slow, but generally fruitful, owing in no small part to the significance which was attached to detailed research and critical evaluation at each new step. In studying the problems of communication which confronted the composer it became quickly apparent that the provision of tools to replace conventional concepts of notation and instrumentation required major initiatives in the sphere of both morphology and musical analysis, not least in identifying those features which will allow the creative process to be quantified in terms which may be easily and accurately translated into practical synthesis procedures.

The existence of such complex areas of difficulty became widely evident with the introduction of the voltage-controlled synthesizer and the resultant flood of unimaginative works which poured forth from many of the new studios. The sudden availability of conveniently packaged systems, accompanied usually by little more than a basic set of operating instructions, provided no artistic basis whatsoever for the aspirations of the novice electronic composer. Many of the more talented newcomers were quickly disheartened, and those who persisted in their endeavours were forced, except at the most favoured studios, to develop their own ideas in complete isolation from those responsible for the system design. Some of the worst operational problems were eased by the introduction of sequencer control facilities, but again progress in narrowing the gap between technology and its creative application was restricted to pioneering studios, in a position to explore the possibilities of computer control.

The research teams responsible for the birth and early development of computer music systems were dominated by scientists rather than musicians. As a result, their artistic achievements were for many years overshadowed by the output from the main analogue studios. The credibility of the new technology was thus not generally appreciated until the early 1980s when, ironically, the initiative was to be seized by the commercial sector. Yet another twist to this tale concerns the change in marketing emphasis from the days of the early voltage-controlled synthesizer to those of the early all-digital MIDI synthesizer. Whereas the former products were initially targeted at the educational sector the latter were from the outset geared towards the needs of the rock and pop industries. Despite this most practitioners would agree that it is the modern digital synthesizer which is the more versatile tool for the serious composer, a reflection not only of an advancing technology but also of a more informed understanding by manufacturers of the needs of both their general and also their more specialist clientele.

The provision of more flexible resources forms only part of the overall equation. Educating a wider circle of users on the benefits to be gained from using them is just as important, and much work remains to be done in this area. Manufacturers of digital synthesizers have been known to remark how few of their products returned for repair show any evidence of more than a superficial investigation of their characteristics beyond the factory presets. For many sampler users, for example, a comprehensive library of standard orchestral sounds is apparently all that they require. This approach is entirely consistent with the craft of the traditional composer working with an ensemble of acoustic instruments but it denies the opportunity to explore the true potential of these synthesis resources and thus discover a far more interesting sound world which can be applied to so many styles of composition. What is inhibiting this educational process is the nature of the interface between the system and its user, and this explains why both institutional and commercial research is now concentrating increasingly on this specific issue.

There are many other problems unique to the electronic medium to which solutions remain elusive. Perhaps the most significant arises from a complementary aspect of communication, the means of contact with a captive audience. The general acceptance of recorded sound in the intimacy of the home suggests an ideal situation for listening to compositions. Outside the sphere of rock and pop music, however, sales of records and cassettes are modest. Some works are becoming available on compact disc but many of these only enjoy a limited circulation and are often only available from specialist suppliers. The rapid demise of the long-playing record is having another effect in that what little repertory still remains in the main catalogues is rapidly disappearing as manufacturers one by one withdraw completely from this particular market. It is no longer possible for a newcomer to assemble a representative collection of such records from current lists, and it is to libraries and other specialized archives that the enquiring researcher now has to turn to access a representative cross-section of works, even those produced as recently as the last decade.

This rather depressing trend has been largely obscured by the burgeoning sales of MIDI synthesizers, which has resulted in increasing numbers of enthusiasts gaining first-hand experience of what such technology can provide, in many instances in the comfort of their own homes. In the 1950s and 60s electronic music was to a large extent an exclusive art form available to just a few, thus according it a particular status as part of the developing genre of contemporary music. Very few creative skills are required in the first instance to produce basic material from a modern synthesizer. A Yamaha SY77, for example, is provided not only with a preset bank of voices but also with a selection of ready-composed works on a floppy disk. With such easy access to the basic tools of the rock and pop music industries cultivating an interest in more serious styles of composition has become that much harder since many of those most likely to be attracted to the medium have found amateur composing or performing with synthesizers at home an altogether more interesting pastime.

Despite a growing cottage industry in the private publication of works on disc or tape, broadcasting and concert performances remain the primary means of disseminating new works by most serious composers. Unfortunately broadcasting authorities in many countries tend to regard such works as even more of a minority interest than contemporary music which uses conventional acoustic instruments. The concert hall has proved a major source of disappointment for many composers of taped works, for tradition has cultivated an expectation of live action as part of any public performance. Experience has shown that the vista of a platform empty except for an arrangement of loudspeakers does not encourage a heightened concentration on the aural dimension unless considerable thought has been given to the diffusion of the material as part of the compositional process. Without a visual aspect the projection of sound has to be handled with special care and any material shortcomings in this respect will only serve to heighten any feelings of detachment or alienation. The social aspects of concert-going are firmly rooted, and habits of a lifetime are hard to change.

The laws of acoustics give rise to a further difficulty, for the diffusion of sounds in large acoustic spaces leads to significant alterations in the perceived images. Many a composer, having realized a work in the confines of a studio, has discovered too late that large-scale projection removes subtleties of texture and dynamics, while spatial effects often assume dramatic proportions. If a work is written specifically for public performance in a large auditorium, subsequent issue on tape or record can lead to the converse problems. The full grandeur and perspective of Varèse's *Poème électronique* can never be recaptured, for it is impossible to reproduce the very special acoustics of the Philips Pavilion for which it was composed.

However excellent the facilities for sound diffusion, for many there is no substitute for the live interpreter. Cage, Wolff, Tudor, Behrman, Mumma, Ashley, Reich are but a few examples of composers who abandoned the studio for the concert hall at a very early stage in their careers, and many others have found the fusion of tape with live electronics or acoustic instruments a more satisfactory medium to work with than just tape alone.

In the final analysis it is the response of the listener which determines whether of not the inspiration of the composer has been successfully communicated. The variety of material which may be incorporated in an electroacoustic work creates a freedom of choice which is unprecedented in traditional music. This very diversity introduces its own problems, for in experiencing the unfamiliar there is an instinctive desire to identify features which relate to known phenomena, drawn from the experiences of everyday life. The pioneers at Cologne were to discover only too clearly the difficulties of creating a musical language based exclusively on the attributes of synthetic sound. While a number of composers have remained committed to the pursuit of this particular objective, the majority have come to place a higher priority on the refinement of links between the synthetic and natural sound worlds, seeking a language which is common to both. As noted in the preceding chapters, digital signal processing is proving of considerable significance in this context, from sampling synthesizers to the IRCAM Musical Workstation.

The digital era has finally come of age and by the millennium most of the remaining technical hurdles should have been solved. The challenge is thus primarily an artistic one, and here there is still much work to be done. Time alone will show whether this revolution in music will yield any lasting solutions to the problems of direction and purpose which confront the contemporary composer.

# Bibliography

The following suggestions for further reading are selected from a wide repertoire of material dealing with aspects of electronic and computer music. One or two additional items have been included, dealing with more general aspects of the art and practice of music which have a particular significance for the medium as a whole.

## Catalogues and Periodicals

Bartle, Barton K., *Computer Software in Music and Music Education: A Guide* (Scarecrow Press, Metuchen, NJ, 1987)

*The Computer Music Journal*, 1– (1977– ). MIT Press, Cambridge, Mass.

*Contemporary Music Review*, 1– (1984– ). Harwood Academic Publishers, Chur, Switzerland

Cross, Lowell, *A Bibliography of Electronic Music* (Univ. of Toronto Press, Toronto, 1967)

Davies, Hugh, *International Electronic Music Catalog* (MIT Press, Cambridge, Mass., 1968)

Davis, Deta S., *Computer Applications in Music: A Bibliography* (A-R Editions, Madison, Wis., 1988; OUP, Oxford, 1993)

*Electronic Music Reports*, 1–4 (1969–71). Institute for Sonology, Utrecht

*Electronic Music Review*, 1–7 (1967–9). Independent Electronic Music Center, Trumansberg, NY

*Gravesaner Blätter/Gravesano Review*, 1– (1955– ). Mainz, Germany

*Interface*, 1– (1972– ). Swets und Zeitlinger, Amsterdam

*Journal of Music Theory*, 1– (1957– ). Yale School of Music, New Haven, Conn.

*Perspectives of New Music*, 1– (1962– ). Annandale, Minn.

*Die Reihe*, 1–8 (1955–62). Universal Edition, Vienna. English translations (1958–66). Theodore Presser Company, Bryn Mawr, Pa.

Risset, Jean C., *An Introductory Catalog of Computer Synthesized Sounds* (Bell Telephone Laboratories, Murray Hill, NJ, 1970)

*Source Magazine*, 1–9 (1967–71). Sacramento, Calif.

Tjepkema, Sandra, *A Bibliography of Computer Music: A Reference for Composers* (Univ. of Iowa Press, Iowa, 1981)

## Books

Appleton, Jon H., and Perera, Ronald C. (eds.), *The Development and Practice of Electronic Music* (Prentice Hall, NJ, 1975)

Backus, John, *The Acoustical Foundations of Music* (Norton, NY, 1969)

Bateman, Wayne, *Introduction to Computer Music* (Wiley, NY, 1980)

Busoni, Ferruccio, *Sketch of a New Aesthetic of Music* (Trieste, 1907. English translation, Schirmer, NY, 1911)

Buxton, William (ed.), *Computer Music 1976/77: A Directory to Current Work* (The Canadian Commission for UNESCO, Ontario, 1977)

Cage, John, *Silence* (Wesleyan Univ. Press, Middleton, Conn., 1961; repub. Caldar and Boyars, London, 1968)

Deutsch, Herbert A., *Synthesis: An Introduction to the History, Theory and Practice of Electronic Music* (Alfred Publishing Co., NY, 1976)

Dobson, Richard, *A Dictionary of Electronic and Computer Music Technology* (OUP, Oxford, 1992)

Dodge, Charles, and Jerse, Thomas A., *Computer Music: Synthesis, Composition and Performance* (Schirmer, London and NY, 1985)

Douglas, Alan L. M., *Electronic Music Production* (Pitman, London, 1973)

Emmerson, Simon (ed.), *Language of Electroacoustic Music* (Macmillan, London, 1986)

Ernst, David, *The Evolution of Electronic Music* (Schirmer, NY, 1977)

von Foerster, Heinz, and Beauchamp, James W. (eds.), *Music by Computers* (Wiley, NY, 1969)

Griffiths, Paul, *A Guide to Electronic Music* (Thames and Hudson, London, 1979)

Harvey, Jonathan, *The Music of Stockhausen* (Faber and Faber, London, 1976)

Hiller, Lejaren, and Isaacson, Leonard, *Experimental Music* (McGraw-Hill, NY, 1959)

Holmes, Thomas, *Electronic and Experimental Music* (Macmillan, NY, 1986)

Howe, Hubert S., Jun., *Electronic Music Synthesis* (Dent, London and NY, 1975)

Judd, Frederick C., *Electronic Music and Musique Concrète* (Neville Spearman, London, 1961)

Keane, David, *Tape Music Composition* (OUP, London, 1980)

Lincoln, Barry B. (ed.), *The Computer and Music* (Cornell Univ. Press, Ithaca, NY, 1970)

Maconie, Robin, *The Works of Karlheinz Stockhausen* (OUP, London, 1976)

Mathews, Max V., and Miller, Joan E., *The Technology of Computer Music* (MIT Press, Cambridge, Mass., 1969)

—— and Pierce, John D., (eds.), *Current Directions in Computer Music Research* (MIT Press, Cambridge, Mass., 1989)

Meyer, Leonard B., *Explaining Music* (Univ. of California Press, Berkeley, Los Angeles, and London, 1973)

Moles, André A., *Information Theory and Aesthetic Perception* (trans. Joel E. Cohen, Univ. of Illinois Press, Urbana, Ill., 1966)

Moore, F., *Elements of Computer Music* (Prentice Hall, NJ, 1989)

Nyman, Michael, *Experimental Music: Cage and Beyond* (Schirmer, London, 1974, repr. 1981)

Olson, Harry F., *Music, Physics and Engineering* (Dover, NY, 1967)

Ouellette, Fernand, *Edgard Varèse* (Caldar and Boyars, London, 1973)

Paynter, John, Howell, Tim, Orton, Richard, and Seymour, Peter (eds.), *Companion to Contemporary Musical Thought* (Routledge, London, 1992)

Pressing, Jeff, *Synthesizer Performance and Real-Time Techniques* (A-R Editions, Madison, Wis., 1992; OUP, Oxford, 1992)

Roads, Curtis, *Composers and the Computer* (W. Kaufmann, Los Altos, Calif., 1985)

—— (ed.), *Music Machine* (MIT Press, Cambridge, Mass., 1989)

—— and Strawn, John (eds.), *Foundations of Computer Music* (MIT Press, Cambridge, Mass., 1987)

Rothstein, Joseph, *MIDI: A Comprehensive Introduction* (A-R Editions, Madison, Wis., 1992; OUP, Oxford, 1992)

Russolo, Luigi, *The Art of Noise* (trans. Robert Filliou, Something Else Press, NY, 1967)

Schaeffer, Pierre, *À la recherche d'une musique concrète* (Éditions du Seuil, Paris, 1952)

—— *Traité des objets musicaux* (Éditions du Seuil, Paris, 1966)

Schillinger, Joseph, *The Mathematical Basis of the Arts* (repr. Da Capo Press, NY, 1976)

Schrader, Barry, *Introduction to Electro-Acoustic Music* (Prentice Hall, NJ, 1982)

Schwartz, Elliott, *Electronic Music: A Listener's Guide* (Praeger, NY, 1973)

Sear, Walter, *A Guide to Electronic Music and Synthesizers* (Omnibus, London, 1977)

Strange, Allen, *Electronic Music* (William C. Brown, Dubique, Iowa, 1972)

Taylor, Charles A., *The Physics of Musical Sounds* (American Elsevier Publishing Co., NY, 1965)

Wells, Thomas H., *The Technique of Electronic Music* (Schirmer, NY, 1981)

Winkel, Fritz, *Music, Sound and Sensation* (trans. Thomas Binkely, Dover, NY, 1967)

Wörner, Karl H., *Stockhausen: Life and Work* (Faber and Faber, London, 1973)

Xenakis, Iannis, *Formalized Music* (Indiana Univ. Press, Bloomington, Ind., 1971)

# Discography

The lists which follow provide a representative guide to the recordings of electronic and computer music which have been issued over the years. Regrettably, with the demise of the long-playing record, most of the entries under *records* have been deleted from current lists, and will only be located in library collections, private collections, or deletion offers. Entries under *compact discs* are current at the time of writing (1992), but these too will in due course be subject to deletion. Readers wishing to research further into recordings produced prior to 1980 are directed to the following publication which contains over 2000 entries:

Kondraki, M., Stankiewicz, M., and Weiland, F., *Electronic Music Discography* (Schott, London, Mainz, NY, and Tokyo, 1979)

## *Records*

AMM: AMM Music (1966) Elektra EUKS 7256
  Live Electronic Music Improvised (1968) Mainstream MS 5002
Anhalt, István: Electronic Composition No. 4 (1961) Allied Record 17
Appleton, Jon: Zoetrope (1974) Folkways FTS 3345
  Mussem's Song (1976) Folkways FTS 3345
  The Sydsing Camklang (1976) Folkways FTS 3345
  In Deserto (1977) Folkways FTS 3345
  Syntrophia (1977) Folkways FTS 3345
Arel, Bülent: Electronic Music No. 1 (1960) CRI S 356, Son Nova S 3
  Stereo Electronic Music No. 1 (1960) Columbia MS 6566
  Dramatic Fragment from 'The Scapegoat' (1961) Son Nova S 3
  Sacred Service: Prelude and Postlude (1961) CRI S 356, Son Nova S 3
  Mimiana II: Frieze (1969) CRI SD 300
  Stereo Electronic Music No. 2 (1970) CRI SD 265, Finnadar 9010 Q
Ashley, Robert: The Wolfman (1964) ESP S 1009 (*Source Magazine* No. 4) Source 1
  Untitled Mixes (1965) ESP S 1009
  Accidents (1967) Source 2
  Purposeful Lady Slow Afternoon (1968) Mainstream MS 5010
Austin, Larry: Hybrid Musics (1980) IRIDA 0022, The New Music Distribution Center, 500 Broadway, NY
Babbitt, Milton: Composition for Synthesizer (1960–1) Columbia MS 6566
  Vision and Prayer (1961) CRI SD 268, CRI S 268
  Philomel (1963–4) Acoustic Research AR 0654 083
  Ensembles for Synthesizer (1963) Columbia MS 7051 Finnadar 9010 Q
  Phonomena (1969–74) New World NW 209
  Reflections (1974–5) New World NW 209

Badings, Henk: Kaïn en Abel (1956) Philips 400 036 AE, Philips ABE 10073

Evolutionem (1957) Epic BC 1118, Philips 835 056 AY, Philips SABL 206

Genese (1958) Epic BC 1118, Philips 835 056AY, Philips SABL 206

Capriccio (1959) Epic BC 1118, Limelight 86055, Philips 835 056 AY, Philips SABL 206

Barraqué, Jean: Étude (1953) Barclay 89005

Bayle, François: Pluriel (1962–3) Philips 836 894 DSY

Archipel (1963) Philips 895 DSY

Vapeur (1963) Boîte à Musique LD 072, Boîte à Musique 5072

L'Oiseau-Chanteur (1964) Candide CE 31025, Philips 836 895 DSY, Varèse VS 81005

Lignes et points (1966) Philips 836 895 DSY

Espaces inhabitables (1966–7) Philips 836 895 DSY

Jeîta ou Murmure des eaux (1970) Philips 6521 016

Behrman, David: Runthrough (1966) Mainstream MS 5010

Wavetrain (1966) (*Source Magazine* No. 3) Source 1

Figure in a Clearing (1977) Lovely Music Ltd., 325 Spring Street, NY, LML 1041

On the Other Ocean (1977) Lovely Music Ltd., 325 Spring Street, NY, LML 1041

Berio, Luciano: Mutazioni (1955) RAI (Elettronica 1956 No. 3)

Perspectives (1957) Compagnia Generale del Disco ESZ 3

Thema—Omaggio a Joyce (1958) Philips 836 897 DSY, Philips 835 485 AY, Turnabout N 34177 S

Différences (1958–60) Mainstream MS 5004, Philips 839 323 DSY, Philips 6500 631

Momenti (1960) Limelight LS 86047, Philips 836 897 DSY, Philips 835 485 AY

Visage (1961) Candide CE 31027, Colombia OS 3320, RCA 61079, Turnabout TV 34046 S

Laborintus II (1965) Harmonia Mundi HM 764

Birtwistle, Harrison: Four Interludes from a Tragedy (1970) L'Oiseau-Lyre DSLO 17

Chronometer (1971) Argo ZRG 790

Boretz, Benjamin: Group Variation II (1973) CRI SD 300

Boucourechliev, André: Texte I (1958) Mercury SR2 9123, Philips 835 486 AY

Texte II (1959) Boîte à Musique LD 071

Boulez, Pierre: Étude (1952) Barclay 89005

Brown, Earle: Octet 1 (1953) CRI SD 330

Four Systems (1954) Columbia MS 7139, EMI Electrola C 065 02469

Times Five (1963) Boîte à Musique LD 072

Brün, Herbert: Anepigraphe (1958) Amadeo AVRS 5006

Klänge unterwegs (1961) Amadeo AVRS 5006

Futility (1964) Heliodor HS 25047

Cage, John: Imaginary Landscape No. 1 (1939) Avakian JCS 1, EMI Electrola C 165 28954

Credo in U.S. (1942) EMI Electrola C165 28954
Radio Mix (1950) Cramps CRS LP 6101
Williams Mix (1952) Avakian JCS 1
Aria with Fontana Mix (1959) Mainstream MS 5005, Time S 8003
Fontana Mix (1959) Turnabout RV 34046 S
Cartridge Music (1960) Mainstream MS 5015, Time S 8009, DGG 137 009
Music for Amplified Toy Pianos (1960) Cramps CRS LP 6101, EMI
   Electrola C 065 02469
Solos for Voice 2 (1960) Odyssey 32 16 0156
Variations II (1963) Colombia MS 7051, CBS France S 3461064
Variations III (1963) DGG 139442, Wergo 60057
Variations IV (1963) Everest 3130
Rozart Mix (1963) EMI Electrola C 165 28954
Fontana Mix-Feed (1964) Columbia MS 7139
Sixty-Two Mesostics re Merce Cunningham (1971) Cramps CRS LP
   6101 (extracts)
Cage, John, with Hiller, Lejaren: HPSCHD (1967–9) Nonesuch H 71224
Carlos, Walter: Dialogues for Piano and Two Loudspeakers (1963)
   Turnabout TV 34004 S
Variations (1964) Turnabout TV 34004 S
Switched on Bach (1968) Columbia MS 7194
The Well Tempered Synthesizer (1969) Columbia MS 7286
Sonic Seasonings (1971–2) Columbia PG 31234
Clementi, Aldo: Collage II (1960) Compagnia Generale del Disco ESZ 3
Davidovsky, Mario: Electronic Study No. 1 (1960) Columbia MS 6566
Electronic Study No. 2 (1962) CRI S 356, Son Nova S 3
Synchronisms No. 1 (1963) CRI SD 204
Synchronisms No. 2 (1964) CRI SD 204
Synchronisms No. 3 (1964–5) CRI SD 204
Electronic Study No. 3 (1965–6) Finnadar 9010 Q, Turnabout TV
   34487 S
Synchronisms No. 5 (1969) CRI SD 268, Turnabout TV 34487 S
Synchronisms No. 6 (1970) Turnabout TV 34487 S
Dobrowolski, Andrzej: Music for magnetic tape and oboe solo (1965)
   Muza Warsaw Fest 244
Dodge, Charles: Changes (1969) Nonesuch H 71245
Earth's Magnetic Field (1970) Nonesuch H 71250
Extensions for Trumpet and Tape (1973) CRI SD 300
Speech Songs (1973) CRI SD 348
The Story of Our Lives (1974) CRI SD 348
In Celebration (1975) CRI SD 348
Druckman, Jacob: Animus I (1965) Turnabout TV 34177 S
Animus II (1967–8) CRI SD 255
Animus III (1969) Nonesuch H 71253
Synapse → Valentine (1969–70) Nonesuch H 71253
Eaton, John: Piece for Solo Synket No. 3 (1965) Decca 710154
Songs for R.P.B. (1965) Decca 710154
Concert Piece for Synket and Symphony Orchestra (1967) Turnabout
   TV 34428 S

Soliloquy (1967) Decca 710165
Thoughts on Rilke (1967) Decca 710165
Blind Man's Cry (1968) CRI SD 296
Duet for Synket and Moog (1968) Decca 710165
Mass (1970) CRI SD 296
Eimert, Herbert: Glockenspiel (1953) DGG LP 16132
Etüde über Tongemische (1953–4) DGG LP 16132
Fünf Stücke (1955–6) DGG LP 16132
Zu Ehren von Igor Stravinsky (1957) Wergo 60006
Variante einer Variation von Anton Webern (1958) Wergo 60006
Selektion 1 (1959–60) Mercury SR 2 9123, Philips 835 486 AY
Epitaph für Aikichi Kuboyama (1960–2) Wergo 60014
Sechs Studien (1962) Wergo 60014
El-Dabh, Halim: Leiyla and the Poet (1961) Columbia MS 6566
Ferrari, Luc: Étude aux accidents (1958) Boîte à Musique LD 070
Étude aux sons tendus (1958) Boîte à Musique LD 070
Visage V (1958–9) Limelight LS 86047, Philips 835 485 AY, Philips
6740 001
Tête et queue du dragon (1959–60) Candide CE 31025, Philips 835
487 AY, Varèse VS 81005
Tautologos I (1961) Boîte à Musique LD 072
Tautologos II (1961) Boîte à Musique LD 071
Composé-composite (1962–3) Philips 836 894 DSY
Hétérozygote (1963–4) Philips 836 885 DSY
Und so weiter (1966) Wergo 60046
J'ai été coupé (1969) Philips 836 855 DSY
Gaburo, Kenneth: Antiphony III (1962) Nonesuch H 71199
Exit Music I: The Wasting of Lucrecetzia (1964) Nonesuch H 71199
Lemon Drops (1965) CRI S 356, Heliodor HS 25047
Exit Music II: Fat Millie's Lament (1965) Nonesuch H 71199
For Harry (1966) CRI S 356, Heliodor HS 25047
Antiphony IV (1967) Nonesuch H 71199
Gerhard, Roberto: Symphony No. 3 'Collages' (1960) Angel S 36558
Ghent, Emanuel: Brazen (—) *New Direction in Music*, Tulsa Studios,
Tulsa, Oklahoma
Glass, Philip: Contrary Motion (1969) Shandar 83 515
Music in Fifths (1969) Chatham Sq LP 1003
Music in Similar Motion (1969) Chatham Sq LP 1003
Two Pages (1969) Folkways 33902, Shandar 83 515
North Star (1977) Virgin V 2085
Gruppo di Improvvisazione Nuova Consonanza: Cantata (1964) DGG
643 541, RCA Italiana MLDS 21243
Credo (1969) DGG 137 007
Hambraeus, Bengt: Konstellationer II (1959) Limelight LS 86032, Philips
838 750
Rota II (1963) Riks LP 7 S
Tetragon (1965) Riks LP 7 S
Henry, Pierre: Concerto des ambiguïtés (1950) Philips 6510 012,
Ducretet-Thomson DUC 8, London DTL 93090 (part)

Batterie fugace (1950–1) Ducretet-Thomson DUC 8, London DTL 93090

Musique sans titre (1950–1) Ducretet-Thomson DUC 8

Tam-tam III (1950–1) Ducretet-Thomson DUC 8, London DTL 93090

Tam-tam IV (1950–1) Ducretet-Thomson DUC 9, London DTL 93121

Antiphonie (1952) Ducretet-Thomson DUC 9, London DTL 93121

Vocalises (1953) Ducretet-Thomson DUC 9, London DTL 93121

Astrologie (1953) Ducretet-Thomson DUC 9, London DTL 93121

Le Voile d'Orphée (1953 version) Ducretet-Thomson DUC 8, London DTL 93090, Philips 836 887 DSY

Orphée (1958 version) Philips 839 484 LY

Entité (1960) Limelight LS 86048, Philips 835 486 AY, Philips 836 887 DSY

Maléfices (1961) Philips 432 762 BE

La Noire à soixante (1961) Philips 836 892 DSY

Le Voyage (1961–2) Limelight LS 86049, Philips 836 899 DSY, Philips 6510 014 (part)

La Reine verte (1963) Philips 6332 015, Philips 6510 014

Variations pour une porte et un soupir (1963) Philips 836 898 DSY, Philips 6510 014 (part)

Le Voile d'Orphée (1966 version) Philips 680 201 NL

Granulométrie (1962–7) Philips 836 892 DSY

Messe de Liverpool (1967) Philips 6501 0001

Apocalypse de Jean (1968) Philips C 3017, Philips 6521 001-3

Ceremony (1969) Philips 849 512

Messe pour le temps présent (1970) Philips 836 893 DSY

Mouvement-rhythme-étude (1970) Philips 6504 052

Mise en musique du cortical art (1971) Philips 6521 022

Musiques pour une fête (1971) Philips 6565 001

Cortical Art III (1973) Philips 6510 015

Machine Dance (1973) Philips 6510 013

Prismes (1973) Philips 6510 016

Henry, Pierre, with Schaeffer, Pierre: Symphonie pour un homme seul (1949–50) Ducretet-Thomson DUC 9, London DTL 93121

Bidule en ut (1950) Ducretet-Thomson DUC 8, London DTL 93090, Philips 6736 006

Henze, Hans Werner: Violin Concerto No. 2 (1971) Decca Headline HEAD 5

Tristan (1973) DGG 2530 834

Hiller, Lejaren: Nightmare Music from 'Time of the Heathen' (1961) Heliodor HS 2549 006

Vocalise (1962–3) Supraphon DV 6221

Computer Cantata (1963) CRI SD 310, Heliodor HS 25053

Machine Music (1964) Heliodor HS 25047

Suite (1966) Heliodor HS 2549 006

Algorithms 1 (1968) DGG 2543 005

An Avalanche (1968) Heliodor HS 2549 006

Computer Music for Percussion and Tape (1968) Heliodor HS 2549 006

Hiller, Lejaren, with Cage, John: HPSCHD (1967–9) Nonesuch H 71224
Holliger, Heinz: Siebengesang (1967) DGG 2530 318
Howe, Hubert S., Jun.: Three Studies in Timbre (1970–3) Opus One,
    No. 47, New Music Distribution Service, 500 Broadway, NY
    Improvisation on the Overtone Series (1977) Opus One, No. 53, New
    Music Distribution Service, 500 Broadway, NY
Kagel, Mauricio: Transición I (1958–60) Limelight LS 86048, Philips 835
    486 AY
    Transición II (1959) Mainstream MS 5003, Time S 8001
    Acustica (1968–70) DGG 2707 059
    Unter Storm (1969) DGG 2530 460
Kayn, Roland: Cybernetics III (1969) DGG 2543 006
Koenig, Gottfried Michael: Klangfiguren II (1955-6) DGG LP 16134
    Terminus II (1966–7) DGG 137 011
    Funktion Grün (1967) DGG 137 011
    Terminus X (1967) Philips 836 993 DSY
    Funktion Gelb (1968) Wergo 324
    Funktion Blau (1969) Philips 6736 006, Philips 6740 002
Křenek, Ernst: Pfingstoratorium—Spiritus Intelligentiae, Sanctus
    (1955–6) DGG LP 16134
    Quintona (1966) Jornadas de Musica Experimental JME ME 2
Lansky, Paul: Mild und leise (1973–4) Odyssey Y 34239
Le Caine, Hugh: Dripsody (1955) Folkways FMS 33436
Ligeti, György: Glissandi (1957) Wergo 60076
    Artikulation (1958) Limelight LS 86048, Philips 835 486 AY, Wergo
    60059
Lucier, Alvin: North American Time Capsule (1967) CBS France S 346
    1066, Odyssey 32 16 0156
    Vespers (1968) Mainstream MS 5010
    I am sitting in a Room (1970) (*Source Magazine* No. 7) Source 3
Luening, Otto: Fantasy in Space (1952) Desto DC 6466, Folkways FX
    6160, Innovation GB 1
    Invention in 12 Notes (1952) Desto DC 6466, Innovation GB 1
    Low Speed (1952) Desto DC 6466, Innovation GB 1
    In the Beginning (1956) CRI SD 268
    Gargoyles (1960) Columbia MS 6566
    Synthesis (1962) CRI SD 219
    Moonflight (1968) Desto DC 6466
Luening, Otto, with Ussachevsky, Vladimir: Incantation (1953) Desto
    DC 6466, Innovation GB 1
    Rhapsodic Variations (1953–4) Louisville 545 5
    A Poem in Cycles and Bells (1954) CRI 112
    Carlsbad Caverns (1955) RCA Victor LPM 1280
    Suite from 'King Lear' (1956) CRI 112
    Concerted Piece (1960) CRI SD 227
Mâche, François-Bernard: Volumes (1960) Boîte à Musique LD 071
    Terre de feu (1963) Boîte à Musique LD 072, Candide CE 31025
Maderna, Bruno: Musica su due Dimensioni (1952) Compagnia
    Generale de Disco ESZ 3

Notturno (1956) RAI (Elettronica 1956 No. 3)

Continuo (1958) Limelight LS 86047, Philips 835 485 AY

Malec, Ivo: Dahovi (1961) Candide CE 31025, Philips 836 891 DSY, Philips 6740 001, Varèse VS 81005

Reflets (1961) Boîte à Musique LD 072, Boîte à Musique 5072

Tutti (1962–3) Philips 836 894 DSY

Cantate pour elle (1966) Philips 836 891 DSY\

Martirano, Salvatore: Underworld (1964–5) Heliodor HS 25047

L's GA (1967–8) Polydor 245001

Mathews, Max: Bicycle Built for Two (1962) Decca DL 79103

Maxfield, Richard: Night Music (1960) Odyssey 32 16 0160

Mayuzumi, Toshiro: Campanology (1959) Nippon Victor SJU 1515

Mandala (1969) Nippon Victor SJX 1004

Messiaen, Olivier: Fête des belles eaux (1937) Erato LDE 3202, Erato STU 70102

Mimaroğlu, İlhan: Bowery Bum (1964) Finnadar 9012, Turnabout TV 34004 S

Intermezzo (1964) Finnadar 9012, Turnabout TV 34004 S

Le Tombeau d'Edgar Poe (1964) Finnadar 9012, Turnabout TV 34004 S

Agony (1965) Finnadar 9012, Turnabout TV 34046 S

Anacolutha: Encounter and Episode II (1965) Finnadar SR 9001

White Cockatoo (1966) Finnadar SR 9001

Preludes I, II, VI, IX, XI, XIII (1966–7) Turnabout 34177 S

Piano Music for Performer and Composer (1967) Turnabout TV 34177 S

Prelude XII (1967) Finnadar SR 9001

Wings of the Delirious Demon (1969) Finnadar SR 9001

Sing me a Song of Songmy (1970) Atlantic SD 1576, Finnadar SR 9001 (part)

Hyperboles (1971) Finnadar SR 9001

Provocations (1971) Finnadar SR 9001

La Ruche (1972) Folkways 33951

To Kill a Sunrise (1974) Folkways 33951

Tract (1972–4) Folkways 33441

Moroi, Makoto: Shosange (1968) Nippon Victor SJX 1004

Mumma, Gordon: Music for the Venezia Space Theatre (1964) Advance FGR 5

Peasant Boy (1965) ESP S 1009

Mesa (1966) CBS France S 346 1065, Odyssey 32 16 0158

Hornpipe (1967) Mainstream MS 5010

Cybersonic Cantilevers (1973) Folkways FTS 33904

Musica Elettronica Viva: Spacecraft (1967–8) Mainstream MS 5002

Sound Pool (1969) BYG 529 326

Neuhaus, Max: Realization of Cage, *Fontana Mix-Feed* (1965) MASS ART M 133

Nono, Luigi: Omaggio a Emilio Vedova (1960) Wergo 60067

La fabbrica illuminata (1964) Wergo 60038

Ricorda cosa ti hanno fatto in Auschwitz (1965) Wergo 60038

A floresta è jovem e cheia de vida (1966) Arcophon AC 6811, DGG 2531 004, Musique Vivante HM 30767

Per Bastiana Tai-Yang Cheng (1967) Wergo 60067

Contrappunto dialettico alla mente (1967–8) DGG 2543 006

Non consumiamo Marx (1969) I Dischi del Sole DS 182 4 CL

Un volto, del mare (1969) I Dischi del Sole DS 182 4 CL

Y entonces comprendió (1969–70) DGG 2530 436, Ricordi SAVC 501

Como una ola de fuerza y luz (1971–2) DGG 2530 436, DGG 2740 229

Nordheim, Arne: Epitaffio (1963) Decca HEAD 23, Limelight LS 86061, Philips 839 250 AY

Respons I (1966–7) Limelight LS 86061, Philips 839 250 AY

Colorazione (1968) Philips 854 005 AY

Solitaire (1968) Philips 6740 004, Philips 854 005 AY

Five Osaka Fragments (1970) Philips 6507 034

Oliveros, Pauline: I of IV (1966) Odyssey 32 16 0160

Oram, Daphne: Electronic Sound Patterns (1962) HMV 7EG 8762

Penderecki, Krzysztof: Psalmus (1961) Supraphon DV 6221

Philippot, Michel: Étude I (1952) Ducretet-Thomson DUC 9, London DTL 93121

Ambiance I (1959) Boîte à Musique LD 070

Ambiance II—Toast funèbre (1959) Boîte à Musique LD 071

Maldoror (1960) Boîte à Musique LD 075–6

Rhinocéros (1960) Vega T 31 SP 8003

Étude III (1962) Candide CE 31025, Varèse VS 81005

Pierce, John: Five against Seven—Random Canon (1961) Decca DL 79103

Variations in Timbre and Attack (1961) Decca DL 79103

Pousseur, Henry: Scambi (version I) (1957) Limelight LS 86048, Philips 835 486 AY

Rimes pour différentes sources sonores (1958–9) RCA Victrola VICS 1239

Electre (1969) Universal Edition UE 13500

Trois Visages de Liège (1961) Columbia MS 7051

Jeu de miroirs de Votre Faust (1966) Heliodor Wergo 2549 021, Wergo 60026

Powell, Mel: Electronic Setting I (1961) Son Nova S 3

Second Electronic Setting (1962) CRI SD 227

Events (1963) CRI SD 227

Randall, Jim: Quartets in Pairs (1964) Nonesuch H 71245

Mudgett: Monologues by a Mass Murderer (1965) Nonesuch H 71245

Lyric Variations (1968) Vanguard VCS 10057

Quartersines (1969) Nonesuch H 71245

Reich, Steve: Its Gonna Rain (1965) Columbia MS 7265

Come Out (1966) Odyssey 32 16 0160

Violin Phase (1967) Columbia MS 7265

Phase Patterns (1970) Shandar 10005

Four Organs (1970) Angel S 36059, Shandar 10005

Reynolds, Roger: Ping (1968) CRI SD 285

Traces (1968–9) CRI SD 285

Riehn, Rainer: Chants de Maldoror (1965-6, revised 1968–9) DGG 137011

Riley, Terry: Dorian Reeds (1966) Mass Art M 131
  Poppy Nogood and the Phantom Band (1968) Columbia MS 7315
  A Rainbow in Curved Air (1969) Columbia MS 7315
  Persian Surgery Dervishes (1971) Shanti 83 501–2

Risset, Jean Claude: Little Boy (1968) Decca 710180
  Mutations (1969) Collection GRM AM 564 09, Turnabout 34427
  Dialogues (1975) Collection GRM AM 564 09
  Inharmonique (1977) Collection GRM AM 564 09
  Inharmonic Soundscapes (1977) *Significant Contemporary Works*, Tulsa, Tulsa Studios, Oklahoma
  Moments Newtoniens (1977) Collection GRM AM 564 09

Salzman, Eric: Helix (1966) Finnadar 9005
  Larynx Music (1967) Finnadar 9005
  The Nude Paper Sermon (1968–9) Nonesuch H 71231

Schaeffer, Myron: Dance 4 : 3 Folkways FMS 33436

Schaeffer, Myron, with Olnick, Harvey, and Walter, Arnold: Summer Idyll (1960) Folkways FMS 33436

Schaeffer, Pierre: Étude au Piano II (1948) Ducretet-Tomson DUC 8, London DTL 93090
  Étude aux casseroles (1948) Ducretet-Thomson DUC 8, London DTL 93090, Philips 6521 021
  Étude aux chemins de fer (1948) Ducretet-Thomson DUC 8, London DTL 93090, Philips 6521 021
  Étude aux tourniquets (1948) Ducretet-Thomson DUC 8, London DTL 93090, Philips 6521 021
  Étude pathétique (1948) Philips 6521 021
  Étude violette (1948) Philips 6521 021
  Suite pour quatorze instruments (1949) Philips 6521 021
  Variations sur une flûte mexicaine (1949) Ducretet-Thomson DUC 8, London DTL 93090
  L'Oiseau RAI (1950) Ducretet-Thomson DUC 9, London DTL 93121, Philips 6521 021
  Étude aux allures (1958) Boîte à Musique LD 070, Philips 6521 021
  Étude aux sons animés (1958) Boîte à Musique LD 070, Philips 6521 021
  Étude aux objects (1959 version) Philips 835 478 AY
  Étude aux objets (1967 version) Candide CE 31025, Varèse VS 81005 (part)

Schaeffer, Pierre, with Henry, Pierre: Symphonie pour un homme seul (1949–50) Ducretet-Thomson DUC 9, London DTL 93121
  Bidule et ut (1950) Ducretet-Thomson DUC 8, London DTL 93090, Philips 6736 006

Smalley, Denis: Pentes (1974) Univ. of East Anglia, Norwich, England, UEA 81063
  Chanson de geste (1978) Univ. of East Anglia, Norwich, England, UEA 81063
  Pulses of Time (1979) Univ. of East Anglia, Norwich, England, UEA 81063

Souster, Tim: Spectral (1972) Transatlantic TRAG 343
  Afghan Amplitudes (1976) Transatlantic TRAG 343
  Arcane Artefact (1976) Transatlantic TRAG 343
  Music from Afar (1976) Transatlantic TRAG 343
  Surfit (1976) Transatlantic TRAG 343
Stockhausen, Karlheinz: Studie I (1953) DGG LP 16133
  Studie II (1954) DGG LP 16133
  Gesang der Jünglinge (1955-6) DGG 16133, DGG 138 811
  Kontakte (1959–60) (tape alone) DGG 138 811
  Kontakte (1959–60) (tape plus instruments) Candide CE 31022, Vox STGBY 638
  Mikrophonie I (1964) Columbia MS 7355, CBS 72647, CBS S 77230, CBS 32 11 0044, DGG 2530 583
  Mixtur (1964) DGG 137 012, DGG ST 643 546
  Mikrophonie II (1965) Columbia MS 7355, CBS 72647, CBS S 77230, CBS 32 11 0044, DGG 2530 583
  Solo (1966) DGG 137 005, DGG 104 992
  Telemusik (1966) DGG 137 012, DGG ST 643 546
  Ensemble (1967) Wergo 60065
  Hymnen (1967) DGG 2707 039, DGG ST 139 421–2
  Prozession (1967) Candide CE 31001, CBS S 77230, Vox STGBY 615, DGG 2530 582
  Aus den sieben Tagen (1968) DGG 270 073, Harmonia Mundi 30899M
  Kurzwellen (1968) DGG 139 451, DGG 139 461
  Spiral (1968) DGG 2561 109, EMI Electrola C 165 02 313–14, Wergo 325
  Mantra (1970) DGG 2530 208
  Pole (1969–70) EMI Electrola C 165 02 313
  Sternklang (1971) Polydor 2612 031
  Trans (1971) DGG 2530 726
  Momente (1961–72) Nonesuch H 71157, Wergo 60024, DGG 3709 055
  Ylem (1972) DGG 2530 442
Subotnick, Morton: Prelude No. 4 (1966) Avant 1008
  Silver Apples of the Moon (1967) Nonesuch H 71174
  The Wild Bull (1968) Nonesuch H 71208
  Touch (1969) Columbia MS 7316
  Laminations (1969–70) Turnabout TV 34428 S
  Sidewinder (1971) Columbia M 30683
Takemitsu, Toru: Vocalism A–I (1955, Revised 1965) RCA VICS 1334
Tenney, James: Five Stochastics Studies (1961) Decca 710180
  Noise Study (1961) Decca DL 79103
Tomita, Isao: Snowflakes are Dancing (1974) RCA ARL 1 0488
Truax, Barry: Nautilus (1976) Imperial Record Corporation, Vancouver SMLP 4033
  Sonic Landscapes (1978) Imperial Record Corporation, Vancouver SMLP 4033
Ussachevsky, Vladimir: Composition (1951–2) Folkways FTX 6169
  Experiment (1951–2) Folkways FTX 6169

Reverberation (1951–2) Folkways FTX 6169
Transposition (1951–2) Folkways FTX 6169
Underwater Valse (1951–2) Folkways FTX 6169
Sonic Contours (1952) Desto DC 6466
Piece for Tape Recorder (1956) CRI 112, Finnadar 9010 Q
Metamorphoses (1957) CRI S 356, Son Nova S 3
Improvisation No. 4711 (1958) Son Nova S 3
Linear Contrasts (1958) CRI S 356, Son Nova S 3
Wireless Fantasy (1960) CRI SD 227
Creation: Prologue (1960–1) Columbia MS 6566
Of Wood and Brass (1964–5) CRI SD 227
Computer Piece No. 1 (1968) CRI SD 268
Two Sketches for a Computer Piece (1971) CRI SD 268

Ussachevsky, Vladimir, with Luening, Otto: Incantation (1953) Desto
    DC 6466, Innovation GB 1
    Rhapsodic Variations (1953–4) Louisville 545 5
    A Poem in Cycles and Bells (1954) CRI 112
    Carlsbad Caverns (1955) RCA Victor LP 1280
    Suite from 'King Lear' (1956) CRI 112
    Concerted Piece (1960) CRI SD 227

Varèse, Edgard: Déserts (1954) Angel S 36786, Columbia MS 6362, CRI
    SD 268
    Poème électronique (1958) Columbia MS 6146

Vercoe, Barry: Synthesism (1969–70) Nonesuch H 71245

Wessel, David: Anthony (1977) New Directions in Music, Tulsa Studios,
    Tulsa, Oklahoma

Wishart, Trevor: Red Bird (1973–7) Philip Martin Books, York,
    England, YES 7

Wuorinen, Charles: Time's Encomium (1969) Nonesuch H 71225

Xenakis, Iannis: Diamorphoses (1957) Boîte à Musique LD 070, Erato
    STU 70530
    Concret PH (1958) Philips 835 487 AY, Erato STU 70530
    Analogique B (1958–9) Philips 835 487 AY
    Orient-Occident (1960) Limelight LS 86047, Philips 835 485 AY,
    Erato STU 70530
    Bohor (1962) Erato STU 70530, Nonesuch H 71246
    Concret P.H. (revised version, 1968) Nonesuch H 71246
    Diamorphoses (revised version, 1968) Erato STU 70530, Nonesuch H
    72146
    Orient-Occident (revised version, 1968) Nonesuch H 71246
    Persepolis (1971) Philips 6521 045

Young, La Monte: 13 I 73 5: 35–6: 14: 03 PM NYC (1969–73) Shandar
    83510
    Drift Study 14 VII 73 9: 27: 27–10: 06: 41 PM NYC (1973) Shandar
    83510

*Rock*

The Beach Boys: Good Vibrations (1966) Reprise 2223
    Smiley Smile (1966–7) Capitol T 2891

The Beatles: Revolver (1967) Parlophone PCS 7009
  Sgt. Pepper's Lonely Hearts Club Band (1967) Capitol MAS 2653,
    Parlophone PCS 7027
  Magical Mystery Tour (1967) Capitol MAL 2835
Emerson, Lake, and Palmer: Pictures at an Exhibition (1971) Cotillion
    ELP 66666, Manticore K33501
  Brain Salad Surgery (1973) Manticore MS 66669
Eno, Brian (Matching Moles, Roxy Music): Another Green World
    (1975) Island ILPS 9351
  Discreet Music (1975) Obscure 3
Froeze, Edgar: Aqua (1973–4) Virgin V 2016, Virgin VR 13 111
The Grateful Dead: Anthem of the Sun (1967–8) Warner Brothers WS
    1749
  Live/Dead (1968) Warner Brothers WS 1830
  Aoxomoxoa (1969) Warner Brothers WS 1790
Hendrix, Jimi: The Jimi Hendrix Experience (1967–8) Polydor 2683 031,
    Reprise RS 6261
Matching Moles: Little Red Record (1972) Columbia KC 32148
Oldfield, Mike: Tubular Bells (1975) Virgin V 2001
Pink Floyd: Atom Heart Mother (1970) EMI Harvest SHVL 781 Meddle
    (1971) EMI Harvest SHVL 795
  The Dark Side of the Moon (1972–3) EMI Harvest SHVL 804
The Rolling Stones: Their Satanic Majesties Request (1967) London
    NPS 2
Soft Machine: Soft Machine (1968) Probe CPLP 4500
  Soft Machine II (1969) Probe CPLP 4505
  Soft Machine VII (1973) Columbia KC 32716
Tangerine Dream: Rubycon (1975) Virgin VR 13 116
  Cyclone (1978) Virgin V 2097
Velvet Underground: Andy Warhol's Velvet Underground Featuring
    Nico (1967–9) MGM 2683 006, Verve V6 5008
Yes: Close to the Edge (1972) (Rick Wakeman) Atlantic K 50012,
    Atlantic SD 7244
  Yes Songs (1973) Atlantic SD 3 100
Frank Zappa and the Mothers of Invention: Uncle Meat (1967–8)
    Bizarre 2024
  Roxy and Elsewhere (1974) Disc ZDS 2202, WEA K 69201

## *Compact Discs (Recommended Selection)*

Appleton, Jon: Brush Canyon, CDCM Centaur CRC 2052
  Degitaru Ongaku, CDCM Centaur CRC 2052
Arfib, Daniel: Le Souffle du Doux, Wergo 2022-50
Austin, Larry: Beachcombers, CDCM Centaur CRC 2078
  Montage: Theme and Variations for Violin and Computer Music on
    Tape, CDCM Centaur CRC 2110
  Sinfonia Concertante: A Mozartean Episode, CDCM Centaur CRC 2029
  Sonata Concertante, CDCM Centaur CRC 2029

Baitz, Rick: Kaleidocycles, CDCM Centaur CRC 2029

Barlow, Clarence: Relationships for Melody Instrs, Wergo WER 2070-50

Bayle, François: Les Couleurs de la Nuit, Harmonia Mundi INA C 1001
Motion-Emotion, Harmonia Mundi INA C 1001
Le Sommeil d'Euclide, Wergo 2025-50

Berger, Jonathan: Diptych, CDCM Centaur CRC 2091

Braxton, Anthony: Composition No. 107, CDCM Centaur CRC 2110

Bresnick, Martin: Lady Neil's Dumpe, CDCM Centaur CRC 2029

Brün, Herbert: i toLD You so!, CDCM Centaur CRC 2045

Butler, Martin: Night Machines, CDCM Centaur CRC 2076

Chadabe, Joel: Modalities, CDCM Centaur CRC 2047

Chafe, Chris: Quadro, CDCM Centaur CRC 2091

Chowning, John: Phoné, Wergo 2012-50
Sabelithe, Wergo 2012-50
Stria, Wergo 2012-50
Turenas, Wergo 2012-50

Clark, Thomas: Peninsular, CDCM Centaur CRC 2029

Dashow, James: Archimedes, Wergo 2018-50
Argento, Wergo 2018-50
Legno, Wergo 2018-50
Mnemonics and Oro, Wergo 2018-50
Sequence Symbols, Wergo WER 2070-50

Davidovsky, Mario: Synchronisms No. 9, Wergo 2022-50

Garton, Brad: Approximate Rhythms, CDCM Centaur CRC 2076
Wasting, CDCM Centaur 2076

Ghent, Emmanuel: Phosphones, Wergo 2022-50

Goebel, Johannes: Vom Übersetzen über den Fluss, Wergo 2025-50

Hiller, Lejaren: An Avalanche for Pitchman, Prima Donna, Player
Piano, Percussionist and Pre-recorded Tape, Wergo 60128
Circus Piece: A Cadential Process, Wergo 60128
Computer Music for Percussion and Tape, Wergo 60128
Expo '85 for Multiple Synthesizers, Wergo 60128
Illiac String Quartet, Wergo 60128
Mix or Match: A Time-Generating Process, Wergo 60128
Persiflage for Flute, Oboe and Percussion, Wergo 60128
Toy Harmonium: A Statistical Process, Wergo 60128
Transitions: A Hierarchical Process, Wergo 60128

Hunt, Jerry: Fluud, CDCM Centaur CRC 2029

Jaffe, David: Telegram to the President, CDCM CRC 2091

Jones, David: Still Life Dancing, CDCM Centaur CRC 2052
Still Life in Wood and Metal, CDCM Centaur CRC 2052

Kabat, Julie: Child and the Moon-Tree, CDCM Centaur CRC 2047

Karpen, Richard: Eclipse, Wergo 2025-50

Kaske, Stephan: Transition No. 2, Wergo 2070-50

Keefe, Robert: The Ephemerides for Harp and Percussion: Moon, 1650-1657, CDCM Centaur CRC 2078

Koenig, Gottfried Michael: Three ASKO Pieces, Wergo 2022-50

Lansky Paul: As If, CDCM Centaur CRC 2110
   Guy's Harp, New Albion NA 030CD
   idle chatter, Wergo WER 2070-50
   just-more-idle-chatter, CDCM Centaur CRC 2076
   Late August, New Albion NA 030CD
   Not So Heavy Metal, New Albion NA 030CD
   Smalltalk, New Albion NA 030CD
   Wasting, CDCM Centaur CRC 2076

Lindroth, Scott: Syntax, CDCM Centaur CRC 2029

Lorrain, Denis: Black it Stood as Night, Wergo 2022-5

McLean, Barton: Demons of the Night, CDCM Centaur CRC 2047
   A Little Night Music, CDCM Centaur CRC 2047
   Visions of a Summer Night, CDCM Centaur CRC 2047

McTee, Cindy: Metal Music, CDCM Centaur CRC 2078

Martirano, Salvatore: Sampler: Everything Goes when the Whistle Blows, CDCM Centaur CRC 2045

Melby, John: Concerto No. 1 for Flute and Computer-Synthesized Tape, CDCM Centaur CRC 2110
   Chor der Waisen, CDCM Centaur CRC 2045

Milburn, Andrew: Elmore, CDCM Centaur CRC 2076
   Wasting, CDCM Centaur CRC 2076

Moravec, Paul: Devices and Desires, CDCM Centaur CRC 2052

Morrill, Dexter: Quartet, CDCM Centaur CRC 2091

Oliveros, Pauline: Lion's Tale, CDCM Centaur CRC 2047

Parmegiani, Bernard: La Création du Monde, Harmonia Mundi INA C 1002

Piekaski, James: Dreamfile, CDCM Centaur CRC 2078

Reynolds, Roger: Transfigured Wind IV, Neuma 450-73/74

Risset, Jean-Claude: Computer Suite from Little Boy, Wergo 2013-50
   Contours, Neuma New Music Series Vol. 1
   Passages, Wergo 2013-50
   Songes, Wergo 2013-50
   Sud, Wergo 2013-50

Roads, Curtis: nscor, Wergo WER 2070-50

Rogers, Rowell: Centoph, CDCM Centaur CRC 2078

Rolnick, Neil: What is the Use?, CDCM Centaur CRC 2039
   Vocal Chords, CDCM Centaur CRC 2047
   A Robert Johnson Sampler, CDCM Centaur CRC 2047

Rosenboom, David: A Precipice in Time, CDCM Centaur CRC 2110
   Systems of Judgement, CDCM Centaur CRC 2077

Rubin, Anna: Crying for Laughing and Golden, Neuma New Music Series Vol. 1

Scaletti, Carla: sunSurgeAutomata, CDCM Centaur CRC 2045

Schindler, Allan: Tremor of Night and Day, CDCM Centaur CRC 2091

Schottstaedt, William: Leviathan, Wergo 2025-50

Teitelbaum, Richard: Golem 1, CDCM Centaur CRC 2039

Tepei, Sever: Cuniculi, CDCM Centaur CRC 2045

Truax, Barry: The Blind Man, Wergo CSR-CD8701
  Aerial, Wergo CSR-CD8701
  Solar Ellipse, Wergo CSR-CD8701
  Riverrun, Wergo CSR-CD8701
  Wars Edge, Wergo CRS-CD8701

Waisvisz, Michel: The Hands, Wergo WER 2070-50

Warren, Alicyn: Contraption, CDCM Centaur CRC 2076

Waschka, Rodney: At Night, however, it Creaks and Breaks, CDCM
  CRC 2078

White, Frances: Still Life with Piano, CDCM Centaur CRC 2076

Winsor, Phil: Anamorphoses, CDCM Centaur CRC 2078
  Dulcimer Dream, CDCM Centaur CRC 2029

Wishart, Trevor: Vox 5, Virgo VC7 91108-2

Wolff, Christian: Mayday Materials, CDCM Centaur CRC 2052

Wyatt, Scott: Still Hidden Laughs, CDCM Centaur CRC 2029

Xenakis, Iannis: Mycenae Alpha, Neuma 450-73/74

# Index